D1327816

The Commission on the Limits of the Continental Shelf

Publications on Ocean Development
Volume 77

A Series of Studies on
the International, Legal, Institutional, and Policy Aspects
of Ocean Development

General Editors: Robin Churchill and Alex Oude Elferink

The titles published in this series are listed at *brill.com/pood*

The Commission on the Limits of the Continental Shelf

Law and Legitimacy

by

Øystein Jensen

BRILL

LEIDEN | BOSTON

14- 1091360 -1

Library of Congress Cataloging-in-Publication Data

The Commission on the Limits of the Continental Shelf : law and legitimacy / Edited by Oystein Jensen.
    p. cm. — (Publications on ocean development ; 77)
    Includes bibliographical references and index.
    ISBN 978-90-04-27415-0 (hardback : alk. paper) — ISBN 978-90-04-27417-4 (e-book : alk. paper)
1. Continental shelf—Law and legislation. 2. United Nations. Commission on the Limits of the Continental
Shelf. I. Jensen, Øystein, editor.

    KZA1660.C65 2014
    341.4'48—dc23

                                                                                          201401986

This publication has been typeset in the multilingual 'Brill' typeface. With over 5,100 characters covering
Latin, IPA, Greek, and Cyrillic, this typeface is especially suitable for use in the humanities.
For more information, please see brill.com/brill-typeface.

ISSN 0924-1922
ISBN 978 90 04 27415 0 (hardback)
ISBN 978 90 04 27417 4 (e-book)

This book is printed on acid-free paper.

MIX
Paper from
responsible sources
FSC
www.fsc.org   FSC® C109576

Printed by Printforce, the Netherlands

Contents

5 The Future of the Commission

Acknowledgements

This book is based on my doctoral thesis—*The Commission on the Limits of the Continental Shelf: Law and Legitimacy*—completed in 2013. First of all, I would like to thank the members of the dissertation adjudication committee: Professor Ellen Hey from Erasmus University of Rotterdam, Professor Ted L. McDorman from the University of Victoria and Professor Ole Kristian Fauchald from the University of Oslo. I am very grateful to them for writing an extensive evaluation report, as well as taking part in my public defence of the dissertation, held on 10 June 2013 at the University of Oslo. They have provided various recommendations, all of which have contributed to improving my text.

I also wish to thank two anonymous reviewers who read and made useful comments on an unrevised version of the doctoral thesis.

As always, I have had the privilege of exceptionally good working conditions at my regular workplace, the Fridtjof Nansen Institute, with its fine administrative and academic resources. In particular, I would like to extend thanks to our librarian Kari Lorentzen, administrative assistant Rigmor Hiorth, and Head of Administration and Information, Claes Lykke Ragner. In addition, I would like to extend special thanks to the leadership at the Fridtjof Nansen Institute, as well as many of the Institute's accomplished researchers; Geir Hønneland and Arild Moe are among those who have provided valuable and stimulating feedback.

Further, I wish to thank Rolf Einar Fife, Director General of the Legal Affairs Department of the Norwegian Ministry of Foreign Affairs, for stimulating discussions on the Commission. Alex G. Oude Elferink of the Netherlands Institute for the Law of the Sea deserves warm thanks for having read through an early draft of my doctoral thesis. I also received invaluable input from Harald Brekke—for many years a member of the Commission—who has read and commented on one part of the manuscript. I am also grateful to Vaughan Stagpoole and John Callan, both with GNS Science in New Zealand, for allowing me to use some of GNS Science's excellent illustrations, on the basis of which several of the figures in this book have been redrawn.

I also wish to thank Marie Sheldon, Senior Acquisitions Editor for International Law and International Relations, and Lisa Hanson, Assistant Editor, both at Brill Nijhoff Publishers in Boston, Massachusetts, for highly professional assistance in various phases of the production of this book.

During the work with the doctoral thesis, I was fortunate in having two academic supervisors. My colleague Davor Vidas, Research Professor and Director of the Law of the Sea Programme at the Fridtjof Nansen Institute, served as co-supervisor. He read drafts, commented, offered valuable ideas and provided encouragement throughout the project. I am deeply grateful to Davor—through many years of working together, he has continued to supervise me in the field of the law of the sea.

My main supervisor was Professor Geir Ulfstein at the University of Oslo. It was my good fortune to have a supervisor known for his outstanding theory contributions in many fields of international law, including the law of the sea and international institutional law. Geir read and provided critical comments, suggestions and ideas throughout the entire process. I am profoundly indebted for his dedicated academic supervision, professionalism, generosity and inspiring research example.

Finally, I wish to thank those people who are most special to me: my dear Tone, and my beloved parents at home in Høyanger.

Polhøgda, January 2014
Øystein Jensen

List of Acronyms and Short Forms

Aarhus Convention	Convention on Access to Information, Public Participation in Decision-making and Access to Justice in Environmental Matters
AB	Appellate Body (of the World Trade Organization)
ACHPR	African Commission on Human and Peoples' Rights
African Charter	African Charter on Human and Peoples' Rights
ATS	Australian Treaty Series
BCBS	Basel Committee on Banking Supervision
CAC	Codex Alimentarius Commission
CBD	Convention on Biological Diversity
CCJE	Consultative Council of European Judges
CLCS	Commission on the Limits of the Continental Shelf
DOALOS	Division for Ocean Affairs and the Law of the Sea, Office of Legal Affairs, United Nations
DRC	Democratic Republic of the Congo
DSR	Dispute Settlement Reports
EC	European Communities
ECHR	European Convention on Human Rights
ECJ	European Court of Justice
ECtHR	European Court of Human Rights
EPC	European Patent Convention
EPO	European Patent Office
GATT	General Agreement on Tariffs and Trade
HRC	Human Rights Committee
ICC	International Criminal Court
ICCPR	International Covenant on Civil and Political Rights
ICJ	International Court of Justice
I.C.J. Reports	Reports of Judgments, Advisory Opinions and Orders of the International Court of Justice
ICNT	Informal composite negotiating text
ICRW	International Convention for the Regulation of Whaling
ILA	International Law Association
ILC	International Law Commission
ILM	International Legal Materials
IMF	International Monetary Fund
IMFAT	International Monetary Fund Administrative Tribunal
IMO	International Maritime Organization
IO	International Organization

IPEA	International Preliminary Examination Authority
IPER	International Preliminary Examination Report
ISA	International Seabed Authority
ISNT	Informal single negotiating text
ITLOS	International Tribunal for the Law of the Sea
IWC	International Whaling Commission
LOS Convention	United Nations Convention on the Law of the Sea
NGO	Non-governmental Organization
OAS	Organization of American States
OLA	United Nations Office of Legal Affairs
OLC	United Nations Office of the Legal Counsel
OSPAR	Convention for the Protection of the Marine Environment of the North-East Atlantic
PCIJ	Permanent Court of International Justice
P.C.I.J. Reports	Reports of the Permanent Court of International Justice
PCT	Patent Cooperation Treaty
RSNT	Revised single negotiating text
SBSTTA	Subsidiary Body on Scientific, Technical and Technological Advice
SPS Agreement	Agreement on the Application of Sanitary and Phytosanitary Measures
STECF	Scientific, Technical and Economic Committee for Fisheries
TBT Agreement	Agreement on Technical Barriers to Trade
UNCLOS I	First United Nations Conference on the Law of the Sea
UNCLOS II	Second United Nations Conference on the Law of the Sea
UNCLOS III	Third United Nations Conference on the Law of the Sea
UNEP	United Nations Environment Program
UNESCO	United Nations Educational, Scientific and Cultural Organization
UNGA	General Assembly of the United Nations
UNRIAA	United Nations Reports of International Arbitral Awards
UNSC	United Nations Security Council
UN Sea-Bed Committee	Committee on the Peaceful Uses of the Seabed and Ocean Floor beyond the Limits of National Jurisdiction
UNSG	Secretary-General of the United Nations
UNTS	United Nations Treaty Series
Vienna Convention	Vienna Convention on the Law of Treaties
WIPO	World Intellectual Property Organization
WTO	World Trade Organization

List of Figures and Table

Conventions and Other International Instruments

African Charter on Human and Peoples' Rights, Banjul, 27 June 1981; entered into force 21 October 1986. Published in *UNTS*, Vol. 1520, p. 217.

Agreement between the Government of the United Kingdom of Great Britain and Northern Ireland and the Government of the Republic of Ireland Concerning the Delimitation of Areas of the Continental Shelf between the Two Countries. Adopted 7 November 1988; entered into force 11 January 1990. In *Law of the Sea Bulletin*, No. 13, p. 48.

Agreement between the United States of America and the Union of Soviet Socialist Republics on the Maritime Boundary, Washington, D.C., 1 June 1990; not yet in force. In *ILM*, Vol. 29, p. 942.

Agreement on Agriculture. Adopted 15 April 1994; entered into force 1 January 1995. Published in *UNTS*, Vol. 1867, p. 410.

Agreement on Maritime Delimitation between the Government of Australia and the Government of the French Republic, Melbourne, 4 January 1982; entered into force 10 January 1983. Published in *ATS*, 1983, No. 3.

Agreement on Technical Barriers to Trade. Adopted 15 April 1994; entered into force 1 January 1995. Published in *UNTS*, Vol. 1868, p. 120.

Agreement on the Application of Sanitary and Phytosanitary Measures. Adopted 15 April 1994; entered into force 1 January 1995. Published in *UNTS*, Vol. 1867, p. 493.

Agreement relating to the implementation of Part XI of the Convention, New York, 28 July 1994; entered into force 16 November 1994. Published in *UNTS*, Vol. 1836, p. 3.

American Convention on Human Rights, San José, 21 November 1969; entered into force 18 July 1978. Published in *UNTS*, Vol. 1144, p. 123.

Consolidated version of the Treaty on the Functioning of the European Union. Adopted 13 December 2007; entered into force 1 December 2009. In *Official Journal of the European Union*, Vol. 51, 2008, p. 47.

Constitution of the International Labour Organisation, Paris, 1 April 1919; entered into force on 28 June 1919. Published in *UNTS*, Vol. 15, p. 35.

Convention against Torture and Other Cruel, Inhuman or Degrading Treatment or Punishment, New York, 10 December 1984; entered into force 26 June 1987. Published in *UNTS*, Vol. 1465, p. 85.

Convention Concerning the Protection of the World Cultural and Natural Heritage, Paris, 23 November 1972; entered into force 17 December 1975. Published in *UNTS*, Vol. 1037, p. 151.

Convention for the Protection and Preservation of the Marine Environment and the North East Atlantic, Paris, 22 September 1992; entered into force 25 March 1998. Reprinted in *ILM*, Vol. 32, p. 1068.

Convention for the Protection of Human Rights and Fundamental Freedoms (as amended), Rome, 4 November 1950; entered into force 3 September 1953. Published in *UNTS*, Vol. 213, p. 222.

Convention on Access to Information, Public Participation in Decision-Making and Access to Justice in Environmental Matters, Aarhus, 25 June 1998; entered into force 30 October 2001. Published in *UNTS*, Vol. 2161, p. 447.

Convention on Biological Diversity, Rio de Janeiro, 5 June 1992; entered into force 29 December 1993. Published in *UNTS*, Vol. 1760, p. 79.

Convention on International Trade of Endangered Species, Washington, D.C., 3 March 1973; entered into force 1 July 1975. Published in *UNTS*, Vol. 993, p. 243.

Convention on the Continental Shelf, Geneva, 29 April 1958; entered into force 10 June 1964. Published in *UNTS*, Vol. 499, p. 311.

Convention on the Elimination of All Forms of Discrimination against Women, New York, 18 December 1979; entered into force 3 September 1981. Published in *UNTS*, Vol. 1249, p. 13.

Convention on the Grant of European Patents, Munich, 5 October 1973; entered into force on 7 October 1977. Published in *UNTS*, Vol. 1065, p. 199.

Convention on the Prevention of Marine Pollution by Dumping of Wastes and Other Matters, London, 29 December 1972; entered into force 30 August 1975. Published in *UNTS*, Vol. 1046, p. 120.

Convention on the Privileges and Immunities of the United Nations, New York, 13 February 1946; entered into force 17 September 1946. Published in *UNTS*, Vol. 1, p. 15 and Vol. 90, p. 327 (corrigendum to Vol. 1).

Convention on the Rights of the Child, New York, 20 November 1989; entered into force 2 September 1990. Published in *UNTS*, Vol. 1577, p. 3.

Convention on the Settlement of Investment Disputes between States and Nationals of Other States, Washington, D.C., 18 March 1965; entered into force 14 October 1966. Published in *UNTS*, Vol. 575, p. 159.

International Convention for the Prevention of Pollution from Ships, London, 2 November 1973, as amended by the Protocol, London, 1 June 1978; entered into force 2 October 1983. Published in *UNTS*, Vol. 61, p. 1340.

International Convention for the Regulation of Whaling, Washington, D.C., 2 December 1946; entered into force 10 November 1948. Published in *UNTS*, Vol. 161, p. 72.

International Convention for the Safety of Life at Sea, London, 1 November 1974; entered into force 25 May 1980. Published in *UNTS*, Vol. 2, p. 1184.

International Convention on the Elimination of All Forms of Racial Discrimination, New York, 7 March 1966; entered into force 4 January 1969. Published in *UNTS*, Vol. 660, p. 195.

International Convention on the Protection of the Rights of All Migrant Workers and Members of their Families, New York, 19 December 1990; entered into force 1 July 2003. Published in *UNTS*, Vol. 2220, p. 3.

International Covenant on Civil and Political Rights, New York, 16 December 1966; entered into force 23 March 1976. Published in *UNTS*, Vol. 99, p. 171 and Vol. 1057, p. 407.

General Agreement on Tariffs and Trade, Geneva, 30 October 1947; entered into force 1 January 1948. Published in *UNTS*, Vol. 55, p. 194.

Optional Protocol to the Convention against Torture and other Cruel, Inhuman or Degrading Treatment or Punishment, New York, 18 December 2002; entered into force 22 June 2006. Published in *UNTS*, Vol. 2375, p. 237.

Optional Protocol to the Convention on the Elimination of Discrimination against Women, New York, 6 October 1999; entered into force 22 December 2000. Published in *UNTS*, Vol. 2131, p. 83.

Optional Protocol to the Convention on the Rights of Persons with Disabilities, New York, 13 December 2006; entered into force 3 May 2008. In UN Doc. A/61/611.

Optional Protocol to the Convention on the Rights of the Child on a Communications Procedure, New York, 19 December 2011; not yet in force. In UN Doc. A/RES/66/138.

Optional Protocol to the International Covenant on Economic, Social and Cultural Rights, New York, 10 December 2008; enter into force 5 May 2013. In UN Doc. A/63/435.

Patent Cooperation Treaty, Washington, D.C., 19 June 1970; entered into force 24 January 1978. Published in *UNTS*, Vol. 1160, p. 231.

Regulations under the Patent Cooperation Treaty (as amended). Adopted 19 June 1970.

Rio Declaration on Environment and Development, Rio de Janeiro, 14 June 1992. Reprinted in *ILM*, Vol. 31, p. 876.

Rome Statute of the International Criminal Court, Rome, 17 July 1998; entered into force 1 July 2002. Published in *UNTS*, Vol. 2187, p. 3.

Rules of Procedure of the Human Rights Committee. Adopted 11 January 2012. In UN Doc. CCPR/C/3/Rev.10.

Rules of Procedure of the Intergovernmental Committee for the Protection of the World Cultural and Natural Heritage. In Doc. WHC.2-2011/5.

Rules of the International Tribunal for the Law of the Sea, as amended. Reprinted in *International Tribunal for the Law of the Sea: Basic Texts* (Martinus Nijhoff Publishers/Brill Publishers, 2004).

Senate Treaty Document 103–139, U.S. Senate, 103D Congress, 2d Session (Washington, D.C.: U.S. Government Printing Office, 1994).

Statute of the Inter-American Court on Human Rights, La Paz, 1 October 1979; entered into force 1 November 1979. Published in *OAS Official Records* (OEA/Ser.P/IX.0.2/80), Vol. 1, p. 88.

Statute of the International Court of Justice; Integral Annex to the *Charter of the United Nations*, San Francisco, 26 June 1945; entered into force 24 October 1945. Published in *UNTS*, Vol. 1 (XVI).

Treaty between the Government of Australia and the Government of New Zealand establishing certain Exclusive Economic Zone and Continental Shelf Boundaries, Adelaide, 25 July 2004; entered into force 25 January 2006. Published in *ATS*, 2006, p. 4.

Treaty Between the Government of the United States of America and the Government of the United Mexican States on the Delimitation of the Continental Shelf in the Western Gulf of Mexico Beyond 200 Nautical Miles, Washington, 9 June 2000; entered into force 17 January 2001. In *Senate Treaty Document 106–39, U.S. Senate, 106th Congress, 2d Session* (Washington, D.C.: U.S. Government Printing Office, 2000).

Treaty between the Kingdom of Norway and the Russian Federation concerning Maritime Delimitation and Cooperation in the Barents Sea and the Arctic Ocean, Murmansk, 15 September 2010; entered into force 7 July 2011. Reprinted in Henriksen, Tore, and Geir Ulfstein, 'Maritime Delimitation in the Arctic: The Barents Sea Treaty', in *Ocean Development & International Law*, Vol. 42, 2011, pp. 1–21.

Treaty between the Republic of Trinidad and Tobago and the Republic of Venezuela on the Delimitation of Marine and Submarine Areas. Adopted 18 April 1990; entered into force 23 July 1991. Published in *UNTS*, Vol. 1654, p. 300.

Treaty concerning the Cession of the Russian Possessions in North America by his Majesty the Emperor of all the Russias to the United States of America, Washington, 30 March 1867; entered into force 20 June 1867. Reprinted in Kemp, Roger L. (ed.), *Documents of American Democracy: A Collection of Essential Works* (McFarland, 2010), pp. 200ff.

Understanding on Rules and Procedures Governing the Settlement of Disputes. Published in *UNTS*, Vol. 1869, p. 401.

United Nations Convention on the Law of the Sea, Montego Bay, 10 December 1982; entered into force 16 November 1994. Reprinted in *ILM*, Vol. 21, p. 1245.

United Nations Framework Convention on Climate Change, New York, 9 May 1992; entered into force 21 March 1994. Published in *UNTS*, Vol. 1771, p. 107.

Vienna Convention on the Law of Treaties, Vienna, 23 May 1969; entered into force 27 January 1980. Published in *UNTS*, Vol. 1155, p. 331.

CHAPTER 1

Introduction

1.1   The Commission on the Limits of the Continental Shelf

The rules of international law concerning the continental shelf that today apply to the vast majority of the world's states are found in the 1982 United Nations Convention on the Law of the Sea (the LOS Convention).[1] This Convention builds on several decades of economic, political and legal developments, of which the final stage—its implementation—is currently ongoing.

Article 76 is among the key provisions of the LOS Convention. Marked by its exceptional complexity, it defines the continental shelf by criteria that differ considerably from those under Article 1 of the 1958 Convention on the Continental Shelf.[2] Notably, Article 76 brings a new *identification* of the outer limits of the continental shelf by reference to geographical and, especially, geological features. The provision establishes the right of coastal states to determine the outer limits of the continental shelf by means of two criteria: based on a distance of 200 nautical miles from the territorial sea baselines, or based on natural prolongation to the end of the continental margin. These two criteria differ in nature. Whereas 200 nautical miles is a distance limit that need not necessarily correspond to that part of the continental shelf which is a natural prolongation of the continent under the sea, the outer edge of the continental margin denotes a geo-morphological feature determinable in terms of geology and susceptible to the natural prolongation test.[3]

For cases where a coastal state intends to claim a continental shelf extending *beyond* 200 nautical miles from the baselines from which the breadth

---

1   United Nations Convention on the Law of the Sea, Montego Bay, 10 December 1982; entered into force 16 November 1994. Reprinted in *ILM*, Vol. 21, p. 1245. In accordance with Article 308, the LOS Convention entered into force 12 months after the date of deposit of the 60th instrument of ratification or accession. The LOS Convention comprises 320 Articles and nine Annexes, governing all aspects of ocean space, such as delimitation of maritime zones, environmental control, marine scientific research, economic and commercial activities, transfer of technology and the settlement of disputes relating to maritime areas and resources. As at 1 January 2014, there were 166 parties to the LOS Convention.

2   Convention on the Continental Shelf, Geneva, 29 April 1958; entered into force 10 June 1964. Published in *UNTS*, Vol. 499, p. 311.

3   Mahmoudi, Said, *The Law of Deep Seabed Mining* (Almqvist & Wiksell International, 1987), p. 73.

---

of the territorial sea is measured, Article 76 of the LOS Convention has also introduced a special *procedure* for so doing. Notably, paragraph 8 introduces a distinct and institutional element to facilitate the implementation of Article 76—the Commission on the Limits of the Continental Shelf (hereafter the Commission).

Article 3 of Annex II to the LOS Convention specifies that the Commission has two separate functions. First, it shall consider the data and other material submitted by a coastal state to substantiate its claim to a continental shelf beyond 200 nautical miles, and, whenever requested, provide scientific and technical advice during the preparation of such data and material. Second, it shall make recommendations concerning the claim submitted by the coastal state 'in accordance with article 76'. Accordingly, the Commission becomes involved when a coastal state 1) is a party to the LOS Convention; 2) intends to establish the outer limits of its continental shelf beyond 200 nautical miles from the baselines from which the breadth of the territorial sea is measured; and 3) submits to the Commission the particulars of outer limits with such extent, along with supporting scientific and technical data.

The procedures under the LOS Convention for establishing the outer limits of the continental shelf beyond 200 nautical miles can be summarized as follows. After the coastal state has provisionally delineated the outer limits on the basis of the provisions of the LOS Convention, it shall (before a determined 10-year deadline) submit information on these limits to the Commission. The Commission follows the procedure provided for in Annex II to the LOS Convention and makes recommendations to the coastal state on matters related to the establishment of the outer limits. The Commission then submits the recommendations to the coastal state. Outer continental shelf limits subsequently established by a coastal state 'on the basis' of the Commission's recommendations are, according to Article 76, paragraph 8, to be legally final and binding.

This book deals with the Commission as a decision-making body as regards the establishment of the limits of the continental shelf beyond 200 nautical miles under the LOS Convention. In doing so it will analyse the Commission's functions and competence on the one hand, and the adequacy of its procedures and composition on the other. For this purpose, the focus is placed on two specific aspects.

First, the legal aspects of the Commission's decision-making, beginning with the Commission's *procedural* regulations. The Rules of Procedure is one of the basic documents of the Commission; continuously reviewed and amended in light of the evolving practice of the Commission. The Rules of Procedure have significant implications for the Commission's consideration of coastal state submissions. But do the Commission's procedural rules conform to the legal instrument on which they are based, i.e. Article 76 and Annex II of the LOS Convention? Issues in the Commission's Rules of Procedure that give rise to questions in this regard are presented and discussed.

In addition, the study of the legal aspects of the Commission's decision-making includes an examination of the *content* of the Commission's recommendations made to coastal states. Examples illustrating how the Commission has adopted interpretations which qualify and deviate from Article 76 are provided.

Lastly—but perhaps most importantly—the study also examines the *legal effects* of the Commission's recommendations. From Article 76 it follows that the Commission shall make recommendations on matters related to the establishment of the outer limits beyond 200 nautical miles, and then submit these recommendations to the coastal state. The key provision in the last sentence of Article 76, paragraph 8, is given in a form that—according to Allott—should bring a sparkle to the eye of any administrative lawyer: 'The limits of the shelf established by a coastal State on the basis of these recommendations shall be final and binding.'[4]

In light of the scope for interpretation of this provision, the legal significance of the Commission's recommendations as regards establishing 'final and binding' outer limits of the continental shelf beyond 200 nautical miles is examined. A separate issue relating to the legal effects of the Commission's recommendations concerns the legal significance of the recommendations as means of interpretation in the context of Article 76 of the LOS Convention, by reference to the general rules on treaty interpretation in international law. Finally, this study examines the potential legal significance of the Commission's recommendations for the delimitation of the continental shelf beyond 200 nautical miles between states with adjacent or opposite coastlines.

The main reason for examining these three elements is to shed light on the Commission as an international body and thus facilitate an answer to the following basic question: Is the Commission an international institution whose role is limited solely to examination of technical aspects within the scope of Article 76—or does the Commission's work in fact resemble that of a legal body?

The *second* focus is on issues of legitimacy related to the Commission and its procedures. Given the Commission's key role in the process of setting the outer limits of the continental shelf under the LOS Convention, we may ask whether the Commission's composition and procedures are adequate in light

---

4   Allott, Philip, 'Power Sharing in the Law of the Sea', in *American Journal of International Law*, Vol. 77, 1983, pp. 1–30, at p. 18.

of its functions and competences. The basic assumption is that authority should be controlled and that the provisions of the LOS Convention pertaining to the composition and procedures of the Commission should therefore satisfy certain requirements.[5]

Legitimacy is examined in relation to both institutional design and procedures, in terms of the following main questions: Do the members of the Commission have professional backgrounds and qualifications that match their allotted duties? Is the Commission, as a whole and its members individually, independent and impartial? Do the procedures of the Commission satisfy appropriate standards of 'due process of law', for instance with regard to transparency? The purpose of this examination is to enable us to answer the following question: Did the drafters of the LOS Convention succeed in creating a legal framework which—in terms of institutional design and procedures—is normatively legitimate, i.e. which protects and recognizes the fundamental interests of all parties affected by the process under Article 76?

Writings of legal publicists regarding the continental shelf in international law are extensive, with a great many scholarly articles on various aspects of the Commission's work. Existing legal literature on the continental shelf therefore contains valuable collections and analyses of the Commission's practice.[6]

---

5   See also Hey, Ellen, 'International Institutions', in Bodansky, Daniel, Jutta Brunnée and Ellen Hey (eds), *The Oxford Handbook of International Environmental Law* (Oxford University Press, 2008), pp. 749–769, at p. 751.

6   See notably McDorman, Ted, 'The Role of the Commission on the Limits of the Continental Shelf: A Technical Body in a Political World', in *The International Journal of Marine and Coastal Law*, Vol. 17, 2002, pp. 301–324; Elferink, Alex G. Oude, and Constance Johnson, 'Outer Limits of the Continental Shelf and "Disputed Areas": State Practice Concerning Article 76(10) of the LOS Convention', in *The International Journal of Marine and Coastal Law*, Vol. 21, 2006, pp. 461–487; Cavnar, Anna, 'Accountability and the Commission on the Limits of the Continental Shelf: Deciding Who Owns the Ocean Floor', in *Cornell International Law Journal*, Vol. 42, 2009, pp. 387–44; Serdy, Andrew, 'The Commission on the Limits of the Continental Shelf and its Disturbing Propensity to Legislate', in *The International Journal of Marine and Coastal Law*, Vol. 26, 2011, pp. 368–369; Suarez, Suzette, *The Outer Limits of the Continental Shelf—Legal Aspects of Their Establishment* (Springer, 2008); Elferink, Alex G. Oude, 'The Establishment of Outer Limits of the Continental Shelf Beyond 200 Nautical Miles by the Coastal State: The Possibilities of Other States to Have an Impact on the Process', in *The International Journal of Marine and Coastal Law*, Vol. 4, 2009, pp. 535–556; and Jares, Vladimir, 'The Work of the Commission on the Limits of the Continental Shelf', in Vidas, Davor (ed.), *Law, Technology and Science for Oceans in Globalisation—IUU Fishing, Oil Pollution, Bioprospecting, Outer Continental Shelf* (Martinus Nijhoff Publishers, 2010), pp. 449–475. See also Churchill, Robin, and Alan Vaughan Lowe, *The Law of the Sea* (Manchester University Press, 1999), pp. 141–159.

These contributions also include the work of a former committee of the International Law Association (ILA). The ILA Committee on the Outer Continental Shelf was in operation from 2000 to 2010, during which time it produced four reports on the rules of the LOS Convention of relevance to the establishment of the outer limits of the continental shelf.[7] During its ten-year mandate, the Committee produced valuable insights and clarified various legal implications of Article 76 of the LOS Convention.[8]

The legal literature has, however, focused predominantly on issues related to the interpretation and application of the substantive definition of Article 76 of the LOS Convention in various regions, as in the Arctic Ocean. Less attention has been paid to the properties of the Commission as an international institution. This study is a first attempt to engage in a deep analysis of the work of the Commission, and introduces a conceptual framework for assessing how it should operate.

The book also discusses timely issues of increasing importance in the field of the law of the sea. The role and significance of the Commission recently came into focus in international litigation, in a case rendered by the International Tribunal for the Law of the Sea (ITLOS) on 14 March 2012, concerning the delimitation of the territorial sea, the exclusive economic zone and the continental shelf between Bangladesh and Myanmar in the Bay of Bengal.[9] Furthermore, during the Third United Nations Conferences on the Law of the Sea (UNCLOS III, 1973–1982), it was indicated that only some 30 states were seen as likely to have continental shelf areas beyond 200 nautical miles. By the 1990s, that number had expanded considerably: as of January 2014, 70 submissions have been made to the Commission.[10] Even more submissions are anticipated, for

---

7   All reports available at www.ila-hq.org/en/committees/index.cfm/cid/33 (accessed 1 January 2014).

8   The 74th Conference of the ILA recommended dissolution of the Committee in 2010. See Resolution No 8/2010 of the ILA, available at www.ila-hq.org/en/committees/index.cfm/cid/33 (accessed 1 January 2014).

9   *Dispute concerning delimitation of the maritime boundary between Bangladesh and Myanmar in the Bay of Bengal (Bangladesh v. Myanmar)*. For the full text of the basic documents, pleadings, transcripts, judgment and of the declarations and dissenting and separate opinions appended thereto, see the website of the ITLOS at www.itlos.org (accessed 1 January 2014). For a comment on the judgment, see Anderson, David H., 'Delimitation of the Maritime Boundary in the Bay of Bengal (Bangladesh/Myanmar)', in *American Journal of International Law*, Vol. 106, 2012, pp. 817–824.

10 Information retrieved from the website of the Division for Ocean Affairs and the Law of the Sea, Office of Legal Affairs, United Nations (DOALOS): <www.un.org/depts/los/clcs_new/commission_submissions.htm> (accessed 1 January 2014).

instance with respect to the potentially profitable seabed areas beyond 200 nautical miles in the Arctic Ocean. For many years to come, the Commission will therefore be occupied with one of the most important international legal questions of our time—in fact, the issue that initiated negotiations on a new convention on the law of the sea in the early 1970s: the determination of the limits between the area of national jurisdiction of sovereign states, on the one hand, and the seabed subject to the common heritage of mankind on the other, legally defined as the 'Area' in Article 1 of the LOS Convention.

1.2   Outline

The book is divided into five chapters. This first chapter provides a general overview of the topic and timeliness of the book. Chapter 2 presents a brief chronology of the development of the legal regime and the outer limits of the continental shelf, focusing on UNCLOS III and on those parts of the negotiations relating to the outer limits of the continental shelf and to the Commission in particular.

Chapter 3 examines legal aspects of the Commission's decision-making, beginning with certain aspects of the Commission's Rules of Procedure. Selected procedural regulations are examined in light of the LOS Convention, including the Commission's regulations on transparency, issues concerning joint submissions, regulations on the submission deadline applying to coastal states, and procedural aspects of the Commission's regulations with respect to continental shelf submissions in cases of pending maritime disputes concerning shelf areas beyond 200 nautical miles.

The second part of Chapter 3 discusses legal aspects of the Commission's substantive decision-making. Features of certain recommendations show that the Commission has adopted interpretations that can indeed be challenged on the basis of Article 76 of the LOS Convention—including how the Commission resolves conflicts of norms between separate paragraphs of Article 76, and the Commission's classification of seafloor highs.

Lastly, Chapter 3 examines the legal effects of the Commission's recommendations and discusses how these recommendations come into play when coastal states seek to establish the outer limits of their continental shelf beyond 200 nautical miles from the territorial sea baselines. In focus here is the legal significance of the recommendations for the purpose of establishing 'final and binding' outer limits of the continental shelf. Subsequently, the Commission's recommendations as relevant means of interpretation with regard to Article 76 of the LOS Convention are discussed, as is the potential significance of the

Commission's recommendations for the delimitation of the continental shelf beyond 200 nautical miles.

Chapter 4 turns to the legitimacy of the Commission and its decision-making. It begins by discussing the membership and composition of the Commission, including an examination of the expertise and professional background of Commission members, their qualifications and issues with respect to representativeness. Chapter 4 then goes on to discuss legitimacy aspects with respect to independence and impartiality. Key aspects here concern nomination and election procedures, how members are remunerated, their tenure and extra-professional activities. Chapter 4 also examines the procedures of the Commission from the perspective of normative legitimacy, discussing admissibility of facts and evidence in the Article 76 process, coastal state participation and the right to be heard, transparency, reasons for recommendations and review.

Finally, Chapter 5 identifies some future challenges for the Commission, also as regards the current debate on dislocation of decision-making in international law, and how Article 76 and the Commission relate to this topic.

The Outer Limits of the Continental Shelf in International Law

2.1   Introduction

This chapter provides an historical account of the rules on the outer limits of the continental shelf in international law, so as to introduce the provisions of the LOS Convention pertaining to the Commission and the outer limits of the continental shelf.

The chapter is divided into five sections. Section 2.2 briefly deals with the early origins of the continental shelf regime under international law. Section 2.3 reviews the evolution from 1945 and until the mid-1960s. Section 2.4 discusses the last and consolidating phase of the historical development related to the regime of the continental shelf in international law. The focus is on the UNCLOS III negotiations directly relevant to the current legal rules on the outer limits of the continental shelf and the Commission: Article 76 and Annex II of the LOS Convention. Some concluding remarks are offered in section 2.5.

2.2   The Early History of the Legal Regime of the Continental Shelf

Towards the end of the 17th century, the perception among European naval powers was that the principle of the freedom of the seas was more beneficial to them than previous failed attempts to establish national monopolies. Most unilateral claims had been withdrawn, and by the turn of the century, Hugo Grotius' ideology of *mare liberum* had become a reality.[1] The principle of the 'free sea' had proven to be of benefit to international trade and shipping.

The continental shelf was nevertheless not yet perceived as a specific matter of interest. Of course, at that time, states did not know and could not imagine the continental shelf concealed valuable assets. The only example of

---

1   Grotius' influential argument in favour of freedom of navigation trade, and fishing is available in Richard Hakluyt's translation *The Free Sea*—edited and with an introduction by David Armage. See Armage, David (ed.), *The Free Sea* (Liberty Fund, 2004).

© KONINKLIJKE BRILL NV, LEIDEN, 2014 | DOI 10.1163/9789004274174_003

utilization of seabed resources in Europe during the 18th century was the occasional fishing of oysters on the banks in the English Channel.[2]

It was the USA which first made an official reference to the continental shelf in a legal context. A report of 17 November 1806 dealt with a US proposal for the expansion of the country's territorial waters.[3] During the 19th century, several other states began adopting laws concerning activities on the seabed. In the *Cornwall Submarines Act* of 1858, the UK invoked the right to build tunnels and mines beneath the seabed outside the limits of its territorial waters.[4] Similar regulations were also adopted by Canada, Australia, Chile and Japan.[5] Domestic legislation concerning pearl fisheries off the coasts of Ceylon can be traced back as early as to 1811.[6] Legislation for sedentary fisheries also applied in Tunisia,[7] Panama and Venezuela.[8] In some cases, these regulations were subject to geographical limitations. For example, the regulation of pearl fisheries in Panama applied to a distance of 120 nautical miles from the coast.[9] Regulation concerning fishing for sponges off the coast of Tunisia applied to a distance of 17 nautical miles.[10] But even though some states at a very early point in time regulated activities on the continental shelf adjacent to their coasts, the claims were so limited that they in reality never challenged the principle of *mare liberum*.[11] Even by the beginning of the 20th century, marine technology had made little significant progress. Commercial activity was still limited to traditional pearl and shell fisheries on banks and close to land.

---

2   Chapman, Wilbert McLeod, 'Concerning Fishery Jurisdiction and the Regime of the Deep-sea Bed', in Burke, William (ed.), *Towards a Better Use of the Oceans: Contemporary Legal Problems in Ocean Development* (Almqvist & Wiksell, 1969), pp. 154ff.

3   McNair, Arnold D., *International Law Opinions* (Cambridge University Press, 1956), pp. 258–331.

4   Higgins, Alexander, and Constantine John Colombos, *The International Law of the Sea* (Longmans, 1943), p. 54; Katin, Ernest, *The Legal Status of the Continental Shelf as Determined by the Conventions Adopted at the 1958 United Nations Conference on the Law of the Sea: An Analytical Study of an Instance of International Law Making* (University of Minnesota Press, 1969), p. 20.

5   Higgins and Colombos, *The International Law of the Sea*, p. 55.

6   O'Connell, Daniel P., *The International Law of the Sea* (Clarendon Press, 1982), p. 451.

7   *Ibid.*, p. 452.

8   See Katin, *The Legal Status of the Continental Shelf as Determined by the Conventions Adopted at the 1958 United Nations Conference on the Law of the Sea: An Analytical Study of an Instance of International Law Making*, p. 18.

9   *Ibid.*, p. 18.

10   O'Connell, *The International Law of the Sea*, p. 452.

11   Smith, Herbert Arthur, *The Law and Custom of the Sea* (Stevens and Sons Limited, 1959), p. 61.

Nevertheless, the number of declarations and state practices explicitly referring to the continental shelf began to increase. Oden de Buen, a Spanish oceanographer, argued in 1916 that coastal state rights within territorial waters should apply to the ocean floor as well.[12] Also in 1916, Russia referred to 'the continental platform of Siberia' in a unilateral statement relating to the rights of certain Arctic islands.[13] The Soviet Union maintained this claim in a statement to the USA in 1924.[14]

The continental shelf was also mentioned when the Assembly of the League of Nations commissioned its Council to study the possibility of codifying specific international legal principles in 1924.[15] The Council established an expert committee that was tasked, *inter alia*, with preparing an overview of 'subjects of international law, the regulation of which by international agreement would seem to be most desirable and realisable at the present moment'.[16] The Council's Sub Committee on Territorial Waters did not explicitly raise the issue of the continental shelf. However, in its work on the limits of the territorial waters, the Committee found reason to note a complicating circumstance:

> [A] certain distance from the coast—a distance which varied to some extent—the bottom of the sea is marked by a sort of great step, almost always abrupt, which divides it into two quite distinct regions. The region extending from this step to the coast-line has been called the 'continental shelf'. The other much vaster, which extend beyond this step, is the abysmal region [...].[17]

By the mid-1930s, new technology made it possible to drill for oil in shallow waters, including in the Gulf of Mexico, the Arabian Gulf and the Gulf of California. Drilling had proven very successful, and initiated further attempts to exploit submarine hydrocarbons, led by US oil companies. Interest was further intensified by the Second World War. During the war, the first known delimitation agreement dealing explicitly with the continental shelf was signed.

---

12   Annand, Ram Prakash, *Legal Regime of the Sea-Bed and the Developing Countries* (A.W. Sijthoff International Publishing, 1976), p. 32.

13   See *Yearbook of the International Law Commission*, Vol. II, 1950, p. 49.

14   *Ibid.* See also Andrassy, Juraj, *International Law and the Resources of the Sea* (Columbia University Press, 1970), p. 49.

15   Resolution of the Fifth Assembly of the League of Nations of 22 September 1924. Reprinted in *American Journal of International Law*, Vol. 20, 1926, pp. 2–3.

16   *Ibid.*

17   Report of the Sub-Committee on Territorial Waters. Reprinted in *American Journal of International Law*, Vol. 20, 1926, p. 126.

On 26 February 1942, the UK—on behalf of then-protectorate Trinidad—signed an agreement with Venezuela that delimited the continental shelf areas in the Gulf of Paria.[18]

2.3   Continental Shelf Claims and the Development of International Law

2.3.1   *The Truman Proclamation and Other Unilateral Claims*

Towards the end of the Second World War, there was little doubt that the sea-bed contained hydrocarbons on a significant scale. The US authorities went along with powerful oil interests and the military. National jurisdictional claims to the seabed, down to at least 200 metres sea depth, would ensure US primacy in areas where it had the greatest economic and industrial interests: the Gulf of Mexico and off the coast of Southern California. These interests eventually prompted President Harry Truman, on 28 September 1945, to issue a proclamation on the 'Policy of the United States with Respect to the Natural Resources of the Subsoil and Sea Bed of the Continental Shelf'.[19]

This proclamation marked a turning point in the evolution of the international legal regime of the continental shelf. For the first time, 'continental shelf' was used as a clearly defined term in an international legal context. The proclamation did not state the width of the continental shelf, but, according to the press release from the White House on the same day, 'the U.S. generally viewed the submerged lands contiguous to the continent and covered by no more than 100 fathoms (600 feet) of waters as the continental shelf'.[20]

As the proclamation made clear, from now on the natural resources of the continental shelf were under US jurisdiction. This was thus a claim to exclusive rights. However, while the proclamation rejected the thesis that the continental shelf was *res nullius* or *res communis*,[21] the claim of exclusive rights of the

---

18   Gutteridge, J.A.C., 'The 1958 Geneva Convention on the Continental Shelf', in *British Yearbook of International Law*, Vol. 35, 1959, pp. 102–123, at p. 102.

19   Reprinted in Whitemann, Marjorie M., *Digest of International Law* (Department of State Publication, 1965), pp. 756–757. A second proclamation was issued by Truman on the same day: 'Policy of the United States with Respect to Coastal Fisheries in Certain Areas of the High Seas'. That proclamation concerned in essence the establishment of conservation zones in those areas of the high seas contiguous to US coasts where fishing activities had been or might be developed and maintained on a substantial scale (*ibid.*).

20   Press release reprinted in *ibid.*, pp. 757–758.

21   Pardo, Arvid, 'Whose Is the Bed of the Sea?', in *American Society of International Law*, Vol. 62, 1968, pp. 216–229, at p. 218.

coastal state did in no way affect the status of the waters *above* the continental shelf, including navigational freedoms. The Truman Proclamation thus did not involve any claim of sovereignty, only jurisdiction and exclusive control.[22]

The Truman Proclamation unleashed a stream of similar unilateral initiatives. Already by 1958, unilateral statements and claims had been issued by more than 50 states, mostly in Latin America and Asia.[23] All national initiatives were tacitly accepted, and no formal reservations were made. But state practice was by no means uniform. Some states limited their claims in line with that of the USA; others went significantly further with regard to the continental shelf's outer limits as well as the nature of jurisdiction. Among the latter were several Latin American and South Asian states which claimed not only exclusive rights over resources, but *sovereignty* to the seabed. Some states also extended these latter claims to include the water column and airspace above.[24] Some did not use the term 'continental shelf', but referred instead to

---

22   On the relationship between 'jurisdiction and exclusive control' and 'sovereignty', see Lauterpacht, Hersch, 'Sovereignty over Submarine Areas', in *British Yearbook of International Law*, Vol. 17, 1950, pp. 376–433, at p. 389.

23   Mahmoudi, *The Law of Deep Seabed Mining*, p. 56.

24   Many continental shelf claims are reprinted in Whitemann, *Digest of International Law*, pp. 793–801. Examples include Article 7 of the Constitution of El Salvador of 7 September 1950, under which '[t]he territory of the Republic within its present boundaries is irreducible. It includes the adjacent seas to a distance of two hundred sea miles from low water line and the corresponding air space, subsoil and continental shelf' (*Constitution of the Republic of El Salvador, 1950* (Pan American Union, 1953), Article 2 of Presidential Declaration of Chile, dated 23 June 1947, providing that '[t]he Government of Chile confirms and proclaims its national sovereignty over the sea adjacent to its coasts whatever may be their depths' (*Presidential Declaration [of Chile] Concerning the Continental Shelf, 23 June 1947.* Reprinted in *Laws and Regulations on the Régime of the High Seas* (Division for the Codification and Development of International Law: United Nations publication, Sales No. 1951.V.2/UN Doc. ST/LEG/SER.B/1), p. 6.), and Presidential Decree No. 781 of Peru of 1 August 1947, which provides that 'national sovereignty and jurisdiction are to be extended over the sea adjoining the shores of national territory whatever its depths and in the extension necessary to preserve, protect, maintain and utilize natural resources and wealth of any kind which may be found in or below those waters' (*Presidential Decree No. 781 [of Peru] Concerning Submerged Continental or Insular Shelf, 1 August 1947.* Reprinted in *Laws and Regulations on the Régime of the High Seas* (Division for the Codification and Development of International Law: UN publication, Sales No. 1951.V.2/ UN Doc. ST/LEG/SER.B/1), p. 16). See also Johnson, D.H.N., 'The Legal Status of the Sea-Bed and Subsoil', in *Zeitschrift für ausländisches öffentliches Recht und Völkerrecht*, Vol. 16, 1957, pp. 474–487.

the 'sea-bed' or 'sea-bed and subsoil of the submarine areas'.[25] And far from all states defined the seaward limit of their continental shelf claims.

2.3.2   The International Law Commission

In response to these unilateral claims to seabed areas, the International Law Commission (ILC) started work to codify the law of the sea. The ILC touched on the issue of the continental shelf at its first session in 1949, when Professor Jean Pierre François remarked that it would be 'very useful for the Commission to study the modern regulations regarding the continental shelf, although that question fell within the scope of the progressive development of international law rather than of its codification'.[26] Several others supported François and agreed that the topic was a suitable matter for the ILC.[27]

There was, however, some disagreement among ILC members as to the basic models and theories for the regulation of the continental shelf. One member suggested that 'the exploitation of the products of the continental shelf might be entrusted to the international community'.[28] Others felt there were insurmountable difficulties relating to such an internationalization model.[29]

At the Commission's third session in 1951, François submitted a second report on various matters concerning the regime of the high seas.[30] The ILC then formulated draft treaty provisions for the continental shelf.[31] According to Article 1,

> the 'continental shelf' refers to the sea-bed and subsoil of the submarine areas contiguous to the coast, but outside the area of territorial waters, where the depth of the superjacent waters admits of the exploitation of the natural resources of the sea-bed and subsoil.[32]

The ILC thus adopted a distinctly *legal* definition of the continental shelf, which did not coincide with the 'geological' definition of the continental shelf. In justification, the ILC said: '[t]he varied use of the term by scientists is in

---

25   McDougal, M.S., and W.T. Burke, *The Public Order of the Oceans* (Yale University Press, 1962), pp. 669–670 and Eckert, R.D., *The Enclosure of Ocean Resources* (Hoover Institution Press, 1979), p. 34.

26   *Yearbook of the International Law Commission*, Vol. I, 1949, p. 43 (para. 63).

27   *Ibid.* (para. 64).

28   *Yearbook of the International Law Commission*, Vol. II, 1950, p. 384 (para. 198).

29   *Ibid.*

30   UN Doc. A/CN.4/42 (*Second Report on the Regime of the High Seas*), p. 139.

31   *Ibid.*, p. 141.

32   *Ibid.*

itself an obstacle to the adoption of the geological concept as a basis for legal regulation of the problem'.[33]

The proposed legal definition was, however, criticized by many because it did not specify a fixed outer limit.[34] After considering the opinions of certain governments, the ILC came to the conclusion that the text previously adopted did not satisfy the requirement of certainty and would likely generate disputes. In 1953, the ILC thus abandoned the criterion of exploitability in favour of a depth criterion of two hundred metres:

> As used in these articles, the term 'continental shelf' refers to the sea-bed and subsoil of the submarine areas contiguous to the coast, but outside the area of the territorial sea, to a depth of two hundred meters.[35]

The ILC explained the new proposal, arguing that a limit of 200 metres in depth would be sufficient, considering the practical possibilities of exploiting the seabed resources.[36]

The issue of the definition of the continental shelf was not discussed again by the ILC until its eighth session in 1956, when it adopted the following definition:

> For the purposes of these articles, the term 'continental shelf' is used as referring to the seabed and subsoil of the submarine areas adjacent to the coast but outside the area of the territorial sea, to a depth of 200 metres

---

33   *Ibid.* The ILC also explained why it nevertheless chose to use the term 'continental shelf': 'The Commission considered whether it ought to use the term 'continental shelf' or whether it would not be preferable, in accordance with an opinion expressed in some scientific works, to refer to such areas merely as 'submarine areas'. It was decided to retain the term 'continental shelf' because it is in current use and because the term 'submarine areas' used alone would give no indication of the nature of the submarine areas in question'. See *ibid.*

34   *Yearbook of the International Law Commission*, Vol. I, 1953, p. 73 (paras. 65–66). One of several states that demonstrated concern was Norway: 'If it is necessary to give coastal States a right of control and jurisdiction for the purpose of exploring and exploiting the natural resources of the sea-bed and subsoil, the best thing would probably be to limit that right to a contiguous zone of a fixed breadth'. See *Yearbook of the International Law Commission*, Vol. II, 1953, p. 261. For other comments by governments on the draft articles on the continental shelf and related subjects prepared by the ILC at its third session in 1951, see *ibid.*, pp. 241–269.

35   *Ibid.*, p. 213.

36   *Ibid.*

(approximately 100 fathoms) or, beyond that limit, to where the depth of the superjacent waters admits of the exploitation of the natural resources of the said areas.[37]

Compared to the previous drafts of 1951 and 1953, the ILC had changed the wording significantly. Notably, the ILC had taken note of the Inter-American Specialized Conference on 'Conservations of Natural Resources: Continental Shelf and Oceanic Waters'—held at Ciudad Trujillo in 1956—according to which the right of the coastal state should be extended beyond the limit of 200 metres, 'to where the depth of the superjacent waters admits of the exploitation of the natural resources of the seabed and subsoil'.[38] The majority of the members of the ILC decided in favour of this addition, although certain members contested the usefulness of the addition, which in their opinion unjustifiably and dangerously impaired the stability of the limit adopted.[39]

2.3.3   UNCLOS I and the Convention on the Continental Shelf

On 21 February 1957, the UNGA decided to convene an international conference on the law of the sea.[40] The purpose of this first UN law of the sea conference, which came to be known as UNCLOS I, was 'to examine the law of the sea, taking account not only of the legal, but also of the technical, biological, economic and political aspects of the problem, and to embody the results of its work in one or more international conventions or such other instruments as it may deem appropriate'.[41] In reality, however, the purpose was somewhat narrower. A later paragraph in the resolution refers to the ILC's 1956 report as 'the basis for its consideration of the various problems involved in the development and codification of the law of the sea'.[42] It later emerged that this, in practice, limited the task of UNCLOS I to deciding *for* or *against* the ILC draft.

As noted above, the ILC had considered fundamentally different methods of delineating the outer limits of the continental shelf. In 1956, the ILC had proposed a two-point criterion for the continental shelf: a 200-metre depth-line, combined with the exploitability criterion. The combination of these two was an attempt on the part of the ILC to unite conflicting perceptions and interests.

---

37   *Yearbook of the International Law Commission*, 1956, Vol. II, p. 264.
38   *Ibid.*, p. 296.
39   *Ibid.*
40   UNGA Res. 1105 (XI) (*International Conference of Plenipotentiaries to Examine the Law of the Sea*), para. 2.
41   *Ibid.*
42   *Ibid.*, para. 9.

The exploitability criterion nevertheless became a hard-fought issue also at UNCLOS I.[43] The most central objection to the criterion was that it in reality did not stipulate any outer limit of the continental shelf. Technology had already advanced to such a level that the 200-metre criterion would not have any practical significance: the exploitability criterion would prevail in practice. Arguments along these lines were put forward by technologically advanced states, but also by nations that were not.[44]

Opposition to the exploitability criterion did not, however, culminate in a united front: the countries opposing it were divided among themselves and unable to agree on an alternative treaty proposal. Instead, a series of unilateral initiatives were proposed,[45] none of which gained majority when the Fourth Committee of UNCLOS I came to vote on the matter. The 1956 ILC draft was adopted by 51 votes in favour, 9 against and 10 abstentions.[46] Those who voted against were France, Belgium, the Netherlands, Italy and West Germany, as well

---

43   See generally *Official Records of the United Nations Conference on the Law of the Sea (Fourth Committee)*, Vol. VI. See UN Doc. A/CONF.13/42.

44   For instance, South Vietnam argued that the criterion of possible exploitation introduced the seeds of uncertainty; modern technical progress is so rapid that it will be difficult to state at any time where the outward limit lies (*ibid.*, p. 24). The delegation from South Vietnam made no secret of their motives and went on to explain that they would prefer to see the criterion of depth alone retained, particularly as the waters off their shores are relatively shallow and do not reach a depth of 200 metres for more than 200 nautical miles. Similar examples of diplomatic honesty are rarely encountered. Also Pakistan claimed that the effect of the criterion of exploitability would be to abolish any definite limit to the continental shelf, replacing it by the possibility of limitless extension subject only to technical considerations (*ibid.*, p. 17). This pattern of criticism was also followed by Canada (*ibid.*, p. 30), France (*ibid.*, p. 32) and West Germany (*ibid.*, p. 38), but the state to express the greatest concern about vast areas of the ocean floor in the open sea becoming subject to national jurisdiction was Lebanon: '[In adopting the criterion of exploitation it is] possible that four-fifths of an area which now forms part of the high seas will become the exclusive preserve of technically developed coastal States, instead of being open to the entire national community as *res communis*. If the clause relating to possible exploitation were retained, it would be unnecessary to mention the 200 metre limit, since the definition would then refer, not to a depth of 200 metres, but to some other, unspecified, depth' (*ibid.*).

45   For instance, Yugoslavia proposed that the exploitability criterion should be replaced by a maximum limit of 100 nautical miles from the coast (*ibid.*). France wanted to remove the exploitability criteria and maintain the 200-metre limit as the sole criterion (*ibid.*). The Netherlands, the UK and India proposed replacing the exploitability criteria with a depth limit of 550 metres, which was believed to be the largest water depth over the geological continental shelf anywhere (*ibid.*, pp. 132 and 135).

46   *Ibid.*, p. 47.

as Japan, South Korea, Argentina and Pakistan. Among those who voted for were the USA and the Soviet Union, the Eastern European states, most Asian and African states, as well as the Latin American states. Norway also voted in favour, which is difficult to understand in light of Norway's strong opposition to the criterion during negotiations, and of the delegation's instructions.[47]

France did not give up, however. In a final attempt to challenge the exploitability criterion before it was laid before the plenary session, the French delegation proposed a vote on the wording 'or, beyond that limit, to where the depth of the superjacent waters admits of the exploitation of the natural resources of the said areas', that is, the exploitability criterion. The Latin American states protested, but the proposal was approved.[48] The exploitability criterion survived, with 48 votes in favour, 20 against and 2 abstentions. When the matter was brought forward in plenary session it was thus a mere formality and the wording of the 1956 ILC draft was adopted by a sufficient majority. Article 1 of the Convention on the Continental Shelf defines the continental shelf as

> the seabed and subsoil of the submarine areas adjacent to the coast but outside the area of the territorial sea, to a depth of 200 meters or, beyond that limit, to where the depth of the superjacent waters admits of the exploitation of the natural resources of the said areas.

As it turned out, however, this provision was to become not much more than a harbinger of new conflict dimensions with respect to the issue of the outer limits of the continental shelf in international law.

2.3.4   Developments from 1958 to 1967

The Second UN Conference on the Law of the Sea (UNCLOS II, 1960) did not address the definition of the continental shelf, and the Convention on the Continental Shelf had no immediate effect on legal developments. Six years were to pass from its adoption to its entry into force, even though only 22 deposits of the Convention were required.[49]

The Convention on the Continental Shelf was therefore also unable to prevent the proliferation of unilateral declarations which went considerably further than its provisions. Since 1958, the seabed had increasingly become

---

47   Traavik, Kim, *Et nytt territorium åpnes—en studie av forhandlingene om kontinental-sokkelkonvensjonen av 1958* (Fridtjof Nansen Institute, 1973), p. 89.

48   *Official Records of the United Nations Conference on the Law of the Sea (Plenary Meetings)*, Vol. II, p. 18. See UN Doc. A/CONF.13/38.

49   See Article 11 of the Convention on the Continental Shelf.

a source of tension in international politics. First, economic, strategic and military reasons propelled interest in the continental shelf. The period from 1958 also saw regional disputes regarding overlapping continental shelf claims. Most pertinent from the perspectives of this study were the disputes submitted to the ICJ in 1967 by the countries bordering the southern waters of the North Sea: the Netherlands, Denmark and West Germany. In the *North Sea Continental Shelf* cases, the ICJ for the first time referred to the principle of 'natural prolongation':

> More fundamental than the notion of proximity appears to be the principle [...] of the natural prolongation or continuation of the land territory or domain, or land sovereignty of the coastal State, into and under the high seas, via the bed of its territorial sea which is under the full sovereignty of that State. There are various ways of formulating this principle, but the underlying idea, namely of an extension of something already possessed, is the same, and it is this idea of extension which is, in the Court's opinion, determinant.[50]

Although the issue at stake was *delimitation* of the continental shelf, the ICJ affirmed the basic prerequisite for a delimitation dispute to arise: the continental shelf must be a natural prolongation of the claiming coastal state in question. Thus, the ICJ's premises were instructive in at least two ways. First, the Court stated what part of the ocean floor could be classified as 'continental shelf' in a legal sense. Second, the Court said something about the geographical extent for a coastal state's claim to the seabed; the outer limits lie where the ocean floor can no longer be said to constitute a natural extension of the land territory from which the claim is made. These remarks by the ICJ on the concept of natural prolongation would prove highly significant in negotiations at the forthcoming UNCLOS III and also for the already ongoing work of the UN on the adoption of a new definition of the continental shelf.

2.4   Limits to Coastal State Claims over the Continental Shelf

2.4.1   *Malta and the UN Sea-Bed Committee*
The issue of the continental shelf was brought up again in the UN in 1967. It was in the form of a *note verbale* from UN delegation of Malta, one of the

---

50   *I.C.J. Reports* 1969, p. 3, at p. 31 (para. 43).

smallest and youngest members of the 'world organization'. In this note, Malta proposed to include in the 22nd UNGA the following item:

> Declaration and Treaty concerning the Reservation Exclusively for Peaceful Purposes of the Sea-bed and the Ocean Floor, Underlying the Seas beyond the Limits of Present National Jurisdiction, and the Use of Their Resources in the Interests of Mankind.[51]

Two months later, on 1 November 1967, Malta's UN Ambassador Arvid Pardo held a speech on the subject, in the First Committee of the UNGA.[52] In his speech, Pardo called for a new international legal order, to be fundamentally based on the concept of the ocean floor as a common heritage of mankind. He also argued for a new treaty that would include a prohibition against the further national annexation of continental shelf areas, as well as rules for the utilization of submarine resources:

> I think it is clear that there can be no doubt that an effective international regime over the sea-bed and the ocean floor beyond a clearly defined national jurisdiction is the only alternative by which we can hope to avoid the escalating tensions that will be inevitable if the present situation is allowed to continue. It is the only alternative by which we can hope to escape the immense hazards of a permanent impairment of the marine environment. It is, finally, the only alternative that gives assurance that the immense resources on and under the ocean floor will be exploited with harm to none and benefit to all.[53]

Malta's proposal got a mixed reception. The UNGA, nevertheless, decided that a further study of these issues would be appropriate. This time, however, the task was not entrusted to the ILC. The matter was seen as being essentially *political* in nature and should thus rest with the UNGA.[54]

---

51   UN Doc. A/6695 ('Examination of the question of the reservation exclusively for peaceful purposes of the seabed and the ocean floor, and the subsoil thereof, underlying the high seas beyond the limits of present national jurisdiction, and the use of their resources in the interests of mankind').

52   UN Doc. A/C.1/PV.1515 ('Statement by Ambassador Pardo').

53   *Ibid.*, p. 2.

54   Evensen, Jens, *Working Methods and Procedures in the Third United Nations Conference on the Law of the Sea* (Martinus Nijhoff Publishers, 1986), p. 435.

On 18 December 1967, the UNGA then unanimously adopted resolution 2340.[55] This resolution provided for the establishment of an *ad hoc* committee to work on the question of the peaceful use of the ocean floor beyond the limits of national jurisdiction, and also prepare a report to include a survey of past and present activities with regard to the seabed, a survey of existing international agreements concerning these areas and an account of the scientific, technical, economical, legal and other aspects of the matter.[56]

The report of the *ad hoc* Committee was adopted on 30 August 1968. The First Committee—the committee dealing with key political and security policy issues—undertook a thorough review of the report, and on 21 December 1968, the UNGA adopted a series of four resolutions, of which Resolution A established the 'Committee on the Peaceful Uses of the Seabed and Ocean Floor beyond the Limits of National Jurisdiction' (the UN Sea-Bed Committee).[57] The *ad hoc* Committee had thus, in the course of only one year, become a permanent Committee of 42 members.

The UN Sea-Bed Committee continued working on seabed issues, like its predecessor. Its first report was finalized at the end of 1969. Discussions at the 24th UNGA culminated in the adoption of a new series of four resolutions. In resolution A, the UNGA determined that 'there exists an area of the sea-bed and ocean floor and the subsoil thereof which lies beyond the limits of national jurisdiction'.[58] Furthermore, this area should be used exclusively for peaceful purposes and its resources utilized for the benefit of all mankind; and, importantly, that

> the definition of the continental shelf contained in the Convention on the Continental Shelf of 29 April 1958 does not define with sufficient

---

55   UN Doc. A/RES/22/2340 ('Examination of the question of the reservation exclusively for peaceful purposes of the sea-bed and the ocean floor, and the subsoil thereof, underlying the high seas beyond the limits of present national jurisdiction, and the use of their resources in the interests of mankind').

56   Oda, Shigeru, *The International Law of the Ocean Development: Basic Documents* (Sijthoff, 1972), pp. 7–8.

57   UNGA Res. 2467 (XXIII) ('Examination of the Question of the Reservation Exclusively for Peaceful Purposes of the Sea-Bed and the Ocean Floor, and the Subsoil Thereof, Underlying the High Seas Beyond the Limits of Present National Jurisdiction, and the Use of Their Resources in the Interests of Mankind').

58   UNGA Res. 2574 (XXIV) ('Question of the Reservation Exclusively for Peaceful Purposes of the Sea-Bed and the Ocean Floor, and the Subsoil Thereof, Underlying the High Seas Beyond the Limits of Present National Jurisdiction, and the Use of Their Resources in the Interests of Mankind').

precision the limits of the area over which a coastal State exercises sovereign rights for the purpose of exploration and exploitation of natural resources, and that customary international law on the subject is inconclusive.[59]

The resolution then requested the UN Secretary-General

> to ascertain the views of Member States on the desirability of convening at an early date a conference on the law of the sea to review the regimes of the high seas, the continental shelf, the territorial sea and contiguous zone, fishing and conservation of the living resources of the high seas, particularly in order to arrive at a clear, precise and internationally accepted definition of the area of the sea-bed and ocean floor which lies beyond the limits of national jurisdiction, in the light of the international regime to be established for that area.[60]

This survey revealed widespread support for a new law of the sea conference. On 17 December 1970, an extended UN Sea-Bed Committee of 86 members was created.[61] At the same time, the UNGA unanimously adopted the 'Declaration of Principles Governing the Sea-Bed and the Ocean Floor, beyond the Limits of National Jurisdiction'.[62] Here, among other things, it was provided that 'there is an area of the seabed and the ocean floor, and the subsoil thereof, beyond the limits of national jurisdiction, *the precise limits of which are yet to be determined*' (emphasis added).[63] The UNGA therefore decided

> to convene in 1973 [...] a conference on the law of the sea which would deal with the establishment of an equitable international regime—including an international machinery—for the area and the resources of the sea-bed and the ocean floor, and the subsoil thereof, beyond the limits of national jurisdiction, a precise definition of the area, and a broad range of related issues including those concerning the regimes of the high seas, the continental shelf, the territorial sea (including the question

---

59   *Ibid.*
60   *Ibid.*
61   *Ibid.*
62   UNGA Res. 2749 (XXV) ('Declaration of Principles Governing the Sea-Bed and the Ocean Floor, and the Subsoil Thereof, Beyond the Limits of National Jurisdiction').
63   *Ibid.* The resolution was passed with 108 states in favour, none against, and 14 abstentions.

of its breadth and the question of international straits) and contiguous
zone [...].[64]

The UN Sea-Bed Committee would from now on concentrate on preparing UNCLOS III. It retained its original name, though its mandate in reality
was considerably extended. In 1973, the Committee adopted a comprehensive report containing various draft articles relating to questions UNCLOS III
should take into consideration. Two main alternatives were mentioned regarding the outer limits of the continental shelf: a Soviet proposal of the 500 metre
isobath or 100 nautical miles from the coast, and the outer edge of the continental margin.[65]

2.4.2   *UNCLOS III*

On 16 November 1973, the UNGA decided to convene a third global conference on the law of sea.[66] UNCLOS III held 11 sessions between 1973 and 1982.
The Second Committee of the Conference was responsible for general questions of the law of the sea. This involved preparing draft treaty articles on
the territorial sea, international straits, the exclusive economic zone and the
continental shelf.

The Second Committee held 59 formal meetings between 1974 and 1982,
of which 46 took place in 1974.[67] The foundation of the work was the many
proposals that were included in the report of the UN Sea-Bed Committee,
as well as new proposals which emerged during the general debate in
plenary sessions.

---

64   UNGA Res. 2750 C (XXV) ('Reservation Exclusively for Peaceful Purposes of the Sea-Bed
      and the Ocean Floor, and the Subsoil Thereof, Underlying the High Seas Beyond the
      Limits of Present National Jurisdiction and Use of Their Resources in the Interests of
      Mankind, and Convening of a Conference on the Law of the Sea').

65   UN Doc. A/9021 ('Report of the Seabed Committee to the General Assembly'), pp. 66–67.
      All suggestions concerning the outer limit of the continental shelf are included in UN
      Doc. A/AC.138/94/Add. 1 ('Report of Sub-Committee I, Annex III, Texts Illustrating Areas
      of Agreement and Disagreement on Items 1 and 2 of the Sub-Committee's Programme of
      Work'), pp. 2–3.

66   UNGA Res. 3067 (XXVIII) ('Reservation exclusively for peaceful purposes of the sea-bed
      and the ocean floor, and the subsoil thereof, underlying the high seas beyond the limits of
      present national jurisdiction and use of their resources in the interests of mankind, and
      convening of the 3rd United Nations Conference on the Law of the Sea-Bed and the
      Ocean Floor beyond the Limits of National Jurisdiction').

67   Nandan, Satya, and Shabtai Rosenne (eds), *United Nations Convention on the Law of the
      Sea, 1982, A Commentary* (Martinus Nijhoff Publishers, 1993), Vol. II, p. 18.

The work of the Second Committee resulted in Articles 2 to 132, parts of Articles 297 and 298, and Annexes I and II of the LOS Convention. Thus the relevant provisions concerning the outer limits of the continental shelf and the Commission were also the result of the work of the Second Committee. In what follows, we shall examine how UNCLOS III dealt with the question of the outer continental shelf limits, including how the *institutionalized* method for ascertaining continental shelf limits in the LOS Convention came into being.

Third Session

After the discussions at the second session, held in Caracas from 20 June to 29 August 1974, the individual countries' views on the issue of the continental shelf had taken form. The initial discussions at the third session revealed two main directions. First, many states wanted the coastal state's sovereign rights to stop at 200 nautical miles. There was no real need for special rules concerning the continental shelf, they maintained, since the rules on the exclusive economic zone would give the coastal state full rights over the resources of the seabed out to 200 nautical miles. The areas beyond, it was argued, should belong to the international community.[68] Second, there were states whose continental margins extended beyond 200 nautical miles from the coast, which held that sovereign rights should apply to the outer edge of the continental margin or to 200 nautical miles where the margin was located within this limit (these were the so-called 'margineers').[69] Basically, they argued that the coastal state under current international law—including the ICJ judgment in the *North Sea Continental Shelf* cases—already had jurisdiction to the part of the continental shelf stretching beyond 200 nautical miles. One would thus not, through a new treaty, relinquish existing rights.

The margineers' view materialized in the form of four informal proposals, each of which claimed that coastal state sovereign rights had to include the entire natural extension of the continental territory—that is, the whole of the seabed area known as the continental margin. The first two were drafted by the USA;[70] the other two by an informal group of juridical experts known

---

68   Also several suggestions for the text of the treaty were made by landlocked and geographically disadvantaged countries. See proposals reproduced in Platzöder, Renate (ed.), *Third United Nations Conference on the Law of the Sea: Documents*, Vol. IX (Oceana Publications, 1982), pp. 238–239.

69   The following nations were members of the group of margineers: Argentina, Australia, Canada, India, Ireland, New Zealand, Norway, Great Britain, Uruguay and the USA.

70   Reproduced in Platzöder, Renate (ed.), *Third United Nations Conference on the Law of the Sea: Documents*, Vol. XI (Oceana Publications, 1982), pp. 498 and 500.

as the 'Evensen group'.[71] All proposals were relatively extensive, and included long and detailed texts. The continental shelf, they all stressed, should be defined legally on the basis of geological criteria, and the outer limit should lie where the continental margin meets the deep ocean floor. The proposals also made reference to what would become Article 76, paragraph 4(a)(ii), of the LOS Convention (the 'Hedberg formula').

Already at the third session, informal conversations also revealed thoughts on the establishment of an *international expert commission* mandated to over-rule the unilateral delineation that each coastal state made on the basis of the new provision. The USA proposed:

> Every delineation pursuant to this Article shall be submitted to the Continental Shelf Boundary Commission for review in accordance with Annex [...]. Acceptance by the Commission of a delineation so submitted, or the final decision of the Commission in accordance with Annex [...] and the seaward boundary so fixed, shall be final and binding.[72]

Also the Evensen group referred to a special boundary commission:

> The coastal State, any State with a particular interest in the matter, or the International Authority, may submit any delineation pursuant to paragraph 4 of this article to the Continental Shelf Boundary Commission for review in accordance with Annex [...]. The decision of the Commission on a delineation so submitted shall be final and binding [...]. It is assumed that the Continental Shelf Boundary Commission is an independent organ, and that its composition would ensure that it dispose of the necessary technical and scientific expertise. The scope of the powers of the Commission, and the questions of possible appeal procedures, of the participation of legal expertise in the Commission, and of the relationship with the proposed dispute settlement procedures under the new Convention, remain to be discussed.[73]

The idea of an international commission came in addition to the issue of *revenue sharing*. Only if those states with an extended continental shelf were willing to accept the distribution of revenue from activities on the seabed,

---

71   *Ibid.*, p. 469.

72   *Ibid.*, p. 500.

73   See 'Fourth Revision' (Informal Group of Juridical Experts), reproduced in Platzöder, *ibid.*,
      p. 281.

would other states allow the sovereign rights of the coastal state to extend to the edge of the continental margin. Thus several delegations from the margineers came together at the third session to discuss the possibility of submitting concrete proposals on revenue sharing. This group, which included Norway and the USA, however, encountered problems in agreeing on formulation of concrete suggestions. No agreement was reached, for instance, as to whether the calculation should be based on net or gross profits. Moreover, some of the margineers—Australia in particular—were dismissive of the whole notion of a system of revenue sharing.[74] In the end, the definition of the continental shelf in the informal single negotiating text (ISNT) from the third session made no reference to the Commission or the concept of revenue sharing.[75]

Fourth Session

It was assumed that the proposed definition of the continental shelf from the third session would be rejected by some delegations, particularly those from Africa, who wanted the 200 nautical mile limit to mark the perimeter of the continental shelf. At the fourth session, the 'margineers' proved, nonetheless, willing to meet them halfway. The USA suggested that a certain percentage of the value of the extracted resources that lay in the range between 200 nautical miles and the outer edge of the 'margin' should go to an international organization, and benefit the poor countries. Another part of such a compromise arrangement would consist in finding a *precise* definition of the continental shelf that would prevent a coastal state from extending its sovereign rights to sediment layers that form part of the deep ocean floor.

On this basis, a group of margin-states had worked on finding a precise definition of the continental shelf. On behalf of this group, Ireland proposed a new definition, based in part on the US proposal during the third session, and partly on ideas provided by the Evensen group. The edge of the continental margin as the outer limit was included; the Hedberg formula was included; and reference was made to a 'Continental Shelf Boundary Commission' tasked with determining whether the coastal state had properly refined the outer limit.

What was innovative about the Irish proposal was its alternative way of delineating the outer edge of the continental margin beyond 200 nautical miles, as compared to the 'Hedberg Formula'. The outer portion of the sediment layer of the continental rise, typically located at great depths, was to be

---

74 See generally Nandan and Rosenne (eds), *United Nations Convention on the Law of the Sea, 1982*, Vol. II, pp. 935–937.

75 UN Doc. A/CONF.62/C.2/L.47 ('United States of America: draft articles for a chapter on the economic zone and the continental shelf').

'cut off' where the thickness of this layer is not in reasonable proportion to the distance from the shore; the foot of the slope was thus described as 'the point of maximum change in the gradient at its base'.[76] The majority of UNCLOS III's participants, however, were not convinced, and the Soviet Union was strongly against.[77] The Irish proposal was not included in the revised negotiating text, which therefore emerged unchanged.[78]

Also at the fourth session, Canada proposed the adoption of an attachment to the definition of the continental shelf, relating to the specialized commission proposed to be established. The attachment consisted of nine articles and was the precursor to what ultimately became Annex II of the LOS Convention. The commission would be composed of 30 members, to be selected by the International Oceanographic Commission and the International Hydrographic Bureau. According to Article 3 of the draft,

[t]he Commission shall [...] certify that the delineation by a coastal State of the seaward boundary of its Continental Shelf beyond 200 nautical miles from the baselines from which the breadth of the territorial sea is measured, is in accordance with article 62 [...].[79]

According to Article 5 of the attachment, it was a 'special committee' of five members of the commission that would verify the limits of the coastal state. If a majority of the special committee was 'satisfied', they would stamp the limits as 'final and binding' and 'conclusive'.[80] However, this proposal from Canada was not included in the revised single negotiating text (RSNT).[81]

76   Text of the 'Irish formula' is reproduced in Nandan and Rosenne (eds), *United Nations Convention on the Law of the Sea, 1982*, Vol. II, pp. 852–853.
77   The Soviet Union put forward its own proposals on the continental shelf at the fourth session: '[The continental shelf comprises] the sea-bed and subsoil of the submarine areas that extend beyond its territorial sea throughout the natural prolongation of its land territory within [the] 500-metre isobath or to a distance of 200 nautical miles from the baselines from which the breadth of the territorial sea is measured in areas where the 500-metre isobath is situated at a distance less than 200 miles from those baselines'. Proposal reproduced in Platzöder, Renate (ed.), *Third United Nations Conference on the Law of the Sea: Documents*, Vol. IV (Oceana Publications, 1982), p. 468.
78   UN Doc. A/CONF.62/WP.8/Rev.1/Part II (RSNT, 1975, Article 64).
79   Reproduced in Platzöder (ed.), Vol. IV, p. 321.
80   *Ibid.*, for Article VI of the Annex.
81   *Third United Nations Conference on the Law of the Sea, Official Records*, Vol. V (New York: United Nations, 1976), p. 153.

Fifth Session

In informal discussions at the fifth session in New York in 1976, the Irish proposal from the fourth session was still seen as an appropriate option. The Irish formula, combined with the Hedberg formula, would mean a definition of the outer edge of the continental margin that secured access to potential oil deposits. During the fifth session, however, these proposals were also criticized, mainly by landlocked states and geographically disadvantaged states. The margineers realized they would lose when it came to a vote. In an effort to meet their opponents halfway, the margineers thus continued to work on a compromise model consisting of three elements.

First, coastal states were to have sovereign rights to the outer edge of the continental margin where this extended beyond 200 nautical miles. Second, to prevent a coastal state from extending its jurisdiction into the deep ocean floor at the expense of 'the common heritage of mankind', the edge of the continental margin was to be defined precisely. Importantly, consideration could also be given to having the limits assessed by an international commission. Third, there should be international income distribution for mineral exploitation in the area between the 200 nautical mile limit and the edge of the margin. A portion of the proceeds or production should reach the developing world by distribution through an international agency.

For a while, an agreed compromise with the aforementioned elements seemed to be within reach. However, towards the end of the discussions, some states reserved their position. As a result, the Committee's Chairman would not draw any final conclusions, though in his report gave the impression that he still had faith that a compromise on this basis would eventually be possible.[82]

Sixth Session

During the sixth session in 1977, the Irish proposal was criticized anew in the negotiating group on the continental shelf. The thickness of the sedimentary at the outer edge of the continental margin was difficult to measure, claimed the Japanese delegation, and the method could therefore not be used as a starting point for establishing the outer edge of the continental margin.[83] Ireland defended its proposal. The proposal was in reality a compromise. Under the

---

82   UN Doc. A/CONF.62/L.17 ('Report by Mr Andres Aguilar, Chairman of the Second Committee, on the work of the Committee'), paras. 11, 13 and 37–39. See also *Third United Nations Conference on the Law of the Sea, Official Records*, Vol. VI (New York: United Nations, 1977), p. 137.

83   *Third United Nations Conference on the Law of the Sea, Official Records*, Vol. VII (New York: United Nations, 1976), p. 37.

Irish formula, the coastal state would not be able to claim the whole of the continental margin as comprising its legal continental shelf. Furthermore, it was pointed out, the method was very practical, and the relevant techniques and practices were already available for establishing the outer edge of the continental margin in accordance with the proposal.[84]

The informal composite negotiating text following the sixth session—'ICNT Article 76'—rendered without change the definition of the continental shelf in the RSNT from 1976. At the sixth session, there were, however, two events of importance to the issue of outer limits of the continental shelf. First, the Second Committee requested the UN Secretariat to undertake a study in the form of maps and statistical charts to illustrate the various alternatives to the present definition of the continental shelf, that is, show on maps and numerically the difference in area between the various approaches to the problem of the limit of national jurisdiction over the continental shelf. The maps would trace a 200-mile line around all elevations permanently above the surface of the sea; a line showing 500-metre isobaths; a line showing the outer edge of the margin; and lines illustrating the effect of the Irish formula.[85] In anticipation of this study, it was perhaps not surprising that many states towards the end of the session were reluctant to make changes to the negotiating text.

Second, the margineers' proposal for a system of revenue sharing beyond 200 nautical miles gained significant traction at the sixth session. There were extensive discussions on the point for taxation and percentages. Eventually, broad agreement on a text about tax level took form. It was also agreed that the International Seabed Authority (ISA) would distribute the incoming revenue.[86]

Seventh Session

At the seventh session of UNCLOS III, support for the Irish formula widened.[87] However, this was to some extent offset by the fact that the Soviet Union

---

84   *Third United Nations Conference on the Law of the Sea, Official Records*, Vol. V, p. 36.

85   Second Committee, 51st meeting, para. 2. See *Third United Nations Conference on the Law of the Sea, Official Records*, Vol. III (New York: United Nations, 1977), p. 40.

86   See Nandan and Rosenne (eds), *United Nations Convention on the Law of the Sea, 1982*, Vol. II, pp. 940–942.

87   For example, Sri Lanka argued that it would accept the rational of the Irish formula, but at the same time raised some issues concerning its application in specific situations. Sri Lanka held that the combined distance/sedimentary layer/thickness criterion could produce equitable results only in cases where the margin thinned out rapidly. It could, however, cause injustice in the case of countries where the continental margin was wide and of considerable thickness throughout. The delegation of Sri Lanka thus felt there should be an opening for exceptions to strict application of the Irish formula. Notably, a

remained opposed to the proposal, and submitted a separate text proposal based on a 300 nautical mile maximum outer limit of the continental shelf.[88] The margineers nevertheless held firm. They would provide the coastal state with a choice in cases where the continental shelf extended beyond 200 nautical miles: either at a distance of 60 nautical miles from the foot of the continental slope, or to a distance at which the sediment layer's thickness made up only 1 per cent of the distance from the foot of the continental slope.

Both the margin states' and Soviet's proposals were referred to in the report of the Chairman.[89] There now seemed to be increasing agreement that an acceptable definition would have to involve two elements: an accurate definition of the continental margin beyond 200 nautical miles, and a form of revenue sharing for the benefit of the developing countries relating to exploitation conducted between 200 nautical miles and the outer edge of the continental margin.

The negotiating group on the continental shelf continued to work at the resumed seventh session in New York, but without making much progress. The meetings were held in parallel with talks between the Soviet Union and the USA on the same issues, with the aim of reaching a mutual compromise. For many, the important talks seemed to be going on between the two superpowers. Also, many states were concerned that the Irish proposal would lead to a type of 'creeping jurisdiction' on the part of coastal states. Importantly, Norway therefore advocated a *deadline* for establishing the outer limits of the continental shelf. Similar arguments were later expressed by other states.

In his report, the Chairman indicated that after the seventh and resumed seventh session, a solution was not any closer; three proposals were discussed in addition to the negotiating text: an Irish proposal; a Soviet proposal for a

---

rigid application of the Irish formula would deprive Sri Lanka of a vast extent of its continental margin. Sri Lanka received considerable support for this view. See *Third United Nations Conference on the Law of the Sea, Official Records*, Vol. IX (New York: United Nations, 1980), p. 71.

88   Reproduced in Platzöder, Renate (ed.), *Third United Nations Conference on the Law of the Sea: Documents*, Vol. V (Oceana Publications, 1982), p. 20. It may also be noted that the Arab Group suggested that '[t]he continental shelf of a coastal State comprises the seabed and subsoil of the submarine areas that extend beyond its territorial sea throughout the natural prolongation of its land territory to a distance of 200 nautical miles from the baselines from which the breadth of the territorial sea is measured'. See Platzöder (ed.), *Third United Nations Conference on the Law of the Sea: Documents*, Vol. IX, p. 371.

89   UN Doc. A/CONF.62/RCNG/1 ('Report to the Plenary by the Chairman of the Second Committee, Annex A'), paras. 6–8.

maximum outer limit of 300 nautical miles; and an Arab proposal for a maximum outer limit of 200 nautical miles.[90]

Eighth Session
At the eighth UNCLOS III session—in Geneva from 19 March to 27 April 1979—major steps were taken towards a final solution. The Soviet Union was among the states to suggest amendments to the Irish proposal, *inter alia*, concerning an absolute maximum limit to the extent of the continental shelf:

> The fixed points comprising the line of the outer limit of the continental shelf on the sea-bed, drawn in accordance with subparagraphs (a) and (b) of paragraph 3, must be situated at a distance either not exceeding 100 nautical miles from the line on the sea-bed, corresponding to the outer limit of the 200-mile economic zone, or not exceeding 60 nautical miles from the 2,500 metre isobath, which is a line connecting depths of 2,500 meters.[91]

A new paragraph was also proposed:

> Information on the limits of the continental shelf beyond the 200-mile economic zone shall be submitted by the coastal State to the Commission on the Limits of the Continental Shelf set up under Annex__ on the basis of equitable geographic representation. The Commission shall make recommendations to coastal States on matters related to the establishment of the outer limits of their continental shelf. The limits of the shelf established by a coastal State *taking into account* these recommendations shall be *final and unalterable*.[92] (Emphasis added)

The Soviet Union's suggestion added to the distance criterion ('not exceeding 100 nautical miles from the line on the sea-bed corresponding to the outer limit of the 200-mile economic zone') a combined depth/distance criterion ('not exceeding 60 nautical miles from the 2,500 metre isobath'). As we see, it was further proposed that the 'Commission on the Limits of the Continental Shelf' should have a role in the process. That the Soviet Union—and thereby

---

90   *Ibid.*, para. 6.
91   Reproduced in Platzöder (ed.), *Third United Nations Conference on the Law of the Sea: Documents*, Vol. IX, p. 377.
92   *Ibid.*

the entire Eastern Bloc—now recognized the role of the Commission, was essential to its future.

The Chairman of the negotiating group, after extensive consultations, drafted the new text proposal. His text nevertheless replaced the words 'final and unalterable' with 'final and binding'. And paragraph 3 *bis* established that the maximum outer limit of the continental shelf was either 350 nautical miles from the baselines or 100 nautical miles from the 2,500 metre isobath.[93] The Chairman also suggested drawing up a new text proposal for the provision on revenue sharing—Article 82—with a view to achieving consensus on the 'the rate of payments and contributions to be made by a coastal State from exploitation of its continental shelf beyond 200 nautical miles'.[94]

The new formulations divided opinion among the group of landlocked and geographically disadvantaged states. The Arab countries maintained their opposition to the proposal. In their view, the outer limit of the continental shelf should be congruent with the limit of the exclusive economic zone at 200 nautical miles. On the whole, however, the Chairman's text received broad support, and was included in the informal composite negotiating text (ICNT/Rev.1).[95]

Under the resumed eighth session in New York, it was confirmed that Article 76, as it now was drafted, would be adopted. But even if the main problems in connection with Article 76 were resolved, issues were raised about how the continental margin should be delineated in relation to 'submarine ridges'. The problem consisted in drafting a provision that would prevent the coastal states from using the depth criterion in Article 76 in an unreasonable manner by 'pushing' the outer limit of its continental shelf along the undersea ridges, in areas with depths not greater than 2,500 metres. At the eighth session, however, no consensus was achieved on how the issue of ridges should be resolved.[96]

---

93   UN Doc. A/CONF.62/L.37 ('Compromise suggestion by the Chairman of negotiating group 6'). See *Third United Nations Conference on the Law of the Sea, Official Records*, Vol. XI, pp. 100–101.

94   UN Doc. A/CONF.62/WP.10/Rev.1 ('Informal composite negotiating text, revision 1'). Reproduced in Platzöder, Renate (ed.), *Third United Nations Conference on the Law of the Sea: Documents*, Vol. I (Oceana Publications, 1982), p. 423.

95   *Ibid.*

96   During the resumed session of the eight session, the Soviet Union (see Platzöder (ed.), *Third United Nations Conference on the Law of the Sea: Documents*, Vol. IX, p. 379), a joint group of ten states (*ibid.*, p. 380) and Bulgaria (*ibid.*, p. 382) put forth proposals for how to deal with the complex question of submarine ocean ridges.

At the resumed eighth session in 1979, it was confirmed that the Commission should have a role in the process of establishing the outer limits of the continental shelf beyond 200 nautical miles. Focus was therefore gradually turning towards the rules and procedures that would apply to its business. The UK proposed a 'Draft Annex for a Commission on the Limits of the Continental Shelf', on the same lines as the Canadian proposal at the fourth session.[97] Discussions about this annex went parallel to discussions about the final wording of Article 76.

Ninth Session

The problems of drafting Article 76 regarding how to delineate the continental shelf in relation to submarine ridges and elevations, continued at the ninth session in the spring of 1980. The margineers,[98] the Soviet Union[99] and Australia[100] proposed two separate solutions to the problem. The Chairman made a compromise solution, a slightly different formulation of the formal negotiating text.[101] A new paragraph 5 *bis* was also proposed:

> Notwithstanding the provisions of paragraph 5, on submarine ridges the outer limit of the continental shelf shall not exceed 350 miles from the baselines from which the breadth of the territorial sea is measured. The paragraph does not apply to submarine elevations that are natural components of the continental margin, such as its plateaux, rises, caps, banks and spurs.[102]

Several states appended remarks. For example, Iceland commented that it 'understood that the new provision regarding submarine ridges meant that the 350-mile limit criterion would apply to ridges which were a prolongation of the land mass of the coastal State'.[103] The US delegation advanced similar views, exemplified by the case of the Chukchi Plateau, to the north of Alaska:

---

97   Reproduced in Platzöder (ed.), *Third United Nations Conference on the Law of the Sea: Documents*, Vol. IV, p. 520.

98   *Ibid.*, p. 524.

99   Two different suggestions by the Soviet Union reproduced in Platzöder (ed.), *Third United Nations Conference on the Law of the Sea: Documents*, Vol. IX, p. 389 and Vol. XI, p. 574.

100   Reproduced in Platzöder (ed.), *Third United Nations Conference on the Law of the Sea: Documents*, Vol. IV, p. 524.

101   Platzöder (ed.), *Third United Nations Conference on the Law of the Sea: Documents*, Vol. XI, p. 576 and Vol. IV, p. 525.

102   UN Doc. A/CONF.62/L.51 ('Report of the Chairman of the Second Committee'), paras. 4–7.

103   See *Third United Nations Conference on the Law of the Sea, Official Records*, Vol. VIII, p. 36.

> [Our] support for the proposal on the continental shelf contained in the report of the Chairman [...] rested on the understanding that it was recognized [...] that features such as the Chukchi plateau situated to the north of Alaska and its component elevations could not be considered a ridge and were covered by the last sentence of the proposed paragraph 5 *bis* of article 76.[104]

In the informal composite negotiating text (ICNT/Rev.2), paragraph 5 *bis* was transformed into a new paragraph 6, in which a distinction was suggested between 'submarine ridges' and 'submarine elevations'. Moreover, a maximum distance from the coast of 350 nautical miles was provided for, but this was not to apply to 'submarine elevations which are natural components of the continental margin'.[105]

The Chairman had also proposed a change to the formal negotiating text of (then) paragraph 7 in the course of the eighth session, replacing the phrase 'taking into account' with 'on the basis of'.[106] In the ICNT/Rev.2, the last sentence of paragraph 7 was incorporated into paragraph 8, last sentence:

> The limits established by a coastal State on the basis of these recommendations shall be final and binding.

Some states reserved their position regarding this change[107] and at the resumed ninth session, discussions continued on the wording of the last sentence of paragraph 8. Germany suggested that the Commission should adopt binding decisions which would determine, with final effect, the outer limits of the continental shelf.[108] The term 'recommendations' should be replaced with 'decisions':

---

104 *Ibid.*, p. 43.

105 UN Doc. A/CONF.62/WP.10/Rev.2 and Corr.2 ('Informal composite negotiating text, revision 2, correction 2). Reproduced in Platzöder, Renate (ed.), *Third United Nations Conference on the Law of the Sea: Documents*, Vol. II (Oceana Publications, 1982), pp. 3 and 48.

106 UN Doc. A/CONF.62/L.51 ('Report of the Chairman of the Second Committee'), paras. 4–7.

107 Nandan and Rosenne (eds), *United Nations Convention on the Law of the Sea, 1982*, Vol. II, p. 870.

108 Reproduced in Platzöder (ed.), Vol. IV, p. 527.

The functions of the Commission shall be: To consider the data and other material submitted by the coastal State [...] and to render decisions in accordance with article 76 [...].[109]

That proposal was rejected and the wording of Article 76 of the informal composite negotiating text (ICNT/Rev. 3) remained unchanged.[110]

The ICNT/Rev.2 had also contained a separate annex ('Annex II') which regulated the procedures of the Commission. New informal proposals for the annex were put forward at the ninth session.[111] The number of Commission members should be reduced from 30 to 21; and Commission members should be selected by the States Parties, not by the International Oceanographic Commission and the International Hydrographic Bureau, after nomination from states. Furthermore, a coastal state should submit as soon as possible, but not later than ten years from the time the Convention entered into force for that state, its submission to the Commission. Changes with respect to the Commission's internal procedures were also proposed. A sub-commission was to submit recommendations to the Commission in plenary, which would then make final recommendations to coastal states. Procedural regulations were also proposed should a coastal state disagree with the recommendations of the Commission: the coastal state should revise or make a new submission to the Commission.

On the basis of these proposals, a new Annex II was adopted in the informal negotiation text.[112] However, not all delegations were convinced an international institution should be involved in the setting of the outer limits of the continental shelf beyond 200 nautical miles. Bahrain objected to the Commission's composition and function.[113] Canada, which at an early stage had been involved in suggesting the Commission and its authority, eventually came to view the Commission's operation with greater concern: were not the coastal state's sovereign rights over the continental shelf in danger of being diluted?

---

109   *Ibid.*

110   UN Doc. A/CONF.62/WP.10/Rev.3* ('Informal composite negotiating text, revision 3'). Reproduced in Platzöder (ed.), Vol. II, pp. 3 and 48.

111   UN Doc. NG6/20 ('Informal Suggestion, anonymous'). Reproduced in Platzöder (ed.), Vol. IX, p. 387.

112   See UN Doc. A/CONF.62/WP.10/Rev.2 ('Informal Composite Negotiating Text, revision 2'), Annex II. Reproduced in Platzöder (ed.), Vol. II, pp. 3 and 17.

113   UN Doc. A/CONF.62/WS/7 ('Statement by the delegation of Bahrain dated 4 April 1980'), para. 10. See *Third United Nations Conference on the Law of the Sea, Official Records*, Vol. XIII, p. 109.

The [...] commission is primarily an instrument which will provide the international community with reassurances that coastal States will establish their continental shelf limits in strict accordance with the provisions of article 76. It has never been intended, nor should it be intended, as a means to impose on coastal States limits that differ from those already recognized in article 76. Thus to suggest that the coastal States limits shall be established 'on the basis' of the commission's recommendations rather than on the basis of article 76, could be interpreted as giving the commission the function and power to determine the outer limits of the continental shelf of a coastal State. We are assured on all sides that this is not the intention [...].[114]

Canada's views were not expressed in what ultimately became the last sentence of Article 76, paragraph 8. The informal negotiating text from the ninth session—the 'Draft Convention'[115]—was also similar in terms of Annex II, as this had been included in the informal negotiating text from the eighth session.[116]

Tenth and Eleventh Sessions
At the resumed tenth session in 1981, the UNCLOS III Drafting Committee proposed various 'technical' changes in the wording of Article 76.[117] Several

---

114   UN Doc. A/CONF.62/WS/4 ('Statement by the delegation of Canada dated 2 April 1980'), para. 15. See *Third United Nations Conference on the Law of the Sea, Official Records*, Vol. XIII, pp. 101–102.

115   UN Doc. A/CONF.62/L.78 ('Draft convention on the law of the sea'), Annex II. See *Third United Nations Conference on the Law of the Sea, Official Records*, Vol. XV, pp. 172–224.

116   See UN Doc. A/CONF.62/WP.10/Rev.2 ('Informal Composite Negotiating Text, revision 2'), Annex II. Reproduced in Platzöder (ed.), Vol. II, pp. 3 and 17.

117   See UN Docs. A/CONF.62/L.67/Add.4 ('Report of the Chairman of the Drafting Committee'), pp. 2–13, A/CONF.62/L.67/Add.4/Corr.1–5 ('Report of the Chairman of the Drafting Committee'), A/CONF.62/L.67/Add.14 ('Report of the Chairman of the Drafting Committee'), pp. 8–9 and A/CONF.62/L.72 ('Report of the President of the Drafting Committee on behalf of the President of the Conference and the Chairmen of the First, Second and Third Committees'). See also *Third United Nations Conference on the Law of the Sea, Official Records*, Vol. XV, p. 151. The Drafting Committee commenced its work at the seventh session of the Conference with the informal examination of negotiating texts, for the purposes of refining drafts, harmonizing recurring words and expressions and achieving, through textual review, concordance of the text of the Convention in the six official languages. The Committee was assisted in its informal work by six language groups comprising both members and non-members of the Drafting Committee, representing the six official languages of the Conference, each group chaired by a coordinator and

of these proposals were included in Article 76 of the Draft Convention—for example, the phrase 'the 200 nautical mile exclusive economic zone' in paragraph 8, was replaced by the wording '200 nautical miles from the baselines from which the breadth of the territorial sea is measured'. Article 76 incorporated various other improvements; the phrase 'opposite and adjacent States' was replaced by 'States with adjacent or opposite coasts', for example.[118] No further changes were made to Article 76 of the Draft Convention, except for some details proposed by the Drafting Committee.[119]

At the eleventh session of UNCLOS III, however, two additional proposals for changes to the Draft Treaty text were made and both rejected: the UK proposed replacing the words 'on the basis of' in paragraph 8, last sentence, with 'taking into account', arguing that the change would restore the provision as it was originally intended.[120] China's attempt to change certain elements of paragraphs 1 and 3 of the Draft Treaty was also rejected.[121]

The eleventh session of UNCLOS III had been declared as the final decision-making session of the Conference.[122] All efforts to reach general agreement had been exhausted, and on 30 April 1982, the USA requested that voting be held on the Draft Convention. In all, 130 states voted in favour of the draft, 4 against (Israel, the USA, Turkey and Venezuela), and 18 abstained. The *United Nations Convention on the Law of the Sea* was thus opened for signature at Montego Bay, Jamaica, on 10 December 1982. Article 76 of the Convention contains the new juridical definition of the continental shelf, and Annex II to the LOS Convention contains the regulations to be followed by the Commission in the performance of its functions.

---

assisted by linguistic experts. See UN Doc. A/CONF.62/121 ('Final Act of the Third United Nations Conference on the Law of the Sea'), p. 148.

118   UN Doc. A/CONF.62/L.78 ('Draft convention on the law of the sea'), Article 76. See *Third United Nations Conference on the Law of the Sea, Official Records*, Vol. XV, p. 172.

119   UN Docs. A/CONF.62/L.152/Add.23 ('Report of the Chairman of the Drafting Committee'), pp. 72–73 and A/CONF.62/L.160 ('Report of the Chairman of the Drafting Committee on behalf of the President and the Chairmen of the First, Second and Third Committees'). See also *Third United Nations Conference on the Law of the Sea, Official Records*, Vol. XVII, p. 225.

120   UN Doc. A/CONF.62/L.126 ('United Kingdom of Great Britain and Northern Ireland: amendments'). See *Third United Nations Conference on the Law of the Sea, Official Records*, Vol. XVI, p. 233.

121   Reproduced in Platzöder (ed.), Vol. V, p. 76.

122   UN Doc. A/CONF.62/121 ('Final Act of the Third United Nations Conference on the Law of the Sea'), para. 41.

2.4.3   *Article 76 of the LOS Convention*

Article 76 defines the continental shelf in a whole new way compared to Article 1 of the Convention on the Continental Shelf. The provision consists of ten paragraphs, most of them (paragraphs 2 to 8), relating exclusively to the limits of the continental shelf where it extends beyond 200 nautical miles from the baselines.

Paragraph 1 establishes the principal rule that the continental shelf comprises the natural extension of the land to the outer edge of the continental margin. The definition combines two distinct criteria: a distance criterion, and a geomorphological criterion. The first is a simple criterion of 200 nautical miles, independent of the geological conditions at the seabed and in line with the coastal state's rights to an exclusive economic zone under Articles 56 and 57 of the LOS Convention. This criterion therefore has independent importance only in cases where the coastal state has not proclaimed an exclusive economic zone, or the continental margin does not extend out to 200 nautical miles. The second criterion—'edge of the continental margin'—is inspired by the ICJ's judgment concerning the continental shelf in the *North Sea Continental Shelf* cases, where the Court described the continental shelf in the legal sense as being the *natural prolongation* of the continental territory.

Paragraphs 2 to 6 limit the extent of the continental shelf. Paragraph 2 refers to the limitations in the extent specified in paragraphs 4 to 6. Paragraph 3 provides for a geomorphological definition of the continental margin: it includes the 'shelf', the 'slope' and the 'rise'. Excluded is 'the deep ocean floor with its oceanic ridges or the subsoil thereof'.

Paragraph 4 outlines the technical rules for how the coastal state shall establish the outer edge of the continental margin when this extends beyond 200 nautical miles. The coastal state must choose one of the two options in paragraph 4 (a)(i) or paragraph 4 (a)(ii). Both options require determination of the 'foot of the slope', which is defined in *litra* (b). It is up to states themselves to choose which option to use. The coastal state is free to choose the alternative that at various points of the continental shelf offers the most favourable result.

Pursuant to the option in Article 76, paragraph 4 (a)(i), the outermost points of the outer limit of the continental margin shall be determined by reference to the thickness of the sedimentary rocks of the continental rise. The continental margin may extend to the area where the sediment thickness at fixed points on the continental rise is at least 1 per cent of the shortest distance from each fixed point to the foot of the continental slope. For example, if the thickness is 1 kilometre in an area of the continental rise, the outer limit of the continental shelf can be established 100 kilometres from the nearest site of 'the foot of the slope'. Application of this formula thus requires sediment measurements on the floor of the vast ocean deep.

The option in Article 76, paragraph 4 (a)(ii), provides that the outer limit may be at maximum of 60 nautical miles from the foot of the slope: a pure distance criterion. However, also for this method, the location of the 'the foot of the slope' must be determined. In the absence of evidence to the contrary, 'the foot of the slope' shall, according to paragraph 4 (b), be set at the point where the change of fall-off is steepest. The rule seems difficult to apply in practice, as local topographical differences may make it difficult to locate the 'correct' measure.

Paragraph 5 sets maximum limits. The maximum outer limits of the continental shelf shall be either 350 nautical miles from the baselines, or a maximum of 100 nautical miles from the 2,500 metre isobath. The coastal state may choose the more favourable option. In this context, the LOS Convention provides a special rule for the continental shelf in the southern part of the Bay of Bengal (Sri Lanka), because, due to the special geological conditions here, application of Article 76 would give a completely unreasonable result.[123]

Paragraph 6 contains a special rule for submarine ridges. The outer limit of the continental shelf on ridges can be located no further than 350 nautical miles from the baselines. Thus the 100 nautical mile + 2,500 metre isobath rule in paragraph 5 does not apply to ridges. This limitation does not, however, apply to subsea 'elevations' that are part of the natural extensions of the continental margin. Therefore, in many situations, the coastal state would prefer having formations at the bottom of the sea considered as submarine elevations rather than submarine ridges.[124]

---

123   *Ibid.*, Annex II.
124   See for instance Message of 7 October 1994, from the President of the USA to the US Senate, where it is argued that the Chukchi plateau north of Alaska and the Bering Strait is an elevation, not a ridge: 'The United States understands that features such as the Chukchi plateau and its component elevations, situated to the north of Alaska, are covered by this exemption, and thus not subject to the 350 mile limitation set forth in paragraph 6. Because of the potential for significant oil and gas reserves in the Chukchi plateau, it is important to recall the U.S. statement made to this effect on April 3, 1980 during a Plenary session of [UNCLOS III], which has never given rise to any contrary interpretation. In the statement, the United States representative expressed support for the provision now set forth in article 76(6) on the understanding that it is recognized that features such as the Chukchi plateau situated to the north of Alaska and its component elevations cannot be considered a ridge and are covered by the last sentence of paragraph 6' (Senate Treaty Document 103–109, at p. 56).

Taking into consideration the two maximum constraint lines for the outer limits of the continental shelf in Article 76, paragraph 5, it follows from paragraphs 1 to 6 that there are in principle four possible outer limits to the continental shelf: 1) 200 nautical miles from the baselines from which the breadth of the territorial sea is measured; 2) the outer edge of the continental margin; 3) 350 nautical miles from the baselines from which the breadth of the territorial sea is measured; and 4) 100 nautical miles from the 2,500 metre isobath.

Paragraphs 7 to 9 give rules on how the coastal state shall establish the outer limits of continental shelf. First, the coastal state delineates its outer limits. According to paragraph 7, the delineation shall be made using straight lines of maximum 60 nautical miles, connecting fixed points, defined by coordinates of latitude and longitude. The coastal state shall then submit information on these limits to the Commission. The Commission follows the procedures set out in Annex II, and makes recommendations to the coastal state. The coastal state shall then establish the limits and deposit marine charts and relevant information with the UNSG. Read in conjunction with Article 1, paragraph 1, and Article 134, paragraph 3, of the LOS Convention, the outer limits of the continental shelf established by a coastal state determine at the same time the extent of the seabed beyond national jurisdiction: the Area.

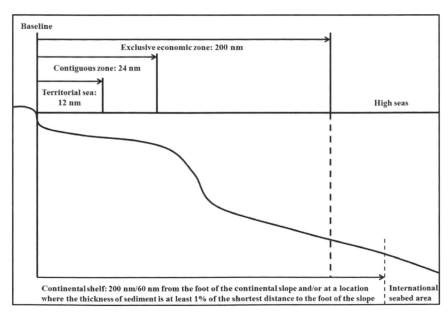

FIGURE 2.1   *Extension of the legal continental shelf under the LOS Convention*
SOURCE: ØYSTEIN JENSEN (2014).

According to paragraph 10, Article 76 is not to affect the issue of delimitation in relation to neighbouring states with overlapping continental shelf claims. This is also expressed in Article 134, paragraph 4, and in Article 9 of Annex II to the LOS Convention.

2.4.4 *Annex II of the LOS Convention*
Annex II of the LOS Convention sets out regulations concerning the Commission—its composition and functions, coastal state obligations in relation to the Commission, and the procedures to be followed by the Commission in preparing recommendations to coastal states.

Article 1 determines that the Commission shall be established, and that its mandate be limited to the question of setting the outer limits of the continental shelf beyond 200 nautical miles.[125] Article 2 concerns the Commission's composition, elections and election period, as well as the coverage of expenses. The Commission shall consist of 21 members who are experts in geology, geophysics and hydrography. Members sit for five-year terms, and re-election is permitted. To the extent considered necessary and useful, the Commission may also cooperate with competent international organizations for the exchange of scientific and technical information which might be of assistance

---

125 It should be noted that the Commission is one of four bodies established by the LOS Convention. Other bodies established by the LOS Convention are the International Tribunal for the Law of the Sea (ITLOS), an independent judicial body established under Part XV of the Convention, to adjudicate disputes arising out of the interpretation and application of the Convention; secondly, the International Seabed Authority (ISA), an autonomous international organization established by the 1994 Agreement relating to the Implementation of Part XI of the LOS Convention, and through which the States Parties shall organize and control activities of the seabed and ocean floor and subsoil thereof beyond the limits of national jurisdiction, that is, the 'Area' as defined by Article 1 of the LOS Convention. Also the ITLOS Trust Fund has been established by the Secretary-General of the UN (UNSG) in accordance with an UNGA resolution (UN Doc. A/RES/55/7: *The Law of the Sea*. See also Doc. CLCS/16), and pursuant to the Agreement on Cooperation and Relationship between the United Nations and the International Tribunal for the Law of the Sea of 18 December 1997 (see UN Doc. A/RES/52/251). The purpose of the trust fund is to provide financial assistance to States Parties for expenses incurred in connection with cases submitted, or to be submitted, to the ITLOS. It can also be questioned whether the Meeting of States Parties to the LOS Convention can be classified as an 'international institution'. Be that as it may, the Meeting is a highly institutionalized form of diplomatic conference to be convened by the UNSG to perform certain tasks set out in the LOS Convention (see Article 319, para. 1 (*litra* e), of the LOS Convention). See further Treves, Tullio, 'The Law of the Sea "System" of Institutions', in *Yearbook of UN Law*, Vol. 2, 1998, pp. 325–340, at pp. 331–332.

in the discharging of the Commission's functions. The Intergovernmental Oceanographic Commission of the UN Educational, Scientific and Cultural Organization (UNESCO) and the International Hydrographic Organization are explicitly mentioned. The Secretariat shall be provided by the UNSG. Expenses of a member are covered by the country that has nominated him or her.

Article 3 specifies the functions of the Commission. The Commission shall evaluate the information and other materials submitted by coastal states concerning the limits of the continental shelf beyond 200 nautical miles, and make recommendations in accordance with Article 76 (as well as the rule in Annex II of the Final Act of the LOS Convention applying to the southern part of the Bay of Bengal). The Commission shall also, upon request, provide technical and scientific advice to the coastal state when it is preparing its submission.

According to Article 4, a state that intends to establish the outer limits of its continental shelf beyond 200 nautical miles shall, as soon as possible, and no later than ten years after the Convention has entered into force for that state, make a submission containing the particulars of such limits to the Commission, supported by scientific and technical data.

Articles 5 and 6 provide rules for the Commission's working methods. The Commission shall work in sub-commissions consisting of seven members. A member who is a national of the state which has referred the matter is automatically excluded from the sub-commission, but may attend the relevant plenary session of the Commission. The recommendations of the sub-commission shall be approved by the Commission in plenary, by a majority of two thirds of the members present and voting. The Commission is then to submit the recommendations in writing to the coastal state. The coastal state shall subsequently, according to Article 7, establish the outer limits of its continental shelf in accordance with Article 76, paragraph 8.

According to Article 8, if the coastal state does not agree with the Commission's recommendations, it shall within reasonable time make a revised or new submission to the Commission. Finally, Article 9 of Annex II restates the provisions contained in Article 76, paragraph 10: the actions of the Commission shall not affect questions regarding the delimitation of the continental shelf between states that are opposite or adjacent to each other.

2.5   Assessment

We have in this chapter seen how the first real attempt to create an international legal regime for the continental shelf came with US President Truman's proclamation in 1945. Prompted by the US initiative, several other coastal states put forward their claims to the continental shelf. Irregular in content, they created confusion as to the legal status of the seabed beyond the territorial sea. International regulation was needed, and the ILC was tasked with drawing up draft rules for the definition of the continental shelf.

UNCLOS I. adopted the Convention on the Continental Shelf in 1958. However, it became clear that this treaty was unable to balance considerations arising from international politics in the course of the 1960s. The main problem of the 1958 Convention was that its provisions did not adequately take into account nor envisaged the technological developments already underway at that time. Its Article 1 defined the outer limits of the continental shelf by a vague criterion, entailing the risk of coastal-state 'grabbing' of seabed areas.[126] The language of this provision is open to several possible interpretations, of which the most extreme—resting solely on the exploitability criterion—would ultimately permit all submarine areas to be claimed someday by coastal states.

Calls to redefine the criteria for determining the outer limits of the continental shelf were made in the second half of the 1960s. However, views of the states were divided. Some coastal states, in favourable geographical positions and with technological possibilities, were pushing for an extensive outer limit, whereas states that lacked these advantages argued for the opposite. The latter group of states were increasingly concerned that the dual criterion under Article 1 of the Convention on the Continental Shelf was insufficiently precise to serve as a rule for setting the outer limits of the continental shelf under international law. A new definition of the continental shelf was needed, they argued, in order to stop the gradual extension of individual national rights over ever-larger parts of the submarine areas.

In 1967, the issue again received global attention when Ambassador Arvid Pardo of Malta spoke before the UNGA. Pardo turned to the world community when he called for a new legal order for the oceans, an order which in a more satisfactory manner would define the limits of national jurisdiction, while also recognizing that the seabed beyond that should be designated as the common heritage of all mankind. This Maltese initiative spurred the UN to establish a provisional *ad hoc* committee to deal with the subsea question and the definition of the continental shelf. The committee was later made permanent, and in 1970, its mandate extended: the now UN Sea-Bed Committee would begin work on a new global conference on the law of the sea.

UNCLOS III commenced in 1973. On the negotiation table with respect to the outer limits of the continental shelf were drafts of treaty provisions from

---

126   Henkin, Louis, *Law for the Sea's Mineral Resources* (Institute for the Study of Science in Human Affairs: Columbia University, 1968), pp. 18–19.

the UN Sea-Bed Committee, the definition in Article 1 from the Convention on the Continental Shelf, the increasing and widespread perception that coastal states had the right to some kind of 'economic jurisdiction' out to 200 nautical miles from their coasts, and the judgment from the ICJ in the *North Sea Continental Shelf* cases from 1969, in which the Court had determined that the 'continental shelf' legally comprised the natural extension of a coastal state's territory.

UNCLOS III involved at least two opposing constellations. On the one side were states that wanted continental shelf rights to the end of the continental margin: the 'margineers'. On the other, the geographically disadvantaged states, land-locked states and most of the African states. Briefly put, this latter group wanted to limit the sovereign rights of the coastal state to 200 nautical miles.

It soon became clear that a compromise would have to be sought, and here the rules of coastal state entitlement to an exclusive economic zone would be crucial. The rules on the 200 nautical mile exclusive economic zone had evolved into customary law from around the mid-1970s. This was a good negotiation card for the margineers, who claimed that rights to the continental shelf should in any case extend that far. But it also was a negotiation card for those who wanted to limit the continental shelf to 200 nautical miles, in the sense that this limit should apply to the shelf as well. It was not necessary to negotiate separate rules for the continental shelf, they argued, since the rules on the exclusive economic zone 'consumed' the claims to the seabed.

However, the margineers were determined to see rights extended to the continental shelf *beyond* 200 nautical miles. In this they drew on the definition in Article 1 of the Convention on the Continental Shelf and the judgment of the ICJ in the *North Sea Continental Shelf* cases. An essential element in this picture during UNCLOS III was also the willingness shown by both the USA and the Soviet Union to accept broad continental shelf rights for coastal states.

The ultimate compromise between the margineers and the states wanting a more geographically restricted continental shelf produced a two-way split. First, there had to be a provision for sharing the revenue arising from gains enjoyed by coastal states in the exercise of their exclusive rights between 200 nautical miles and the outer edge of continental margin. This became Article 82 of the LOS Convention, under which coastal states commit to pay a tax on economic activities beyond 200 nautical miles.

Second, the outer limit of the continental shelf had to be established with the greatest possible degree of *precision*. Landlocked states, developing countries and geographically disadvantaged states would not accept imprecise regulation that in reality did not entail any real outer limit of the continental shelf. Therefore, Article 76 contains detailed rules on the extent of the continental shelf, enabling a more sophisticated and clearly defined determination of outer limits than those under Article 1 of the Convention on the Continental Shelf. The physical extension of coastal state jurisdiction to the seabed is no longer indefinite, although the outer limits of the continental shelf may be established at a very seaward position.

In addition, an essential component of this last part of the compromise was the creation of the Commission on the Limits of the Continental Shelf—a 21-person expert body to facilitate implementation of the LOS Convention by making recommendations to coastal states on matters related to the establishment of the outer limits of the continental shelf beyond 200 nautical miles from the territorial sea baselines.[127] The creation of an expert commission to be involved in the establishment of the outer limits of the continental shelf is indeed one of the most far-reaching innovations of the whole LOS Convention. And it is precisely the decision-making and legitimacy of this unique international institution that comprises the focal point of the chapters that follow.

---

127   See also McDorman, Ted, 'The Continental Shelf Regime in the Law of the Sea Convention: A Reflection on the First Thirty Years', in *The International Journal of Marine and Coastal Law*, Vol. 27, 2012, pp. 743–751, at pp. 744–745.

Legal Aspects of the Commission's Decision-Making

3.1 Introduction

The first session of the Commission on the Limits of the Continental Shelf was held at the UN Headquarters in New York, from 16 to 20 June 1997.[1] The Commission has thus been an operative treaty body for almost 20 years, and played an important role in the process of implementing the continental shelf regime under the LOS Convention.

The Commission—composed exclusively of scientists—is often considered to be more of a technical than a legal body. In that sense, the Commission's business would not seem to have particular *legal* implications, and should not be of much interest from a dogmatic legal science point of view. However, the formal frame of the Commission's activities is enshrined in a treaty, specifically Article 76 and Annex II of the LOS Convention. As a result, *legal issues always* constitute part of the background when the Commission conducts its work.

Basically, the legal significance of the Commission's work unfolds on three levels, of which the most interesting, in my view, is the *legal effects* of the Commission's recommendations. Indeed, the characteristics of the Commission as a decision-making body are highly related to what extent its recommendations produce legal consequences. The key formulation in the LOS Convention that regulates the relationship between the Commission's recommendations and the outer limits of the continental shelf established by a coastal state is the third sentence of Article 76, paragraph 8: 'The limits of the shelf established by a coastal State on the basis of these recommendations shall be final and binding'. This provision calls for an analysis of the legal effects of the Commission's recommendations in the view of the coastal states pursuing to establish their outer limits 'on the basis of' the Commission's recommendations.

In addition to the implication of the phrase 'on the basis of', however, it is also a question as to what extent the Commission's recommendations are relevant as a means of interpretation—their value *res interpretata*—in light of the general rules on treaty interpretation in international law. Another question is

---

1 Doc. CLCS/1.

whether the Commission's recommendations have, or should have, any effect on the delimitation of the continental shelf between states with adjacent and opposite coasts.

The following chapter focuses on two other legal aspects related to the Commission's decision-making. First, according to Article 3, paragraph 1 (*litra* a), of Annex II to the LOS Convention, the Commission shall consider the data and other material submitted by coastal states concerning the outer limits of the continental shelf in areas where those limits extend beyond 200 nautical miles. This implies a duty on the Commission to take continental shelf submissions to treatment and process them according to internal procedures. However, the LOS Convention does not regulate each and every procedural question. Article 76 and Annex II provide only general rules—a rudimentary framework—as to the procedures to be followed by the Commission and the coastal state in delineating the outer limits of the continental shelf. As a result, the Commission itself has elaborated more detailed procedural rules. This wide-ranging 'law-making' in terms of procedural rules prompts a closer examination of the relationship between the Commission's rules of procedure and the overall legal framework provided by the LOS Convention.

Second, according to Article 3, paragraph 1 (*litra* a), of Annex II to the LOS Convention, the Commission's recommendations to coastal states shall be 'in accordance with article 76 and the Statement of Understanding adopted on 29 August 1980 by the Third United Nations Conference on the Law of the Sea'. This implies that the Commission is to base its views concerning the outer limits of the continental shelf on the provisions of the LOS Convention. Specific recommendations to coastal states therefore also indicate how the Commission has interpreted and applied Article 76 in a particular case. The Commission's decision-making by way of recommendations therefore calls for a closer examination of the relationship between specific recommendations and Article 76 of the LOS Convention.

3.2   Outline

In pursuing all these inquiries—legal effects, procedural aspects and substantive aspects—the remainder of this chapter is structured as follows: In section 3.3, I present a brief overview of the Commission's Rules of Procedure and discuss issues in those regulations that give rise to questions in relation to the LOS Convention. Instead of elaborating on the Commission's procedural rules in detail, I examine the degree of consistency between the Commission's Rules of Procedure and the LOS Convention. For this purpose, I offer some examples from the Rules of Procedure that can be considered to depart from or qualify the rules of the LOS Convention. The presentation will thus be limited to an examination of concrete procedural rules and whether the Commission has gone too far in relation to the mandate contained in the LOS Convention. While these examples have already given rise to some debate in the legal literature, they are not meant to constitute an exhaustive list.

In section 3.4, I look into potential discrepancies between the Commission's recommendations and the LOS Convention's criteria concerning the outer limits of the continental shelf. Several examples are provided here too, showing how the Commission sometimes deviates from, qualifies or adopts controversial interpretations of the provisions of the LOS Convention. Again, it must be noted, the examples presented here are not necessarily the only instances of the Commission adopting controversial interpretations of Article 76. These examples too have generated theoretical discussions and appear to be controversial among coastal states.

In section 3.5, I examine the legal effects of the Commission's recommendations, beginning with the relevance of its recommendations for the purpose of establishing 'final and binding' outer limits within the context of Article 76, paragraph 8, of the LOS Convention. Subsequently, the Commission's recommendations are investigated as a means of interpretation in a broader perspective, that is, as regards general rules of treaty interpretation in international law. Finally, I ask whether and to what extent the Commission's recommendations might be relevant to the process of delimiting the continental shelf between states with adjacent or opposite coasts. Section 3.6 offers some concluding remarks.

3.3   Legal Aspects of the Commission's Procedural Decision-Making

3.3.1   *The Rules of Procedure of the Commission*
A short overview of the Commission's procedural rules contained in Annex II to the LOS Convention was presented in Chapter 2. Annex II regulates the functioning of the Commission only in general terms, and so, as mentioned, the Commission has refined and expanded these provisions. Accordingly, the Rules of Procedure is one of the basic documents of the Commission.[2]

---

2   Doc. CLCS/40/Rev.1 contains the latest version of the Rules of Procedure of the Commission, embodying amendments and additions adopted by the Commission as of 11 April 2008. Annexes I and II to the present Rules were adopted by the Commission at its fourth session, in 1998. Annex III was adopted by the Commission at its thirteenth session in 2004, and

Even before the Commission started work, draft Rules of Procedure had been prepared by the Division for Ocean Affairs and the Law of the Sea (DOALOS),[3] at the request of the Meeting of States Parties to the LOS Convention.[4] These were applied provisionally until the Commission adopted its own rules.[5] The Rules of Procedure have since been continuously reviewed and amended by the Commission in light of developing practice at the Commission and in order to address new matters not initially foreseen.

The current version of the Rules of Procedure consists of a main body of 59 rules on the Commission's session and meetings, how often the Commission shall hold meetings, the venue and agenda. The Rules of Procedure also prescribe more detailed regulations as to the members of the Commission—their term of office, expenses and their duty to act independently. Section IV contains separate rules for the officers of the Commission: for example, the Commission shall elect from among its members a chairperson and four vice-chairpersons. There are rules for DOALOS in section V, working languages (section VI) and private and public meetings (section VII). Several provisions in the Rules of Procedure concern the Commission's conduct of business and voting (sections VIII and IX), sub-commissions and other subsidiary bodies (section X). Section XI contains regulations pertaining to submissions by coastal states including the form and language of the submission, procedures in case of disputes between states with opposite or adjacent coasts or in other cases of unresolved land or maritime disputes, regulations on the Commission's consideration of the submission and rules relating to the attendance by the coastal state at the consideration of its submission. The Rules of Procedure have separate sections for the Commission's advice to coastal states (section XII), the Commission's cooperation with international organizations (section XIII) or for cases in which the Commission seeks the advice of specialists (section XIV). Section XV sets out the procedures for adoption of

replaced the *modus operandi* of the Commission (Doc. CLCS/L.3) and the internal procedure of the sub-commission of the Commission (Doc. CLCS/L.12). The present Rules and their Annexes supersede and replace Docs. CLCS/L.3 and CLCS/L.12 as well as all previously issued docs. containing the Rules of Procedure of the Commission and their revisions or corrections (Docs. CLCS/3, CLCS/3/Corr.1, CLCS/3/Rev.1, CLCS/3/Rev.2, CLCS/3/Rev.2/Corr.1, CLCS/3/Rev.3, CLCS/3/Rev.3/Corr.1 and CLCS/40).

3   UN Doc. SPLOS/CLCS/WP.1 ('Draft Rules of Procedure of the Commission on the Limits of the Continental Shelf').

4   UN Doc. SPLOS/14 ('Report of the fifth Meeting of States Parties'), para. 44.

5   Jares, Vladimir, 'The Work of the Commission on the Limits of the Continental Shelf', in Vidas, Davor (ed.), *Law, Technology and Science*, pp. 449–475, at p. 452.

other regulations, guidelines and annexes to the Rules of Procedure. Finally, section XVI specifies the procedure for amending the Rules of Procedure.

The Rules of Procedure also contain three annexes. Annex I has more detailed rules on submissions in case of dispute between states with opposite or adjacent coasts or in other cases of unresolved land or maritime disputes. For instance, the Commission shall be informed of such disputes by a coastal state making a submission. Annex I also offers solutions for so-called partial and joint submissions.

Annex II deals with issues of confidentiality, and therefore contains rules of considerable importance to both the Commission and the submitting coastal state. The annex has rules concerning what shall be classified as confidential data and information in a submission (Rule 2), rules on the duty to preserve confidentiality (Rule 4) and also regulations on the enforcement of rules on confidentiality through a Standing Committee on Confidentiality composed of five Commission members (Rule 5). In case of an alleged breach of confidentiality by a member of the Commission, the Commission may institute proceedings, and an investigating body consisting of three or five of its members is to be set up. Having completed its examination of the case, the investigating body shall prepare a report on its findings, to be presented by the Chairperson of the Committee on Confidentiality to the Commission. The Commission shall then inform the Meeting of States Parties to the LOS Convention of the allegations and the results of the investigation, together with its recommendations.

Annex III contains the *modus operandi* for the consideration of a submission made to the Commission. Section VII of the *modus operandi* includes a useful summary flow chart of the procedures concerning a submission made to the Commission.

3.3.2   Competence to Adopt Procedural Regulations

Before looking into the substantive contents of a selection of the Commission's rules, it is worth noting that the Commission's competence to adopt procedural regulations, in addition to those contained in Article 76 and Annex II, does not follow explicitly from the LOS Convention. To determine the Commission's actual competence to adopt such rules, it is therefore necessary to address certain principles of international institutional law.

In the *Reparation for Injuries* case in 1949, the ICJ observed with regard to the UN that

> the rights and duties of an entity such as the Organization must depend upon its purpose and functions as specified or implied in its constituent

documents and developed in practice [...]. Under international law, the Organization must be deemed to have those powers which, though not expressly provided in the Charter, are conferred upon it by necessary implication as being essential to the performance of its duties.[6]

Accordingly, the ICJ confirmed the UN's right to bring legal claims externally.[7] And in the *UN Administrative Tribunal* case in 1954, the ICJ affirmed that the UN also had the competence to establish a subsidiary organ.[8] Also in *Legality of the Use by a State of Nuclear Weapons* case, the ICJ underscored how the

> necessities of international life may point to the need for organizations, in order to achieve their objectives, to possess subsidiary powers which are not expressly provided for in the basic instrument which govern their activities. It is generally accepted that international organisations can exercise such powers, known as 'implied' powers.[9]

The question is, however, whether this doctrine of 'implied powers' also applies to the Commission.[10] The Commission is not an international organization (IO). Insofar as the drafters deliberately chose not to create an IO—but a 'simplified' treaty body—we should be cautious in applying a doctrine which in practice only has been applied to IOs.

On the other hand, the LOS Convention does not forbid the Commission to adopt supplementary rules for its proceedings. As mentioned above, the first Rules of Procedure were in fact adopted at the request of the Meeting of States Parties to the LOS Convention. Thus it is difficult 'to find any intention of the parties *not* to apply the doctrine' of implied powers to the Commission.[11]

It should also be noted here that certain other general rules and principles relating to institutions and organizations which have evolved from legal practice or can be derived from customary international law, have been applied to

---

6   *I.C.J. Reports* 1949, p. 174, at pp. 180 and 182.
7   See further Ulfstein, Geir, 'Treaty Bodies and Regimes', in Hollis, Duncan B., *The Oxford Guide to Treaties* (Oxford University Press, 2012), pp. 428–447, at p. 433.
8   *I.C.J. Reports* 1954, p. 47, at p. 53.
9   *I.C.J. Reports* 1996, p. 66, at pp. 78–79.
10   The ILA Committee on the Outer Continental Shelf argued that the Commission has to be presumed to have the competences that is required to carry out its task, but did not address the issues of the Rules of Procedure specifically. See Report of the ILA Conference in Berlin, 2004, para. 3.3. Available at the website of the ILA: <www.ila-hq.org> (accessed 1 January 2014).
11   Ulfstein, 'Treaty Bodies and Regimes', pp. 433–434.

the Commission as well. One example is the rules of privileges and immunities of organizations and their personnel emanating from the Convention on the Privileges and Immunities of the United Nations.[12] On privileges and immunities of the members of the Commission, the UN Legal Council (OLC) has concluded that 'by established precedent in respect of similar treaty organs, the members of the Commission on the Limits of the Continental Shelf can be considered to be experts on mission covered by article VI of the General Convention [on the Privileges and Immunities of the United Nations]'.[13] In this regard, then the OLC equated the status of the members of the Commission with that of experts on mission in accordance with one of the basic legal instruments of the UN.[14]

3.3.3   *The 10-Year Time Limit for Making a Submission*
The first controversial issue in the Commission's Rules of Procedure concerns the deadline set by the LOS Convention for making a continental shelf submission to the Commission. According to Article 4 of Annex II to the LOS Convention, a coastal state which intends to establish the outer limits of the continental shelf beyond 200 nautical miles in accordance with Article 76 shall, as soon as possible, and no later than 10 years after the Convention has entered into force for that state,[15] submit the particulars of these limits to the Commission, supported by scientific and technical evidence.

'[A]s soon as possible' and 'within 10 years' from the time of ratification are therefore deadlines with which States Parties are obliged to comply. The 10-year time limit in Article 4 of Annex II has, however, been subject to what can be described as intrusive undermining by States Parties and, moreover, also by the Commission itself. Through its Rules of Procedure, the Commission has contributed to render more or less illusory the deadlines provided for by the text of the LOS Convention.

First—even though the focus here is on the Commission—some attention will be paid to the decisions taken by the *States Parties* in relation to the time

---

12   Convention adopted in New York on 13 February 1946; entered into force 17 September 1946. Published in *UNTS*, Vol. 1, p. 15 and Vol. 90, p. 327 (corrigendum to Vol. 1).

13   Doc. CLCS/5, para. 5.

14   See also letter of 15 May 1998 from the Chairman of the Commission addressed to the President of the eight Meeting of States Parties to the LOS Convention (UN Doc. SPLOS/28: 'Letter dated 15 May 1998 from the Chairman of the Commission on the Limits of the Continental Shelf addressed to the President of the Eighth Meeting of States Parties').

15   See Article 308, para. 2, of the LOS Convention.

limit under Article 4 of Annex II. At the Tenth Meeting of States Parties in May 2000, one delegation voiced concerns regarding the practical difficulty of complying with the time limit set in Article 4. It was proposed that the Meeting should consider the difficulties faced by certain countries, particularly developing countries, in complying with the time limit for making submissions to the Commission. It was pointed out that the letter of Article 4 placed a maximum time limit of 10 years from the entry into force of the LOS Convention for the submitting state, but in view of the limited technical expertise of certain countries, particularly the least developed countries, the Meeting should evaluate means by which assistance could be provided with respect to the scientific and technical expertise required by those preparing submissions, or consider an extension of the time limit.[16] The Meeting expressed general support for these concerns and decided to include on its agenda for the Eleventh Meeting the following item: 'Issues with respect to Article 4 of Annex II to the United Nations Convention on the Law of the Sea'. DOALOS was requested to prepare a background paper.[17]

---

16   UN Doc. SPLOS/60 ('Report of the tenth Meeting of States Parties'), para. 61.

17   *Ibid.*, para. 62. In addition to the document prepared by DOALOS, the eleventh Meeting of States Parties also had before it *notes verbales* from the Government of Seychelles regarding the extension of the time period for submissions and a position paper on the time frame for submissions put forward by the states members of the Pacific Island Forum (Australia, Fiji, Marshall Islands, Federated States of Micronesia, Nauru, New Zealand, Papua New Guinea, Samoa, Solomon Islands, Tonga and Vanuatu). See UN Doc. SPLOS/73 ('Report of the eleventh Meeting of States Parties'), para. 69. It was emphasized that a crucial theme of the LOS Convention was that developing states should not, through lack of resources or capacity, be disadvantaged in respect of access to or use of their resources. Therefore, it would be inconsistent with the LOS Convention if developing states were unable to define the limits of their extended continental shelf owing to a lack of resources or capacity. In that regard, it was underscored that the LOS Convention contained important provisions on transfer of technology so as to ensure that developing states were able to exercise their rights and fulfil their obligations under the Convention (*ibid.*, para. 70). It was emphasized that many countries would obviously not be able to make a submission within the 10-year time-frame and argued that states had had a clear idea of how to prepare their submissions only after the Commission had adopted its Scientific and Technical Guidelines in 1999. It was also recalled that the election of the members of the Commission had not taken place until May 1997, nearly three years after the entry into force of the LOS Convention (*ibid.*, para. 71). In this light, the states of the Pacific Island Forum proposed that, first, the States Parties should agree to extend the 10-year period of Article 4. Such an extension should be agreed through a decision of the Meeting of States Parties or through an understanding on the interpretation of Article 4. Second, this understanding should include an agreement that the 10-year period would not begin

The Eleventh Meeting generally supported a step-by-step approach. The first step was to address the issue of selecting the date for calculating the 10-year time limit, which could be done at that Meeting. The second step was to deal with the issue of a possible extension of the 10-year time limit, which would require sound legal clarification, and clarification of the procedures to be followed.[18] Also examined was the procedural issue of how to give effect to any decision extending the 10-year time period. Four possible procedures were put forward. The first was to adapt an amendment in accordance with Article 312 of the LOS Convention. The second was an amendment by means of the simplified procedure provided for in Article 313. Third, an agreement relating to the implementation of Article 4 was discussed. And fourth, a decision could be taken by the Meeting of States Parties along the lines of the procedure that the Meeting earlier had used regarding the postponement of the election of the members of the ITLOS and the Commission.[19]

---

to run for any state, regardless of its date of ratification or accession, until the date of adoption of the Commission's Scientific and Technical Guidelines. Third, the time for making a submission would be further extended beyond 10 years if a State Party had been unable, for technical reasons, to comply in good faith with the time limit (*ibid.*, para. 71). Many delegations supported the arguments put forward in the position paper of the states of the Pacific Island Forum that the Meeting should consider issues with respect to Article 4 and take such a decision on the starting date for the calculation of the 10-year time period for making submissions that would ameliorate the difficulty in complying with the 10-year deadline (*ibid.*, para. 72).

18   *Ibid.*, para. 73. Many delegations agreed that the starting date should be 13 May 1999, i.e. the date of adoption of the Scientific and Technical Guidelines of the Commission. They pointed out that the Guidelines gave guidance to states as to the particulars to be expected to be included in submissions. One delegation emphasized, however, that the adoption of the Scientific and Technical Guidelines was not a prerequisite or a condition for making a submission (*ibid.*, para. 74). Some delegations also pointed out that there was no legal consequence provided by the LOS Convention if a state did not make a submission to the Commission. It was underscored that the rights of the coastal state over its continental shelf were inherent, and that non-compliance with the 10-year time period specified in Article 4 would not affect those rights, which did not depend on occupation, effective or notional, or any express proclamation, as stated in Article 77, para. 3, of the LOS Convention (*ibid.*, para. 75). Others emphasized that at the current stage, the adoption of the decision that the 10-year period would not begin to run for any State Party, regardless of its date of ratification or accession, until the date of adoption of the Commission's Scientific and Technical Guidelines, would have already ameliorated substantially the situation for the first group of states by extending their deadline, in fact, for an additional five years (*ibid.*, para. 77).

19   *Ibid.*, para. 78. Many delegations were of the view that it fell within the competence of the Meeting to adopt by consensus a decision expressing general agreement on the starting date

In light of the discussions, and a further proposal from Papua New Guinea, an open-ended working group prepared a draft decision,[20] subsequently adopted by the Meeting of States Parties on 29 May 2001 as 'Decision regarding the date of commencement of the 10-year period for making submissions to the Commission on the Limits of the Continental Shelf set out in Article 4 of Annex II to the United Nations Convention on the Law of the Sea'.[21] The decision provides that, for a state for which the Convention entered into force *before 13 May 1999*, the date of commencement of the 10-year time period for making submissions to the Commission referred to in Article 4 of Annex II would be 13 May 1999—the date of adoption of the Commission's Scientific and Technical Guidelines.[22] The decision is reflected in the Rules of Procedure of the Commission, Rule 45 (*litra* a) of which provides that 'the 10-year time period referred to in Article 4 of Annex II to the Convention shall be taken to have commenced on 13 May 1999'. This meant that states which had ratified the LOS Convention prior to 1999 were given extra time to submit their continental shelf submissions to the Commission. And—despite all good intentions—the black-letter law of the 10-year time limit in Article 4 of Annex II had suddenly become subject to a peculiar legal innovation.[23]

---

for calculating the 10-year time period. Such a decision, they stated, would be of a procedural nature similar to the ones the Meeting had taken with respect to the postponement of the election of members of ITLOS and the Commission. However, one delegation was of the view that the issue of the starting date was of direct relevance to the rights and obligations of States Parties to the LOS Convention and therefore could not be considered as simply a procedural decision (*ibid.*, para. 79). The Chairman of the Commission stated that the 10-year deadline was a matter that fell within the competence of states; the Commission would be guided by whatever deadline was decided upon by the States Parties on the condition that the decision was legally correct (*ibid.*, para. 80).

20 UN Doc. SPLOS/L.22 ('Draft decision on the day of commencement of the ten-year period for making submissions to the Commission on the Limits of the Continental Shelf set out in article 4 of Annex II to the United Nations Convention on the Law of the Sea').

21 UN Doc. SPLOS/72 ('Decision regarding the date of commencement of the ten-year period for making submissions to the Commission on the Limits of the Continental Shelf set out in article 4 of Annex II to the United Nations Convention on the Law of the Sea').

22 UN Doc. SPLOS/73 ('Report of the eleventh Meeting of States Parties'), para. 81.

23 Several states for which the LOS Convention entered into force before that date have nevertheless decided to comply with the 'original' deadline. There are probably several explanations for this. First, compiling a dossier of the information required under Article 76 of the LOS Convention is a complex and long-term task with regard to the scientific methodology, the planning and organization. Technology already used in the preparation of a submission would not necessarily be appropriate if the submission were to be delayed, and returning to square one in planning and organization would

Implementation of Article 4 was further accommodated by the States Parties at their Eighteenth Meeting. This Meeting—recalling the decision of the eleventh Meeting regarding the date of commencement of the 10-year period described above—had to recognize that some coastal states, in particular developing countries, continued to face particular challenges in submitting information to the Commission in accordance with Article 4, including the 'postponement' given by the decision of 29 May 2001.[24] Thus it was decided by the Meeting that

> the time period referred to in Article 4 of Annex II to the Convention and the [Decision regarding the date of commencement of the 10-year period for making submissions to the Commission on the Limits of the Continental Shelf set out in Article 4 of Annex II to the United Nations Convention on the Law of the Sea], may be satisfied by submitting to the Secretary-General *preliminary information indicative of the outer limits of the continental shelf beyond 200 nautical miles* and a description of the status of preparation and intended date of making a submission in accordance with the requirements of Article 76 of the Convention and with the Rules of Procedure [...].[25] (Emphasis added)

---

require further rounds of long-term planning and fresh research, neither particularly desirable from a financial or organizational point of view (see Jensen, Øystein, 'Towards Setting the Outer Limits of the Continental Shelf in the Arctic: On the Norwegian Submission and Recommendations by the Commission', in Vidas (ed.), *Law, Technology and Science for Oceans in Globalisation*, p. 523). A second reason might be of a legal nature, connected to the May 2001 decision of the Meeting of State Parties. That decision can neither be regarded as a formal amendment to the LOS Convention (see Articles 312 and 312 of the LOS Convention), nor as an agreement relating to the implementation of Article 4 of Annex II. As noted above, what the Meeting did was to adopt a decision similar to the ones with respect to the postponement of the election of members of ITLOS and the Commission. But would this decision bind those states that became parties to the LOS Convention after the Eleventh Meeting of the State Parties? Or would there be an opening for those states to oppose submissions made with a delay in relation to the original schedule under Article 4 of Annex II to the LOS Convention? Questions of that sort would not arise in the case of a 'timely' submission (*ibid.*).

24   UN Doc. SPLOS/183 ('Decision regarding the workload of the Commission on the Limits of the Continental Shelf and the ability of States, particularly developing States, to fulfil the requirements of article 4 of Annex II to the Convention, as well as the decision contained in SPLOS/72, paragraph (a)').

25   *Ibid.*

This decision may look as if it was meant to favour only developing countries, given that it was based on the recognition that 'some coastal States, in particular developing countries, including small island developing States, continue to face particular challenges in submitting information to the Commission [...] due to a lack of financial and technical resources and relevant capacity and expertise'.[26] However, industrialized coastal states have also taken advantage of the opportunity to suspend the 10-year time limit in Article 4, by submitting only 'preliminary information'– as was the case for instance with France's preliminary information of 8 May 2009 in relation to Saint Pierre and Miquelon, French Polynesia and Wallis and Futuna:

> Les informations préliminaires indicatives sur la limite extérieure du plateau continental au-delà de 200 milles marins des lignes de base à partir desquelles est mesurée la largeur de la mer territoriale de la Polynésie française et du territoire des îles Wallis et Futuna sont soumises par le Gouvernement de la République Française au Secrétaire Général des Nations unies, en se référant à la décision de la Réunion des Etats parties de la Convention des Nations Unies sur le droit de la mer (SPLOS/183). Ces informations préliminaires sont fournies sans préjudice des demandes complètes concernant la Polynésie française et les îles Wallis et Futuna, que la France se réserve le droit de déposer à une date ultérieure auprès de la Commission des Limites du Plateau Continental conformément à l'Article 76, paragraphe 8, et à l'article 4 de l'Annexe II de la Convention.[27]

A similar interpretation was invoked by Spain in relation to the seabed areas beyond 200 nautical miles off the west coast of the Canary Islands:

> De acuerdo con la disposición de SPLOS/183 del 20 de Junio de 2008, España puede presentar antes del 13 de Mayo de 2009, únicamente información preliminar indicativa de los límites exteriores de la plataforma continental más allá de las 200 millas marinas y una descripción del estado de preparación y de la fecha prevista de envío de la presentación, para cualquiera de las áreas parciales que considere oportuno.[28]

---

26   *Ibid.*
27   Preliminary information submitted by France, available at the Commission website: <www.un.org/Depts/los/clcs_new/submissions_files/preliminary/fra2009infos_pre liminaires_polynesie_wallis_f.pdf> (accessed 1 January 2014).
28   Preliminary information submitted by Spain, available at the Commission website: <www.un.org/Depts/los/clcs_new/submissions_files/preliminary/esp_can_2009_pre liminaryinfo.pdf> (accessed 1 January 2014).

On this basis, it thus seems that the decisions of the *States Parties* in relation to Article 4 of Annex II to the LOS Convention have led to a *de facto* amendment of a clear-cut treaty provision.[29]

---

29   See also Treves, Tullio, 'The Development of the Law of the Sea since the Adoption of the UN Convention on the Law of the Sea: Achievements and Challenges for the Future', in Vidas, Davor (ed.), *Law, Technology and Science for Oceans in Globalisation*, pp. 41–58, at p. 49. Before proceeding to the Commission's decisions relating to Article 4 of Annex II, it is worth briefly noting that both the appropriateness and legality of the above mentioned decisions of the Meeting can be discussed. With regard to the appropriateness, it is obvious that changes have been initiated by the fact that the deadline set out in Article 4 has emerged as much too short for some coastal states. It can be argued that the deadline extension thus makes sense in that all states now have the opportunity to make 'timely' submissions. UNCLOS III—in setting 10 years from the date of ratification as the maximum deadline for making a submission—perhaps did not predict the challenges related to the implementation of Article 76 at the national level, and the time actually needed for the most disadvantaged states to design their shelf submissions. On the other hand, it can be argued that the Meeting—by deciding that the filing of 'preliminary information' is sufficient to stop the deadline from running—actually has terminated the implementation of Article 76 indefinitely, which would be unfortunate. Preliminary information will not provide the Commission with full shelf submissions to work with, only a notice that a full shelf submission someday will arrive. But it is still unclear *when* the preliminary information submitted by many coastal states in 2009 will be transformed into fully fledged submissions. The Meeting's second decision may thus have unintended consequences. While the intention was only to give coastal states a longer time to prepare their shelf submissions, it is a risk that the decision will actually be a 'pretext' and that implementation of Article 76 will be postponed indefinitely. It is also appropriate to attach some comments to which *legal* effects—if any—are related to the decisions of the States Parties. Shall coastal states follow the 10-year deadline or the Meeting's decisions? The Meeting has not followed the formal amendment procedures in the LOS Convention. However, it would have been possible to amend the LOS Convention 10 years after it entered into force, that is, from November 2004 (see Article 212, para. 1, of the LOS Convention). Formally, Article 4 of Annex II therefore continues to apply and the deadline which the states parties shall use will still depend on an interpretation of this provision. However, it is debatable whether the deadline in Article 4 of Annex II must be interpreted so that '10 years' should not be taken literally, but instead be interpreted in the light of the Meeting's decisions, considering the significance of these decisions as subsequent agreements or subsequent practice expressing the agreement of the parties regarding the LOS Convention's interpretation (in accordance with Article 31, para. 3 (*litras* a and b), of the Vienna Convention). The Vienna Convention does not in this regard specify that any particular 'form' of agreement or practice is required. Hence, any good evidence that the parties to the LOS Convention have reached agreement on the interpretation seems admissible (see Gardiner, *Treaty Interpretation*, p. 220). However, if one considers that Article 4 shall be construed so that the contents of the decisions of the Meetings are applicable, then one will provide context—subsequent agreements—decisive weight at

Also the Commission, however, has contributed to undermine the submission deadline under Article 4 of Annex II to the LOS Convention. The relevant provision is Rule 3 of Annex I to the Rules of Procedure, under which the Commission accepts that an incomplete shelf submission will suspend the 10-year deadline:

> A submission may be made by a coastal State for a portion of its continental shelf in order not to prejudice questions relating to the delimitation of boundaries between States in any other portion or portions of the continental shelf for which a submission may be made later, notwithstanding the provisions regarding the 10-year period established by Article 4 of Annex II to the Convention.

This provision thus allows a submission in respect of a 'portion' (or, we may assume, portions) of the continental shelf. The rule appears to be the result of the Commission's sensitivity in relation to unresolved maritime boundary issues. Rule 3 arises as a consequence of Rule 46 of the Rules of Procedure, which specifies that if there is a delimitation dispute, or other cases of unresolved land or maritime disputes, involved in any submission relating to the outer continental shelf, the Commission may, *prima facie*, be unable to make recommendations on the submitted information. Rule 46 refers to Annex I and in Rule 5 (*litra* a) of Annex I it is provided that a submission by any of the states concerned in the dispute shall not be considered and qualified by the Commission without prior consent of all states involved in the dispute.

The core of Rule 3 of Annex I is thus that the coastal state may provide a partial submission that covers only certain parts of the total continental shelf beyond 200 nautical miles in order not to prejudice delimitations in other portions of the continental shelf for which a submission may be made later, notwithstanding Article 4 of Annex II to the LOS Convention. However, there is no provision in the LOS Convention which gives the coastal state any right to 'postpone the deadline' simply because maritime boundary issues are involved. This, arguably, reveals a contradiction between the Commission's procedural rules and the LOS Convention's provisions on this point. Article 76, paragraph 10, and Article 9 of Annex II, stipulate that the *Commission's* actions should not touch on questions concerning maritime boundary issues. In Rule 3, however, the Commission has offered an opt-out clause to the submitting coastal state.

---

the cost of the 'ordinary meaning to be given to the terms'. Ten years means ten years. An important question of a more general matter is also whether the parties in this way should be allowed to circumvent the formal amendment procedures of the LOS Convention.

That might be at the expense of other states, if these wish to take advantage of the consequences that might follow from a breach of the 10-year deadline provided for in Article 4 of Annex II to the LOS Convention.[30]

For example, one could ask whether the Commission is entitled to examine continental shelf claims that are submitted too late with regard to Article 4. The Commission's view is obviously that this will not be a relevant issue, since, under Rule 3, it allows states to file their shelf submissions *after* the deadline in Article 4 has expired. The Commission has made no effort to discuss these matters and its rule simply seems to join the ranks of 'deadline extensions' created by the Meetings of States Parties. However, insofar as the Commission under Rule 3 of Annex II waives the 10-year time limit of Article 4 to the advantage of coastal states—enabling them to submit particulars of the outer limits notwithstanding the deadline prescribed by Article 4 of Annex II to the LOS Convention—the balance between the rights and obligations of coastal states and other states created by the Rules of Procedure is again thrown out of kilter, as Serdy has emphasized and criticized.[31]

The 'rule of conflict' between the Commission's Rules of Procedure would arguably not be a technically difficult legal question if it were put to the test. The Commission's procedural rules will not supersede the provisions of the LOS Convention if there is contradiction: the Rules of Procedure are clearly 'subordinate' to the rules in the LOS Convention.[32] However, the Commission's rules have had significant practical effects. The Irish submission related to the Porcupine Abyssal Plain area of the Atlantic region in 2005 was the first example of a partial submission being made under Rule 3 of Annex I.[33] In Ireland's view, that particular portion of the shelf was not the subject of any dispute and consideration by the Commission would thus not prejudice matters relating to the delimitation of boundaries between Ireland and any other states.[34]

---

30   See Serdy, Andrew, 'The Commission on the Limits of the Continental Shelf and its Disturbing Propensity to Legislate', in *The International Journal of Marine and Coastal Law*, Vol. 26, 2011, pp. 355–383, at p. 369.

31   *Ibid.*

32   Elferink, Alex G. Oude, and C. Johnson, 'Outer Limits of the Continental Shelf and "Disputed Areas": State Practice Concerning Article 76(10)', in *The International Journal of Marine and Coastal Law*, Vol. 21, 2006, pp. 461–487, at p. 467. See also Doc. CLCS/46, para. 8.

33   Executive summary of the Irish submission, available at the website of the Commission: <www.un.org/Depts/los/clcs_new/submissions_files/submission_irl.htm> (accessed 1 January 2014).

34   'Continental Shelf Notification' accompanying the submission of Ireland, referred to at the website of the Commission: <www.un.org/Depts/los/clcs_new/submissions_files/irl05/IRL_CLCS_04_2005_csn_e.pdf> (accessed 1 January 2014).

Another example of the use of partial submissions is that made by France in respect of French Guiana and New Caledonia in 2007.[35] Also, the UK made a partial submission in respect of Ascension Island in 2008.[36] The joint submission to the Commission in 2006 by France, Ireland, Spain and the UK regarding the outer continental shelf limits in the area of the Celtic Sea and Bay of Biscay also constitutes an example of a partial submission under Rule 3 of Annex I.[37] As stated in the notes accompanying the submission,

> for each of these four coastal States the enclosed joint submission represents a partial submission in respect of a portion only of the outer limits of the continental shelf appurtenant to all four coastal States that lie beyond 200 nautical miles from their baselines from which the breadth of their respective territorial seas are measured. This portion of shelf is not the subject of any dispute and, in the view of the four coastal States, its consideration by the Commission will not prejudice matters relating to the delimitation of boundaries between the four coastal States and any other States.[38]

The notes accompanying the submission also stated:

> In accordance with paragraph 3 of Annex I to the Rules of Procedure of the Commission, in order not to prejudice unresolved questions relating to the delimitation of boundaries between France, Ireland, Spain and the United Kingdom of Great Britain and Northern Ireland and some of their neighbours in other portions of the continental shelf appurtenant to France, Ireland, Spain and the United Kingdom of Great Britain and Northern Ireland, submissions for those portions shall be made at a later date.[39]

Thus, the Commission has contributed to the fact that, for several coastal states, the Convention's deadline in its original form—10 years—simply has

---

35   Doc. CLCS/56.

36   Doc. CLCS/60.

37   Executive Summary of the Irish submission, available at the website of the Commission: <www.un.org/Depts/los/clcs_new/submissions_files/submission_frgbires.htm> (accessed 1 January 2014).

38   'Continental Shelf Notification' accompanying the submission of France, Ireland, Spain and the United Kingdom, referred to at the website of the Commission: <www.un.org/Depts/los/clcs_new/submissions_files/frgbires06/clcs06_2006e.pdf> (accessed 1 January 2014).

39   *Ibid.*

no significance in respect of certain seabed areas. The implementation of Article 76 is put on hold.

An issue that arises in the extension of the practice with partial implementation of the LOS Convention's deadline is what the Commission actually has meant by the term 'later' in Rule 3 of Annex I. One interpretation is that it means that when the maritime boundary is resolved, the remaining part of the continental shelf claim must be presented to the Commission. Such an understanding can be underpinned by the provision's underlying rationale, i.e. that the deadline postponement in Rule 3 is the result of unresolved maritime boundary issues. Therefore, when the maritime boundary issues in question are finalized, the remaining part of the continental shelf claim must be submitted. Another interpretation, however, could be that 'later' gives the coastal state a free margin with respect to the time for submitting the remaining portion of the continental shelf submission to the Commission. It would therefore help reduce some of the 'discrepancy' between Rule 3 and the LOS Convention if the former, for example, had used the formulation 'as soon as possible', after the pattern of Article 4 of Annex II to the LOS Convention.

3.3.4 *Joint Submissions*
Many coastal states have or could have overlapping claims and/or unresolved boundaries with neighbouring states. The Commission has made rules that encourage these states to submit 'joint submissions', notably according to Rule 4 of Annex I to the Rules of Procedure:

> Joint or separate submissions to the Commission requesting the Commission to make recommendations with respect to delineation may be made by two or more coastal States by agreement: (a) Without regard to the delimitation of boundaries between those States; or (b) With an indication, by means of geodetic coordinates, of the extent to which a submission is without prejudice to the matters relating to the delimitation of boundaries with another or other States Parties to this Agreement.

This rule may promote timely implementation of the deadline in Article 4 of Annex II to the LOS Convention, since unresolved maritime boundary question will not be an obstacle for submissions to the Commission. On the practical and technical levels, there are also clear advantages for states in being able to make use of joint data collection arrangements and expertise, as well as potential resource savings in terms of the division of labour. State practice also has indicated considerable interest in joint submissions. In addition to the above-mentioned submission made by the UK, France, Ireland and Spain, a joint submission has been made by the Republic of Mauritius and the Republic of Seychelles in the region of the Mascarene Plateau;[40] and a joint submission has been made by the Federated States of Micronesia, Papua New Guinea and Solomon Islands concerning the Ontong Java Plateau.[41] Other joint submissions include Malaysia and Vietnam's for the southern part of the South China Sea,[42] and France and South Africa's in the area of the Crozet Archipelago and Prince Edward Islands.[43]

Allowing 'joint submissions' is, however, a legal innovation that is not known from the LOS Convention's text, and was not discussed as an option during UNCLOS III. Article 76 and Annex II consistently use the singular forms, 'the coastal State' and 'it'. Under the LOS Convention, establishing the outer limits of the continental shelf is intended to be a unilateral matter, as it is for the delineation of the outer limits of other maritime zones under the Convention. Thus, Rule 4 of Annex I complements the LOS Convention's provisions and enables a type of joint procedure alien to the system of the Convention.

In essence, Rule 4 may prove useful for coastal states with overlapping continental shelves extending beyond 200 nautical miles from the baselines. It could, for example, accelerate the preparation and submission of claims of individual coastal states, in that all overlapping shelf submissions in an area can be collected under a common umbrella, which in turn may discourage single states from attempting to delay proceedings for tactical reasons. But—is Rule 4 a lawful provision in light of the LOS Convention?

Joint submissions are not explicitly prohibited by the LOS Convention, nor is Rule 4 likely to obstruct the implementation of other substantive provisions of the LOS Convention, such as deadlines. Rule 4 merely provides coastal states with a right to choose. In my view, the provision therefore complements the LOS Convention—not directly conflicts with it.

It is interesting to note, however, that in practice the Commission seems to have taken a major step towards undermining the advantages to states from

---

40   Executive summary available at the website of the Commission: <www.un.org/Depts/los/ clcs_new/submissions_files/musc08/sms_es_doc.pdf> (accessed 1 January 2014).

41   Executive summary available at the website of the Commission: <www.un.org/Depts/los/ clcs_new/submissions_files/fmpgsb32_09/exsumdocs/fmpgsb2009executivesummary .pdf> (accessed 1 January 2014).

42   Executive summary available at the website of the Commission: <www.un.org/Depts/los/ clcs_new/submissions_files/mysvnm33_09/mys_vnm2009excutivesummary.pdf> (accessed 1 January 2014).

43   Executive summary available at the website of the Commission: <www.un.org/Depts/ los/clcs_new/submissions_files/frazaf34_09/frazaf2009exec_sum_resume.pdf> (accessed 1 January 2014).

making joint continental shelf submissions under Rule 4 of Annex I. In relation to the joint submission of France, Ireland, Spain and the UK, the Chairman of the Commission noted that

> the total area of continental shelf resulting from the outer limits of the continental shelf proposed in a joint submission cannot be larger than the sum of the individual areas of continental shelf resulting from the outer limits of the continental shelf that each of the States would have proposed if they had made separate submissions. In other words, in any joint submission, each coastal State has to establish its own set of criteria for the feet of the continental slope, applied formulas, constraints and respective outer limits.[44]

Here it is thus provided that each submitting state will still be requested to show what portion of the area landward of the jointly submitted outer limit would have fallen within a putative individually submitted limit. Then—as remarked by Serdy—one may ask what the coastal state really has to gain from a joint submission under Rule 4 of Annex I.[45]

3.3.5 *Transparency Regulations*

Interestingly, the Commission has imposed upon coastal states requirements as to transparency not required under the LOS Convention. According to Rule 50 of the Commission's Rule of Procedure, the UNSG

> shall, through the appropriate channels, promptly notify the Commission and all States Members of the United Nations, including States Parties to the Convention, of the receipt of the submission, and make public the executive summary including all charts and coordinates referred to in paragraph 9.1.4 of the Guidelines and contained in that summary, upon completion of the translation of the executive summary referred to in rule 47, paragraph 3.

The Commission has also adopted Rule 11, paragraph 3, of Annex III to the Rules of Procedure, providing for public disclosure of the summary of the recommendations:

---

44   Doc. CLCS/56, para. 28.
45   Serdy, 'The Commission on the Limits of the Continental Shelf and its Disturbing Propensity to Legislate', p. 370.

The recommendations prepared by the subcommission shall include a summary thereof, and such summary shall not contain information which might be of a confidential nature and/or which might violate the proprietary rights of the coastal State over the data and information provided in the submission. The Secretary General shall make public the summary of the recommendations upon their approval by the Commission.

Ultimately, Rule 54, paragraph 3, of the Commission's Rules of Procedure determines:

> Upon giving due publicity to the charts and relevant information, including geodetic data, permanently describing the outer limits of the continental shelf deposited by the coastal State in accordance with article 76, paragraph 9, of the Convention, the Secretary-General shall also give due publicity to the recommendations of the Commission which in the view of the Commission are related to those limits.

These rules of the Commission for the purpose of openness are indeed procedural innovations concerning an issue of considerable importance to both the coastal state and the outside world. But, pursuant to the LOS Convention, it is only the *outer limits* established by the coastal state that shall be given due publicity, not any information contained in the submission of the coastal state or the recommendations of the Commission.[46] The Commission has thus imposed upon the States Parties—or at least attempted to impose upon them—additional commitments regarding transparency that do not explicitly follow from the LOS Convention.

While increased transparency—as will be argued later—is preferred *lex ferenda* and from a normative legitimacy perspective, questions nevertheless arise in relation to the lawfulness of the Commission's additional regulations on this point. Insofar as the LOS Convention contains no explicit prohibition against public disclosure of recommendations and submissions, the above mentioned regulations cannot be said to *contradict* the LOS Convention. The provisions nevertheless complement Article 76 and Annex II in an area which might be sensitive and controversial to states that prefer secrecy during the submission process. Neither, remarkably, is there any formal requirement to obtain the consent of the coastal state prior to disclosure of information contained in the submission or the recommendations. From Rule 50, Rule 11 and

---

46   See Article 76, para. 9, of the LOS Convention.

Rule 54, it appears that the Commission takes it for granted that public disclosure must apply.

So far, the rules on openness have proven to be of great practical importance. This may be because states find the regulations acceptable, but partly also because it is DOALOS that is tasked with providing disclosure of the summaries of submissions and (summaries of) recommendations. In practical terms, then, the provisions are by no means a burdensome obligation to the coastal state in question.

For quite a long time, however, at least one coastal state has resisted disclosure under Rule 11, paragraph 3, of Annex III to the Rules of Procedure. While the recommendations to Brazil were adopted on 4 April 2007,[47] no summary of the recommendations could be found on the Commission's website until late 2013. Now, this might be because the summary of the recommendations—with amendments—was adopted by the Commission only on 24 August 2011.[48] All the same, approximately two years lapsed from the summary was finalized until it was made public, indicating, perhaps, a more deliberate opposition on the part of the Brazilian government regarding transparency regulations—so perhaps the Commission's procedural rules do not have a content which is acceptable to all States Parties after all.

3.3.6   Third States' Right of Veto
In the LOS Convention, it is made clear that the provisions on setting the outer limits of the continental shelf shall not affect the issue of delimitation between states with overlapping continental shelf claims. Article 76, paragraph 10, provides that '[t]the provisions of [Article 76] are without prejudice to the question of delimitation of the continental shelf between States with opposite or adjacent coasts'. According to Article 9 of Annex II, '[t]he actions of the Commission shall not prejudice matters relating to the delimitation of boundaries between States with opposite or adjacent coasts'.

The Commission has also adopted in its Rules of Procedure provisions for situations in which a submission concerns a seabed area of unresolved maritime delimitations. Rule 5 (*litra* a) of Annex I to the Rules of Procedure reads:

> In cases where a land or maritime dispute exists, the Commission shall not consider and qualify a submission made by any of the States

---

47   Doc. CLCS/54.
48   Information regarding the submission made by Brazil, available at the website of the Commission: <www.un.org/Depts/los/clcs_new/submissions_files/submission_bra.htm> (accessed 1 January 2014).

concerned in the dispute. However, the Commission may consider one
or more submissions in the areas under dispute with prior consent given
by all States that are parties to such a dispute.

In light of this provision, it can be argued that the Commission has gone beyond
the proper limits set out in the LOS Convention by declining to examine submissions affected by a dispute without the consent of all parties to the dispute.
The intention is praiseworthy, and obviously based on Article 76, paragraph 10,
and Article 9 of Annex II, that is, so that its performance shall not 'prejudice'
matters related to maritime delimitation.

First, however, Rule 5 (*litra* a) provides that all states that are 'parties to
[...] a dispute' have a right of veto as to whether the Commission shall consider and evaluate a submission at all. The Commission may consider a submission in the area under dispute only if 'prior consent' has been given by all
states that are parties to the dispute. This is not provided for under the LOS
Convention. On the contrary, according to Article 76, paragraph 8, of the
LOS Convention, the Commission 'shall issue recommendations to coastal
States'.[49] The Commission's obligation is thus not conditional upon the consent of other states. And the mandatory language in paragraph 8—'shall'—will
probably lead submitting states to actually expect that the Commission starts
its examination.[50]

The Commission seems to have based Rule 5 (*litra* a) of Annex I on a very
broad interpretation of the concept of 'prejudice' in Article 76, paragraph 10,
and Article 9 of Annex II. Or, put differently, Rule 5 is the expression of a
'defensive' Commission, which, on its own behalf, has increased the risk of
total paralysis in the face of coastal state submissions. In consequence of this
clause, other states, merely by notifying a dispute, will have the right to veto
whether the Commission shall proceed to examine a submission at all.

There is also a clear contradiction here as regards the scope of application of
Rule 5 as compared to the relevant provisions of the LOS Convention. Article 76,
paragraph 10, and Article 9 of Annex II, respectively, have rules about the

---

49   See also Article 3, para. 1 (*litra* a), of Annex II to the LOS Convention.
50   There are several cases in which states have taken the advantage of 'blocking' the
      Commission from proceeding with considering submissions where there exists a dispute
      in the delimitation of the continental shelf between opposite or adjacent states or in
      other cases of unresolved land or maritime disputes, as between Argentina and the UK,
      and between Iceland and Denmark on the Hatton-Rockall area. See McDorman, Ted, 'The
      Continental Shelf Regime in the Law of the Sea Convention: A Reflection on the First
      Thirty Years', p. 749.

'delimitation of the continental shelf' and 'delimitation of boundaries'. By contrast, Rule 5 is concerned with 'land or maritime dispute[s]'. These are, however, not concurrent concepts. There are many 'land or maritime dispute[s]' that are not about maritime delimitation. One example is pending issues regarding the exercise of jurisdiction on the continental shelf, as with the adjacent seabed areas around Svalbard.[51] Likewise, 'dispute'—but not 'delimitation of the continental shelf' or 'delimitation of boundaries'—may concern issues that are extrinsic to Article 76, such as the question of sovereignty over the Falkland Islands, or whether title to Antarctic territory can or does exist.[52]

On the other hand, not all delimitation issues can be categorized as 'disputes' in a legal sense, that is, in which 'the claim of one party is positively opposed by the other'.[53] A relevant illustration has been given by Serdy; the continental shelf submission made by Palau in 2009.[54] The Philippines had requested the Commission to refrain from considering the submission in view of the dispute brought about by an overlap in the jurisdictional continental shelves of the two coastal states.[55] However, Palau, while acknowledging that it and the Philippines shared an overlapping exclusive economic zone, argued that this did not constitute a dispute.[56] Palau had formally notified the Federated States of Micronesia, Japan and Indonesia in advance of its submission, and

---

[51] See generally Churchill, Robin, and Geir Ulfstein, 'The Disputed Maritime Zones around Svalbard', in Nordquist, Myron H., Tomas H. Heidar and John Norton Moore (eds), *Changes in the Arctic Environment and the Law of the Sea* (Martinus Nijhoff Publishers, 2010), pp. 551–593. See also Ulfstein, Geir, *The Svalbard Treaty: From Terra Nullius to Norwegian Sovereignty* (Scandinavian University Press, 1995) and Churchill, Robin, and Geir Ulfstein, Marine *Management in Disputed Areas: The case of the Barents Sea* (Routledge, 1992), pp. 23–53.

[52] Serdy, Andrew, 'Some Views Are More Equal Than Others: Submission to the Commission on the Limits of the Continental Shelf and the Strange Loss of Confidence in Article IV of the Antarctic Treaty', in *Australian Yearbook of International Law*, Vol. 28, 2009, pp. 181–195, at p. 192.

[53] See *South West Africa Cases*. Published in *I.C.J. Reports* 1962, p. 319, at p. 328.

[54] Serdy, 'The Commission on the Limits of the Continental Shelf and its Disturbing Propensity to Legislate', pp. 362–363. Submission available at the website of the Commission: <www.un.org/Depts/los/clcs_new/submission_files/submission_plw_41_2009.htm> (accessed 1 January 2014).

[55] *Note verbale* dated 4 August 2009, available at the website of the Commission: <www.un.org/Depts/los/clcs_new/submissions_files/plw41_09/clcs_41_2009_los_phl.pdf> (accessed 1 January 2014).

[56] *Note verbale* dated 22 July 2010, available at the website of the Commission: <www.un.org/Depts/los/clcs_new/submissions_files/plw41_09/clcs_41_2009_los_plw.pdf> (accessed 1 January 2014).

underscored at the presentation of its submission to the Commission that no such *note verbale* had been received from those states.[57] Thus, none of Palau's other neighbours, with which delimitation was also to take place, had raised objections, and so Palau claimed that the submission had been made without prejudice to the question of the delimitation of the continental shelf between Palau and other states.[58] The Commission, however, addressing the modalities for the consideration of the submission, and taking into account the *note verbale* of the Philippines referred to above, decided to defer further consideration of the submission until such time as the submission would be next in line for consideration, as queued in the order in which it was received.[59]

It must be assumed that the Commission, also in the way it has chosen to approach submissions related to continental shelves that are subject to disputes, has adopted procedural rules with the best intentions. It can be argued, however, that the Rules of Procedure, with regard to Rule 5 (*litra* a) of Annex I, provide for a solution which not only stands in contradiction to the provisions of the LOS Convention, but could also undermine a fundamental purpose of the Convention, as expressed in its preamble: the strengthening of peace, security, cooperation and friendly relations among all nations. The point stressed in the legal literature seems to be that a rule which captures disputes other than those only related to maritime delimitation matters may in fact have the consequence of 'exacerbating existing disputes or even create disputes where none existed'.[60] Thus, the Commission's Rules of Procedure would perhaps in a more sensible way have promoted stability in the oceans—and been in better harmony with the non-prejudice clause of Article 76, paragraph 10, and Article 9 of Annex II—if one of the other draft provisions proposed in the course of the drafting of Annex I had been adopted, i.e.: 'Even in cases where a land or maritime dispute exists, the Commission shall examine and qualify a submission made by any of the States concerned in the dispute'.[61] However, only one Commission member favoured that solution.[62]

---

57   Doc. CLCS/68, para. 30.

58   *Ibid.*

59   Doc. CLCS/68, para. 31.

60   Serdy, 'The Commission on the Limits of the Continental Shelf and its Disturbing Propensity to Legislate', pp. 363–364, referring to UN Doc. SPLOS/24 ('Report of the seventh Meeting of States Parties'), para. 31.

61   Doc. CLCS/3, p. 21.

62   Serdy, 'The Commission on the Limits of the Continental Shelf and its Disturbing Propensity to Legislate', pp. 363–364.

The Commission's regulations giving states the right of 'veto' was also highlighted in the ITLOS case between Bangladesh and Myanmar concerning the delimitation of the maritime zones in the Bay of Bengal. One question was whether the Tribunal should exercise its jurisdiction to delimit the continental shelf beyond 200 nautical miles *before* the Commission had adopted recommendations to the states in the dispute. The question arose because Bangladesh had informed the Commission, in a *note verbale* dated 23 July 2009, that, for the purpose of Rule 46 of the Rules of Procedure of the Commission, and of Annex I thereto, there was a dispute between the Parties, and the Commission should therefore not 'consider and qualify the submission made by Myanmar without the prior consent given by all states that were parties to the dispute'.[63]

The Commission, taking into account Bangladesh's position, had deferred the consideration of the submission made by Myanmar.[64] The Commission had also decided to defer the consideration of the submission of Bangladesh

> in order to take into account any further developments that might occur in the intervening period, during which the States concerned might wish to take advantage of the avenues available to them, including provisional arrangements of a practical nature as outlined in annex I to the rules of procedure.[65]

Accordingly, the situation was that the Commission—due to its rules on the right of veto under Rule 5 (*litra* a) of Annex I—was not able to continue with the examination of the two submissions. So when the case of delimitation was put to the ITLOS, the Commission had not examined either of the two continental shelf claims beyond 200 nautical miles in the Bay of Bengal.

Interestingly, the ITLOS then used the Commission's Rules of Procedure to justify it exercising its jurisdiction to delimit the continental shelf beyond 200 nautical miles:

> The consequence of these decisions of the Commission is that, if the Tribunal declines to delimit the continental shelf beyond 200 nm under Article 83 of the Convention, the issue concerning the establishment of the outer limits of the continental shelf of each of the Parties under

---

63   *Dispute concerning delimitation of the maritime boundary between Bangladesh and Myanmar in the Bay of Bengal (Bangladesh v. Myanmar)*, Judgment, para. 387. Available at <www.itlos.org> (accessed 1 January 2014).

64   *Ibid.*, para. 388. See also Doc. CLCS/64, p. 10 (para. 40).

65   Doc. CLCS/72, p. 7 (para. 22).

Article 76 of the Convention may remain unresolved. The Tribunal notes that the record in this case affords little basis for assuming that the Parties could readily agree on other avenues available to them so long as their delimitation dispute is not settled...A decision by the Tribunal not to exercise its jurisdiction over the dispute relating to the continental shelf beyond 200 nm would not only fail to resolve a long-standing dispute, but also would not be conducive to the efficient operation of the Convention...In the view of the Tribunal, it would be contrary to the object and purpose of the Convention not to resolve the existing impasse. Inaction in the present case, by the Commission and the Tribunal, two organs created by the Convention to ensure the effective implementation of its provisions, would leave the Parties in a position where they may be unable to benefit fully from their rights over the continental shelf.[66]

Thus, the ITLOS concluded that

the Tribunal [...], in order to fulfil its responsibilities under Part XV, Section 2, of the Convention in the present case, [...] has an obligation to adjudicate the dispute and to delimit the continental shelf between the Parties beyond 200 nm. Such delimitation is without prejudice to the establishment of the outer limits of the continental shelf in accordance with Article 76, paragraph 8, of the Convention.[67]

Here, the ITLOS uses the Commission's procedural rules as an argument for continuing the delimitation beyond 200 nautical miles: when the Commission has made itself paralyzed, the Tribunal cannot similarly abstain from taking action. Apparently, the Tribunal feels that the duty to delimit is reinforced by the fact that the Commission has 'suspended' the examination of the two states' continental shelf submissions until there is explicit consent from each of them.

The judgment can thus perhaps also be taken as a 'criticism' of the Commission's rules concerning veto, as contained in Rule 5 (*litra* a) of Annex I. Instead of enabling states to block the Commission's handling of a submission, the Commission should rather have promoted the expedite examination of states' continental shelf submissions. In this connection we may recall the wording of Article 76, paragraph 8:

---

66   Judgment, paras. 390–392.
67   Judgment, para. 394.

The Commission shall make recommendations to coastal States [...].[68]

In my view, it is therefore clear that the Commission, by adopting Rule 5 (*litra* a) of Annex I, has not been sufficiently mindful of its stated duties under the LOS Convention. In making the examination of a submission and the drafting of recommendations conditional on the agreement of other states, the Commission will (if the right to veto is used) be violating its obligations under the Convention. The Commission 'shall' make recommendations to coastal states, regardless of the opinions of other states.

Further to this, Rule 5 (*litra* a) of Annex I is problematic from a broader perspective. A neighbouring state may, or so it would seem, exercise its right of veto indefinitely. As long as the veto is sustained, then no recommendations will be adopted. The outer limits of the continental shelf beyond 200 nautical miles will not be established with final and binding effect. The additional implication is perhaps that not all States Parties will be able to benefit fully from their rights over the continental shelf.

The Commission's rules on veto could therefore obstruct the application of Article 76, which in turn could thwart the Convention's implementation, thereby undermining its object and purpose. With Rule 5 (*litra* a), the Commission has therefore failed to take sufficient account of considerations of purpose in the choice of solutions—a crucial point when the ITLOS felt obliged to continue the delimitation of the continental shelf beyond 200 nautical miles in the *Bay of Bengal* case. In my view, the Commission should have felt obliged by the same considerations, and refrained from incorporating Rule 5 (*litra* a) of Annex I into the Rules of Procedure with its current wording.

3.4   Legal Aspects of the Commission's Substantive Decision-Making

3.4.1   *The Commission's Recommendations*
The Scientific and Technical Guidelines are—in addition to the Rules of Procedure—one of the basic documents of the Commission.[69] The Guidelines

---

68   See also Article 3, para. 1 (*litra* a), of Annex II to the LOS Convention.

69   During its second session in September 1997, the Commission set up several technical working groups to formulate scientific and technical guidelines as to the data and information to be included in coastal state submissions. The Commission established an Editorial Working Group on its Scientific and Technical Guidelines in 1998. At its fourth session, the Commission resumed its work on the Scientific and Technical Guidelines and decided to adopt them provisionally (Doc. CLCS/L.6). It was also agreed that, pending

generally deal with relevant provisions of Article 76, and are thus useful to the Commission in the examination of coastal state submissions, and to coastal states in preparing submissions. However, it is the *recommendations* of the Commission that are the key link in the relationship between the coastal state and the Commission. Only in its recommendations does the Commission express its views on how Article 76 is to be interpreted and applied to a given continental shelf area. The recommendations entail significant legal effects, not least as regards establishing 'final and binding' outer limits of the continental shelf beyond 200 nautical miles under the LOS Convention—an important point to which I return later. Their content is therefore of crucial importance, particularly to the coastal state making the submission. It should also be recalled that, as specified in Article 3 of Annex II to the LOS Convention, the Commission shall always adopt recommendations 'in accordance with article 76' of the LOS Convention.

As of 1 January 2014, the Commission had issued 18 recommendations to coastal states.[70] Many more are yet to come, but the Commission has already

---

formal adoption at the fifth session, the Guidelines could be applied provisionally. The Scientific and Technical Guidelines were finally adopted by the Commission on 13 May 1999 and were published in Doc. CLCS/11.

70   These are as follows: on 27 June 2002 in response to the submission made by the Russian Federation on 20 December 2001 (Doc. CLCS/34), on 4 April 2007 in response to the submission made by Brazil on 17 May 2004 (Doc. CLCS/54), on 9 April 2009 in response to the submission made by Australia on 15 November 2004 (Doc. CLCS/58), on 5 April 2007 in response to the submission made by Ireland (in respect of Porcupine Abyssal Plain) on 25 May 2005 (Doc. CLCS/54), on 22 August 2008 in response to the submission made by New Zealand on 19 April 2006 (Doc. CLCS/60), on 24 March 2009 in response to the joint submission made by France, Ireland, Spain and the UK in respect of the area of the Celtic Sea and the Bay of Biscay on 19 May 2006 (Doc. CLCS/62), on 27 March 2009 in response to the submission made by Norway on 27 November 2006 (Doc. CLCS/62), on 2 September 2009 in response to the submission made by France in respect of areas of French Guiana and New Caledonia on 22 May 2007 (Doc. CLCS/64), on 31 March 2009 in response to the submission made by Mexico in respect of the western polygon in the Gulf of Mexico on 13 December 2007 (Doc. CLCS/62), on 15 April 2010 in response to the submission made by Barbados on 8 May 2008 (Doc. CLCS/68), on 15 April 2010 in response to the submission made by the UK in respect of the Ascension Island on 9 May 2008 (Doc. CLCS/66), on 28 March 2011 in response to the submission made by Indonesia in respect of the North West of Sumatra Island on 16 June 2008 (Doc. CLCS/70), on 30 March 2011 in response to the joint submission by the Republic of Mauritius and the Republic of Seychelles in the region of the Mascarene Plateau on 1 December 2008 (Doc. CLCS/70), on 30 March 2011 in response to the submission made by Suriname on 5 December 2008 (Doc. CLCS/70), on 12 April 2012 in response to the submission made

on several occasions adopted recommendations which raise various legal issues in light of the substantive criteria set out in Article 76. In what follows, I explore a few examples of the Commission's recommendations, all of which serve to show the manner in which the Commission's interpretation and application of Article 76 can sometimes be seen to be controversial, and not necessarily correct *lex lata*. At the very least, the Commission's recommendations do not always coincide with the perception of the submitting coastal state regarding the placement of the outer limits of the continental shelf. Importantly, and as with the procedural matters dealt with in the previous section, these examples, too, have already generated some debate in the legal literature. Again, the examples are not intended as an exhaustive list of cases in which the Commission's interpretation and application of Article 76 is questionable.

3.4.2   *Linking the Outer Limit to the 200 Nautical Mile Limit*

Continental margins are generally not straight, but rather interrupted by ridges, plateaus, embayments, canyons or other features. The delineation of the outer edge of the continental margin in accordance with Article 76, paragraph 4, of the LOS Convention will reflect this and may be correspondingly complicated. In order to simplify the potentially very curved and complex character of the outer limit established in accordance with that provision, Article 76, paragraph 7, provides for the use of 'straight bridging lines' between fixed points, which are

> [...] straight lines not exceeding 60 nautical miles in length, connecting fixed points, defined by co-ordinates of latitude and longitude.

Paragraph 7 thus helps to 'smooth' curvatures and construct an outer limit which is simple and right-angled. The risk, however, seems to be that certain parts of the deep ocean floor may fall on the landward side of the outer limit and thus technically become part of the coastal state's legal continental shelf. The way paragraph 7 is drafted may therefore result in, for instance, that seabed areas which have not been surveyed as being within 60 nautical miles of a foot of the continental slope position—and therefore are not part

---

by the Philippines in the Benham Rise region on 8 April 2009 (Doc. CLCS/74), on 13 April 2012 in response to the revised submission made by Barbados on 25 July 2011 (Doc. CLCS/74), on 19 April 2012 in response to the submission made by Japan on 12 November 2010 (Doc. CLCS/74) and on 19 April 2012 in response to the submission made by France in the areas of the French Antilles and the Kerguelen Islands on 5 February 2009 (Doc. CLCS/74).

of the 'continental margin' according to the method prescribed in Article 76, paragraph 4(a)(ii)—nonetheless end up on the landward side of the outer limit delineated by the coastal state. Thus, Article 76, paragraph 7, of the LOS Convention not only simplifies the outer limit in practical terms—it also has the consequence that parts of the deep ocean floor will become part of the submitting coastal state's 'continental shelf' within the context of Article 76.

A controversial issue in the Commission's recommendations is whether straight bridging lines of 60 nautical miles may be used to link the endpoint of the outer limit to the coastal state's 200 nautical mile limit in order to maximize the area enclosed as continental shelf—regardless of whether this enclosed area of seabed lies beyond the continental margin as defined by paragraph 4.[71] The Commission has not accepted this. In the summary of its recommendations to Australia, the Commission included the following reservation, under the heading 'General principles on which these recommendations are based':

> Australia is of the view that it is possible to use lines not more than 60 M in length to join fixed points on the formula line beyond 200 M to any fixed point on the 200 M line. However the Commission is of the view that the determination of the *last* segment of the outer limits of the continental shelf shall be established either by the intersection of the formula line, in accordance with Article 76, paragraphs 4 and 7, and the 200 M limit from the baselines from which the breadth of the territorial sea is measured, or it shall be determined by the line of shortest distance between the last fixed formula point and 200 M limit. In all cases, the segment cannot exceed 60 M in length in accordance with Article 76, paragraph 7.[72] (Emphasis added)

In other words, when linking the outer limit to the 200 nautical mile limit, the Commission recommends that the last segment of the outer limit (the 'link') shall be either the intersection of the formula line (established in accordance

---

71   According to Serdy, this is a topical issue for a significant number of the coastal states that have filed submissions. It is not, however, a concern for coastal states whose outer limit neither begins nor ends nor touches the submitting state's 200 nautical mile-limit. The end point of the outer limits is, for example by a neighbouring state's 200 nautical mile limit or a maritime boundary. See Serdy, 'The Commission on the Limits of the Continental Shelf and its Disturbing Propensity to Legislate', p. 375.

72   Summary of the recommendations made to Australia, para. 8. Available at the website of the Commission: <www.un.org/Depts/los/clcs_new/submissions_files/aus04/aus_summary_of_recommendations.pdf> (accessed 1 January 2014).

with Article 76, paragraphs 4 and 7) and the 200 nautical mile limit, *or* the line of shortest distance between the last fixed formula point and the 200 nautical mile limit.

In line with this general remark, the Commission would therefore not accept the method used by Australia in its continental shelf submission of linking the outer limit to the 200 nautical mile limit for a total of eight regions. For example, in the Naturaliste Plateau Region—a plateau extending westwards from the southwestern coast of the Australian continent—the Commission stated that it did

> not agree with the method submitted by Australia for the connection of outer limit continental shelf points beyond 200 M to the 200 M limit line at points NAT-ECS-1 and NAT-ECS-R1–138, since this methods creates area of continental shelf that falls outside of the continental margin as defined in Article 76, paragraphs 4 and 7.

The Commission thus recommended that

> points NAT-ECS-1 and NAT-ECS-R1–138 and their respective connecting lines be replaced by the points and lines that conform to the outer edge of the continental margin. The Commission further recommends that Australia proceeds to establish the outer limits of the continental shelf in the Naturaliste Plateau Region accordingly.[73]

The position of the Commission has, however, already been criticized in legal theory since 'there being nothing in paragraph 7 of Article 76 to suggest that [using straight bridging lines of 60 nautical miles from the last fixed point on the outer limit to any point on the 200 nautical mile line so as to maximize the enclosed area] is not permissible'.[74] That the Commission declined to apply paragraph 7 in this way is thus controversial. Nor does the Commission's approach

---

73   Summary of the recommendations made to Australia, para. 90. Available at the website of the Commission: <www.un.org/Depts/los/clcs_new/submissions_files/aus04/aus_summary_of_recommendations.pdf> (accessed 1 January 2014). For corresponding reservations of the Commission, see para. 19 (the Argo Region), para. 35 (Great Australian Bight Region), para. 54 (Kerguelen Plateau Region), para. 67 (Lord How Rise Region), para. 77 (Macquarie Ridge Region), para. 106 (South Tasmanian Rise Region) and para. 144 (Wallaby and Exmouth Plateaus Region).

74   Serdy, 'The Commission on the Limits of the Continental Shelf and its Disturbing Propensity to Legislate', p. 373.

conform with that of several other coastal states, for all for whom this problem is relevant.[75] Whether other states will rely on the Commission's approach when establishing the outer limit in national law—or on how it originally delineated this part of the outer limit in its submission—remains to be seen.

Australia, however, seems to have 'postponed' the problem in relation to certain seabed areas where this problem arose. When Australia on 2 November 2012 deposited with the UNSG, pursuant to Article 76, paragraph 9, of the LOS Convention, information describing the outer limits of its continental shelf, it emphasised that the outer limits of a limited number of areas of extended continental shelf had not yet been established and thus remained to be resolved.[76] These areas include the Wallaby and Exmouth Plateaus Region and the Kerguelen Plateau Region—that is, two of the areas where Australia had linked the last segment of the outer limit to the 200 nautical mile limit by the method the Commission found unacceptable. The Commission may therefore expect these areas to be subject to a revised submission, in which Australia revisits the Commission's recommendations related to the linking of last segment of the outer limit to the 200 nautical mile limit.[77]

In my view, the legal problem related to the method for linking the outer limit to the 200 nautical mile limit, is basically one of a conflict of norms. On the one hand, there is the 'technical' solution prescribed by paragraph 7, under which the coastal state may use straight bridging lines, seemingly without exceptions, and thus also from the last fixed point on the outer limit to any point on the 200 nautical mile limit. Reading paragraph 7 in isolation, one may therefore argue that the Commission should have accepted the position taken by Australian in its submission. The wording indicates that paragraph 7 applies to any part of the outer limit, also to the last segment of it. It is true that in the Naturaliste Plateau region, a rather large area beyond the continental margin happened to fall on the landward side of the outer limit when Australia drew a straight line from the last fixed point on the outer limit to the 200 nautical mile limit. But here it can be argued that if areas of deep ocean floor—no matter

---

75   See for instance the submissions of Barbados, the Federated States of Micronesia, Ghana, Indonesia, the Maldives, the Solomon Islands, South Africa, Tonga, Vietnam and Yemen. All available at the website of the Commission: <www.un.org/Depts/los/clcs_new/commission_submissions.htm> (accessed 1 January 2014).

76   See circular communication available at the DOALOS website: <www.un.org/Depts/los/LEGISLATIONANDTREATIES/PDFFILES/mzn_s/mzn92ef.pdf> (accessed 1 January 2014).

77   Deposit by Australia, pursuant to Articles 76, para. 9, and 84 of the LOS Convention, of relevant information permanently describing the outer limits of its continental shelf is available at the DOALOS website: <www.un.org/Depts/los/LEGISLATIONANDTREATIES/STATEFILES/AUS.htm> (accessed 1 January 2014).

what their size—become part of the submitting coastal state's legal continental shelf by the use of straight bridging lines, this is simply the 'inevitable result of the way paragraph 7 is drafted'.[78]

On the other hand, it can be argued that the Commission was correct in its conclusion when it recommended Australia to not use straight bridging lines to maximize the area of continental shelf by drawing such a line from the last fixed point on the outer limit to any point on the 200 nautical mile limit, because, according to the Commission, the method created an area of continental shelf that falls outside of the continental margin as defined by Article 76.

I am inclined to agree with the Commission. First, because of the context in which paragraph 7 appears. Article 76 provides that the legal continental shelf extends as far as to 'the outer edge of the continental margin' (Article 76, paragraph 1) and that it shall not include 'the deep ocean floor' (Article 76, paragraph 3). Those 'main' provisions of Article 76 must therefore prevail, one could argue, and be used as 'safety valves' if paragraph 7 is used by a coastal state to ensure the greatest possible foothold of sovereign rights on the deep ocean floor.

That brings us to the second argument: the object and purpose of paragraph 7. It was not intended to be used by the coastal state to achieve the biggest possible area of continental shelf. The purpose was—as pointed out above—to enable a more practical and easy delineation. It can therefore be argued that the Commission's approach promotes the object and purpose of paragraph 7, although the consequence is to shift the outer limit landward, and at the cost of the coastal state.

This may very well also have been the underlying reason the Commission decided to reject Australia's way of joining the outer limit and the 200 nautical mile limit by the use of straight bridging lines in accordance with paragraph 7. What is problematic about the Commission's recommendations, as referred to above, however, is—first—the absence of legal reasoning. By saying only that the Australian method creates an area of continental shelf that falls outside of the continental margin, the Commission does not fully explain *why* it rejects the Australian view as to how the outer limit can be linked with the 200 nautical mile limit.

Second—and that is perhaps a more serious matter—it is not clear what makes the *last segment* of the outer limit extraordinary in regard to the application of paragraph 7. This is curious, since the coastal state is allowed to draw

---

78   Serdy, 'The Commission on the Limits of the Continental Shelf and its Disturbing Propensity to Legislate', p. 374.

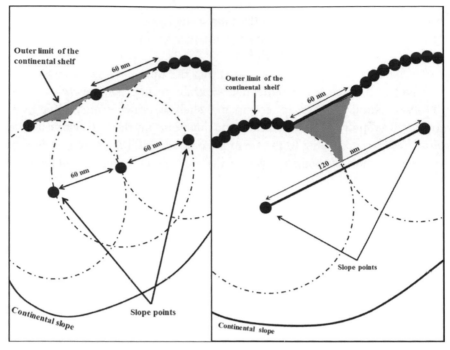

FIGURE 3.1 *Application of Article 76, paragraph 7, of the LOS Convention*
Smoothing of the outer limit of the continental shelf by straight bridging lines
between fixed points. Areas of the continental shelf that are within 60 nautical miles
of a foot of the continental slope position are part of the continental shelf. Areas in
grey are parts of the continental shelf that have not been surveyed as being within 60
nautical miles of a foot of the continental slope position, but are delineated by
straight bridging lines.
SOURCE: ØYSTEIN JENSEN (2014). THE FIGURES HAVE BEEN REDRAWN ON THE BASIS
OF ILLUSTRATIONS APPEARING ON THE WEBSITE OF GNS SCIENCE: <WWW.GNS.CRI
.NZ/STATIC/UNCLOS/BRIDGING.HTML> (ACCESSED 1 JANUARY 2014).

straight bridging lines at other segments of the outer limit that result in parts
of the deep ocean floor ending up on the landward side of the outer limit. The
Commission is therefore not consistent in the application of paragraph 7.

3.4.3   *Other Conflicts of Norms Caused by Paragraph 7*

The Commission has also addressed a related aspect of the issue referred to in
section 3.4.2 above. In specific situations, the area enclosed by straight bridging lines of 60 nautical miles may, in accordance with paragraph 7, include
relatively large areas of deep ocean floor, notably where embayments occur in
the continental margin. If the distance between the fixed points established

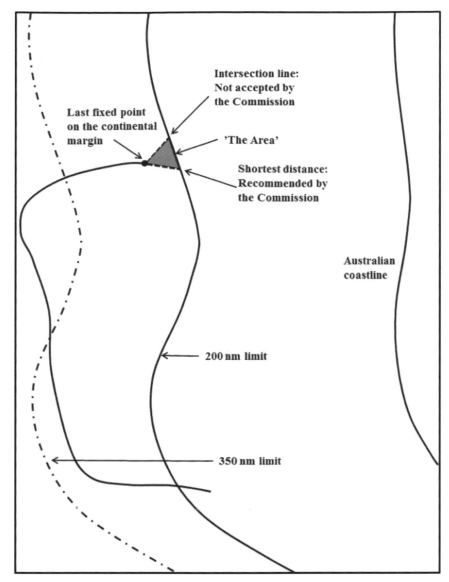

FIGURE 3.2 *Linking the 200 nautical mile limit and the outer limit in the Naturaliste Plateau Region*

The Commission's view on how the 200 nautical mile limit and the outer limit should be joined in the Naturaliste Plateau Region: Intersection of 200 nautical miles and the continental margin, or the shortest distance between last fixed point on the continental margin and the 200 nautical mile limit.

SOURCE: ØYSTEIN JENSEN (2014). THE FIGURE HAS BEEN REDRAWN ON THE BASIS OF ILLUSTRATIONS APPEARING ON THE WEBSITE OF GNS SCIENCE: <WWW.GNS.CRI.NZ/ STATIC/UNCLOS/BRIDGING.HTML> (ACCESSED 1 JANUARY 2014).

by the coastal state at the entrance of such an embayment does not exceed 60 nautical miles, it follows from paragraph 7 that the coastal state may draw a line straight across the entrance of such embayments. The question again is whether seabed areas in this embayment, which are not 'continental margin' in accordance with paragraph 4, still become part of the legal continental shelf of the coastal state.

This very question was put to the test in the Commission's recommendations to New Zealand. In the Northern Region, New Zealand had established fixed points for the determination of the outer edge of the continental margin in accordance with Article 76, paragraph 4, of the LOS Convention. New Zealand then smoothed the outer limits by drawing straight bridging lines in-between the fixed points in accordance with paragraph 7. Between two of these points, New Zealand had drawn a line straight across the entrance to the South Fiji Basin. Parts of the seabed areas so enclosed, however, constituted in a geomorphological sense the deep ocean floor, not continental margin. The Commission refused to allow these areas to become part of the continental shelf:

> The Commission agrees with the determination of the fixed points listed in Table 1.A, Annex III, delineating the outer edge of the continental margin of New Zealand. However, the Commission does not agree to include the whole of that part of the South Fiji Basin that is located to the south of Points N177 and N178 in Table 2, Annex III as part of the continental shelf of New Zealand.[79]

Despite the fact that New Zealand had established fixed points in accordance with paragraph 4, and linked these points together in accordance with Article 7, the Commission emphasized the nature of the seabed so enclosed, i.e. the definition of the continental shelf in Article 76, paragraphs 1 and 3. Thus, those parts of the seabed which had the geomorphological character of deep ocean floor—and not continental margin—were not recommended by the Commission to be a part of the legal continental shelf of New Zealand, even though there was nothing wrong with New Zealand's combined application of paragraphs 4 (a)(ii) and 7, and the resulting enclosure of the entire embayment as part of its continental shelf. The Commission did not accept that areas with the character of deep ocean floor found on the landward side

---

79   Summary of recommendations to New Zealand, para. 148. Available at the website of the Commission: <www.un.org/Depts/los/clcs_new/submissions_files/nzl06/nzl_summary_of_recommendations.pdf> (accessed 1 January 2014).

of the outer limit should form part of the legal continental shelf. The geomorphological definition of the continental margin in paragraph 3 seems to have prevailed, resulting in a large hole in New Zealand's continental shelf in this area (similar to 'Area A' Figure 3.3).

Also this conclusion may thus be considered to be controversial and at the cost of the coastal state, and it has been criticized as such in legal theory.[80] In my opinion, however, also here the Commission would have been able to avoid some of the criticism if it had taken the trouble to justify its conclusion more clearly. The unanswered question is *why* the Commission recommends that paragraph 7 should allow certain seabed areas that have the character of deep ocean floor (see 'Area B' in Figure 3.3) to become part of the legal continental shelf, whereas other areas—incorporated on the landward side of the outer limit on the basis of the same criteria—are not accepted (see 'Area A' in Figure 3.3). This is particularly so because the only difference between the former and the latter seabed areas is in fact one of scale.

As I see it, while the Commission's conclusion is substantially correct, it should preferably have justified its recommendations within contextual considerations, by referring to the 'principal' rules in Article 76, paragraphs 1 and 3, i.e. that the legal continental shelf extends only as far as to 'the outer edge of the continental margin' (paragraph 1), and then that the legal continental shelf shall not include 'the deep ocean floor' (paragraph 3). Second, the Commission should have attached importance to the *purpose* of Article 76, paragraph 7, i.e. that the provision is not intended to 'maximize' the coastal state's foothold of sovereign rights to the deep ocean floor: straight bridging lines are intended to enable an easier, more practical delineation.

3.4.4   The Commission's Dismissal of 2,500 Metre Isobaths

Also controversial has been the Commission's approach in dealing with certain 2,500 metre isobaths for the purpose of constructing the depth constraint lines (i.e. the maximum permitted extension of the legal continental shelf based on the depth criterion) under Article 76, paragraph 5, of the LOS Convention. Locating the 2,500 metre isobath is a crucial element in a coastal state's effort to claim an extended continental shelf under Article 76. Article 76, paragraphs 5 and 6, set the maximum limits on the extent of continental shelf: the outer limits shall not lie beyond 350 nautical miles from the baselines from which the territorial sea is measured, or 100 nautical miles from the 2,500 metre isobath. In the first case, this is relatively simple—that

---

Serdy, 'The Commission on the Limits of the Continental Shelf and its Disturbing Propensity to Legislate', pp. 376–377.

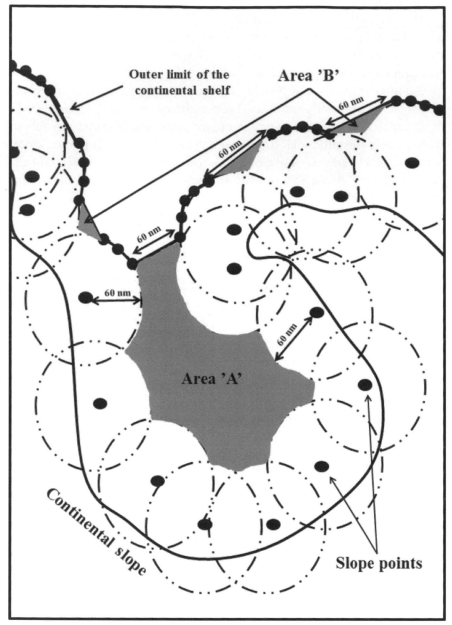

FIGURE 3.3 *Article 76, paragraph 7, of the LOS Convention applied to embayments*
Outer limit of the continental shelf delineated by straight bridging lines between
fixed points. 'Area A' includes a large embayment included in the continental shelf by
a straight bridging line. 'Area B' shows how the arcs defining the outer limit of the
continental shelf are smoothed by straight bridging lines. The only difference
between 'Area A' and 'Area B' is one of scale.
SOURCE: ØYSTEIN JENSEN (2014). THE FIGURE HAS BEEN REDRAWN ON THE BASIS OF
ILLUSTRATIONS APPEARING ON THE WEBSITE OF GNS SCIENCE: <WWW.GNS.CRI.NZ/
STATIC/UNCLOS/BRIDGING.HTML> (ACCESSED 1 JANUARY 2014).

is, to set the maximum limit by measuring the distance from the coast. In the second case, however, the coastal state must identify the depth curve of 2,500 metres. Paragraph 5 defines the 2,500 metre isobath as 'a line connecting the depth of 2,500 metres.'

First of all—but this is a matter relating to the content of paragraph 4.4.2 of the Commission's Guidelines, and not specific recommendations—we should note that, with regard to isobaths that are complex or repeated in multiples, the Commission has clarified its preferred interpretation of Article 76, paragraph 5:

> The selection of the most salient points along the 2,500 m isobath for the purpose of delineating the 100 M limit may be straightforward when isobaths are simple. However, when isobaths are complex or repeated in multiples, the selection of points along the 2,500 m isobath becomes difficult. Such situations arise as a result of geological and tectonic processes shaping the present continental margins. They can create multiple repetitions of the 2,500 m isobath, for example, by faulting, folding and thrusting along continental margins. Unless there is evidence to the contrary, the Commission may recommend the use of the *first* 2,500 m isobath from the baselines from which the breadth of the territorial sea is measured that conforms to the general configuration of the continental margin. (Emphasis added)

The focal point here seems first to consist in determining whether isobaths fall into one of two categories: whether the 2,500 metre isobaths are simple, or are complex or repeated in multiples. That is a factual question. However, it is a matter of law when the Commission (unless there is evidence to the contrary) decides to use the *first* 2,500 metre isobath from the baselines that conforms to the general configuration of the continental margin—and not the second, third, fourth, etc. When isobaths are repeated in multiples, the Commission thus starts from the option that is least advantageous for the coastal state. That starting point, however, seems debatable. Article 76, paragraph 5, does not specify from *which* depth curve 100 nautical miles shall be measured where several depth curves of 2,500 metre can be identified in the same area.

Second—and this is indeed a debatable matter—the Commission has in specific recommendations rejected coastal state application of certain 2,500 metre isobaths *solely because they lay seaward of the foot of the slope*, even though such a rule does not follow from the wording of Article 76, paragraph 5. One example is found in the recommendations to Norway. To estimate the outer limits of its continental shelf in the Banana Hole area, Norway had used both distance and depth constraints, as per Article 76, paragraph 5, of the LOS Convention.[81] The Commission in general agreed with the way Norway had combined these constraint criteria in order to establish the outer limits. Concerning the southernmost part of the Banana Hole, however, the Commission held that between two fixed outer limits points a small triangular area constituting the submerged prolongation of the territory of Jan Mayen lay beyond the distance constraint line, and could not be said to be part of the Norwegian continental shelf on the basis of the depth-constraint criterion alone.

The Commission's reasoning is interesting. In its recommendations to Norway, the Commission opined that the Jan Mayen Micro-Continent/Iceland Plateau was a submarine elevation in the sense of Article 76, paragraph 6, and therefore that the depth criterion in paragraph 5 was applicable:

> [T]he JMMC/IP composite high is a submarine elevation that is a natural component of the continental margin of Jan Mayen in the sense of Article 76, paragraph 6. Hence, to delineate the outer limits of the continental shelf, a valid depth constraint could be applied.[82]

In this case, however, the Commission recommended that an isobath could be invoked as 'valid' only if there was sufficient evidence to demonstrate that it was located landward of the foot of the continental slope and thus, in the view of the Commission, could be considered to conform to the general configuration of the continental margin. The Commission could not, on the basis of the material submitted by Norway,

> verify that the isobaths lying south of [slope point JM8 . . .] are landward of the foot of the continental slope [. . .] and therefore conform to the general configuration of the continental margin. Thus, the Commission recommends that these isobaths not be used as a basis to delineate the outer limits of the continental shelf for Jan Mayen in the southernmost area.[83]

---

81   Jensen, 'Towards Setting the Outer Limits of the Continental Shelf in the Arctic', in Vidas (ed.), *Law, Technology and Science for Oceans in Globalisation*, p. 533.

82   Summary of recommendations to Norway, para. 77. Available at the website of the Commission: <www.un.org/Depts/los/clcs_new/submissions_files/nor06/nor_rec_summ .pdf> (accessed 1 January 2014).

83   *Ibid.*, para. 74.

Accordingly, solely because Norway could not prove that the relevant 2,500 metre isobath lay landward of the relevant foot of the slope point, the Commission recommended not using that isobath to delineate the outer limits of the continental shelf—even though it is located on a submarine elevation that is a natural component of the continental margin. Norway was instead recommended to apply the distance criterion of 350 nautical miles as the maximum constraint line in that part of the Southern Banana Hole area.[84]

This raises a matter of principle nature: Are isobaths that conform to the general configuration of the continental margin valid only if they lie landward of the foot of the continental slope? Conversely, are 2,500 metre isobaths seaward of the foot of the continental slope automatically inadmissible? Nothing in Article 76 indicates that such a restriction shall be read into paragraph 5. And, as explained in the legal literature, this conclusion may in some cases lead to strange results where the 2,500 metre isobath is 'close to land, but the foot of the slope is significantly seaward of it and another such isobath lies beyond'.[85] Thus, the approach by the Commission—which perhaps will eventually become transformed into a mandatory test for determining whether an isobath is 'valid'—does not appear consistent with a plain reading of paragraph 5 or with what the drafters had intended.

For Norway's part, however, the rejection of the isobath is likely to mean little in practice. The part of the continental shelf which with the Commission's recommendations fell outside Norwegian jurisdiction when Norway was forced to apply the distance criterion of 350 nautical miles and not the depth constraint of 2,500 metre isobaths + 100 nautical miles, is located to the south of a provisional maritime boundary agreement between the Faroe Islands and Norway in the southern part of the Banana Hole.[86] Faroe Islands' continental shelf claim beyond 200 nautical miles would thus have to be completely dismissed for Norway to have any interest in pursuing the Commission's reasoning as regards the validity of the said isobath. The discussion on the Commission's

---

84   Serdy, 'The Commission on the Limits of the Continental Shelf and its Disturbing Propensity to Legislate', p. 372.

85   *Ibid.*, referring to Kunoy, Bjørn, Martin V. Heinesen and Finn Mørk, 'Appraisal of Applicable Depth Constraint for the Purpose of Establishing the Outer Limits of the Continental Shelf', in *Ocean Development & International Law*, Vol. 41, 2010, pp. 357–379, at pp. 369–374.

86   On 20 September 2006 the Minister of Foreign Affairs of Norway, the Minister for Foreign Affairs of Denmark together with the Prime Minister of the Government of the Faroes and the Minister for Foreign Affairs of Iceland signed Agreed Minutes that set out an agreed procedure for determining future delimitation lines in the southern part of the Banana Hole. See Jensen, 'Towards Setting the Outer Limits of the Continental Shelf in the Arctic', in Vidas (ed.), *Law, Technology and Science for Oceans in Globalisation*, p. 534.

recommendations here, however, is of a principled nature, without concern for whether a coastal state gains or loses.

3.4.5   Classification of Seafloor Highs

Also the Commission's application of the LOS Convention's provisions on seafloor highs seems somewhat controversial. Article 76, paragraphs 3 and 6, distinguish three types of seafloor highs: oceanic ridges of the deep ocean floor, submarine elevations that are natural components of the margin, and submarine ridges. These distinctions are important because they have a direct influence the size of the area of continental shelf beyond 200 nautical miles.

According to Article 76, paragraph 3, oceanic ridges are not part of the continental margin, and thereby also not part of the continental shelf.[87] For submarine ridges, the more advantageous maximum limit of 100 nautical miles from the 2,500 metre isobath does not apply according to Article 76, paragraph 6. However, this limitation is not applicable to submarine elevations, which, according to paragraph 6, constitute 'elevations that are natural components of the continental margin'. Thus, the coastal state is best served by a seafloor high being considered a submarine elevation. It is less beneficial if the high is considered as a submarine ridge. And it is not at all positive for the coastal state if a seafloor high is classified as an oceanic ridge according to the last sentence of Article 76, paragraph 3, as it will then not be considered to form part of the continental margin at all. Summing up, the continental shelf of coastal states can extend to 200 nautical miles on oceanic ridges, to 350 nautical miles on submarine ridges, and to either 350 nautical miles or 100 nautical miles from the 2,500 metre isobath on submarine elevations.

Fundamentally, paragraph 7.1.8 of the Commission's Guidelines provides that the

> distinction between 'submarine elevations' and 'submarine ridges' or 'oceanic ridges' shall not be based on their geographical denominations and names used so far in the preparation of the published maps and charts and other relevant literature. Such a distinction for the purpose of Article 76 shall be made on the basis of scientific evidence taking into account the appropriate provisions of these Guidelines.

---

87   Unless they are within 200 nautical miles from the baselines. It may also be attempted to include oceanic ridges as part of the continental shelf by the use of straight bridging lines. The issue will then be the same as under section 3.4.2 and 3.4.3 discussed above.

Furthermore, as regards the *evidence* necessary to distinguish among seafloor highs, paragraph 7.2.10 of the Guidelines states that

> the Commission feels that in cases of ridges its view shall be based on such scientific and legal considerations as natural prolongation of land territory and land mass, morphology of ridges and their relation to the continental margin as defined in paragraph 4, and continuity of ridges.

Let us turn now to specific recommendations which to date have involved the application of the provisions of Article 76, paragraphs 3, 5, and 6, of the LOS Convention.[88] In the recommendations to the UK with respect of Ascension Island, the Commission developed views and understandings related to the characteristics of 'the deep ocean floor with its oceanic ridges'—in that case, to that of the Atlantic Ocean in particular.[89] As regards the distinction between submarine ridges and submarine elevations that are natural components of the continental margin, the Commission has in several recommendations given consideration to these two categories. In fact, the distinction was about to be put to the test in the very first submission to be considered by the Commission. In this submission, made by Russia, the Lomonosov Ridge and the Alpha-Mendeleev Ridge in the Arctic Ocean were treated as submarine elevations, with the 2,500 metre isobath + 100 nautical mile rule invoked as constraint line for parts of the outer limit.[90] The Commission nevertheless recommended that Russia should make a new submission in respect of its extended continental shelf in that area in light of the sparse information submitted.[91]

---

88 For example those of Australia, New Zealand, the joint submission in the Bay of Biscay (France, Ireland, Spain, and the UK), Norway, France (New Caledonia) and the UK (Ascension). Summaries available at the website of the Commission: <www.un.org/Depts/los/clcs_new/commission_recommendations.htm> (accessed 1 January 2014).

89 Summary of the recommendations to the UK in respect of Ascension Island, available at the website of the Commission: <www.un.org/Depts/los/clcs_new/submissions_files/gbr08/gbr_asc_isl_rec_summ.pdf> (accessed 1 January 2014).

90 Executive summary of Russia's submission, p. 2. Available at the website of the Commission: <www.un.org/Depts/los/clcs_new/submissions_files/submission_rus.htm> (accessed 1 January 2014).

91 UN Doc. A/57/57/Add.1 ('Report of the Secretary-General of the United Nations to the Fifty-seventh Session of the United Nations General Assembly Under the Agenda Item Oceans and the Law of the Sea'), para. 41.

The first situation in which the Commission expressly indicated how seafloor highs were to be categorized was therefore with the Australian submission.[92]

The first point worth noting regarding the Commission's recommendations is that the Commission in some cases gives the coastal state the benefit of the doubt in determining whether a seafloor high is a ridge or an elevation. In the recommendations to Australia related to the seabed areas Wallaby Composite High—even though its geological origin remained somewhat uncertain—the Commission agreed with Australia that, on the basis of the morphological and geological evidence presented, the feature should be classified as a natural component of the continental margin:

> [O]n the basis of the data and information presented the geological information of the whole Wallaby Composite High still remains unresolved. Nevertheless, *on the basis of morphological and geological information presented*, the Commission agrees that the Wallaby Composite High is to be regarded as a submarine elevation that is a natural component of the continental margin in the sense of Article 76, paragraph 6, qualifying for the application of the depth criterion constraint.[93] (Emphasis added)

Similar reasoning was applied in Norway's recommendations in respect of the areas of the Jan Mayen Micro-Continent/Iceland Plateau:

---

92   The recommendations to New Zealand also involved the consideration of several seafloor highs, including the Kermadec and Colville Ridge system, and the Three Kings Ridge with the Fantail Terrace in the Northern Region; the Wishbone Ridge in the Eastern Region; and the Challenger Plateau and Lord Howe Rise, including the Gilbert Seamount, in the Western Region. In the recommendations to Norway, the Commission evaluated the status of the Vøring Plateau, the Vøring Spur, and the Jan Mayen Micro-Continent/Iceland Plateau (JMMC/IP) composite high in the area of the Banana Hole in the Norwegian and Greenland Seas as seafloor highs. In the recommendations to France (in respect of French Guiana and New Caledonia), the Commission considered the status of the Lord Howe Rise. And in the recommendations related to the joint submission made by Mauritius and Seychelles concerning the Mascarene Plateau region, the Commission examined the nature of the Mascarene Plateau. All summaries of recommendations available at the website of the Commission: <www.un.org/Depts/los/clcs_new/commission_recommendations.htm> (accessed 1 January 2014).

93   Summary of recommendations, para. 137. Available at the website of the Commission: <www.un.org/Depts/los/clcs_new/commission_recommendations.htm> (accessed 1 January 2014).

> Based on the morphological and geological evidence in the Submission, the additional material provided by Norway [...] and the literature, the Commission agrees that on balance the JMMC/IP composite high is a submarine elevation that is a natural component of the continental margin of Jan Mayen in the sense of Article 76, paragraph 6. Hence, to delineate the outer limits of the continental shelf, a valid depth constraint could be applied to fixed points used to establish the outer edge of the continental margin that are derived from the JMMC/IP composite high; in particular, Jan Mayen South-East FOS 8.[94] (Emphasis added)

The Commission seems to express a degree of uncertainty with regard to the nature of the seafloor highs in question. Nevertheless, it concluded in favour of Norway and Australia, with the approval of the more generous depth criterion. However, the Commission did not in its (summary of) recommendations detail how the morphological evidence could bridge a gap in the geological evidence. Nor did the Commission explain how the 'balance' had been achieved in these cases, and why such an approach had not been used in the other cases involving similar problems.[95] From the summaries of the recommendations, it is impossible to determine the Commission's rationale for concluding as it did.

The examples mentioned above, however, appear to be exceptions that only apply in situations where it is impractical or virtually impossible for coastal states to produce sufficient evidence as regards the seafloor high in question.[96] In cases where the data and materials submitted do not allow the Commission to decide on the classification of a seafloor high, it seems that the Commission will recommend the distance criterion, that is, a *tentative application of the less favourable ridge-provision (the first sentence of paragraph 6)* to all submarine features of the continental margin that extend beyond 350 nautical miles from the baselines, irrespective of whether they are ridges or not.[97] For instance, in

---

94   Summary of recommendations to Norway, para. 77. Available at the website of the Commission: <www.un.org/Depts/los/clcs_new/commission_recommendations.htm> (accessed 1 January 2014).

95   Gao, Jianjun, 'The Seafloor High Issue in Article 76 of the LOS Convention: Some Views from the Perspective of Legal Interpretation', in *Ocean Development & International Law*, Vol. 43, 2012, pp. 119–145, at p. 132.

96   Brekke, Harald, and Philip Symonds, 'Submarine Ridges and Elevations of Article 76 in Light of Published Summaries of Recommendations of the Commission on the Limits of the Continental Shelf', in *Ocean Development & International Law*, Vol. 42, 2011, pp. 289–306, at p. 300.

97   See Serdy, 'The Commission on the Limits of the Continental Shelf and its Disturbing Propensity to Legislate', p. 377.

the summary of Australia's recommendations—related to the Joey Rise—the Commission underscored this 'rule of presumption' by referring to its Scientific and Technical Guidelines, under which the coastal state shall prove how the relevant part of the seabed has been formed. Australia had not provided sufficient evidence, and the Commission recommended the distance criterion of 350 nautical miles as applicable:

> Australia classifies the Joey Rise as a submarine elevation that is a natural component of the continental margin in the sense of Article 76, paragraph 6. Based on morphology only, Australia holds the view that the Joey Rise is not a ridge and, in addition, Australia maintains that the rise is formed under the rifting and breakup of the continent in accordance with paragraph 7.3.1.b of the Guidelines. The view of the Commission, however, is that the data presented on origin of the Joey Rise is too sparse to be conclusive. Therefore, the Commission does not consider it proven that the Joey Rise should be regarded as a submarine elevation that is a natural component of the continental margin in the sense of Article 76, paragraph 6, qualifying for the application of the depth criterion constraint.[98]

The Commission therefore recommended:

> The application of those parts of that combined constraint line which are based on the 2500 metre isobaths on the Joey Rise is not justified since the nature of that submarine high with regard to Article 76, paragraph 6, is not considered proven. The Commission recommends that the combined constraint line to be applied should be adjusted accordingly.[99]

Judging from the practice of the Commission, it seems that if the evidence submitted by the coastal state is insufficient to judge whether one is dealing with a submarine elevation, the doubt will be to the disfavour of the coastal state; the Commission will conclude that the distance criterion shall apply instead of the more advantageous depth criterion—that is, the first sentence of paragraph 6 ('ridge') instead of the second ('elevations that are natural components of the continental margin'). The outer limits of the continental shelf will be at maximum 350 nautical miles from the territorial baselines. Seafloor highs beyond

---

98   Summary of recommendations to Australia, para. 138. Available at the website of the Commission: <www.un.org/Depts/los/clcs_new/submissions_files/submission_aus.htm> (accessed 1 January 2014).

99   *Ibid.*, para. 141.

that limit will, for lack of evidence, be treated as submarine ridges in the sense of the LOS Convention. As far as the Commission is concerned, it is not of interest whether they actually are ridges or not: it is the standard of proof that has not been met by the coastal state.[100]

The Commission thus also acts as 'killjoy' *vis-à-vis* the coastal state, but at the same time as a 'spreader of joy' to the benefit of the international community, in recommending the option which crops the size of the Area least. However, in my view, this practice of not going for the most favourable option for the coastal state in the absence of conclusive evidence gives rise to further questions of a more principled nature.

First, if the submitting coastal state does not manage to prove that the relevant seafloor high beyond 350 nautical miles is a submarine elevation, that need not mean that the seafloor high in question is in fact a ridge. Why, then, does the Commission 'automatically' recommend that the distance criterion be applied, i.e. treating the relevant seafloor high as a ridge *lex lata* by subsuming it under first sentence of Article 76, paragraph 6, of the LOS Convention? Should not the Commission recommend that the coastal state provide more conclusive evidence, instead of 'forcing' it to use the less advantageous 350 nautical mile constraint line?

---

100   In the Commission's recommendations to Australia it is also interesting to see the rejection of the morphological evidence to substantiate the classification of submarine elevations that are a natural component of the continental margin. The Commission called for geological or geophysical data, which are controversial. Some argue that it is only morphology that should be decisive for the choice of whether we are dealing with a ridge or an elevation (see Gudlaugsson, S.T., 'Natural Prolongation and the Concept of the Continental Margin for the Purposes of Article 76', in Nordquist, M.H., J.N. Moore and T.H. Heidar (eds), *Legal and Scientific Aspects of Continental Shelf Limits* (Martinus Nijhoff Publishers, 2004), pp. 61–90). As Australia argued, one can also argue that it is only 'ridge-like structures'—structures that are similar to submarine ridges—that shall be subject to a test of geological continuity, whereas all other seafloor highs which lie landward of the outer edge of the continental margin in accordance with Article 76, para. 4, can be classified as 'natural components of the continental margin' and thus become part of the continental shelf on the basis of the depth constraint criteria. Australia's point was just this: In their submission they argued on the basis of morphological evidence where the seabed did not resemble ridges at all, but on the basis of morphology *and* geology where the seabed had ridge-like structures. The Commission, for its part, seems to be of the opinion that one must cite geological evidence even when speaking about seafloor highs that are not 'ridge-like'. See summary of recommendations to Australia, paras. 47–50. Available at the website of the Commission: <www.un.org/Depts/los/clcs_new/submissions_files/submission_aus.htm> (accessed 1 January 2014).

Second, it can be argued that this approach on the part of the Commission places an excessive burden on the coastal state, since the Commission appears to expect the coastal state to prove that a seafloor high stretching beyond 350 nautical miles is *not* a submarine ridge. The Commission's provisional application of the ridge provision may have the consequence—as explained by Serdy—of 'reversing the onus of the proof',[101] in the sense that the coastal state is not necessarily expected to prove that a seafloor high seaward of 350 nautical miles *is* a submarine elevation, but that it must instead prove that the relevant seafloor high *is not* a submarine ridge.

Third, this could be seen as another example of the Commission interpreting and applying Article 76 to the disadvantage of the coastal state unless there is sufficient evidence to the contrary, i.e. *prima facie* going for the less advantageous option. Thus the threshold for the Commission in giving the coastal state the benefit of the doubt seems to remain high.

3.5   Legal Effects of the Commission's Recommendations

3.5.1   *Recommendations and the Submission Process*
3.5.1.1   Introduction
Article 4 of Annex II to the LOS Convention provides:

> Where a coastal State intends to establish, in accordance with Article 76, the outer limits of its continental shelf beyond 200 nautical miles, it shall submit particulars of such limits to the Commission along with supporting scientific and technical data as soon as possible but in any case within 10 years of the entry into force of this Convention for that State.[102]

The coastal state thus has an obligation to make a submission to the Commission where it intends to establish the outer limits beyond 200 nautical miles from the baselines. Once the Commission has made recommendations to the coastal state, the LOS Convention does not, however, prescribe the exact way in which the coastal state shall act. First, the coastal state may choose to delineate the outer limits of its continental shelf by means of the distance criteria contained in Article 76, paragraph 1, of the LOS Convention, i.e. establish the outer limits 200 nautical miles from the baselines from which the breadth

---

101   Serdy, 'The Commission on the Limits of the Continental Shelf and its Disturbing Propensity to Legislate', p. 377.

102   See also Rule 45 of the Rules of Procedure of the Commission.

of the territorial sea is measured. In that situation, the Commission's recommendations will not come into play.

Second, it may be that the coastal state does not proceed to establish the outer limits once the Commission has issued its recommendations. The recommendations will also then be without any legal impact. However, no outer limits of the continental shelf will be established in this situation and the precise physical definition of the continental shelf in question will remain unsettled, with the attendant difficulties for the coastal state in exercising its sovereign rights over the continental shelf beyond 200 nautical miles.[103]

The most immediate option for a coastal state is to proceed to establish the outer limits of its continental shelf beyond 200 nautical miles, once the Commission has issued its recommendations. This is the procedure that the coastal state will be best served by, since, according to the third sentence of Article 76, paragraph 8, of the LOS Convention, the 'limits of the shelf established by a coastal State on the basis of these recommendations shall be final and binding'. The converse can be deduced as follows: Outer continental shelf limits other than those established 'on the basis of' the Commission's recommendations will *not* become 'final and binding'.[104] In what follows, the legal

---

103 See Elferink, Alex G. Oude, 'Article 76 of the LOSC on the Definition of the Continental Shelf: Questions Concerning its Interpretation from a Legal Perspective', in *The International Journal of Marine and Coastal Law*, Vol. 21, 2006, pp. 269–285. Meanwhile, however, the sovereign rights of the coastal state are not lost in the absence of outer limits defined according to Article 76. Article 77, para. 3, of the LOS Convention provides that 'the rights of the coastal state over the continental shelf do not depend on occupation, effective or notional, or on any express proclamation'. But while the rights may exist, the *exercise* of sovereign rights clearly is dependent on defined outer limits.

104 What 'final and binding' implies is not explicitly addressed in the LOS Convention. Apart from the coastal state concerned, this provision is also of interest to other States Parties, the ISA and states that are not parties to the LOS Convention. For the coastal state, the reference to 'final' entails that the outer limit line shall no longer be subject to change, but becomes permanently fixed. The wording of 'final' implies as such non-mutability in perpetuity of the geographical position of the outer limits established. The coastal state will therefore be duty bound, cf. the phrase 'shall be', to abstain from adjusting the determined limits. This is reinforced by Article 76, para. 9, of the LOS Convention, which provides that the coastal state shall deposit charts and relevant information with the UNSG 'permanently' describing the outer limits of its continental shelf. Thus, the provision read in its context speaks in favour of a fixed and changeless delineation also if the external factors determining the shelf's limits should undergo change, for example if the territorial baselines are moved or physical events alter the seabed. For the coastal state, the term 'binding' implies an obligation to accept the outer limit line concerned. The coastal state will be bound to comply with the limit and must tailor its actions in

significance of Commission's recommendations in the context of this most probable alternative is explored.

3.5.1.2 Legal Significance for Establishing 'Final and Binding' Outer Limits
3.5.1.2.1 *Introduction*

The legal effect to be accorded the Commission's recommendations within the context of the third sentence of Article 76, paragraph 8, of the LOS Convention depends upon the meaning of the term 'on the basis of'. Basically, two situations can be distinguished. First, if the coastal state incorporates the outer

---

relation to the geographical location of the final limits, notably in terms of seabed activity. For example, relating all seabed activities between 200 nautical miles and the outer limits established, the coastal state shall make payments or contributions in respect of the exploitation of the non-living resources (see Article 82, para. 1, of the LOS Convention). As to the significance of 'final and binding' in respect of other States Parties to the Convention, the terms will mean an obligation to accept the outer limit line established: other States Parties must respect the coastal state's continental shelf rights on the landward side of the outer limit. Also here, the deposition of charts and other relevant information with the UNSG signifies completion of the process of establishment of the outer limits, and the outer limits are at least from that moment final and binding on other States Parties. As far as states that are not parties to the LOS Convention are concerned, outer limit lines cannot become 'final and binding' on these states by operation of Article 76, para. 8, as a consequence of the *pacta tertiis nec nocent nec prosunt* rule. Article 34 of the Vienna Convention confirms the paramount principle of international law that a treaty 'does not create either obligations or rights for a third state without its consent'. Also the ISA has an interest in the extent of the Area. According to Articles 136 and 137 of the LOS Convention, the Area and its resources are the common heritage of mankind, on whose behalf the ISA shall act. As provided, no state shall claim or exercise sovereignty or sovereign rights over any part of the Area or its resources, nor shall any state or natural or juridical person appropriate any part thereof. No such claim or exercise of sovereignty or sovereign rights nor such appropriation shall be recognized. The Area is defined as 'the seabed and ocean floor and subsoil thereof, beyond the limits of national jurisdiction' in Article 1 of the LOS Convention. The completion of the process of establishment of the outer limits of the outer continental shelf by the coastal state—cf. Article 76, para. 9, of the LOS Convention—thus also defines the outer limits of the Area (see Article 134, paras. 3 and 4, of the LOS Convention). While the LOS Convention does not give the ISA rights in the Area as such, the Convention charges it to organize and control activities in the Area (see Mahmoudi, *The Law of Deep Sea-Bed Mining*, p. 77 and Nelson, L.D.M., 'Claims to the Continental Shelf beyond the 200-Mile Limit', in Götz, Volkmar, Peter Selmer and Rüdiger Wolfrum (eds), *Liber Amicorum Günther Jaenicke— Zum 85 Geburtstag* (Springer, 1998), pp. 573–588, at p. 575). Therefore, the establishment of 'final and binding' outer limits of the continental shelf directly affects the physical size of the area that is managed by the ISA.

limits of the related segment of the continental shelf into domestic law *exactly* as recommended, the limits of the continental shelf must be considered to have been established 'on the basis of' the Commission's recommendations. The same will be the case if the coastal state adjusts the limits initially delineated in its submission to be in complete conformity with the recommendations of the Commission. Outer limits that are established precisely as recommended by the Commission are by definition established 'on the basis of' the Commission's recommendations.

The second situation to be distinguished—and which is the more interesting one in terms of legal interpretation—is when the coastal state does not heed the Commission's recommendations to the letter. Several examples to date have shown that the Commission has found that the information submitted by the coastal state should result in *different* outer limit lines than those contained in the coastal state's submissions, and has subsequently indicated this in its recommendations. The question is then whether the coastal state must adopt the recommended outer limit lines in order to act in conformity with the requirement that these limits are to be established 'on the basis of' the Commission's recommendations.

One example may serve to illustrate the problem. In regard to Australia's recommendations we saw above that the Commission did not accept the method used by Australia to link together the ending points of the outer limit beyond 200 nautical miles with the 200 nautical mile line. Instead of the most advantageous connection between the outer limit and the 200 nautical mile line, the Commission recommended that the 200 nautical mile line be connected with the outer limit along the outer edge of the continental margin or through a connection line which represented the shortest distance between the last fixed point on the outer limit and the 200 nautical mile line. For the outer limits to be established 'on the basis of' the Commission's recommendations, how then shall Australia's domestic regulation on the outer limit be drafted?

First, Australia could claim that 'on the basis of' means that no consistency is required between the outer limits established and the content of the Commission's recommendations. The justification used here would be that 'on the basis of' only means that the coastal state has an obligation to consider the Commission's recommendations as one of several possible interpretations, but that the coastal state ultimately is free to do as it will—of course, as long as the limits established do not 'extend beyond the limits provided for in paragraphs 4 to 6' of Article 76.[105] Australia could therefore argue that the term 'on the basis of' only expresses a *procedural obligation*, that is, an obligation to bring the

---

105   Article 76, para. 2, of the LOS Convention.

recommendations before the national authority or authorities within whose competence the matter lies for the enactment of continental shelf legislation.

Second, Australia could claim that the term 'on the basis of' contains a margin of discretion, allowing the coastal state to not follow exactly this part of the Commission's recommendations. This could be justified by arguing that the coastal state's outer limit represents a very minor deviation from the Commission's recommendations and that the coastal state is not bound to implement strictly all parts of the recommendations: as long as the most essential parts of the Commission's recommendations are implemented, the coastal state would not be violating the criterion 'on the basis of'.

What is meant by the term 'on the basis of' has previously been discussed in legal theory.[106] The ILA's Committee on the Outer Continental Shelf has also considered this question.[107] However, no in-depth legal analysis has been carried out—and no author has issued firm conclusions. Yet the issue is indeed one of the most essential under Article 76. The aim in the following is therefore to present my interpretation of 'on the basis of', based on the means of interpretation offered by the law of international treaties, i.e. the rules on treaty interpretation codified in the Vienna Convention on the Law of Treaties.[108]

---

106   See for instance McDorman, Ted, 'The Role of the Commission on the Limits of the Continental Shelf: A Technical Body in a Political World', pp. 314–315, Clingan, T.A., 'Dispute Settlement Among Non-Parties to the LOS Convention with Respect to the Outer Limits of the Continental Shelf', in Clingan, T.A., (ed.), *The Law of the Sea: What Lies Ahead?* (Honolulu, 1988), pp. 497–499, at p. 497, Smith, Robert W., and G. Taft, 'Legal Aspects of the Continental Shelf', in Cook and Carleton (eds), *Continental Shelf Limits: The Scientific and Legal Interface*, p. 20, Oxman, B.H., 'The Third United Nations Conference on the Law of the Sea: The Eighth Session (1979)', in *American Journal of International Law*, Vol. 74, 1980, pp. 1–47, at p. 22 and Suarez, Suzette, *The Outer Limits of the Continental Shelf—Legal Aspects of their Establishment* (Springer, 2008), pp. 210–212.

107   See for instance Report of the ILA Conference in Berlin, 2004, para. 6.6. Available at the website of the ILA: <www.ila-hq.org> (accessed 1 January 2014).

108   Vienna Convention on the Law of Treaties, Vienna, 23 May 1969; entered into force 27 January 1980. Published in *UNTS*, Vol. 1155, p. 331. It must be noted that the LOS Convention was concluded *after* the entry into force of the Vienna Convention. Thus, according to Article 4 of the Vienna Convention, it applies to the LOS Convention. However, not all States Parties to the LOS Convention are parties to the Vienna Convention. The LOS Convention must in relation to those states be interpreted on the basis of interpretation principles of customary international law. Then again, it is widely accepted that the rules on treaty interpretation contained in Articles 31–33 of the Vienna Convention constitute 'a general expression of the principles of customary international law relating to treaty interpretation'. See Sinclair, Ian, *The Vienna Convention on the Law of Treaties* (Manchester University Press, 1984), p. 153. Recognition of the rules on

3.5.1.2.2 *Wording*

According to the general rule of interpretation of treaties codified in Article 31 of the Vienna Convention, the starting point of treaty interpretation is the ordinary meaning to be given to the terms of the LOS Convention. The ordinary meaning of 'on the basis of' indicates that the coastal state at least has a procedural obligation if the outer limits, within the context of Article 76, are to become final and binding. The term 'basis' is generally defined as the 'starting point for a discussion'.[109] Accordingly, the term implies that the coastal state must make a start at considering the recommendations—by bringing them before the body empowered by the state with jurisdiction to legislate or to take other action related to the implementation of the LOS Convention.[110] Otherwise, the wording is open as to whether the coastal state has a margin of discretion or if 'on the basis of' implies that the coastal state must heed the Commission's recommendations to the letter.

---

interpretation of the Vienna Convention as customary international law is today well evidenced in judgments and opinions of the ICJ, and likewise in arbitral awards and decisions of national courts ((see for instance in *Avena and other Mexican Nationals*: 'The Court now addresses the question of the proper interpretation of the expression 'without delay' in the light of arguments put to it by the Parties. The Court begins by noting that the precise meaning of 'without delay', as it is to be understood in Article 35, paragraph 1 (b), is not defined in the Convention. This phrase therefore requires interpretation according to the customary rules of treaty interpretation reflected in Articles 31 and 32 of the Vienna Convention on the Law of Treaties' (*I.C.J. Reports* 2004, p. 12, at p. 48 (para. 83). In *Sovereignty over Pulau Ligitan and Pulau Sipadan*, the ICJ made reference to the rules on interpretation of the Vienna Convention although only one party to the litigation was party to the convention: 'The Court notes that Indonesia is not a party to the Vienna Convention [...]. The Court would nevertheless recall that, in accordance with customary international law, reflected in Articles 31 and 32 of that Convention, a treaty must be interpreted in good faith [...]. Moreover, with respect to Article 31, paragraph 3, the Court has had occasion to state that this provision also reflects customary law [...] Indonesia does not dispute that these are the applicable rules' (*I.C.J. Reports* 2002, p. 625, at pp. 645–646 (para. 37)). On the applicability of the rules on interpretation of the Vienna Convention, see further Gardiner, Richard, *Treaty Interpretation* (Oxford University Press, 2008), pp. 12–19.

109 Hornby, A.S., *Oxford Advanced Learner's Dictionary of Current English* (Oxford University Press, 1989).

110 Even though there is no specific requirement to bring the recommendations before any such authorities within a specific period of time. Notably, the LOS Convention is silent on when exactly the coastal state shall notify back and deposit with the UNSG charts and relevant information, including geodetic data, describing the outer limits of its shelf. In practice, years may lapse.

To claim that the outer limits must conform *in toto* to those recommended by the Commission would perhaps require another phrasing. It would then have been more appropriate to restrict the status of 'final and binding' to limits that were established 'in accordance with', 'consistent with', 'in conformity with', 'in line with', etc., the recommendations. In this regard, reference can be made to Article 94, paragraph 5, of the LOS Convention, which requires flag states to 'conform to' so-called 'generally accepted international regulations, procedures and practices' governing, *inter alia*, the construction, equipment and seaworthiness of ships. The LOS Convention makes extensive use of this technique, implicitly requiring states to incorporate recommendations, resolutions, rules and standards of the International Maritime Organization (IMO), including treaties such as the International Convention for the Prevention of Pollution from Ships (MARPOL 73/78)[111] or the International Convention for the Safety of Life at Sea (SOLAS).[112] Although the IMO has no authority to make formally binding decisions on the States Parties to the LOS Convention, the Convention—by implied reference—renders some IMO decisions obligatory.[113] That the wording 'on the basis of' is used in Article 76, instead of (for instance) 'conforming to', perhaps indicates less than an absolute commitment to implement the entire contents of the recommendations of the Commission.

In support of such an interpretation it can also be argued that the legal interpreter should choose the least intrusive or least 'binding' interpretation for the coastal state. This is also expressed by the Permanent Court of International Justice (PCIJ) and the ICJ in their long-standing dicta that restrictions on state sovereignty are not to be presumed lightly: first in the *Lotus* case, which the majority of legal writers, according to Prosper Weil, have viewed as presenting 'a lethal danger to the future of international law'.[114] The relevant passage of the judgment reads:

> International law governs relations between independent states. The rules of law binding upon states therefore emanate from their own

---

111   International Convention for the Prevention of Pollution from Ships, London, 2 November 1973, as amended by the Protocol, London, 1 June 1978; entered into force 2 October 1983. Published in *UNTS*, Vol. 61, p. 1340.

112   International Convention for the Safety of Life at Sea, London, 1 November 1974; entered into force 25 May 1980. Published in *UNTS*, Vol. 2, p. 1184.

113   Boyle, Alan, 'Some Reflections on the Relationship of Treaties and Soft Law', in *International & Comparative Law Quarterly*, Vol. 48, 1999, pp. 901–913, at p. 906.

114   Weil, Prosper, 'The Court cannot Conclude Definitively...Non Liquet Revisited', in *Columbia Journal of Transnational Law*, Vol. 36, 1998, pp. 109–119, at p. 113.

free will as expressed in conventions or by usages generally accepted as expressing principles of law and established in order to regulate the relations between these coexisting independent communities or with a view to the achievement of common aims. Restrictions upon the independence of states cannot therefore be presumed.[115]

However, the principle of restrictive interpretation of treaty obligations in deference to the sovereignty of states—*in dubio mitius*—was not included in the Vienna Convention. Several legal scholars have also seen the principle of effectiveness—*ut res magis valeat quam pereat*—a principle of treaty interpretation superior to that of *in dubio mitius*. For instance, Cassese has written that

> the authors of the Vienna Convention set great store by the principle of 'effectiveness' (*ut res magis valeat quam pereat*), whereby a treaty must be given an interpretation that enables its provision to be 'effective and useful', that is, to have the appropriate effect. This principle is plainly intended to expand the normative scope of treaties, to the detriment of the old principle whereby in case of doubt limitations of sovereignty were to be strictly interpreted.[116]

And in the 2009 *Dispute Regarding Navigational and Related Rights* concerning navigational and related rights on the river San Juan, the ICJ stated:

> In the second place, the Court is not convinced by Nicaragua's argument that Costa Rica's right of free navigation should be interpreted narrowly because it represents a limitation of the sovereignty over the river conferred by the Treaty on Nicaragua, that being the most important principle set forth by Article VI. While it is certainly true that limitations of the sovereignty of a State over its territory are not to be presumed, this does not mean that treaty provisions establishing such limitations, such as those that are in issue in the present case, should for this reason be interpreted *a priori* in a restrictive way. A treaty provision which has the purpose of limiting the sovereign powers of a State must be interpreted like any other provision of a treaty, i.e. in accordance with the intentions of its authors as reflected by the text of the treaty and the other relevant factors in terms of interpretation [...]. There are thus no grounds for supposing, *a priori*, that the words 'librenavegación [...] con objetos de

---

115 *P.C.I.J. Reports*, Series A, No. 10, p. 18.
116 Cassese, Antonio, *International Law* (Oxford University Press, 2005), p. 179.

comercio' should be given a specially restrictive interpretation, any more than an extensive one.[117]

It is tempting to note how phrasing similar to that used in Article 76, paragraph 8, of the LOS Convention has been interpreted and applied in other contexts. Legal practice that directly concerns the term 'on the basis of' as it appears in Article 76 does not exist. From a general perspective, however, the ITLOS in the *MOX Plant Case* shed some light on interpretation of the LOS Convention's provisions as regards similar terms in other treaties. The Tribunal stressed the separate and distinct nature of each treaty regime, indicating that how a term is used in other contexts is of minimal value:

> [E]ven if the OSPAR Convention, the EC Treaty and the Euratom Treaty contain rights or obligations to or identical with the rights and obligations set out in the [LOS] Convention, the rights and obligations under those agreements have a separate existence from those under the [LOS] Convention [...] the application of international law rules on interpretation of treaties to identical or similar provisions of different treaties may not yield the same results, having regard to, *inter alia*, differences in the respective contexts, objects and purposes, subsequent practices of parties and *travaux préparatoires*.[118]

This should not be taken to mean, however, that it is totally irrelevant how 'similar' terms of other treaties have been interpreted. On the contrary. Already in the Arbitral Tribunal in a Franco-Belgian case from 1937, one treaty was interpreted by reference to another treaty.[119] And according to Article 31, paragraph 3 (*litra* c), of the Vienna Convention, in the interpretation of a treaty, account shall be taken, together with the context, of 'any relevant rules of international law applicable in the relations between the parties'. This provision is commonly linked to the 'principle of systemic integration', which according to the ILC indicates the need to take into account the normative environment more widely:

> [A]lthough a tribunal may only have jurisdiction in regard to a particular instrument, it must always *interpret* and *apply* that instrument in its

---

117   *I.C.J. Reports* 2009, p. 213 (paras. 47–48).

118   *The MOX Plant Case (Ireland v United Kingdom)*, Request for Provisional Measures, Order of 3 December 2001, paras. 50–52. Reprinted in *ILM*, Vol. 41, 2002, p. 405.

119   Award of 1 March 1937. Published in *UNRIAA*, Vol. III, p. 1701, at p. 1713.

relationship to its normative environment—that is to say 'other' international law. This is the principle of systemic integration to which article 31 (3) (c) VCLT gives expression.[120]

So, what then about the interpretation of the term 'on the basis of' in Article 76, paragraph 8, of the LOS Convention? The practice of the jurisprudential system of the World Trade Organization (WTO) might offer some insights enabling a better understanding of the wording. Notably, one difficult issue for WTO panels and the Appellate Body (AB) has been the scope of national authorities to set health and environmental standards which fall within traditional state sovereignty and yet have an impact upon free trade.[121] In this context, the duty of states to *base* technical regulations on international standards has been subject to the legal findings of both WTO panels and the AB.

One early illustration of the problem of what 'based on' implies is a case which arose when the European Communities (EC) banned the sale of US beef taken from cattle treated with certain growth hormones: *EC—Measures Concerning Meat and Meat Products (Hormones)*. The USA requested consultations with the EC, claiming that measures taken by the EC under 'Council Directive Prohibiting the Use in Livestock Farming of Certain Substances Having a Hormonal Action' restricted or prohibited imports of meat and meat products from the USA, which was inconsistent with Articles III or XI of the General Agreements on Tariffs and Trade (GATT),[122] Articles 2, 3 and 5 of the WTO Agreement on the Application of Sanitary and Phytosanitary Measures (SPS Agreement),[123] Article 2 of the WTO Agreement on Technical Barriers to Trade (TBT Agreement)[124] and Article 4 of the WTO Agreement on Agriculture.[125]

---

120 UN Doc. A/CN.4/L.682 ('Fragmentation of International Law: Difficulties Arising from the Diversification and Expansion of International Law: Report of the Study Group of the International Law Commission'), para. 423.

121 Cass, Deborah, *The Constitutionalization of the World Trade Organization: Legitimacy, Democracy, and Community in the International Trading System* (Oxford University Press, 2005), p. 199.

122 Agreement adopted 30 October 1947; entered into force 1 January 1948. Published in *UNTS*, Vol. 55, p. 194.

123 Agreement adopted 15 April 1994; entered into force 1 January 1995. Published in *UNTS*, Vol. 1867, p. 493.

124 Agreement adopted 15 April 1994; entered into force 1 January 1995. Published in *UNTS*, Vol. 1868, p. 120.

125 Agreement adopted 15 April 1994; entered into force 1 January 1995. Published in *UNTS*, Vol. 1867, p. 410.

When the case reached the appeal level, the AB used the definition of 'basis' from *The New Shorter Oxford English Dictionary on Historical Principles* as the starting point for interpreting the term 'based on', as used in Article 3.1 of the SPS Agreement:

> A thing is commonly said to be 'based on' another thing when the former 'stands' or is 'founded' or 'built upon' or 'is supported by' the latter.[126]

From this definition, the AB concluded that

> there must be a very strong and very close relationship between two things in order to be able to say that one is 'the basis for' the other'.[127]

Furthermore, according to the AB:

> [...] it can certainly be said—*at a minimum*—that something cannot be considered 'as a basis for' something else if the two are contradictory. Therefore, if under Article 2.4 [of the TBT Agreement], the technical regulation and the international standard contradict each other, it cannot properly be concluded that the international standard has been used 'as a basis for' the technical regulation. (Emphasis added)[128]

As shown by Suarez,[129] the interpretation by the panel and the AB in the *EC—Trade Description of Sardines* is also interesting.[130] Peru had challenged EC regulations that maintained that only the species *Sardina Pilchardus Walbaum*, not other similar fish species, could be marketed in the EC under the name 'sardines'.[131] An international standard set by the Codex Alimentarius

---

126 Appellate Body Report, *European Communities—Measures Concerning Meat and Meat Products*. Published in *DSR* (1998), Vol. I, p. 135 (in para. 163).

127 *Ibid.*, para. 245.

128 *Ibid.*, para. 248. The AB thus only needed to determine whether there was a 'contradiction' between the international standard (of the Codex Alimentarius Commission: CAC) and the EC Regulation. The AB analysed the two regulations and concluded that the EC Regulation was contradictory to the international standard.

129 Suarez, Suzette, *The Outer Limits of the Continental Shelf—Legal Aspects of Their Establishment* (Springer, 2008), pp. 210–212.

130 Appellate Body Report, *European Communities—Trade Description of Sardines*. Published in *DSR* (2002), Vol. VIII, p. 3359.

131 Council Regulation (EEC) No 2136/89 of 21 June 1989 laying down common marketing standards for preserved sardines. In *Official Journal L 212, 22/07/1989*, pp. 79–81.

Commission (CAC), however, maintained that such species could be sold throughout the world under the name 'sardines' provided that a modifying phrase proceeded the designation, specifying a country, a geographic area, the species, or the common name. Thus, under the CAC standard, Peru should have been able to sell its product in EC markets under the name 'Pacific sardines', 'Peruvian Sardines' or 'Sardines—*Sardinossagax*.' The fish had already been sold in Germany as 'Pacific Sardines' until the Commission launched its challenge under EC regulations, which triggered the complaint from Peru, and thus the WTO dispute.

The WTO panel and the AB found that the EC had failed to comply with Article 2.4 of the TBT Agreement because the EC did not base its internal technical regulations on the CAC standard, and had failed to demonstrate that this international standard would not be effective or appropriate in fulfilling the EC's legitimate objectives of ensuring market transparency, consumer protection and fair competition. Article 2.4 of the TBT Agreement reads:

> Where technical regulations are required and relevant international standards exist or their completion is imminent, Members shall use them, or the relevant parts of them, *as a basis* for their technical regulations except when such international standards or relevant parts would be an ineffective or inappropriate means for the fulfilment of the legitimate objectives pursued, for instance because of fundamental climatic or geographical factors or fundamental technological problems. (Emphasis added)

The EC regulation established a requirement that preserved sardines must be prepared exclusively from *Sardina Pilchardus Walbaum*. The AB then had to consider several issues, including one relevant to the question of the meaning of 'on the basis of': Were the standards applied to preserved sardines and sardine-type products set by the CAC used *as a basis* for the EC regulation for purposes of Article 2.4 of the TBT Agreement?

The WTO panel first considered the matter by referring to *Webster's New World Dictionary* on the meaning of the term 'basis'. It found that 'basis' meant

> the principal constituent of anything, the fundamental principle or theory, as of a system of knowledge.[132]

Applying this understanding, the panel held that the CAC standard had not been used 'as a basis' for the EC regulation. To this, the EC argued:

---

132 *European Communities—Trade Description of Sardines*, para. 240.

The European Communities maintains that a 'rational relationship' between an international standard and a technical regulation is sufficient to conclude that the former is used 'as a basis for' the latter. According to the European Communities, an examination based on the criterion of the existence of a 'rational relationship' focuses on 'the qualitative aspect of the substantive relationship that should exist between the relevant international standard and the technical regulation'. In response to questioning at the oral hearing, the European Communities added that a 'rational relationship' exists when the technical regulation is informed in its overall scope by the international standard.

However, the AB agreed with the panel that an international standard is used 'as a basis for' a technical regulation 'when it is used as the principal constituent or fundamental principle for the purpose of enacting the technical regulation'.[133] The AB cited certain definitions of the term 'basis', and concluded:

> From these various definitions, we would highlight the similar terms 'principal constituent', 'fundamental principle', 'main constituent', and 'determining principle'—all of which lend credence to the conclusion that there must be a very strong and very close relationship between two things in order to be able to say that one is 'the basis for' the other.'[134]

Thus also, the AB rejected the EC's argument that a 'rational relationship' between an international standard and a technical regulation is sufficient for concluding that the former is used 'as a basis for' the latter:

> [W]e see nothing in the text of Article 2.4 to support the European Communities' view, nor has the European Communities pointed to any such support. Moreover, the European Communities does not offer any arguments relating to the context or the object and purpose of that provision that would support its argument that the existence of a 'rational relationship' is the appropriate criterion for determining whether something has been used 'as a basis for' something else.[135]

With regard to the requirement in Article 2.4 of the TBT Agreement that member states shall use relevant international standards, 'or the relevant parts of them', as a basis for their technical regulations, the AB also observed:

---

133 *Ibid.*, paras. 240–245.
134 *Ibid.*, para. 245
135 *Ibid.*, para. 247.

In our view, the phrase 'relevant parts of them' defines the appropriate focus of an analysis to determine whether a relevant international standard has been used 'as a basis for' a technical regulation. In other words, the examination must be limited to those parts of the relevant international standards that relate to the subject-matter of the challenged prescriptions or requirements. In addition, the examination must be broad enough to address all of those relevant parts; the regulating Member is not permitted to select only some of the 'relevant parts' of an international standard. If a part is relevant, then it must be one of the elements which is a basis for the technical regulation.[136]

---

136   *Ibid.*, para. 250. The WTO panels and the AB have also, in several cases, held that national measures restrictive of trade in agricultural and food products have not been *based on* correct *scientific risk assessments*, in accordance with Article 5.1 of the SPS Agreement. On 5 October 1995, Canada requested consultations with Australia in respect of Australia's prohibition of imports of salmon from Canada based on a quarantine regulation. Canada alleged that the prohibition was inconsistent with Articles XI and XIII of GATT, and also inconsistent with Article 5.1 of the SPS Agreement (Appellate Body Report, *Australia— Measures Affecting Importation of Salmon.* Published in *DSR* (1998), Vol. VIII, p. 3327). The AB, although reversing the panel's finding because the panel had examined the wrong measures (heat-treatment requirement), still found that the correct measure at issue— i.e. Australia's import prohibition—violated Article 5.1 (and, by implication, Article 2.2 of the TBT Agreement) because it was not 'based on' a risk assessment requirement under Article 5.1. Another example is the 1998 dispute between the USA and Japan over Japanese measures prohibiting the importation of fresh apricots, cherries, plums, pears, quince, peaches, apples, and walnuts from the continental USA (Panel Report, *Japan—Measures Affecting Agricultural Products*, in *DSR* (1999), Vol. I, p. 315). The USA alleged that Japan prohibited the importation of each variety of a product requiring quarantine treatment until the quarantine treatment had been tested for that variety, even if the treatment had proved to be effective for other varieties of the same product. The USA alleged violations of Articles 2, 5 and 8 of the SPS Agreement, Article XI of GATT, and Article 4 of the Agriculture Agreement. The measure at issue was thus varietal testing requirement (i.e. Japan's Plant Protection Law), under which the import of certain plants was prohibited because of the possibility of their becoming potential hosts of codling moth. The AB upheld the panel's finding that Japan's varietal testing requirement had been maintained without sufficient scientific evidence in violation of Article 2.2. (Appellate Body Report, *Japan—Measures Affecting Agricultural Products*, published in *DSR*, Vol. I, p. 277). The AB also agreed with the panel's legal standard for the analysis of Article 2.2: the obligation in Article 2.2 not to maintain an SPS measure without 'sufficient scientific evidence' required that there be a rational or objective relationship between the SPS measure and the scientific evidence. Also, having found that the panel improperly applied judicial economy to the US claim under Article 5.1 in relation to apricots, pears, plums and quince—the four products that were not examined by the panel—the AB completed the legal analysis and found that Japan's measure violated Article 5.1 for these four products

In sum, the practice of WTO panels and AB does not suggest that the ordinary meaning of the words 'based on' means uniformity of standards; 'based on' is—according to the AB in the *Hormones* case—different from the words 'conforming to',[137] so that a national measure does not have to be exactly the same as the international standard in order to be consistent with the latter. Countries may set health standards that differ from the prevailing international standard without violating the SPS Agreement. National health measures thus do not have to correspond precisely with international standards in order to be in conformity with them.[138]

In my opinion, the practice of WTO is interesting in at least two aspects with regard to the understanding of the term 'on the basis of' in the third sentence of Article 76, paragraph 8, of the LOS Convention. First, it can be argued that if the national legislation on the outer limits of the continental shelf shall be based on the Commission's recommendations it is not sufficient that there exists only a vague or abstract relationship between the two. We can say that something is 'based on' something else only if the first constitutes the *determining principle* for the second—or, as set forth in the practice of the AB, that there must be a *very strong and very close relationship* between the national and the international standard in order to be able to say that the latter is used as the basis for the former. This leans in the direction of giving greater weight to the Commission's recommendations.

---

as it was not based on a proper risk assessment. A last example that treats the question of what 'based on' implies in this context is *Japan—Measures Affecting the Importation of Apples* (Published in *DSR* (2003), Vol. IX, p. 4391). On 1 March 2002, the USA requested consultations with Japan regarding restrictions allegedly imposed by Japan on imports of apples from the USA. The US complaint arose from Japan's maintaining quarantine restrictions on apples imported into Japan, restrictions said to be necessary to protect against introduction of fire blight. Among the measures the USA complained of were the prohibition of imported apples from orchards in which any fire blight was detected, the requirement that export orchards be inspected three times yearly for the presence of fire blight and the disqualification of any orchard from exporting to Japan should fire blight be detected within a 500 metre buffer zone surrounding such an orchard. The USA claimed, *inter alia*, that these measures were inconsistent with the obligations of Japan under Article 2.2 of the SPS Agreement. The AB upheld the Panel's finding that the measure was maintained 'without sufficient scientific evidence' inconsistently with Article 2.2, as there was a clear disproportion—and thus no rational or objective relationship—between Japan's measure and the 'negligible risk' identified on the basis of scientific evidence.

137   *EC—Measures Concerning Meat and Meat Products*, in *DSR*, Vol. I, 1998, p. 135 (para. 163).
138   Cass, *The Constitutionalization of the World Trade Organization: Legitimacy, Democracy, and Community in the International Trading System*, p. 199.

Second, we should note that in deciding whether something is based on something else, it has been argued that a type of relevance criterion applies. When asking if states apply international standards as a basis for their national regulations, the AB has stated that the 'based on' criterion is met only if the national law implements the *relevant parts* of the international standard. Thus, if an element of the international standard is relevant, then it must also be one of the elements on which the national regulation is based.

In the context of Article 76, it can therefore also be argued that the outer limits can be said to be established on the basis of the Commission's recommendations only if the national legislation conforms to all *relevant* aspects of the recommendations. This in turn prompts the question whether any part of the Commission's recommendations may be considered irrelevant, or less relevant than others. Are not all elements of the Commission's recommendations of the same crucial importance to the main issue at stake here, which is the *physical location* of the outer limit of the continental shelf beyond 200 nautical miles? In my opinion, the wording 'on the basis of' does not fit well with an arrangement under which the coastal state can selectively sample and disregard certain parts of Commission recommendations because it considers them less important or less relevant than other parts.

3.5.1.2.3   *Terms of the Treaty in Their Context*
According to Article 31, paragraph 1, of the Vienna Convention, the terms of a treaty shall also be interpreted in their context. On the one hand, it can be argued that the term 'on the basis of' read in context supports the conclusion that the coastal state should have some flexibility in establishing final and binding outer limits of the continental shelf. After all, what the Commission adopts are 'recommendations', not decisions. A recommendation is usually something which the recipient may see fit to take into account, without necessarily being obliged to do so: 'Recommendations refer to an action which is advisory in nature rather than one having any binding effect'.[139] This is in line with general international practice, where 'recommendations' indicate only non-binding instruments adopted by international institutions.[140]

---

139   *Black's Law Dictionary* (West Publishing, 1979), p. 1144.
140   See for instance the Convention for the Protection and Preservation of the Marine Environment and the North East Atlantic (OSPAR Convention). Adopted in Paris, 22 September 1992; entered into force 25 March 1998. Reprinted in *ILM*, Vol. 32, p. 1068. Article 13, para. 5, of the OSPAR Convention states explicitly that 'recommendations shall have no binding force'. On the contrary, it follows from the same Article's paras. 2 and 4 that 'decisions' have binding force on parties to the Convention. A different issue is when

On the other hand, the term 'on the basis of' read in context may also support the conclusion that the coastal state is not allowed any margin of discretion in establishing final and binding outer limits. Here reference must be made to Article 8 of Annex II to the LOS Convention:

> In case of disagreement by the coastal State with the recommendations of the Commission, the coastal State shall, within a reasonable time, make a revised or new submission to the Commission.

Thus, if the coastal state disagrees with the recommendations, this disagreement is to be resolved in another way than by the coastal state departing from the Commission's recommendations and establishing the outer limit with reference to a possible built-in margin of discretion contained in the term 'on the basis of'. Disagreement between the Commission and the coastal state adds up to a 'ping-pong' procedure of submission—recommendations—resubmission—recommendations.[141] There is no legislated endpoint to this process.[142] The 'ping-pong' process can thus in principle continue for any number of

states consent to be bound by otherwise non-binding legal instruments. One example is the standards issued by the aforementioned CAC. Standards and other decisions adopted by the CAC (e.g. guidelines and codes of practice) are not as such legally binding for the members of the CAC, but when a food standard is approved and released by the CAC as a recommendation, states enjoy discretion as to whether or not to formally accept it. Formal acceptance makes the recommendation binding upon the state in question. See generally Stewart, Terence, and David Johanson, 'The SPS Agreement of the World Trade Organization and International Organizations: The Roles of the Codex Alimentarus Commission, the International Plant Protection Convention, and the International Office of Epizootics', in *Syracuse Journal of International Law and Commerce*, Vol. 26, 1998, pp. 27–53. See also, Sloan, Blaine, 'The Binding Force of a "Recommendation" of the General Assembly of the United Nations', in *British Yearbook of International Law*, Vol. 25, 1948, pp. 1–33. On the legal effects of unilateral declarations, see the argument made by the PCIJ in *Legal Status of Eastern Greenland (Norway v Denmark)*, published in *P.C.I.J. Reports*, Series A/B, No. 53, p. 71 and the opinion delivered by the ICJ in the *Nuclear Tests Case (Australia v. France)*. See *I.C.J. Reports* 1974, p. 253, at p. 457.

141   Gardiner, Piers R.R., 'The Limits of the Area Beyond National Jurisdiction—Some Problems with Particular Reference to the Role of the Commission on the Limits of the Continental Shelf', in Blake, G.H. (ed.), *Maritime Boundaries and Ocean Resources* (Croom Helm, 1987), pp. 63–76, at p. 69.

142   Klemm, Ulf-Dieter, 'Continental Shelf, Outer Limits', in Bernhardt, Rudolf (ed.), *Encyclopedia of Public International Law*, Vol. I, 1992, pp. 804–806, at p. 806.

rounds,[143] and the main point in our context is therefore that Article 8 determines that *any* disagreement the coastal state might have on the occasion of the Commission's recommendations shall result in a new and revised submission. The context thus shows us that the drafters of the LOS Convention had not foreseen the possibility that a coastal state would disagree with the recommendations, but proceed to establish the outer limits disregarding the recommendations. In my opinion, this strongly indicates that 'on the basis of' does not imply any margin of discretion in establishing the outer limits.

Take, for instance, the aforementioned shelf claim of Australia. Australia has expressed doubt as to the correctness of certain recommendations concerning its continental shelf beyond 200 nautical miles, including the method that involves how to link the last segment of the outer limit with the 200 nautical mile limit. It has been indicated—by a Senior Officer in DOALOS—that Australia will accept only those parts of the Commission's recommendations that it finds to be in line with the LOS Convention's provisions.[144] In defence of such an interpretation, Australia could argue that it has only an obligation to establish the outer limits 'on the basis of' *recommendations which the coastal state finds to have a sound legal foundation*, and can reject recommendations which have not such a foundation.[145] Australia could claim that the limits should become 'final and binding' as long as they are established in accordance with Article 76, paragraphs 1 to 7, and not because they have been established on the basis of recommendations of a technical Commission of experts. This seems also reasonable, since the Commission indeed could be wrong in its interpretation, and Australia right. On the other hand, if each coastal state has the opportunity to select such recommendations as it considers to be correct, then that would abruptly reduce the Commission's recommendations to facultative interpretative suggestions that could be accepted or rejected depending on individual interpretations.

Article 76, therefore—as mentioned—provides for a different approach which involves the making of a new or revised submission. That is how the coastal state is given the opportunity to argue that the Commission has made mistakes. And

---

143   See Smith, Robert W., and G. Taft, 'Legal Aspects of the Continental Shelf', in Cook, P.J., and C.M. Carleton (eds), *Continental Shelf Limits: The Scientific and Legal Interface* (Oxford University Press, 2000), pp. 17–24, at p. 20 (who note that the process could go on 'indefinitely').

144   Jares, 'The Work of the Commission on the Limits of the Continental Shelf', in Vidas (ed.), *Law, Technology and Science for Oceans in Globalisation*, pp. 463 and 467.

145   Serdy, 'The Commission on the Limits of the Continental Shelf and its Disturbing Propensity to Legislate', p. 382.

it is through new recommendations that the Commission has an opportunity to admit that it was wrong in the first place. If the latter situation occurs, agreement will be achieved between the Commission and the coastal state. However, if the Commission stands by its initial recommendations, discrepancy will persist. The LOS Convention's system is still clear: if the coastal state wishes final and binding outer limits, it bears the risk that the Commission—like any other institution which interprets and applies treaty provisions—could be wrong or adopt a different interpretation in its decision-making. This is the solution that the treaty-makers preferred, instead of leaving the interpretation of Article 76 solely in the hands of the coastal state.

Referring to the example of Australia above, it is particularly interesting to note how Australia is now likely to proceed in response to recommendations with which it does not agree: by making a new and revised submission. Australia has established the outer limits of its extended continental shelf for nearly all areas in consistency with the recommendations of the Commission. Australia has not, however, proceeded to establish the outer limits in those areas where Australia disagrees with the recommendations (that is, two areas in which the aforementioned problem of linking the last segment of the outer limit to the 200 nautical mile limit arose: the Wallaby and Exmouth Plateaus and the Kerguelen Plateau). Instead, Australia has deferred domestic implementation and indicated that these seabed areas will be subject to a revised submission.[146]

3.5.1.2.4   *Object and Purpose*

According to Article 31 of the Vienna Convention, a treaty shall be interpreted in light of its object and purpose. In the context of Article 31, 'object and purpose' is used, *inter alia*, to reinforce the interpretative principle that the text of a treaty should be interpreted to reflect the goals embodied in the LOS Convention as a whole.[147] With regard to the term 'on the basis of', it can be argued that 'object and purpose' are relevant for at least two reasons.

First, the preamble of the LOS Convention refers to the needs and interests of mankind as a whole, and that the area of the seabed and ocean floor and the subsoil thereof, beyond the limits of national jurisdiction, as well as its resources, are the common heritage of mankind, the exploration and exploitation of which shall be carried out for the benefit of all states, irrespective

---

146   See section 3.4.2 above.

147   Jonas, Davis S., and Thomas N. Saunders, 'The Object and Purpose of a Treaty: Three Interpretive Options', in *Vanderbilt Journal of Transnational Law*, Vol. 43, 2010, pp. 565–609, at p. 608.

of their geographical location. This suggests a desire to promote more of a 'collective' approach to issues related to the law of the sea. The interests of other states, it can be argued, thus speak against the adoption of any margin of discretion. The placement of the physical limit where the outer continental shelf meets the deep seabed concerns the interests of all mankind, i.e. the size of the Area.[148] We can identify specific concerns when considering the norm in question: Article 76 is clearly 'outward-looking', seeing the setting of continental shelf limits not merely as the internal affair of one coastal state. Article 76 is designed to safeguard one society—the entire international community—against unlawful encroachments by another society—the individual coastal states. In this context, the Commission could be seen as representing the common interest of all states (at least those that are parties to the LOS Convention), so any degree of deference to the delineating state under the term 'on the basis of' should not be allowed.[149]

Second, another protection-worthy purpose that finds support in the Convention's preamble and which suggests that no margin of discretion should be allowed, are the principles of rule of law and non-discrimination. The first is, strictly speaking, not a guarantee, as the Commission may make mistakes in its legal application. But the purpose of non-discrimination is a point in the sense that the Commission, through established procedures and substantive policies, can contribute to the consistent and uniform treaty application of Article 76: that equal continental shelf areas be treated equally. Conversely, allowing any discretion will keep alive individual interpretations and possibly promote less accountability in the application of Article 76. States take decisions as to the application of international law in light of overriding national interests.[150] The degree to which an individual coastal state may be 'trusted' with the exercise of discretion regarding the manner of application of Article 76 could thus always be considered doubtful. Individual coastal states might take advantage of a margin of discretion. The recommendations of the Commission may thus work as a tool to safeguard against incoherence. Leaving the establishment of outer continental shelf limits exclusively in the hands of the coastal state might render the rule of law illusory. This is perhaps especially so with regard to areas of international law which require uniform application

---

148   Article 1 of the LOS Convention.

149   See Cot, Jean-Pierre, 'The Law of the Sea and the Margin of Appreciation', in Nidiaye, Tafsir Malik, and Rüdiger Wolfrum (eds), *Law of the Sea, Environmental Law and Settlement of Disputes* (Martinus Nijhoff Publishers, 2007), pp. 389–404.

150   Shany, Yuval, 'Toward a General Margin of Appreciation Doctrine in International Law?', in *The European Journal of International Law*, Vol. 16, 2005, pp. 907–940, at pp. 923–924.

as a matter of utility. Thus in my view, these considerations of object and purpose also indicate strongly that 'on the basis of' is not meant to imply any margin of discretion for the coastal state.

3.5.1.2.5   Preparatory Works

The actual intention of the parties when the LOS Convention was formulated—evidenced through the *travaux préparatoires*—may be sought in an attempt to interpret a treaty.[151] The drafting history of Article 76,

---

151   International courts and tribunals have relied on preparatory works as relevant sources of interpretation, although Article 32 of the Vienna Convention establishes that recourse to supplementary means of interpretation, including the preparatory work of the treaty and the circumstances of its conclusion, is allowed solely in order to confirm the meaning resulting from the application of Article 31, or to determine the meaning when the interpretation according to Article 31 leaves the meaning ambiguous or obscure, or leads to a result which is manifestly absurd or unreasonable (see Gardiner, *Treaty Interpretation*, pp. 301–350). It has been noted that 'in almost every case involving the interpretation of a treaty one or both of the parties seeks to invoke the preparatory work' (see McNair, Arnold D., *The Law of Treaties* (Oxford University Press, 1961), p. 412). In the use of preparatory works, it is, however, important to distinguish between documents that can clearly be linked to official negotiations, such as successive published draft texts of the LOS Convention, and documents and materials that are of an informal character and cannot be regarded as *travaux préparatoires* in the sense as used in Article 32 of the Vienna Convention. The nature of the working methods and procedures during UNCLOS III raises significant challenges in relation to this issue, i.e. how to determine which materials have the character of negotiating documents. The LOS Convention is, to quote Philip Allott, 'not quite in the happy position of the Treaty Establishing the European Economic Community, for example, which has no effective *travaux* at all and whose interpretation and application has been much assisted by their absence. Nor is it in the familiar position of leading codification treaties, such as the Vienna Convention on the Law of Treaties, where the four-stage *travaux* [...] are well known and their relevance well understood' (see Allott, Philip, 'Power Sharing in the Law of the Sea', p. 7). It is rather to be noted that the *ad hoc* negotiating procedures at UNCLOS III—in working groups (restricted and open-ended), negotiating groups, confrontations between interest groups, 'friends of the chairman' of a committee, the President's bureau, appointed and even self-appointed sorts of mediators—did create a good amount of random and disorderly material, including highly miscellaneous conference documents, together with contemporaneous and retrospective accounts purporting to describe the evolution of the texts (*ibid.*). With respect to the LOS Convention, it is thus not only the challenges associated with the way the preparatory works can be used as a legal source of interpretation, but actually also which material is deemed to be seen as such. On the use of preparatory works, see also Amerasinghe, C.F., 'Interpretation of Texts in Open

paragraph 8, provides some hints as regards the interpretation of the term 'on the basis of'.

On the one hand, the *travaux préparatoires* would seem to indicate that the coastal state must have a certain margin of discretion as regards the Commission's recommendations when it acts to establish the outer limits. A proposal by the US, Canada and Japan that would have given the Commission right not only to review the delineation of the outer limits by the coastal state but also to authorize it to decide whether or not to accept the delineation and then formally make the limits final and binding, was not accepted by UNCLOS III.[152] Nor was Canada's proposal, that if the evidence supplied by the coastal state was viewed as satisfactory by the Commission, such certification should be conclusive.[153] Singapore's proposal, that 'taking into account these recommendations' should be replaced with 'shall be in accordance with these recommendations', was also rejected,[154] as was the German proposal that paragraph 8 should read

> [i]nformation on the limits of the continental shelf beyond 200 nautical miles shall be submitted by the coastal state to the Commission on the Limits of the Continental Shelf [...]. The decisions of the Commission on matters related to the establishment of the outer limits of the continental shelf shall be final and binding.[155]

On the other hand, states were not willing to accept a weak link between the coastal state's outer limits and the recommendations. The USSR had proposed that

International Organizations', in *British Yearbook of International Law*, Vol. 45, 1994, pp. 175–209, at p. 200).

152 Reproduced in Platzöder, Renate (ed.), *Third United Nations Conference on the Law of the Sea: Documents*, Vol. XI, p. 500.

153 *Ibid.*

154 Reproduced in Platzöder, Renate (ed.), *Third United Nations Conference on the Law of the Sea: Documents*, Vol. IX, p. 384.

155 *Ibid.* Several authors also indicate that the coastal state will enjoy a degree of discretion under the term 'on the basis of'. See in particular Smith and Taft 'Legal Aspects of the Continental Shelf', in Cook and Carleton (eds), *Continental Shelf Limits: The Scientific and Legal Interface*, p. 20 and Elferink, Alex G. Oude, 'Article 76 of the LOSC on the Definition of the Continental Shelf: Questions Concerning its Interpretation from a Legal Perspective', p. 281.

information on the limits of the continental shelf shall be submitted by the coastal state to the Commission on the Limits of the Continental Shelf. The Commission shall make recommendations to the coastal state on matters related to the establishment of the outer limits of the continental shelf. The limits of the shelf established by the coastal state taking into account these recommendations shall be final and unalterable.[156]

This inspired a compromise text proposal from the Chairman of Negotiating Group No. 6:

> Information on the limits of the continental shelf [...] shall be submitted to the Commission [...]. The Commission shall make recommendations to the coastal state related to the establishment of the outer limits. The limits of the shelf established by a coastal state taking into account these recommendations shall be final and binding.[157]

The words 'taking into account' were unacceptable to several states. They feared such wording would imply that the coastal state could establish final limits binding on the rest of the world simply by 'taking into account', but possibly in significant respects rejecting the Commission's recommendations.[158] This possible shift in the balance of power from the Commission to the coastal state was the subject of further negotiations where certain parties again wanted to strengthen the legal significance of the recommendations. The Chairman of the Second Committee thus proposed replacing the words 'taking into account' with 'on the basis of'.[159]

Why these changes were made is nowhere explained in the official records of UNCLOS III. As tribunals are generally cautious regarding assertions as to any conclusions to be drawn from a change in wording during the drafting process of a treaty without explanation, this should apply also in our case.[160] Canada, for example, which along with Japan and the USA in the

---

156   Reproduced in Platzöder, Renate (ed.), *Third United Nations Conference on the Law of the Sea: Documents*, Vol. IX, p. 384.

157   *Ibid.*

158   Oxman, 'The Third United Nations Conference on the Law of the Sea: The Eighth Session (1979)', p. 22.

159   UN Doc. A/CONF.62/L.51 ('Report of the Chairman of the Second Committee'). Reproduced in Platzöder, Renate (ed.), *Third United Nations Conference on the Law of the Sea: Documents*, Vol. XV, p. 83.

160   See Gardiner, *Treaty Interpretation*, p. 336.

above-mentioned proposal had proposed at an early stage of UNCLOS III a 'strengthened' Commission, expressed concern for the converse towards the end of the negotiations.[161]

So, if the legislative history of the terms of the treaty tells us anything, it is, first, that states would not accept a Commission of experts authorized to render binding decisions regarding a coastal state's outer limits. Second, the preparatory works indicate that the link between a coastal state's outer limits and the Commission's recommendations was *strengthened* by replacing the words 'taking into account' with 'on the basis of'.

3.5.1.2.6   *Subsequent Practice*

Does subsequent practice in the application of Article 76 provide a basis for establishing a common intention of the parties as to the meaning of the term 'on the basis of' in paragraph 8? As of 1 January 2014, only four states— Australia, Ireland, Mexico and the Philippines—appear to have deposited information regarding the outer limit of the continental shelf with the UNSG pursuant to Article 76, paragraph 9 of the LOS Convention. On 19 August 2009, Ireland deposited a list of geographical coordinates of points, including geodetic data, accompanied by an illustrative map, permanently describing the outer limits of the continental shelf beyond 200 nautical miles from the baselines in the area abutting the Porcupine Abyssal Plain.[162] On 20 May 2009, Mexico deposited a chart and relevant information, including geodetic data, permanently describing the outer limits of its continental shelf beyond 200 nautical miles in respect of the western polygon in the Gulf of Mexico.[163] On 2 July 2012, the Philippines deposited with the UNSG, pursuant to Article 76, paragraph 9, a chart and relevant information, including geodetic data, permanently describing the outer limits of its continental shelf beyond 200 nautical miles in respect of the Benham Rise.[164] And on 2 November 2012, the UNSG

---

161   UN Doc. A/CONF.62/WS/4 ('Statement by the delegation of Canada dated 2 April 1980'), para. 15. See *Third United Nations Conference on the Law of the Sea, Official Records*, Vol. XIII, pp. 101–102.

162   Retrieved from the DOALOS website: <www.un.org/Depts/los/LEGISLATIONAND TREATIES/PDFFILES/mzn_s/mzn73.pdf> (accessed 1 January 2014).

163   From the DOALOS website: <www.un.org/Depts/los/LEGISLATIONANDTREATIES/ PDFFILES/mzn_s/mzn72.pdf> (accessed 1 January 2014).

164   From the DOALOS website: <www.un.org/Depts/los/LEGISLATIONANDTREATIES/ PDFFILES/mzn_s/mzn88ef.pdf> (accessed 1 January 2014).

received the deposit by Australia of the outer limits of its continental shelf beyond 200 nautical miles.[165]

The deposited outer limits of the continental shelf of Mexico[166] and the Philippines[167] show full geographical consistence between the outer limits established nationally and the Commission's recommendations.[168] Australia also claims that the outer limits which it has established so far are in accordance with the Commission's recommendations.[169] As regards Ireland, however, the coordinates of the deposited outer limit[170] indicate that certain minimal adjustments have been made in relation to the Commission's recommendations.[171]

This *may* indicate that Australia, Ireland, Mexico and the Philippines do not have a common understanding of the term 'on the basis of'. However, the sparse practice available as of today limits the significance of subsequent practice as a source of interpretation. Subsequent practice by a few individual States Parties also has some probative value, but in cases where the wording is ambiguous, additional practice will be needed if one is to place any decisive or significant weight on such practice.[172]

3.5.1.2.7   Conclusions
How, then, may we conclude? The deliberately vague wording provides no clear answer as to whether there must be a full match between the coastal state's continental shelf limits beyond 200 nautical miles and the outer limits recommended by the Commission, in order for the former to be established

---

165   From the DOALOS website: <www.un.org/Depts/los/LEGISLATIONANDTREATIES/ PDFFILES/mzn_s/mzn92ef.pdf> (accessed 1 January 2014).

166   From the DOALOS website: <www.un.org/Depts/los/LEGISLATIONANDTREATIES/ PDFFILES/DEPOSIT/mex_mzn72_2009.pdf> (accessed 1 January 2014).

167   From the DOALOS website: <www.un.org/Depts/los/LEGISLATIONANDTREATIES/ PDFFILES/MAPS/phl_mzn88_2012.jpg> (accessed 1 January 2014).

168   From the Commission website: <www.un.org/Depts/los/clcs_new/submissions_files/ mex07/mex_rec.pdf> (accessed 1 January 2014).

169   From the DOALOS website: <www.un.org/Depts/los/LEGISLATIONANDTREATIES/ PDFFILES/mzn_s/mzn92ef.pdf> (accessed 1 January 2014).

170   From the DOALOS website: <www.un.org/Depts/los/LEGISLATIONANDTREATIES/ PDFFILES/DEPOSIT/irl_mnz73_2009.pdf> (accessed 1 January 2014).

171   From the website of the Commission: <www.un.org/Depts/los/clcs_new/submissions_ files/irl05/irl_rec.pdf> (accessed 1 January 2014).

172   Ruud and Ulfstein, *Innføring i folkerett* (Universitetsforlaget, 2011), p. 95. See also Gardiner, *Treaty Interpretation*, p. 236, and Brownlie, Ian, *Principles of Public International Law* (Oxford University Press, 2003), p. 605.

'on the basis of' the latter. On the one hand, if strict compliance was meant, a different wording should have been chosen. On the other hand, however, an ordinary linguistic understanding of the term 'on the basis of' does not preclude the conclusion that absolute consistence is required.

It has been argued that the preparatory works of the LOS Convention open for both understandings of the term. On the one hand, the treaty makers would not accept a Commission without any influence as regards the placement of the outer limits if they eventually were to become legally 'final and binding' in character. On the other hand, as we have seen, several proposals for a Commission that could make binding decisions upon coastal states were rejected. Developments at UNCLOS III would indicate increasing powers devolving to the Commission as the negotiations progressed. The inclusion of the term 'on the basis of'—to the exclusion of other proposed wordings, such as 'taking into account'—was a key component in this respect.

Referring to subsequent state practice in the application of Article 76, it is too early to entertain a sufficiently reasoned opinion about how the States Parties understand the term. A strong argument for holding that 'on the basis of' does not imply any margin of discretion for the coastal state, however, is, in my view, the weight of the other protection-worthy interests in light of the object and purpose of the LOS Convention. A weighty argument in favour of strict consistence is also the Commission's 'control function' on behalf of third states. A further key point is that the Commission, through its recommendations, contributes to equal treatment and consistency in the application of Article 76.

A contextual understanding of the term 'on the basis of' also pulls in the direction that the coastal state should not have any margin of appreciation. In case of disagreement with the Commission's recommendations, what is prescribed is a procedure of returning submissions—not that the dissenting coastal state shall proceed to fix the outer limit by reference to any 'margin of discretion'. Thus, in my opinion, the most weighty arguments indicate that a coastal state wishing 'final and binding' outer limits within the context of Article 76, paragraph 8, must establish the outer limits exactly where the Commission recommends.

3.5.2   Value of the Commission's Recommendations as a Means of Interpretation
3.5.2.1   Introduction
In the previous section the legal effects of the Commission's recommendations were analysed in light of the criterion 'on the basis of'. It was concluded that the provision of Article 76, paragraph 8, of the LOS Convention provides

that the coastal state must establish the outer limits in consistency with the Commission's recommendations if these outer limits are to be legally 'final and binding'. However, the legal status of the Commission's recommendations can be discussed in a broader perspective than solely with respect to examining the wording of the criterion 'on the basis of'. Regardless of whether the coastal state aims to establish the outer limits 'on the basis of' the Commission's recommendations, one may ask whether the Commission's recommendations are relevant for interpreting Article 76. To what extent shall coastal states—or for that matter, any others interpreting the LOS Convention—attach interpretative value to the Commission's recommendations on the basis of the general rules of treaty interpretation in international law?

The extent of interpretative value—*res interpretata*—of the Commission's recommendations can be approximated by examining the extent to which those who interpret Article 76 actually emphasize the Commission's recommendations as a means of interpretation. This will involve, *inter alia*, examining the extent to which the authority of the coastal state responsible for implementing Article 76 into national law has taken the Commission's recommendations into consideration when deciding how to interpret Article 76. Or one can examine the extent to which a national or international court has emphasized the Commission's recommendations in deciding how Article 76 should be interpreted.

The degree to which the Commission's recommendations have actually influenced the interpretative practice of national authorities, however, cannot be determined without undertaking thorough empirical research involving interviews with relevant actors or surveys of relevant national preparatory works. The constraints of the present study have not allowed this. Moreover, we recall that as of 1 January 2014, only four coastal states have established the outer limits beyond 200 nautical miles in their national legislation—an empirical basis too thin to allow anything but rudimentary conclusions based on state practices.

Investigating the recommendation's significance as a means of interpretation in court proceedings—at the national as well as the international level— throws up a problem of a different character. As far as is known, no national court has been asked to question the interpretation of Article 76. And at the time of the verdict in the ITLOS case *Bay of Bengal,* the Commission had yet to issue recommendations to the coastal states involved. The question of how Article 76 should be interpreted in that situation thus had to be solved without any interpretive aid from the Commission's recommendations.[173]

---

173   It is remarkable, however, the extent to which the ITLOS referred to the Commission throughout its judgment. Fundamentally, the Tribunal recognized that 'the Commission

An examination of the Commission's recommendations as a means of interpretation *in light of the rules on treaty interpretation in international law* is, however, independent of the extent to which the recommendations *de facto* influence those who interpret Article 76—be they a legal scholar, a judge, representatives of the coastal state, etc. The rules on treaty interpretation apply to all and sundry; it is therefore a question of principle how much weight the Commission's recommendations should or should not be accorded in the interpretation of Article 76. The question in the remainder of this section is therefore to what extent the Commission's recommendations fit into the 'traditional' sources of international law for the purposes of treaty interpretation. The starting point for the discussion is necessarily the general rules on treaty interpretation in the Vienna Convention.

3.5.2.2   Subsequent Practice in the Application of the LOS Convention

Article 31 of the Vienna Convention specifies the interpretation elements that *shall* be taken into account in the interpretation of treaties—and here, practices and decisions of international institutions are not explicitly mentioned among the mandatory means of interpretation. Article 31, paragraph 3 (*litra* b), of the Vienna Convention determines, however, that account shall be taken, together with the context, of 'any subsequent practice in the application of the treaty which establishes the agreement of the parties regarding its interpretation'. The starting point is thus that any practice that relates to 'the application of the treaty' and 'which establishes the agreement of the parties regarding its interpretation' is relevant as means of interpretation. Therefore, the Vienna

---

plays an important role under the Convention' (Judgment, para. 375). Furthermore, in asserting the meaning of 'natural prolongation', the ITLOS made specific reference to the Commission's Scientific and Technical Guidelines (Judgment, para. 438). The Tribunal also referred to the submissions to the Commission of both Bangladesh and Myanmar in asserting the facts of the case (Judgment, para. 449). As we have seen previously, the ITLOS also used the Commission's procedural rules as an argument for continuing the delimitation of the continental shelf beyond 200 nautical miles (Judgment, para. 390). Thus, the Tribunal did not only refer to the Commission regarding scientific and technical issues arising in the implementation of Article 76. It is therefore also idle to speculate on the extent to which the ITLOS would have relied on the recommendations of the Commission if these had already been adopted at the time of the judgment. Notably, when the Tribunal found support for its interpretation of 'natural prolongation' with reference to the test of appurtenance in the Scientific and Technical Guidelines of the Commission, it is likely that the ITLOS also would have drawn on the Commission's recommendations since it then would have had access to how the Commission had interpreted and applied Article 76 to the matter at hand.

Convention gives subsequent practice a substantive place in the ascertainment of the ordinary and natural meaning, insofar as it states that such practice is to be taken into account in establishing such meaning.[174] The question is, however, whether the Commission's practice can be understood as subsequent practice under Article 31, paragraph 3 (*litra* b), of the Vienna Convention.

Article 31, paragraph 3 (*litra* b), does not explicitly state *whose* practice is to be taken into account. Basically, 'any subsequent practice' is relevant. The Commission's practice by way of recommendations *could* thus also constitute 'relevant practices' in the terms of Article 31.

The mere existence of a practice is nevertheless not sufficient. The second requirement is that the subsequent practice must be attributable to the 'parties', i.e. the States Parties to the LOS Convention. The Commission's practice by way of its recommendations must therefore also be an expression of state practice if it is to be relevant as a means of interpretation under this rule. This is consistent with the idea that the concordant practice of the *parties* is a good evidence of the correct interpretation of the treaty in question.[175]

We cannot conclude that the Commission's recommendations as such should be considered as the practice of the *parties*. It is the Commission, not the states, that adopts recommendations on the outer limits of the continental shelf. There is thus a fundamental difference between subsequent practice originating directly from states and practice originating with the Commission.[176] What remains debatable is whether states may use the

---

174   Amerasinghe, 'Interpretation of Texts in Open International Organizations', p. 198.

175   Gardiner, *Treaty Interpretation*, p. 225.

176   Concerning the interpretation by human rights treaty bodies, however, the ILA Committee on International Human Rights Law and Practice has remarked that the 'reference in Article 31 to subsequent practice—as with so many other provisions in the [Vienna Convention]—is written as if no monitoring body had been established by a treaty, as if no third-party interests existed, and as if it were only for other States to monitor each other's compliance and to react to non-compliance. Human rights treaties *do* differ in some important respects from the presumed ideal type of a multilateral treaty that underpins the formulation of the individual provisions of the [Vienna Convention]. Given these differences, it appears arguable that in interpreting these types of treaties (with third-party beneficiaries and an independent monitoring mechanism), relevant subsequent practice might be broader than subsequent *State* practice and include the considered views of the treaty bodies adopted in the performance of the functions conferred on them by the States parties' (see Report of the Berlin Conference, 2004, p. 629. Available at www.ila-hq.org/. Accessed 1 January 2014). Justifying that decisions of human rights treaty bodies are relevant subsequent practice, the Committee further remarked that 'the general comments and general recommendations of the treaty bodies are circulated to all States parties following their adoption, generally in the form of the

recommendations of the Commission to express their opinion about the interpretation of Article 76, and that the Commission's recommendations should therefore be seen as representing 'the agreement of the parties'. In that case, the interpretation adopted by the Commission in its recommendations must be taken into account in the interpretation of the LOS Convention according to Article 31, paragraph 3 (*litra* b), of the Vienna Convention.

Attribution of the Commission's practice to the LOS Convention's States Parties may be considered controversial, for at least two reasons.[177] Firstly, if we view the Commission's practice as an expression of the 'agreement of the parties', the implication would be—as mentioned—that the Commission's recommendations under Article 31, paragraph 3 (*litra* b), 'shall' (i.e. must) be taken into account as a means of interpretation of the LOS Convention. In reality, this would represent a partial circumvention of the non-binding status of the recommendations, and thus also of the substantive provisions of the LOS Convention. True, the States Parties to the LOS Convention have agreed to the mechanisms of decision-making by the Commission—but they have not committed themselves to an *obligation* to take account of the content of specific recommendations. In this context, we should note that with regard to human

---

annual report of the committee concerned to the General Assembly or to the Economic and Social Council. States have the opportunity to express their views on the correctness of the interpretations at that stage, as well as in their reports under the treaty and in their discussions with the committees during the consideration of those reports. Some States parties have occasionally expressed their disagreement with general comments adopted by the Human Rights Committee, for example the *General comment* relating to the right to life on the possession of nuclear weapons, and its *General comment* on reservations [...] so one could argue that the acquiescence of States parties in those statements could be seen as establishing the agreement of the parties on the interpretation of those provisions' (*ibid.*). See also Hall, Christopher Keith, 'The Duty of States Parties to the Convention against Torture to Provide Procedures Permitting Victims to Recover Reparations for Torture Committed Abroad', in *The European Journal of International Law*, Vol. 18, 2007, pp. 921–937; and Mechlem, Kerstin, 'Treaty Bodies and the Interpretation of Human Rights', in *Vanderbilt Journal of Transnational Law*, 2009, Vol. 42, pp. 905–947, at p. 920ff (arguing that treaty bodies are the main interpreters of human rights treaties and the principal generators of 'subsequent practice' in the sense of Article 31, para. 3 (*litra* b), of the Vienna Convention, and that it would be inappropriate to limit 'practice' to subsequent *state* practice alone).

177 On the subsequent practice argument in respect of international institutions, see generally Alvarez, J.E., 'Constitutional Interpretation in International Organizations', in Coicaud, Jean-Marc, and Veijo Heiskanen (eds), *The Legitimacy of International Organizations* (UN University Press, 2001), pp. 104–154, at pp. 117ff.

rights treaty bodies, it has been argued that caution should be exercised in identifying their practice as 'agreement of the parties'.[178]

One thing, however, is that one 'shall' take into account the Commission's practice as a means of interpretation in the light of the rules of treaty interpretation. But, according to Article 31, paragraph 1, of the Vienna Convention, the starting point for understanding Article 76 is still to be taken in the wording, context and object and purpose. Taking into account the Commission's recommendations as a means of interpretation does not mean that the recommendations are transformed from being recommendatory into being binding: the recommendations only become one of the means to which the treaty interpreter must have recourse in interpreting Article 76.

Secondly—and this I consider a stronger argument against allowing Article 31, paragraph 3 (*litra* b), to apply—the Commission's composition and independence from states suggest that the Commission's practice should not be attributable to the state parties. The Commission adopts its recommendations beyond the control of states. Twenty-one experts serve on the Commission.[179] They are nominated, elected and have their salaries and other expenses paid by the nominating states.[180] However, the Commission members are not government representatives: Article 2 of Annex II to the LOS Convention specifies that they are to serve in their 'personal capacity'. States have no formal authority to instruct either the Commission in plenary or individual Commission members.

The Commission's composition and independence stand in sharp contrast to 'political' international institutions composed of government representatives, like the UNGA or indeed bodies such as the Meeting of States Parties to the LOS Convention. When these organs hammer out decisions, these decisions can be seen as expressions of 'the agreement of the parties regarding [their respective treaties'] interpretation'—because states are represented in such institutions, and states are directly involved in the forging of decisions through voting, often on how a treaty should be interpreted.

An example from section 3.3.3 may serve to illustrate the difference (though this is not related directly to the Commission's recommendations). When the Meeting of States Parties adopted an interpretation of the 10-year deadline

---

178   Van Alebeek, Rosanne, and André Nollkaemper, 'The Legal Status of Decisions by Human Rights Treaty Bodies in National Law', in Keller, Helen, and Geir Ulfstein (eds), *UN Human Rights Treaty Bodies—Law and Legitimacy* (Cambridge University Press, 2012), pp. 356–413, at p. 409.

179   Article 2 of Annex II to the LOS Convention.

180   *Ibid.*

under Article 4 of Annex II to the LOS Convention, it resembled to a far greater degree 'subsequent practice in the application of the treaty which establishes the agreement of the parties regarding its interpretation' than when the Commission through its Rules of Procedure adopted *de facto* amendments to the deadline prescribed by Article 4 of Annex II. The practice of the Meeting of States Parties may be relevant as a means of interpretation under Article 31, paragraph 3 (*litra* b)—but probably without any significance because of the clear wording of Article 4. On the other hand, the Commission's practice—here in the form of its Rules of Procedure—can hardly be said to be an expression of any 'agreement of the parties regarding [the LOS Convention's] interpretation', without firm evidence to indicate that the rules were a direct result of the will of states.

It has also been the attitude of the ICJ in several decisions—both before and after the Vienna Convention codified the rules on treaty interpretation in 1969—that the practice of international institutions consisting of government representatives may constitute an interpretive factor together with the context, if the wording does not give a firm answer. For instance, in the Advisory Opinion of the ICJ in *Competence of the General Assembly Regarding Admission to the United Nations,* the Court—albeit only in an *obiter dicta*—felt satisfied with its conclusion in the fact that 'the organs to which Article 4 entrusts the judgment of the Organization have consistently interpreted the text' in the manner which the Court had concluded was the proper interpretation.[181] In the Advisory Opinion *Certain Expenses of the United Nations,* the ICJ accepted this dictum as authority for reasoning that subsequent practice was to be equated with a practice pursued by the organs of the UN.[182] And in the Advisory Opinion in *Legal Consequences for States of the Continued Presence of South Africa in Namibia (South West Africa) Notwithstanding Security Council Resolution 276 (1970),* the ICJ held that 'the proceedings of the Security Council extending over a long period supply abundant evidence that presidential rulings and the positions taken by members of the Council, in particular its permanent members, have consistently and uniformly interpreted the practice of voluntary abstention by a permanent member as not constituting a bar to the adoption of resolutions [...].'[183] Moreover, even in cases where the application of the treaty is performed by institutions consisting of States Parties, the question arises whether states that were outvoted in the organs

---

181   *I.C.J. Reports* 1950, p. 4, at p. 9.
182   *I.C.J. Reports* 1962, p. 151. See dissenting opinion of Judge Spender, *ibid.,* p. 194.
183   *I.C.J. Reports* 1971, p. 16, at p. 22 (para. 22).

concerned remain bound by the practice as an expression of how a treaty is to be interpreted.[184]

Conversely, there is to my knowledge no case law indicating that the practice of independent expert bodies—such as the Commission—has been understood as an interpretive element in the framework of Article 31, paragraph 3 (*litra* b), of the Vienna Convention. This is in line with the argument above, that there should be strong evidence that the practices of the institution actually represent the will of state—hereunder that states have formal opportunity to influence the outcome of the institution's decisions, and actually make use of this opportunity. Therefore we must conclude that the Commission's recommendations cannot be considered 'subsequent practice' in the application of the LOS Convention establishing the agreement of the States Parties regarding interpretation of the Convention.

3.5.2.3   Object and Purpose

Although our conclusion means that the Commission's recommendations cannot be seen as an expression of the parties' practice—and thus be given significance as a means of interpretation under the narrow definition of Article 31, paragraph 3 (*litra* b)—we still need to decide whether we should emphasize the Commission's practices in order to promote the objectives of the LOS Convention, i.e. the intention of the parties in establishing the Commission with its exclusive competence to make recommendations to coastal states concerning the establishment of the outer limits of the continental shelf beyond 200 nautical miles. Such a 'purposive' interpretation would be consistent with Article 31, paragraph 1, of the Vienna Convention, according to which a treaty is to be interpreted in light of its 'object and purpose'.[185]

Here we should note that the ICJ has not always found it necessary to discuss the relationship between state practice and a treaty body's practice in order to ascribe emphasis to the latter's practice as a means of interpretation. In the Advisory Opinion *Legal Consequences of the Construction of a Wall in the Occupied Palestinian Territory,* the ICJ found that the construction of a wall being built by Israel in the Occupied Palestinian Territory, including in and around East Jerusalem, and its associated regime, was contrary to

---

184   Crawford, James, *Brownlie's Principles of Public International Law* (Oxford University Press, 2012), p. 382. See also Amerasinghe, 'Interpretation of Texts in Open International Organizations', p. 200.

185   Ulfstein, Geir, 'Den rettslige betydningen av avgjørelser fra menneskerettslige konvensjonsorganer', in *Lov og Rett*, Vol. 51, 2012, pp. 552–570, at p. 554.

international law.[186] A key question in the case was whether the International Covenant on Civil and Political Rights (ICCPR) was applicable in the Occupied Palestinian Territory.[187] Article 2 of the ICCPR concerns the Covenant's scope of application, and the Court had to determine whether this provision was to be interpreted as covering only individuals who are both present within a state's territory and subject to the jurisdiction of that state, or if it should be construed as covering individuals present within a state's territory and also those outside that territory but subject to that state's jurisdiction.[188] The Court concluded that the ICCPR was applicable also in respect of acts done by a state in the exercise of its jurisdiction outside its own territory.[189]

In reaching this conclusion, the Court started out by emphasizing that 'it would seem natural' that States Parties to the ICCPR should be bound to comply with its provisions also when the jurisdiction of states is being exercised outside the national territory.[190] The ICJ also referred to the practice of the Human Rights Committee (HRC), the body of independent experts that monitors implementation of the ICCPR:

> The constant practice of the Human Rights Committee is consistent with this [conclusion]. Thus, the Committee has found the Covenant applicable where the State exercises its jurisdiction on foreign territory. It has ruled on the legality of acts by Uruguay in cases of arrest carried out by Uruguayan agents in Brazil or Argentina [...]. It decided to the same effect in the case of the confiscation of a passport by a Uruguayan consulate in Germany [...].[191]

It is not possible to infer anything from the judgment about *why* the Court believed that the practice of the HRC—here in the form of two 'Views'—had an impact on the interpretation of Article 2 of the ICCPR. The Court invoked no specific interpretation rule to substantiate why the Committee's practice

---

186   *I.C.J. Reports* 2004, p. 136.
187   Covenant adopted in New York on 16 December 1966; entered into force 23 March 1976. Published in *UNTS*, Vol. 99, p. 171 and Vol. 1057, p. 407.
188   Article 2, para. 1, of the ICCPR reads: 'Each State Party to the present Covenant undertakes to respect and to ensure to all individuals within its territory and subject to its jurisdiction the rights recognized in the present Covenant, without distinction of any kind, such as race, colour, sex, language, religion, political or other opinion, national or social origin, property, birth or other status'.
189   *I.C.J. Reports* 2004, p. 180 (para. 111).
190   *Ibid.*, p. 179 (para. 109).
191   *Ibid.*

was relevant. Nor is it possible to say anything about the weight attributed
to the HRC's practice in relation to the other interpretation factors that were
used, including the treaty's wording, considerations of object and purpose,
and the legislative history of the treaty.

The ICJ also applied the practice of the HRC (and the African Commission
on Human and Peoples' Rights: ACHPR) as a means of interpretation in the
2010 case *Ahmadou Sadio Diallo* .[192] Also here the ICJ found no reason to discuss the relationship between the treaty bodies' practices and states practices
aimed at applying Article 31, paragraph 3 (*litra* b), of the Vienna Convention.
However, what makes the *Diallo* case particularly interesting is that—unlike
the *Wall* case—the Court explained *why* it placed weight on the practices of
the treaty bodies as a means of interpretation, and also explained the *weight to
be attributed* to that practice as an interpretive factor in the interpretation of
the relevant treaties.

The *Diallo* case involved proceedings commenced against the Democratic
Republic of the Congo (DRC) by the Republic of Guinea relating to violations
of the rights of the Guinean businessman Ahmadou Sadio Diallo. Guinea had
alleged that the DRC committed serious violations of international law following the arrest, detention and expulsion of Mr Diallo from the DRC. The ICJ
found unanimously that, in respect of the circumstances in which Mr Diallo
was expelled from Congolese territory, the DRC violated Article 13 of the ICCPR
and Article 12, paragraph 4, of the African Charter on Human and Peoples'
Rights (African Charter),[193] each provision of which seeks to protect aliens or
non-nationals from arbitrary and unlawful expulsion.[194] The ICJ further unanimously found that the DRC had violated Article 9, paragraphs 1 and 2, of the
ICCPR, and Article 6 of the African Charter, both of which aim to protect the
right to liberty and security of a person, as a result of the circumstances under
which Mr Diallo was arrested and detained in 1995/1996. The ICJ thus con-

---

192   *I.C.J. Reports* 2010, p. 639.

193   African Charter on Human and Peoples' Rights adopted in Banjul on 27 June 1981; entered
      into force 21 October 1986. Published in *UNTS*, Vol. 1520, p. 217.

194   Article 13 of the ICCPR reads: 'An alien lawfully in the territory of a State party to the
      present Covenant may be expelled there from only in pursuance of a decision reached in
      accordance with law and shall, except where compelling reasons of national security
      otherwise require, be allowed to submit the reasons against his expulsion and to have his
      case reviewed by, and be represented for the purpose before, the competent authority or
      a person or persons especially designated by the competent authority'. Likewise, Article 12,
      para. 4, of the African Charter reads: 'A non-national legally admitted in a territory of a
      State party to the present Charter, may only be expelled from it by virtue of a decision
      taken in accordance with the law.' See *I.C.J. Reports* 2010, p. 639, at p. 663 (para. 64).

cluded that the DRC was obliged to make appropriate reparations in the form of compensation to the Republic of Guinea for its violations of these rules.

In examining the alleged violations of Article 13 of the ICCPR and Article 12, paragraph 4, of the African Charter, the ICJ started its interpretation by referring to 'the terms' of the two provisions.[195] It seems the use of the wording was sufficient to justify the Court's conclusion that a breach of the relevant human rights obligations had occurred. However, the ICJ also found reason to point out that its wording-based interpretation was

> fully corroborated by the jurisprudence of the Human Rights Committee established by the Covenant two ensure compliance with that instrument by the States parties [...].[196]

The Court also stressed that

> [s]ince it was created, the Human Rights Committee has built up a considerable body of interpretative case law, in particular through its findings in response to the individual communications which may be submitted to it in respect of States parties to the Optional Protocol, and in the form of its 'General Comments'.[197]

As mentioned, unlike in the *Wall* case, the ICJ found in the *Diallo* case reason to say something about *why* one should ascribe interpretive weight to the practices of the HRC and ACHPR in interpreting the ICCPR and the African Charter, and what *weight* such practice should be awarded as a means of interpretation:

> Although the Court is in no way obliged, in the exercise of its judicial functions, to model its own interpretation of the Covenant on that of the Committee, it believes that it should ascribe great weight to the interpretation adopted by this independent body that was established specifically two supervise the application of that treaty. The point here is to achieve the necessary clarity and the essential consistency of international law, as well as legal security, to which both the individuals with guaranteed rights and the States obliged to comply with treaty obligations are entitled.

---

195   *Ibid.*, p. 663 (para. 65).
196   *Ibid.*, para. 66.
197   *Ibid.*

Likewise, when the Court is called upon, as in these proceedings, to apply a regional instrument for the protection of human rights, it must take due account of the interpretation of that instrument adopted by the independent bodies which have been specifically created, if such has been the case, to monitor the sound application of the treaty in question.[198]

First, we should note that the ICJ considers that it in its interpretation of the ICCPR should ascribe 'great weight' to the practice of the HRC. The Court refers both to the 'General Comments' of the HRC and findings in response to individual communications.[199] The ICJ also states that one should 'take due account' of the practice of the ACPHR, in that regard, referring *inter alia,* to the case *Kenneth Good v. Republic of Botswana.*[200] The ICJ does not explain why the practice of the HRC deserves to be given 'great weight' while the practices of the ACHPR shall only be taken 'due account' of, beside noting that the latter practice relates to a 'regional instrument'. Still, the most noteworthy thing about the ruling is that the Court believes it should ascribe 'great weight' to the interpretation adopted by the HRC.

Second, as mentioned, in *Diallo* the ICJ does not discuss the relationship between treaty body practices and state practices, and whether the former can be seen as the 'subsequent practice [...] establishing the agreement of the parties regarding its interpretation' within the framework of Article 31, paragraph 3 (*litra* b), of the Vienna Convention. The Court cites, however, the parties' intention in creating the said treaty bodies: they were established specifically in order to supervise the application of their respective treaties. Therefore—according to the ICJ—by emphasizing the treaty bodies' practice one can ensure 'the necessary clarity', 'the essential consistency' and 'legal security' in the application of the treaty provisions. Thus, without any explicit reference to rules of interpretation, the Court's explanation for stressing the treaty bodies' practice seems to be rooted in the parties' intentions in creating the HRC and the ACPHR, i.e. purposive considerations in accordance with Article 31, paragraph 1, of the Vienna Convention, according to which a treaty shall be interpreted in light of its object and purpose.[201]

---

198   *Ibid.,* p. 664 (paras. 66–67).

199   *Ibid.,* para. 66.

200   *Ibid.,* para. 67.

201   Ulfstein, Geir, 'Individual Complaints', in Keller, Helen, and Geir Ulfstein (eds), *UN Human Rights Treaty Bodies—Law and Legitimacy,* pp. 73–115, at p. 98. See also Ulfstein, 'Den rettslige betydningen av avgjørelser fra menneskerettslige konvensjonsorganer', p. 554.

In light of the *Diallo* case, the central question thus becomes whether, in interpreting Article 76, one should take into consideration the Commission's recommendations as a means of interpretation because in so doing one would promote the states' intention in creating the Commission. Or put differently: would the intent of the states in creating the Commission not be undermined if the recommendations were *not* taken into account in interpreting Article 76?

According to Article 3 of Annex II to the LOS Convention, the Commission shall make recommendations to coastal states 'in accordance with article 76 and the Statement of Understanding adopted on 29 August 1980 by the Third United Nations Conference on the Law of the Sea.' One of the purposes of establishing the Commission was therefore for it to submit recommendations to coastal states. Obviously, if coastal states do not heed these recommendations, this function of the Commission would be superfluous. Conversely, if states emphasize the Commission's recommendations in interpreting Article 76, that will serve to promote the parties' intentions in creating the Commission.

That putting emphasis on the Commission's practice as a means of interpretation can be justified on the basis of an interpretation based on object and purpose in accordance with Article 31, paragraph 1, of the Vienna Convention, was also the starting point for the ICJ with regard to the HRC and the ACPHR in the *Diallo* case. It was the treaty bodies' function and purpose in creating these that led the ICJ to underscore the institutional practices as interpretive elements. More precisely, the reasoning of the Court was that the HRC and the ACHPR had been created in order to 'supervise' their respective treaties, and emphasizing their practices would help ensure the 'necessary clarity', the 'essential consistency' and 'legal security' to which states and individuals are entitled.[202]

A similar approach could be used with respect to the Commission's recommendations. The conclusion to be drawn thus far is therefore that by putting emphasis on the Commission's recommendations, one helps promote the parties' intentions in creating the Commission. This is in accordance with Article 31, paragraph 1, of the Vienna Convention, according to which the wording of a treaty shall be interpreted in light of its object and purpose.

Let us turn now to the question of how much weight one should place on the Commission's recommendations as a means of interpretation. In *Diallo*, the Court concluded that 'great weight' should be given to the HRC's practice—a strong statement. However, in order to produce an interpretive outcome that can effectively promote the purpose of the Commission's existence, there are

---

202   See *I.C.J. Reports* 2010, p. 639, at p. 664 (para. 66).

good reasons for placing at least as much weight on the Commission's practice as an interpretive factor in the interpretation of Article 76.

Now while we could cite the composition of the Commission as a reason for *not* putting so much emphasis on its practice as a means of interpretation—there being no requirements as to formal legal qualifications as the Commission is constituted purely as a scientific body—its composition is not of interest in light of an interpretation based on the parties' intention in creating it. It is the Commission's *function* that should determine the weight its recommendations are accorded as regards interpretation.

In *Diallo,* the ICJ did not refer to the formal qualifications of the members of either the HRC or the ACHPR. It was the treaty bodies' function that was cited as justifying the weight of their decisions, not their members' professional qualifications. Of course, the judges may have had in mind the composition of these treaty bodies in delivering their judgement. In the ICCPR, for example, there is an explicit requirement that the HRC shall consist of highly qualified lawyers.[203] Therefore, it must be assumed, the members of the HRC, besides specializing in human rights, will be cognizant of the rules of general treaty interpretation. The composition of the HRC resembles that of an international court, as was presumably known to the ICJ judges. The point here, however, is that there is nothing in the judgment to indicate that the formal background of the HRC's members had anything to do with why the Committee's practice should be accorded great weight in the interpretation of the ICCPR. The focus was on *why* states had created these organs. The same reasoning should apply, in my view, in relation to the Commission, in determining the weight to accord to its practice as a means of interpretation.

One specific argument in favour of giving the Commission's recommendations weight as a means of interpretation in the light of purposive considerations is the need for uniform application of the rules of Article 76. Such a goal is not explicitly expressed in the LOS Convention, but, as I have argued above, the states' purpose in creating the Commission was also to ensure uniform treatment of all continental shelf claims. Here reference may also be made to the *Diallo* case and the statement relating to considerations of 'consistency' in the interpretation and application of international law.

By emphasizing the Commission's practice, states could help facilitate a practice of equal treatment with respect to continental shelf submissions. This is because the Commission shall consider *all* submissions regarding continental

---

203   Article 28, para. 2, of the ICCPR.

shelf limits beyond 200 nautical miles.[204] In order for the Commission's practice to serve as an efficient mechanism for establishing a common standard for all outer limits, however, the Commission must act consistently from case to case. But if we assume the Commission does that, then giving weight to its practices as an interpretive factor will certainly help promote the objective that Article 76's concepts shall be given an autonomous meaning, which in turn will help ensure a consistent global standard in the implementation of the content of Article 76.

There is another reason why considerable weight should be given to the Commission's recommendations as an interpretive factor, and that is because the Commission has been given a central role as a treaty interpreter in the application of Article 76. Purposive considerations in accordance with Article 31, paragraph 1, of the Vienna Convention, then, mean that this role should be promoted by stressing the Commission's recommendations in the interpretation of Article 76.

The Commission's role as a treaty interpreter is specified in the provision governing the Commission's basic functions—Article 3 of Annex II to the LOS Convention: the function of the Commission is to 'make recommendations *in accordance with article 76* and the Statement of Understanding adopted on 29 August 1980 by the Third United Nations Conference on the Law of the Sea' (emphasis added). The states' intention here is that when the Commission adopts recommendations, the content of these recommendations accords with Article 76. In other words, there is a clear assumption that the Commission's recommendations are correct. This perception finds support in Article 76, paragraph 8, of the LOS Convention: *only* those outer limits that have been established on the basis of the Commission's recommendations will become legally final and binding.

These provisions say something about the role states have accorded the Commission under the LOS Convention. The Commission was not created solely in order to make vague indications or give partially correct information with regard to the application of Article 76. The Commission's function is to inform coastal state exactly where the outer limits beyond 200 nautical miles shall lie; its recommendations shall thus be 'in accordance with article 76'. It can be argued that the Commission therefore—within the framework of the LOS Convention—has been given a vital role as the 'authoritative interpreter' of Article 76. Purpose considerations then strongly indicate support for this role by emphasizing the Commission's interpretations—that is, its

---

204   Article 4 of Annex to the LOS Convention provides that all states intending to establish the outer limits beyond 200 nautical miles *shall* make a submission to the Commission.

recommendations. Otherwise, the Commission's role under the Convention would be undermined, and thus also the intention of the parties.

The implication is, on the other hand, that a coastal state which interprets the LOS Convention *differently* from the Commission must present very good reasons for its dissenting opinion. For instance, the coastal state may argue that the Commission has interpreted a term of Article 76 contrary to what an ordinary and objective understanding of the term implies. Then the dissenting coastal state can find support for its conclusion by relying on that a treaty shall be interpreted in accordance with the ordinary meaning to be given to the terms (in accordance with Article 31, paragraph 1, of the Vienna Convention), instead of relying on the Commission's recommendations. So, even if the Commission's recommendations are to be attributed significant weight due to the role given to the Commission under Article 76, its recommendations will still just be one of several sources of interpretation. Thus also, other means of interpretation—individually or collectively—may override the content of the Commission's recommendations.

My conclusion, however—based on considerations of object and purpose in light of the role given to the Commission under the LOS Convention—is that its recommendations must be given significant weight as interpretive factors in assessing the meaning of Article 76.

3.5.2.4   Subsidiary or Supplementary Means of Interpretation

The question here is whether the Commission's recommendations constitute 'supplementary means of interpretation' within the meaning of Article 32 of the Vienna Convention. Article 32 mentions potential supplementary interpretative elements which the treaty interpreter may choose to emphasize in order to confirm the meaning resulting from the application of Article 31, or determine the meaning when the interpretation according to Article 31 leaves the meaning ambiguous or obscure, or leads to a result which is manifestly absurd or unreasonable. What is problematic here, however, is the meaning of the term 'supplementary'. The preparatory work of the treaty and the circumstances of its conclusion are explicitly mentioned as supplementary means. The only contextual hint as to what 'supplementary' entails, however, is the word 'including'. The question thus remains: Does 'including' mean that other supplementary means of interpretation must be similar to those explicitly mentioned in Article 32, that is, legislative history and the circumstances of the conclusion of the treaty? Or may the expert recommendations of the Commission be used as interpretive factors in order to confirm the meaning resulting from the application of Article 31, or to determine the meaning when the interpretation according to Article 31 leaves the meaning ambiguous or obscure, or leads to a result which is manifestly absurd or unreasonable?

The Commission's recommendations are obviously of another kind than the legislative history and the circumstances of the LOS Convention's conclusion. The interpretive principle *eiusdem generis*—that a rule is restricted to things of the same type as the listed items—therefore indicates that relevant means of interpretation in the meaning of Article 32 are factors connected to the creation of the LOS Convention, not to its practical application or implementation at a later stage. That would then exclude the Commission's recommendations as a potential means of interpretation under Article 32. However, the French text of the Vienna Convention—which, according to its Article 85, is equally authentic with the English text—seems to indicate that the legislative history and the circumstances of conclusion are explicitly mentioned in Article 32 merely because these are the most important or most obvious complementary interpretation elements, but not necessarily the only ones:

> Il peut être fait appel à des moyens complémentaires d'interprétation, et notamment aux travaux préparatoires et aux circonstances dans lesquelles le traité a été conclu [...].[205]

Earlier legal theory has argued that Article 32 of the Vienna Convention must be used with care—for example, Sinclair, who claimed that 'recourse is only permissible in carefully controlled circumstances'.[206] More recent legal theory, by contrast, argues that Article 32 should not be applied restrictively with regard to which means of interpretation may influence treaty interpretation. Villiger has claimed that 'it is difficult to imagine situations where the means of Article 32 may not be employed'.[207] Therefore I suggest that the list of factors mentioned in Article 32 is not exhaustive, and that the Commission's recommendations should not be excluded outright as a potentially relevant means of interpretation under this rule. But this discussion is clearly of less relevance since the conclusion in the previous section was that the Commission's recommendations—given the object and purpose in creating the Commission— are to be accorded significant weight in interpreting Article 76—referring to Article 31, paragraph 1, of the LOS Convention.

---

205 Gardiner, *Treaty Interpretation*, p. 311.

206 Sinclair, *The Vienna Convention on the Law of Treaties*, p. 142.

207 Villiger, M.E., *Commentary on the 1969 Vienna Convention on the Law of Treaties* (Martinus Nijhoff Publishers, 2009), p. 447. See also Gardiner, *Treaty Interpretation*, pp. 311–312.

3.5.3 Significance of the Commission's Recommendations for the Delimitation of the Outer Continental Shelf between States

3.5.3.1   Introduction

Within the context of the LOS Convention, the *delineation* of the outer limits of the continental shelf beyond 200 nautical miles is a process that involves only the coastal state, and which requires that state to comply with the procedural and substantive terms of Article 76. By contrast, the *delimitation* of overlapping continental shelf areas, involving two or more neighbouring states with opposite or adjacent coasts, is a different process: under Article 83, a delimitation agreement is required in order to achieve an 'equitable solution' on the basis of international law.

This distinction is expressed in Article 76, paragraph 10, of the LOS Convention: 'the provisions of this article are without prejudice to the question of delimitation of the continental shelf between areas with opposite or adjacent coasts.' Further, according to Article 9 of Annex II to the LOS Convention, '[t]he actions of the Commission shall not prejudice matters relating to delimitation of boundaries between States with opposite or adjacent coasts.'

The distinction between delineation and delimitation has also extensively been given consideration in the Commission's own procedural rules. Rule 46 of the Rules of Procedure states that 'in case there is a dispute in the delimitation of the continental shelf between opposite or adjacent States or in other cases of unresolved land or maritime disputes, submissions may be made and shall be considered in accordance with Annex I to these Rules.'[208] Annex I of the Rules of Procedure then imposes additional requirements on the coastal state.[209]

As we have seen previously, the Commission has thus indeed taken the Convention's 'non-prejudice' clause seriously and its Rules of Procedure require not only that the Commission be informed if the incoming submission deals with an area where there is a pending maritime boundary line, it is also so that the Commission cannot start to examine the submission unless all parties to the dispute agree to this. In addition, the Commission's sensitivity with

---

208   And in para. 2 of the same provision: 'The actions of the Commission shall not prejudice matters relating to the delimitation of boundaries between States.'

209   First, the state must inform the Commission that its submission concerns an area which is disputed by one or more third states (see Rule 2, *litra* a); second, the coastal state shall assure the Commission that its submission will not prejudice matters relating to the delimitation of boundaries between states (see Rule 2, *litra* b); and, third, all states that are parties to the dispute over the area must consent that the Commission shall consider the submission (see Rule 5, *litra* a).

regard to submissions relating to overlapping continental shelf areas has—
as also noted above—led to rules that invite coastal states to submit partial
submissions,[210] or joint submissions.[211]

Despite the sharp distinction between *delineation* and *delimitation* of the
outer continental shelf, there is a link between the legal title and delimitation. This was most recently affirmed by the ITLOS in the *Bay of Bengal* case
between Bangladesh and Myanmar. First the Tribunal noted:

> There is a clear distinction between the delimitation of the continen-
> tal shelf under Article 83 and the delineation of its outer limits under
> Article 76. Under the latter Article, the Commission is assigned the func-
> tion of making recommendations to coastal States on matters relating
> to the establishment of the outer limits of the continental shelf, but
> it does so without prejudice to delimitation of maritime boundaries.
> The function of settling disputes with respect to delimitation of mari-
> time boundaries is entrusted to dispute settlement procedures under
> Article 83 and Part XV of the Convention, which include international
> courts and tribunals.[212]

The ITLOS, however, also underscored the following point:

> Delimitation presupposes an area of overlapping entitlements. Therefore,
> the first step in any delimitation is to determine whether there are enti-
> tlements and whether they overlap.[213]

In the following, the issue is therefore if the Commission's recommendations
could or should affect the delimitation of the continental shelf beyond 200
nautical miles, even though the LOS Convention specifies that the actions
of the Commission shall not 'prejudice' matters relating to the delimitation
of boundaries between states. Specifically: whether and to what extent can
geological or geomorphological factors pertaining to the entitlement over
the outer continental shelf—confirmed through recommendations of the
Commission—play a role in determining what an 'equitable' delimitation is in
the context of Article 83 of the LOS Convention?

---

210 See Rule 3 of Annex I to the Rules of Procedure.
211 *Ibid.*, Rule 4.
212 Judgment para. 376.
213 *Ibid.*, para. 397.

3.5.3.2   Prospects for Maritime Delimitations beyond 200 Nautical Miles
At UNCLOS III, a list was prepared, anticipating that at least 33 countries had
potential delimitation lines beyond 200 nautical miles.[214] Prescott has made
a list that shows the existence of at least 29 potential boundary disputes pertaining to the continental shelf beyond 200 nautical miles.[215] However, as for
delimitation agreements already in effect relating to the continental shelf
beyond 200 nautical miles, the list is not that long: as yet, only a few maritime
delimitations beyond 200 nautical miles have been settled by agreement,[216]

---

214   UN Doc. A/CONF.62/C.2/L.98 and Add.1–3 ('Preliminary study illustrating various
       formulae for the definition of the continental shelf'). See also *Third United Nations
       Conference on the Law of the Sea, Official Records*, Vol. XI, p. 189.

215   Prescott, V., 'Natural Rights to Hydrocarbon Resources of the Continental Margin Beyond
       200 Nautical Miles', in Blake, G.H. (ed.), *Boundaries and Energy: Problems and Prospects*
       (Kluwer Law International, 1998), 1998, pp. 51–81, at p. 64.

216   The *Agreement on Maritime Delimitation between the Government of Australia and the
       Government of the French Republic* (adopted in Melbourne, 4 January 1982; entered into
       force 10 January 1983. Published in *ATS*, 1983, No. 3) established a delimitation line that
       extends beyond 200 nautical miles in the two seas. First, between Kerguelen Island
       (France) and McDonald and Heard Islands (Australia) in the Indian Ocean. The
       northeastern segment of the median line extends beyond 200 nautical miles and delimits
       a portion of the shelf on the so-called Kerguelen-Gaussberg Ridge. Second, the
       delimitation agreement concerns a shelf area beyond 200 nautical miles in the Coral Sea
       between New Caledonia (France) and Australia (see also Charney, J.I., and L.M. Alexander
       (eds), *International Maritime Boundaries* (Martinus Nijhoff Publishers, 1993), p. 905).
       Also the *Agreement between the Government of the United Kingdom of Great Britain and
       Northern Ireland and the Government of the Republic of Ireland Concerning the Delimitation
       of Areas of the Continental Shelf between the Two Countries* (adopted 7 November 1988;
       entered into force 11 January 1990. Reprinted in *Law of the Sea Bulletin*, No. 13, p. 48)
       delimits seabed areas beyond 200 nautical miles. One delimitation line lies between
       Ireland and Scotland, and relates to the areas of the Rockall Trough and the Hatton-
       Rockall Plateau. The second delimitation agreement delimits the continental shelf area
       beyond 200 nautical miles in the Celtic Sea (see also Charney, J.I., and L.M. Alexander
       (eds), *International Maritime Boundaries*, p. 1767). The *Treaty between the Republic of
       Trinidad and Tobago and the Republic of Venezuela on the Delimitation of Marine and
       Submarine Areas* (adopted 18 April 1990; entered into force 23 July 1991. Published in
       UNTS, Vol. 1654, p. 300) delimits the continental shelf in the Atlantic Ocean eastward in
       the area between the two states from the Serpent's Mouth. The easternmost section of the
       delimitation line extends beyond 200 nautical miles to the point the two states consider
       to be the outer limit of the continental shelf. Article II of the demarcation line agreement
       states that it may be relevant to share additional seabed areas between themselves in the
       future, to the extent that the delimitation line can be extended further 'in conformity
       with the provisions of International Law' (see also Charney, J.I., and L.M. Alexander (eds),

International Maritime Boundaries, p. 675). Also the USA and the former Soviet Union have delimited their maritime areas in the Bering Sea, the Arctic Ocean, the Pacific Ocean and the Chukchi Sea, by the *Agreement between the United States of America and the Union of Soviet Socialist Republics on the Maritime Boundary* (adopted in Washington, D.C., 1 June 1990. Not yet in force. Reprinted in *ILM*, Vol. 29, p. 942. See also Charney, J.I., and L.M. Alexander (eds), *International Maritime Boundaries*, p. 447). In the Arctic Ocean it is determined that the delimitation line is to follow a northbound meridian. Reference is made to the 1867 Convention under which Russia sold Alaska to the USA ((*Treaty concerning the Cession of the Russian Possessions in North America by his Majesty the Emperor of all the Russias to the United States of America*, Washington, D.C., 30 March 1867; entered into force 20 June 1867. Reprinted in Kemp, Roger L. (ed.), *Documents of American Democracy: A Collection of Essential Works* (McFarland, 2010), pp. 200ff)). Just how far north the delimitation agreement extends cannot be inferred from the wording, but Russia was using the delimitation line with the USA as the eastern maximum, all the way to the North Pole, in its continental shelf submission to the Commission in 2001, that is, far beyond 200 nautical miles. In addition, Russia and the USA have delimited seabed areas beyond 200 nautical miles in the central Bering Sea by the aforementioned 1867 Convention. And in June 2000, Mexico and the USA signed a demarcation line agreement, whereby parts of the seabed beyond 200 nautical miles in the Gulf of Mexico were delimited ((*Treaty Between the Government of the United States of America and the Government of the United Mexican States on the Delimitation of the Continental Shelf in the Western Gulf of Mexico Beyond 200 Nautical Miles*, Washington, D.C., 9 June 2000; entered into force 17 January 2001. Reprinted in *Senate Treaty Document 106–39, U.S. Senate, 106th Congress, 2d Session* (Washington, D.C.: U.S. Government Printing Office, 2000). See also Charney, J.I., and R. W. Smith (eds), *International Maritime Boundaries* (Martinus Nijhoff Publishers, 2002, p. 2619)). Even more recently, Norway and Russia signed a demarcation line agreement which delimited seabed areas beyond 200 nautical miles in the Barents Sea and the Arctic Ocean ((*Treaty between the Kingdom of Norway and the Russian Federation concerning Maritime Delimitation and Cooperation in the Barents Sea and the Arctic Ocean*, Murmansk, 15 September 2010; entered into force 7 July 2011. Reprinted in Henriksen, Tore, and Geir Ulfstein, 'Maritime Delimitation in the Arctic: The Barents Sea Treaty', in *Ocean Development & International Law*, Vol. 42, 2011, pp. 1–21. See also Jensen, Øystein, 'Treaty Between Norway and the Russian Federation concerning Maritime Delimitation and Cooperation in the Barents Sea and the Arctic Ocean', in *The International Journal of Marine and Coastal Law*, Vol. 26, 2011, pp. 151–168)). New Zealand and Australia have also delimited maritime boundaries beyond 200 nautical miles (see *Treaty between the Government of Australia and the Government of New Zealand establishing certain Exclusive Economic Zone and Continental Shelf Boundaries*, Adelaide, 25 July 2004; entered into force 25 January 2006. Published in *ATS*, 2006, p. 4). In addition, a provisional delimitation agreement pertaining to continental shelf areas beyond 200 nautical miles between Norway, Iceland and the Faroe Islands in respect of the overlapping claims to the extended continental shelf in the southern part of the Norwegian Sea must be mentioned (see Jensen, 'Towards Setting the Outer Limits of the Continental Shelf in the Arctic', in Vidas (ed.), *Law, Technology and Science for Oceans in Globalisation*, pp. 533–534).

and only one boundary case beyond 200 nautical miles has been settled by adjudication or arbitration.[217] As remarked by Anderson, however:

> The delimitation, as between neighboring states, of the continental shelf beyond 200 n.m. is a topic that will doubtless receive greater attention as the work of the Commission gathers momentum.[218]

And so it seems. To date, the area of outer continental shelf encompassed by the 70 submissions made to the Commission exceeds 25 million km^2.[219] Approximately 10% of that area is included in two or more submissions, which would indicate a sizeable potential for overlapping continental shelf claims beyond 200 nautical miles.[220]

3.5.3.3 The (Ir)relevance of Geological and Geomorphological Considerations in the Consolidated Law of Maritime Boundary Delimitation

International case law, led by the ICJ, has in recent decades helped clarify the difficult legal issues relating to the delimitation of overlapping continental shelf areas.[221] In short, court practice confirms a unified method. As the first step, a provisional equidistance-line is calculated as the mathematically most reasonable starting point, though without thereby implying a legal presumption in its favour. Second, it is assessed whether there are relevant factors entailing that the equidistance-line would lead to an inequitable result. For example, court practice has opened up for adjusting or moving the median line based on the conduct of the parties or in the case of great disparity in the coastal lengths of the parties. The relevant factors that might justify a departure from the median line are not restricted. The ICJ has applied a type of *equidistance-relevant factor* rule in order to achieve an equitable solution:

---

217   That is, the aforementioned *Bay of Bengal* case.
218   Anderson, David, 'Developments in Maritime Boundary Law and Practice', in Charney, J.I., David A. Colson, Lewis M. Alexander and Robert W. Smith (eds) *International Maritime Boundaries* (Martinus Nijhoff Publishers, 2005), pp. 3199–3222, at p. 3215.
219   Schoolmeester, Tina, and Elaine Baker (eds), 'Continental Shelf: The Last Maritime Zone' (UNEP/GRID-Arendal, 2009), p. 28. Available at: www.unep.org/dewa/pdf/AoA/Continental_Shelf.pdf (accessed 1 January 2014).
220   *Ibid.*
221   For a comprehensive survey, see Jiuyong, Shi, 'Maritime Delimitation in the Jurisprudence of the International Court of Justice', in *Chinese Journal of International Law*, Vol. 9, 2010, pp. 271–291.

Such a result may be achieved by first identifying the equidistance line, then correcting that line to take into account special circumstances or relevant factors.[222]

What, then, about the relevance of geological and/or geomorphological considerations to the bilateral delimitation of the continental shelf between neighbouring states? In the *North Sea Continental Shelf* cases, the ICJ considered the geological and geomorphological nature of the area under dispute, to establish whether there were any features dis-uniting the natural prolongation of the seabed. The ICJ held that potential discontinuities would be relevant to the delimitation of the continental shelf, but no such features were found:

[I]t can be useful to consider the geology of that shelf in order to find out whether the direction taken by certain configurational features should influence delimitation because, in certain localities, they point-up the whole notion of the appurtenance of the continental shelf to the State whose territory it does in fact prolong.[223]

In the *Tunisia–Libya* case the ICJ also stressed that

identification of natural prolongation may, where the geographical circumstances are appropriate, have an important role to play in defining an equitable delimitation, in view of its significance as the justification of continental shelf rights in some cases.[224]

Nevertheless, the parties' arguments that geological conditions on the seabed should have relevance for the delimitation of the seabed, were not given weight in this case. The problem was that such circumstances could not be easily proven, and were thus not deemed relevant to the delimitation issue.

Also, the relevance of geological facts to the purpose of maritime delimitation was seriously hampered by the development of exclusive economic zones from the mid-1970s onwards. In reality, a significant portion of the continental shelf concept was 'consumed', since coastal states were secured sovereign rights in the waters and on the seabed out to 200 nautical miles, regardless of

---

222 Speech by Judge Gilbert Guillaume, President of the ICJ, to the Sixth Committee of the UNGA on 31 October 2001. Available at: <www.icj-cij.org/court/index.php?pr=81&pt=3&p1=1&p2=3&p3=1&PHPSESSID=> (accessed 1 January 2014).

223 *I.C.J. Reports* 1969, p. 51, para. 95.

224 *I.C.J. Reports* 1982, p. 47, para. 44.

the nature of the seabed. Thus, the ICJ in the *Libya–Malta* case stated that the geological features of the seabed would be uninteresting for the delimitation of the continental shelf *within* 200 nautical miles:

> Since the development of the law enables a State to claim that the continental shelf appertaining to it extends up to as far as 200 miles from its coast, whatever the geological characteristics of the corresponding sea-bed and subsoil, there is no reason to ascribe any role to geological or geophysical factors within that distance either in verifying the legal title of the States concerned or in proceeding to a delimitation as between their claims. This is especially clear where verification of the validity of title is concerned, since, at least in so far as those areas are situated at a distance of under 200 miles from the coasts in question, title depends solely on the distance from coasts of the claimant States of any areas of sea-bed claimed by way of continental shelf, and the geological or geomorphological characteristics of those areas are completely immaterial. It follows that, since the distance between the coasts of the Parties is less than 400 miles, so that no geophysical feature can lie more than 200 miles from each coast, the feature referred to as the 'rift zone' cannot constitute a fundamental discontinuity terminating the southward extension of the Maltese shelf and the northward extension of the Libyan as if it were some natural boundary.[225]

The *Libya–Malta* case thus indicated that geological and geomorphological factors would have no significance in delimitation disputes. The situation was, and still is, that the vast majority of delimitation disputes relate to sea areas where the distance between the respective states' baselines is less than 400 nautical miles. Therefore, the relevance of geology and geomorphology seemed to be evaporating in the law of maritime boundary delimitation.

3.5.3.4   Re-Emergence of the Concept of Natural Prolongation and the Impact of the Commission's Recommendations

However, in no way did the *Libya–Malta* case deal the deathblow to geology and geomorphology as relevant factors in delimiting the continental shelf. What had led Highet to ask 'whatever became of natural prolongation?', was exactly that as long as delimitation disputes concerned only seabed areas within

---

225   *I.C.J. Reports* 1985, p. 35, para. 39.

200 nautical miles, there was no need for geological arguments.[226] Importantly, the ICJ in *Libya–Malta* did *not* reject the idea that geological features were relevant in the determination of what constituted an 'equitable solution' with respect to potential delimitations *beyond* 200 nautical miles from the baselines.

And if the rules on exclusive economic zones prevented the relevance of geology and geomorphology for the purpose of maritime delimitation in several previous decades, the implementation of Article 76 has now brought the concept of natural prolongation back again. Article 76 obliges coastal states to make submissions if they intend to establish the outer limits of their continental shelf beyond 200 nautical miles, which in turn has the consequence of forcing potential maritime delimitation disputes on the 'outer' continental shelf to the surface. The issue of whether geological or geomorphological features may have any place in the mix of what case law refers to as 'relevant factors' has again become relevant. But the implementation of Article 76—including the Commission's recommendations—also brings something completely new: We now have a detailed treaty provision which states which geological or geomorphological factors are legally relevant to the coastal state's title to the seabed, and there is a Commission to verify the existence—and relevance—of such factors.

Thus we must ask: Will not factors such as the location of the foot of the slope or the depths of sediments be relevant as regards where the delimitation line should lie—similar to, for instance, how a state's coastal length could form the basis for adjusting the position of the equidistance-line to achieve an 'equitable solution' within the meaning of Article 83 of the LOS Convention?

Three examples—all inspired by the work of Colson—shall here serve to illustrate how the Commission's recommendations could affect maritime delimitation of the continental shelf beyond 200 nautical miles.[227] The first example shows how the Commission could impact future delimitation negotiations. Two other examples illustrate how the Commission's recommendations may lead to geological or geomorphological factors being introduced that

---

226   Highet, Keith, 'Whatever became of natural prolongation', in Dallmeyer, Dorinda, and Louis De Vorsey (eds), *Rights to Oceanic Resources: Deciding and Drawing Maritime Boundaries* (Martinus Nijhoff Publishers, 1989), pp. 87–100.

227   See Colson, David A., 'Delimitation of the Outer Continental Shelf Between States with Opposite or Adjacent Coasts', in Nordquist, Myron H., John N. Moore and Tomas H. Heidar (eds), *Legal and Scientific Aspects of Continentals Shelf Limits*, pp. 287–297, at. pp. 292–293, and Colson, David, 'The Delimitation of the Outer Continental Shelf Between Neighboring States', in *American Journal of International Law*, Vol. 97, 2003, pp. 91–107, at p. 103.

could affect the decisions of a court or tribunal with regard to what constitutes an 'equitable solution' in the context of Article 83.

In example 1, let us imagine two states located 600 nautical miles opposite each other. States X and Y each have proclaimed their exclusive economic zones of 200 nautical miles, so that an outer continental shelf area of equivalent size lies between them. States X and Y make their submissions to the Commission. The Commission finds that the continental shelf of state Y plunges down to the deep ocean floor only 50 nautical miles off its coast. The continental shelf of state X, on the other hand, proves to extend beyond its 200 nautical mile limit, all the way under the 200 nautical mile intersection, intruding even into the 200 nautical mile zone of state Y. In this situation, the Commission will recommend that the continental shelf of state Y should cover the seabed only out to 200 nautical miles. Because of the discontinuity in the natural prolongation 50 nautical miles from the coast, state Y could not claim any part of the outer continental shelf in the intersection between the two states. Geological and geomorphological conditions on the seabed—as confirmed through the Commission's recommendations—provide state X with firm grounds for claiming that the main condition of natural prolongation effectively hinders any continental shelf claim of state Y beyond 200 nautical miles.

In example 2, let us once again imagine two coastal states located 600 nautical miles opposite each other. State X and state Y have both proclaimed exclusive economic zones of 200 nautical miles. According to the criteria in Article 76, it can firmly be concluded that the foot of the continental slope lies everywhere beyond the 200 nautical mile strip in the middle. Therefore, the Commission recommends that the outer edge of the continental margin of the two states should lie completely beyond the disputed area: in other words, that the entire seabed area beyond 200 nautical miles from each state forms part of the submerged prolongation of each state's landmasses and is legally 'continental shelf'. If we assume no other relevant factors affect the delimitation, a plausible result would be that an equidistance line should apply as the 'equitable solution'. The Commission's role here can be summarized as follows: It confirms that the seabed beyond 200 nautical miles is legal continental shelf, and it confirms that all of the continental shelf area between the two states' exclusive economic zones is a continuous continental margin. All other things being equal, it can be argued that the Commission through its recommendations— albeit without saying anything explicitly about delimitation—has cleared the ground for arguing that a court or tribunal should delimit the outer continental shelf between state X and Y in two equal parts.

A relevant example that illustrates precisely this situation can be found in the Commission's recommendations to Norway related to the 'Loophole' area in the central part of the Barents Sea. The Loophole is a shallow-water shelf area located north of mainland Norway and Russia. Based on regional considerations and the technical and scientific information contained in Norway's submission of 2006, the Commission considered the Loophole to lie totally landward of any foot of the continental slope associated with the continental margins of Norway and Russia. Accordingly, the foot of the slope was deemed to lie beyond the Loophole, and the Commission supported the conclusion set forth in the Norwegian submission: that all the area in question was, without doubt, part of the continental margin, and therefore also legally continental shelf. On this basis, the outer edge of the continental margin was considered to lie completely beyond the Loophole area, so that the entire Loophole formed part of the submerged prolongation of the landmasses of mainland Norway (and Svalbard), in accordance with Article 76 of the LOS Convention. With regard to the delineation of the outer limits of the continental shelf—especially taking into consideration the constraint criteria in Article 76, paragraph 5, of the LOS Convention—the Commission thus agreed with Norway's application of the 'depth constraint' rule, according to which the entire Loophole is to be seen as situated landward of the 2,500 metre isobath. Thus also the entire area of the seabed and subsoil of the Barents Sea that lies beyond 200 nautical miles from the baselines of Norway—the Loophole—was considered by the Commission to be part of the continental margin.

Whether the Commission's recommendations had any significance for the 2010 delimitation agreement between Norway and Russia in the Barents Sea and the Arctic Ocean is not known.[228] However, it is not inconceivable that the Commission's recommendations to Norway contributed to a determination in the then ongoing bilateral delimitation negotiations between Norway and Russia as to which 'relevant circumstances' should affect the adjustment of the delimitation line. Keeping the Commission's recommendations in mind, the two states could perhaps forget about the relevance of any geological or geomorphological circumstances and with greater certainty focus on other factors of relevance for shifting the median line westwards or eastwards.[229]

---

228   Summary of recommendations to Norway, p. 7. Available at the website of the Commission: <www.un.org/Depts/los/clcs_new/submissions_files/nor06/nor_rec_summ.pdf> (accessed 1 January 2014).

229   On the agreement, see Henriksen and Ulfstein, 'Maritime Delimitation in the Arctic: The Barents Sea Treaty', and Jensen, 'Treaty between Norway and the Russian Federation concerning Maritime Delimitation and Cooperation in the Barents Sea and the Arctic Ocean'.

In the last example (see Figure 3.4), state X and state Y lie 500 nautical miles opposite each other. The two states have proclaimed exclusive economic zones of 200 nautical miles, leaving an intersection of 100 nautical miles of outer continental shelf between them. Let us assume that both states make their submissions to the Commission, which recommends the following: The foot of the continental slope of state X is located 240 nautical miles from the baselines of state X, that is, at the continental shelf in the intersection subject to delimitation. The foot of the continental slope of state Y, on the other hand, lies only 190 nautical miles from the baselines of state Y, that is, landward of the outer limit of the 200 nautical mile exclusive economic zone.

All else being equal, what would be an 'equitable' delimitation line in this case? A median line measured from the baselines of both states? Or a median line measured from the respective states' foot of the continental slope? The entire area beyond 200 nautical miles is legal continental shelf because of the method prescribed for calculating the position of the outer edge of the continental margin under Article 76, paragraph 4. State X could indeed argue, however, that it has a bigger continental shelf than state Y. Would not the information on the location of the foot of the slope of each state provide a dispute settlement body with sufficient arguments for stating that, in this case, an 'equitable' delimitation line would be a median line measured not from the baselines from which the breadth of the territorial sea is measured, but rather from the respective foot of each continental slope?

The ILA Committee on the Outer Continental Shelf raised the issue of whether the foot of the continental slope provides an alternative 'baseline' for establishing an equidistance line. As stated by the Committee, the 'reason for suggesting this option is that under Article 76 of the LOS Convention the outer limit of the outer continental shelf is not linked directly to the baseline of the territorial sea, as is the case for the territorial sea and 200 nautical mile zones, but depends on the location of the foot of the continental slope'.[230] That this reasoning is not so far-fetched is also illustrated by the fact that the architect of the foot-of-the-slope + 60 nautical mile rule in Article 76, paragraph 4—Hollis Hedberg—once argued that the foot of the continental slope on both sides should be the starting point for measuring a median line between Mexico and the USA in the Gulf of Mexico.[231] Given the text of Article 76 and the growing number of recommendations by the Commission, Hedberg's reasoning may

---

230 Report of the Committee on the Outer Continental Shelf of the ILA, New Delhi Conference, 2002, p. 9. Available at <www.ila-hq.org> (accessed 1 January 2014).

231 Hedberg, Hollis D., 'Ocean Floor Boundaries', in *Science*, Vol. 204, 1979, pp. 135–144, at p. 135.

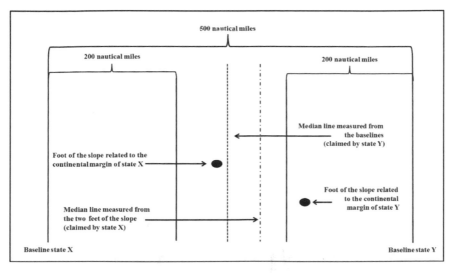

FIGURE 3.4 *Alternative median lines delimiting the continental shelf beyond 200 nautical miles*
SOURCE: ØYSTEIN JENSEN (2014).

eventually attract renewed attention; a court or tribunal might also be led to conclude that the foot of the slope on both sides can be seen as a relevant factor to be taken into account when determining what constitutes an 'equitable' solution in the delimitation of the continental shelf beyond 200 nautical miles in a situation like the one described above.

3.6   Assessment

In this chapter, various legal aspects of the Commission's decision-making have been analysed in order to show how the normative activity of the Commission unfolds on different levels. We have seen that the LOS Convention's rules regarding procedures for establishing the outer limits of the continental shelf beyond 200 nautical miles are remarkably non-specific, offering only a broad framework. The Commission has, however, elaborated procedural regulations through its own Rules of Procedure—a document currently consisting of a main body of 59 paragraphs and three annexes. Most of the Commission's procedural rules pertain to its inner workings and are thus of significance only to the Commission itself. However, the Rules of Procedure do not merely re-state what is already prescribed by the LOS Convention: they provide for certain procedural innovations, some of which may have significant practical and legal effects for the submission process and thus for the coastal state.

In some cases the rules are to the coastal state's advantage. In others, however, the Commission's procedural rules emplace new 'obligations' on coastal states not contained in the LOS Convention.

A first example concerned the deadline in the LOS Convention for making a submission with respect to the outer limits of the continental shelf beyond 200 nautical miles. Article 4 of Annex II to the LOS Convention explicitly states that such submissions shall be made to the Commission no later than ten years after the coastal state in question ratified the Convention. Despite the LOS Convention's clarity on this point, however, the Commission has contributed to both postponing and blurring the deadline concerning this matter—and that in addition to the relaxing of conditions adopted by the Meeting of States Parties. Specifically, the Commission permits a coastal state to submit only a _partial_ continental shelf claim in order not to prejudice questions relating to the delimitation of boundaries between states, notwithstanding the provisions regarding the 10-year time period established by the LOS Convention. The core of the Commission's regulation is that a submission relating to only a part of the continental shelf suspends the 10-year deadline, and that the coastal state may submit information for the remaining part(s) of the outer continental shelf at any later time.

Additional examples were presented of the Commission adopting procedural innovations that do not explicitly follow from the LOS Convention. Coastal states are allowed to make 'joint submissions'. The Commission has also provided for rules on transparency that are not explicitly mentioned in the Convention. The Rules of Procedure provide, *inter alia*, that a summary of the coastal state's submission shall be made public; also, the full recommendations are to be made public when the outer limits have been established by the relevant coastal state. And finally, we saw how the Commission has given other states a right of veto in relation to whether the Commission should start processing a submission in cases where there is a land or maritime dispute related to a continental shelf claim.

There is no reason to question the Commission's intentions in adopting these regulations, for example to facilitate greater transparency in the proceedings and ensure the submission process does not impact sensitive maritime delimitations and other jurisdictional issues related to the continental shelf beyond 200 nautical miles. Nor is there any explicit ban against the aforementioned regulations in the LOS Convention. However, it is a matter of principle whether the Commission should adopt procedural rules that have no explicit support in the LOS Convention.

One thing is regulations that affect only the Commission and its internal procedures. Another matter is regulations which affect the rights and duties of states. The rules on joint submission are perhaps the least 'radical' of the aforementioned examples, since the possibility of filing joint submissions exclusively can be seen as an advantage for the coastal state. As regards the regulations about disclosure of the summaries of submissions and (summaries of) recommendations, however, it can be argued that the Commission has created a regime to which the states did not originally sign up, and one that may intrude upon the sphere of coastal states by making them implicitly consent to disclosure. The Commission has thereby indirectly contributed to the potential discrediting of coastal states which do not accept disclosure, by giving the impression that they have something to hide. In my view, this may be considered an unreasonable burden, since the LOS Convention itself contains no rules regarding disclosure of either submissions or recommendations.

The rule that a coastal state may postpone its submission regarding parts of its continental shelf claim subject to disputes is, in my view, also problematic. Bluntly put: the consequence of the Commission's regulation on this point may be to slow the implementation of Article 76 in several sea areas, since a significant proportion of continental shelf areas beyond 200 nautical miles are subject to overlapping claims. The ambiguous wording 'later' in Rule 3 of Annex II to the Rules of Procedure means that the coastal state may postpone submission of parts of its continental shelf claim indefinitely, without regard to the time limit set in Article 4. The Commission may refer to the adoption by the Meeting of States Parties of decisions which *de facto* imply a subversion of the LOS Convention's deadline. Nevertheless, the Commission's rules stand as an independent contribution that is likely to undermine the 'timely' implementation of Article 76, contrary to the clear intention of the drafters in adopting a specified deadline for making a submission on the outer limits of the continental shelf.

The example of other states' 'veto' marks a far step away from the LOS Convention, which (in Article 76, paragraph 10) expressly states that the Commission shall have no mandate in relation to delimitation issues. Why then has the Commission found it necessary and appropriate to give a state the right to deny the Commission the opportunity to start processing a continental shelf submission, simply because that state is involved in a delimitation dispute with the submitting coastal state? According to the LOS Convention, the Commission *shall* make recommendations to coastal states, regardless of the positions of other states.

The Commission, however, seems to believe that it is entitled to bring its own examination of a continental shelf submission to a halt on the request of a neighbouring state. In turn, the risk is therefore that a coastal state will be deprived of its opportunity to establish the outer limits of its continental shelf beyond 200 nautical miles on the basis of recommendations provided by the Commission—outer limits which are legally 'final and binding' in character. Thus, through this regulation, the Commission (temporarily) fails to comply with its cardinal function under the LOS Convention—to make recommendations to the coastal state. The regulation also reveals the discrepancy between the Commission's Rules of Procedure and the LOS Convention. Since the Commission has a duty to make recommendations to the coastal state, a rule that makes the Commission's processing of a continental shelf submission conditional upon the consent of one or more other states seems to be in direct conflict with the Convention.

Mention should also be made of the more far-reaching implications of the Commission's regulations on this point, as illustrated in the *Bay of Bengal* case. When the ITLOS was to decide whether to exercise its jurisdiction to delimit the continental shelf beyond 200 nautical miles in the Bay of Bengal, Rule 5 (*litra* a) of Annex I to the Rules of Procedure was used as an argument in favour. The Tribunal was of the opinion that, when the Commission did not exercise its jurisdiction, then the ITLOS could not also refrain from exercising its jurisdiction. The result, the ITLOS argued, would be perpetuation of the *status quo*, indefinitely, with regard to both the question of the outer limits of the continental shelf and the question concerning the delimitation of the continental shelf between the two states. Also on this point then, we see that the Commission's Rules of Procedure have the potential to prevent timely implementation of the provisions of the LOS Convention.

We also addressed the Commission's substantive decision-making through issuing recommendations to individual coastal states; the intention was to examine the relationship between the content of selected recommendations and the substantive elements of Article 76 of the LOS Convention. It must be concluded that the Commission does far more than simply make a 'scientific' assessment of coastal state submissions. Essentially, the Commission performs typical legal tasks which resemble those of legal administrative, or even judicial, bodies. In applying Article 76 to concrete cases, the Commission is dealing with complicated issues of treaty interpretation. It makes assertions about the law; and the review of recommendations shows that the outcomes of the Commission's interpretation in many cases can be regarded as legally controversial.

It has been shown, for instance, that when the endpoint of an outer limit is to be linked to the 200 nautical mile limit, the question arises as to whether, under the LOS Convention, the coastal state is allowed to draw a straight line of 60 nautical miles (in accordance with Article 76, paragraph 7) from the outer limit endpoint to the 200 nautical mile limit, maximizing the shelf area but at the same time including seabed areas beyond the outer edge of the continental margin determined in accordance with Article 76, paragraphs 4 to 6. The Commission has not accepted this. Thus—according to the Commission—paragraph 7 does not mean that coastal states may incorporate as part of their continental shelf seabed areas located beyond the continental margin, although the application of paragraph 7 could lead to such a result.

There is reason to question whether the Commission's approach is correct. On the one hand, it seems that the Commission interprets these provisions in context: an outer limit which is established correctly in a 'technical' sense in accordance with paragraph 7 is still not accepted by reference to paragraphs 1 to 6, which—in brief—imply that seabed areas outside the continental margin shall not be part of the continental shelf. On the other hand—and this is the main problem—the Commission is inconsistent in its application of these rules. For instance, it seems to have no difficulty in accepting the use of straight bridging lines at other parts of the outer limit, notably by joining together circular arcs measured from different slope points. The real reason why the Commission in some cases does not allow the use of paragraph 7 may thus be that when the application of this provision leads to what the Commission feels is an unreasonably favourable result for the coastal state, the Commission feels compelled to object. However, if paragraph 7 prevails as *lex specialis* in some cases, it should perhaps be considered as a matter of principle, binding the Commission in all cases when the norm conflict between paragraph 7 and paragraphs 1 to 6 is put to test—regardless of the size of the seabed area in question. In any case, the Commission is clearly dealing with complicated *legal* questions, not only matters of geology! The main point should therefore be sufficiently clear: the Commission is not merely a body of geologists proceeding on the basis of a scientific checklist. The application of Article 76 means that the Commission must consider a whole range of complex interpretative questions and decide on conflicts of norms.

Two other examples showed the Commission interpreting Article 76 to the *disadvantage* of the coastal state. Beyond the more overarching point that the Commission is heavily involved in treaty interpretation and that it, by and large, acts as a legal institution, we thus find that it often interprets the LOS Convention in a different way than individual coastal states. This approach may be considered sensible if the objective is to prevent excessive unilateral claims to the seabed. Given the Commission's competence, however, the only relevant point should be whether it gives recommendations 'in accordance with article 76'—as its function is spelled out in Article 3 of Annex II. And as shown, the legal correctness of selected recommendations can indeed be questioned. It must be emphasized, however, that on the basis of a limited number of examples, no firm or general conclusions can be drawn regarding the Commission's application of Article 76.

Having examined the Commission's procedural regulations and the contents of specific recommendations in light of the LOS Convention, we then scrutinized the legal effects of the Commission's recommendations. Here the main finding is that the Commission's recommendations do have significant legal effects, in three ways: on the purpose of establishing final and binding outer limits of the continental shelf in concrete cases; as means of interpretation of Article 76; and potentially also on the delimitation of overlapping continental shelf areas beyond 200 nautical miles.

The legal effects of the recommendations are indeed significant in relation to the coastal state's establishment of legally 'final and binding' outer limits of the continental shelf—that is, in the context of Article 76, paragraph 8, of the LOS Convention. Under this rule, the term 'on the basis of' is the decisive criterion for the range of legal significance attached to the Commission's recommendations. We have seen that what is provided for in Article 76, paragraph 8, is that *if* the coastal state proceeds to establish the outer limits 'on the basis of' the Commission's recommendations, then these outer limits are final and binding. The interesting scenario is thus if the coastal state in fact seeks to establish outer limits with final and binding character—and then the key issue becomes what the term 'on the basis of' means. Thus also, the prime legal significance of the Commission's recommendations is accorded by way of another factor than their formal status as legal instruments.

The term has not previously been subject to an in-depth legal analysis or much scholarly attention, nor has the question been the subject of a judicial examination of any kind. Therefore, a well-founded conclusion with regard to the meaning of the term 'on the basis of' would in itself further one's understanding of Article 76 and the Commission's competences under the Convention. The aim was therefore to interpret the term so as to be able to conclude with one of the following two interpretive options. The term 'on the basis of' may mean either that the coastal state enjoys a certain margin of discretion when establishing the outer limits. It may also mean that a coastal state must heed the Commission's recommendations to the letter in order for the outer limits it has established to become final and binding.

In my opinion, the most weighty means of interpretation would indicate that 'on the basis of' implies that there must be strict consistence between the outer limit established by the coastal state and the outer limits recommended by the Commission. Thus, the latter interpretation is, in my view, the correct option: 'on the basis of' involves *no* margin of discretion for the coastal state. This conclusion may seem radical, and to my knowledge no other writer has reached a similar conclusion. Clearly, this result strengthens the legal effects of the recommendations and the normative influence of the Commission. The term 'on the basis of' represents a substantive obstacle to coastal states' liberty to proceed independently in establishing 'final and binding' outer limits of their continental shelf beyond 200 nautical miles. As emphasized, paragraph 8 does not provide that the coastal state has an *obligation* to proceed in establishing the limits or, for that matter, base its limits on the Commission's recommendations. It may do as it chooses. But the coastal state must—according to my interpretation of the term 'on the basis of'—follow the Commission's recommendations if the outer limits it establishes are to become final and binding in character. Or we could say, in the context of Article 76, paragraph 8, of the LOS Convention, some outer limits are more equal than others.

We have also seen the extent to which the Commission's recommendations shall be considered relevant means of interpretation with regard to Article 76 in light of the general rules on treaty interpretation in international law. We found that the treaty interpreter must lay significant weight on the Commission's recommendations as a means of interpretation, which then also clearly strengthens their legal effects.

The Commission's recommendations *cannot* be seen as an expression of the parties' practice and thus relevant as a means of interpretation under Article 31, paragraph 3 (*litra* b), of the Vienna Convention—that is, as subsequent practice establishing the agreement of the parties regarding the interpretation of the LOS Convention. However, according to the main rule on treaty interpretation contained in Article 31, paragraph 1, of the Vienna Convention, the LOS Convention is to be interpreted in light of its object and purpose. Notably, the ICJ in the *Diallo* case ruled that the practice of the HRC should be accorded 'great weight' due to the intention of the parties in establishing it to supervise the ICCPR.

Similarly, the Commission has been established in order to make recommendations 'in accordance with article 76'. And since the Commission has been given a key role as treaty interpreter in the application of Article 76, purposive considerations in accordance with Article 31, paragraph 1, of the Vienna Convention mean this role is best promoted by emphasizing the Commission's recommendations in the interpretation of Article 76: The Commission has not been created merely to provide vague indications or partially correct information with regard to the application of Article 76. Its function is—according to Article 3 of Annex II to the LOS Convention—to inform coastal states, upon considering their submissions, exactly where the outer limits beyond 200 nautical miles shall lie. Considerations of purpose therefore strongly indicate that this role should be supported because the role of the Commission under the

Convention would otherwise be undermined, and in turn the original intention of the parties. In light of considerations of object and purpose—and in
light of relevant case law—regardless of whether the party is a coastal state
seeking to establish outer limits 'on the basis of' the Commission's recommendations, or in another setting is about to interpret Article 76 on the basis of the
rules of treaty interpretation in international law, the conclusion remains: the
recommendations of the Commission are to be accorded weight as a normative instrument.

The last issue taken up here concerned the potential legal significance of
the Commission's recommendations for the delimitation of the continental
shelf between neighbouring states. The establishment of the outer limits of
the continental shelf beyond 200 nautical miles and the delimitation of the
continental shelf beyond 200 nautical miles are two different processes, governed by different rules under the LOS Convention. The new criteria and procedures for establishing the outer limits under Article 76 have, however, also
brought something new to the concept of delimitation. First of all, Article 76
clarifies which factual circumstances—geological and geomorphological—
are legally relevant to a determination of the extent of the continental shelf
extension beyond 200 nautical miles. Second, the Commission has been set up
to confirm the existence of such circumstances by way of recommendations
made to coastal states. Thus, not only has the concept of natural prolongation
re-emerged within the frame of reference dominated by Article 76 of the LOS
Convention, it may also be held that geological and geomorphological features
of the seabed—for instance, the location of the foot of the slope—should have
significance for what is considered an 'equitable' maritime boundary beyond
200 nautical miles under Article 83 of the LOS Convention, in the sense that
such circumstances can be conceived of as 'relevant factors', similar to, for
instance, geographical circumstances or coastal length. In that case, the recommendations and practice of the Commission may play a crucial role.

Legitimacy of the Commission and Its Decision-Making

4.1   Introduction

The empowerment of institutions with wider functions and competences in the sphere of international governance has been a main reason for the growing interest in the *legitimacy* of such institutions.[1] The previous chapter showed that the Commission has gained important functions and competences

---

1   For an analysis of factors responsible for the increasing attention to legitimacy, see Zürn, Michael, 'Global Governance and Legitimacy Problems', in *Government and Opposition*, Vol. 39, 2004, pp. 260–287. Examination of the legitimacy of international institutions includes the WTO (see for instance Cass, *The Constitutionalization of the World Trade Organization: Legitimacy, Democracy, and Community in the International Trading System*; Conti, Joseph A., 'Producing Legitimacy at the World Trade Organization: Role of Expertise and Legal Capacity', in *Socio-Economic Review*, Vol. 8, 2009, pp. 131–155; Esty, Daniel C., 'The World Trade Organization's Legitimacy Crisis', in *World Trade Review*, Vol. 1, 2002, pp. 7–22; Howse, Robert, 'Adjudicative Legitimacy and Treaty Interpretation in International Law: The Early Years of WTO Jurisprudence', in Weiler, Joseph H.H. (ed.), *The EU, the WTO, and the NAFTA* (Oxford University Press, 2000), pp. 35–70; Howse, Robert, 'The Legitimacy of the World Trade Organization', in Coicaud, Jean-Marc, and Veijo Heiskanen (eds), *The Legitimacy of International Organizations* (UN University Press, 2001), pp. 355–407; Howse, Robert, and Kalypso Nicolaïdis, 'Legitimacy and Global Governance: Why Constitutionalizing the WTO Is a Step Too Far', in Porter, Roger B., Pierre Sauve, Arvind Subramanian and Americo Beviglia Zampetti (eds), *Efficiency, Equity, and Legitimacy: The Multilateral Trading System at the Millennium* (Brookings Institution Press, 2001), pp. 227–252; Picciotto, Sol, 'The WTO's Appellate Body: Legal Formalism as a Legitimation of Global Governance', in *Governance*, Vol. 18, 2005, pp. 477–503); treaty bodies of multilateral environmental agreements (see for instance Brunnée, Jutta, 'COPing with Consent: Lawmaking Under Multilateral Environmental Agreements', in *Leiden Journal of International Law*, Vol. 15, 2002, pp. 1–52) and the UNSC (see for instance Caron, David, 'The Legitimacy of the Collective Authority of the Security Council', in *American Journal of International Law*, Vol. 87, 1993, pp. 552–588; Hurd, Ian, 'Myths of Membership: The Politics of Legitimation in UN Security Council Reform', in *Global Governance*, Vol. 14, 2008, pp. 199–217; Jodoin, Sébastien, 'Enhancing the Procedural Legitimacy of the U.N. Security Council: A Normative and Empirical Assessment', in *Sri Lanka Journal of International Law*, Vol. 17, 2005, pp. 1–54; Sato, Tetsuo, 'The Legitimacy of Security Council Activities under Chapter VII of the UN Charter at the End of the Cold War', in Coicaud, Jean-Marc, and Veijo Heiskanen (eds), *The Legitimacy of International Organizations*, pp. 309–354; and Voeten, Erik, 'The Political Origins of the UN Security

© KONINKLIJKE BRILL NV, LEIDEN, 2014 | DOI 10.1163/9789004274174_005

under the LOS Convention. These findings—combined with the fact that the Commission is now dealing with an increasing number of continental shelf submissions—prompt a discussion of the Commission in terms of legitimacy as well.

This chapter examines the legitimacy of the Commission and its decision-making, specifically possible legitimacy deficits in the Commission's composition and decision-making. We ask, is there a proper balance between the Commission's functions and competences on the one hand, and its composition and procedures on the other?

To date, little attention has been given to these questions in the legal literature.[2] Most have focused on hard-core *legal* issues, such as those raised in the previous chapter, as well as issues related to the application of the substantive definition of Article 76 in various maritime regions of the world, such as in the Arctic Ocean. Much less attention has been paid to potential weaknesses in the institutional structure and procedures of the Commission. Thus, a broad and critical study of the legitimacy of the composition and the work of the Commission based on recognized criteria will, it is assumed, be a useful addition to the current literature.

The following discussion of the composition and procedures of the Commission can be read as a self-standing analysis of legitimacy. However, the examination also relates to the material covered in the previous chapter. Indeed, more reference to the Commission as regards its composition and procedures might be relevant also for analysing, say, the legal effects of its recommendations. While these issues are interrelated I have chosen to split the two analyses because I see them as two basically different conceptual inquiries. Chapter 3 applies standard treaty interpretive analysis to an examination of the legal aspects of the Commission's decision-making, whereas the discussion of legitimacy in this chapter is essentially an *institutional* study.

Council's Ability to Legitimize the Use of Force', in *International Organization*, Vol. 59, 2005, pp. 527–557).

2 One notable example is, however, Cavnar, Anna, 'Accountability and the Commission on the Limits of the Continental Shelf: Deciding Who Owns the Ocean Floor', in *Cornell International Law Journal*, Vol. 42, 2009, pp. 387–440. Other examples include Macnab, Ron, 'The Case for Transparency in the Delimitation of the Outer Continental Shelf in Accordance with UNCLOS Article 76', in *Ocean Development & International Law*, Vol. 35, 2004, pp. 1–17; Elferink, Alex G. Oude, 'Openness' and Article 76 of the Law of the Sea Convention: The Process Does Not Need to Be Adjusted', in *Ocean Development & International Law*, Vol. 40, 2009, pp. 36–50; and Elferink, Alex G. Oude, 'The Establishment of Outer Limits of the Continental Shelf Beyond 200 Nautical Miles by the Coastal State: The Possibilities of Other States to Have an Impact on the Process', in *The International Journal of Marine and Coastal Law*, Vol. 24, 2009, pp. 535–556.

Thus there might appear some tensions between the conclusions reached in the two chapters. For instance, while it was concluded in Chapter 3 that the Commission's recommendations are to be given weight as interpretive means when interpreting Article 76, Chapter 4 indicates that the Commission may be criticized for its lack of legal expertise. And while some doubts were raised concerning the Commission's initiatives aimed at increasing transparency in Chapter 3, the analysis of legitimacy presented below indicates that greater transparency may indeed be called for.

4.2   Outline

The remainder of this chapter is structured as follows: Section 4.3 explains how legitimacy in relation to the Commission and its decision-making will be assessed. This involves first explaining what legitimacy is taken to mean within the context of this study, and then briefly identifying relevant legitimating factors in light of the Commission's functions and competences. Finally, it involves establishing a comparative legal perspective; identifying international bodies with similarities to the Commission in terms of functions and competences. Throughout the examination, this comparative perspective will help to illustrate which normative standards and characteristics should apply to the Commission, i.e. its institutional design and procedures.

Section 4.4 turns to the substantive examination of legitimacy in terms of the Commission's membership and composition. The basic question concerns the type of qualifications Commission members should have to enable them to deal with continental shelf submissions and adopt recommendations, and to what extent these qualifications are satisfied in practice. Section 4.5 examines the Commission's independence and impartiality. The Commission's procedures are analysed in section 4.6 with a focus on issues assumed to be most controversial in the context of the Commission's work, such as transparency, reason-giving and review. Finally, section 4.7 offers some concluding remarks.

4.3   Legitimacy

4.3.1   *Normative Legitimacy*

While legitimacy in international law has been extensively discussed, there is no agreed definition of the concept.[3] There exists a plethora of approaches

---

3   Literature on legitimacy in international law includes Franck, T.M., *The Power of Legitimacy Among Nations* (Oxford University Press, 1990); Kumm, Mattias, 'The Legitimacy of

concerning the elements that may induce legitimacy for a given authority.[4] Basically, legitimacy can be said to have two fundamentally distinct dimensions.[5] The sociological dimension of legitimacy is concerned with the extent to which an institution, a rule, etc., is 'accepted'. For instance, if states and other actors widely support and endorse the Commission's procedures, we could say the procedures are 'legitimate' in a sociological sense. We could also ask whether the authority of the Commission is seen as useful insofar as the Commission's work promotes the realization or achievement of policy goals—a type of cognitive legitimacy.[6] Measuring legitimacy on the basis of acceptance or usefulness is an empirical exercise, most often dealt with by political scientists.

However, the perspective on legitimacy to be applied here is exclusively *normative*. The examination will not focus on whether the Commission and its decision-making are legitimized through social sanction—if states or other actors actually espouse its authority.[7] The approach should also be distinguished from an analysis of effectiveness or whether the Commission's authority is legitimized by pragmatism: whether or not its exercise of authority is deemed useful, for instance because the Commission's work promotes the

---

International Law: A Constitutionalist Framework of Analysis', in *European Journal of International Law*, Vol. 15, 2004, pp. 907–931; Goldsmith, Jack L., and Eric A. Posner, *The Limits of International Law* (Oxford University Press, 2005); Franck, T.M., 'The Power of Legitimacy and the Legitimacy of Power: International Law in an Age of Power Disequilibrium', in *American Journal of International Law*, Vol. 100, 2006, pp. 88–106; Bodansky, Daniel, 'The Legitimacy of International Governance: A Coming Challenge for International Environmental Law?', in *American Journal of International Law*, Vol. 93, 1999, pp. 596–624; and Brunnée, Jutta, and S.J. Toope, *Legitimacy and Legality in International Law* (Cambridge University Press, 2010).

4 Wolfrum, Rüdiger, 'Legitimacy of International Law and the Exercise of Administrative Functions: The Example of the International Seabed Authority, the International Maritime Organization (IMO) and International Fisheries Organizations', in *German Law Journal (Special Issue: The Exercise of Public Authority by International Institutions)*, Vol. 9, 2008, pp. 2039–2080, at p. 2040.

5 Bodansky, Daniel, 'Legitimacy', in Bodansky, Daniel, Jutta Brunnée and Ellen Hey (eds), *The Oxford Handbook of International Environmental Law* (Oxford University Press, 2008), pp. 704–743, at p. 709.

6 See generally Black, Julia, 'Constructing and contesting legitimacy and accountability in polycentric regulatory regimes', in *Regulation & Governance*, Vol. 2, 2008, pp. 137–164.

7 Bodansky, 'Legitimacy', in Bodansky, Brunnée and Hey (eds), *The Oxford Handbook of International Environmental Law*, at p. 709. On social sanction, see Reus-Smith, Christian, 'International Crises of Legitimacy', in *International Politics*, Vol. 44, 2007, pp. 157–174, at p. 158.

realization or achievement of policy goals. While these descriptive perspectives would offer different insights into possible legitimacy concerns for the Commission, such empirical studies have limited value as regards whether the rules pertaining to the Commission's composition and decision-making are acceptable in light of a more objective perspective grounded in legal-political theory.[8] Using a normative approach to legitimacy, I seek to turn a critical spotlight on these regulations by evaluating them with reference to comparable international legal systems—and with a view to determining if they recognize and protect the legitimate interests of all parties affected by the process of establishing the outer limits under Article 76 of the LOS Convention. This approach to normative legitimacy relates to the law *de lege ferenda*—the law as it should be if the rules were changed to accord with good policy.

A particular characteristic of normative legitimacy in relation to the Commission and its procedures should be mentioned here. Unlike legality, legitimacy is always a matter of degree: 'Legitimacy runs the scale from complete acclaim to complete rejection.'[9] Any categorical rejection or affirmation of legitimacy is therefore not possible. While we may point to specific issues in relation to the Commission's procedures that confer more or less legitimacy on the regulations, we cannot unconditionally conclude that these regulations are either 'legitimate' or 'illegitimate'. Legitimacy must be viewed along a sliding scale—so the Commission and its procedures may emerge as more, or less, legitimate.[10]

4.3.2   Legitimating Factors

State consent has been the traditional basis for legitimizing international treaties.[11] Accordingly, we can trace the legitimacy of an international institution back to the treaty that created it.[12] However, it has been argued that when international institutions are entrusted with ever broader functions and competences, the legitimizing effect of the original state consent

---

8   Keller, Helen, and Geir Ulfstein, 'Introduction', in Keller, Helen, and Geir Ulfstein (eds), *UN Human Rights Treaty Bodies—Law and Legitimacy* (Cambridge University Press, 2012), pp. 1–15, at p. 9.

9   Herz, John, 'Legitimacy—Can We Retrieve It?', in *Comparative Politics*, Vol. 10, 1978, pp. 317–343, at p. 320.

10   Klabbers, Jan, Anne Peters and Geir Ulfstein, *The Constitutionalization of International Law* (Oxford University Press, 2009), pp. 40–41.

11   *Ibid.*, p. 7.

12   Bodansky, Daniel, 'Legitimacy in International Law and International Relations', paper for the 2011 Annual Meeting of the American Political Science Association, p. 11. Available at: <papers.ssrn.com/sol3/papers.cfm?abstract_id=1900289> (accessed 1 January 2014).

is weakened.[13] Accordingly, many international lawyers and international relations scholars now seem to reject state consent as a *sufficient* basis of legitimacy.[14]

Equally, it can be argued that the empowerment of the Commission under the LOS Convention undermines state consent as a sufficient source of legitimacy. The LOS Convention provides the Commission with a sufficient grounding to perform its functions., but the transfer of decision-making authority— combined with the legal effects of the Commission's recommendations— involves a significant surrender of autonomy. This gives rise to serious concerns about legitimacy, 'since, in giving its consent, a state does not know what particular constraints may be imposed on it in the future'.[15]

However, there are also other factors which may infuse the work of the Commission with legitimacy and mitigate the inadequacy of state consent as a legitimizing factor. For instance, considering that the main function of the Commission is to make recommendations 'in accordance with article 76' of the LOS Convention, the Commission's composition can be a legitimizing factor. If it is composed of individuals with the necessary expertise and qualifications to perform this task optimally, that will help legitimize the Commission and its work.

Other factors likely to lend legitimacy to the work of the Commission include its independence and impartiality. For instance, in making recommendations in accordance with Article 76 of the LOS Convention, the work of the Commission should be dedicated to this task only. The independence and impartiality of the members of the Commission will help ensure the Commission focuses on the correct legal interpretation and application of Article 76. Conversely, lack of independence and impartiality may comprise the performance of the Commission's functions, for instance so that its work

---

13   Weiler, Joseph H.H., 'The Geology of International Law—Governance, Democracy and Legitimacy', in *Zeitschrift für ausländisches öffentliches Recht und Völkerrecht*, Vol. 64, 2004, pp. 547–562, at p. 557.

14   See for instance Bodansky, 'The Legitimacy of International Governance: A Coming Challenge for International Environmental Law'; Buchanan, Allen, and Robert O. Keohane, 'The Legitimacy of Global Governance Institutions', in *Ethics & International Affairs*, Vol. 20, 2006, pp. 405–437, Weiler, 'The Geology of International Law—Governance, Democracy and Legitimacy'; and Zürn, 'Global Governance and Legitimacy Problems'. See also Keller and Ulfstein, 'Introduction', in Keller and Ulfstein (eds), *UN Human Rights Treaty Bodies—Law and Legitimacy*, at pp. 7–8.

15   Bodansky, 'Legitimacy', in Bodansky, Brunnée and Hey (eds), *The Oxford Handbook of International Environmental Law*, at p. 714.

becomes based on legally irrelevant factors, like promoting extraneous political or economic interests of individual states.

Another factor which may infuse the work of the Commission with legitimacy is the quality of its procedures. Due process of law promotes fair procedures. In the context of the Commission this relates to whether the LOS Convention—and the supplementary Rules of Procedure—has built a regime that provides fundamental procedural guarantees for those affected by the process. The recommendations of the Commission have significant legal effects— both in individual cases and by adding to the understanding of Article 76 in general (a type of precedential effect). Thus, an established course for proceedings designed to safeguard the legal interests of all affected stakeholders—for instance with regard to transparency, participation or review—may mitigate possible inadequacies in other legitimizing factors.

4.3.3   *Comparative Perspective*

The aforementioned legitimizing factors—composition, independence and impartiality, and due process—constitute the overall structure for the ensuing analysis. One question remains: which precedents should influence our perceptions of what constitute appropriate standards of, for instance, due process?

As noted by Hlavac, international institutions vary greatly in their capacities and functions, so 'what legitimacy demands of them, may change too'.[16] Thus, in establishing the main points of comparison, we should—as far as possible— be aware of the similarities and differences of the Commission's functions and competences with the functions and competences of other international institutions. Relevant variables here might include the type (for instance legislative or judicial), depth (binding or non-binding) or scope (general or specific) of authority exercised by the Commission.[17]

The primary function of the Commission is, as noted, to make recommendations in accordance with Article 76 of the LOS Convention. The Commission thus has a *legal* mandate which is positively related to treaty interpretation. The Commission should therefore be distinguished from treaty bodies which

---

16   Hlavac, Monica, 'A Developmental Approach to the Legitimacy of Global Governance Institutions', in Reidy, D.A., and W.J. Riker (eds), *Coercion and the State* (Springer, 2008), pp. 203–233, at p. 210.

17   Bodansky, 'Legitimacy in International Law and International Relations', p. 14.

have a political[18] or purely scientific mandate.[19] In adopting recommendations, the work of the Commission to a certain extent may even resemble that of traditional judicial bodies, such as international courts or tribunals, or the bodies of the dispute settlement system of the WTO.[20] Accordingly, the Commission cannot—in light of its functions—be seen as merely a technocratic body of experts;[21] and it has already been observed that the Commission exercises a type of 'judicial' function by making recommendations to coastal states.[22] The Commission also differs from institutions specifically established,[23] or

---

18   For instance the World Heritage Committee, established under Article 8 of the Convention Concerning the Protection of the World Cultural and Natural Heritage (adopted in Paris, 23 November 1972; entered into force 17 December 1975. Published in *UNTS*, Vol. 1037, p. 151) to design and update the list of properties forming part of the world's cultural heritage and natural heritage on the basis of what the Committee 'considers as having outstanding universal value in terms of such criteria as it shall have established' (Article 11, para. 2, of the World Heritage Convention).

19   For instance the Subsidiary Body on Scientific, Technical and Technological Advice (SBSTTA), which under Article 25 of the Convention on Biological Diversity (CBD) shall assist the Conferences of the Parties (CBD adopted in Rio de Janeiro, 5 June 1992; entered into force 29 December 1993. Published in *UNTS*, Vol. 1760, p. 79), or the Subsidiary Body for Scientific and Technological Advice, which under Article 9 of the UN Framework Convention on Climate Change shall give advice to the Conferences of the Parties (Convention on Climate Change adopted in New York, 9 May 1992; entered into force 21 March 1994. Published in *UNTS*, Vol. 1771, p. 107).

20   See generally Wolfrum, Rüdiger, Peter-Tobias Stoll and Karen Kaiser (eds), *WTO— Institutions and Dispute Settlement* (Martinus Nijhoff, 2006).

21   For this view, however, see Smith, Robert W., Noel Newton St. Claver Francis and Richard Haworth, 'The Continental Shelf Commission', in Nordquist, Myron H., and John Norton Moore (eds) *Ocean Policy: New Institutions, Challenges and Opportunities* (Martinus Nijhoff, 1999), pp. 135–169, at pp. 141–142, and Zinchenko, Alexei A., 'Emerging Issues in the Work of the Commission on the Limits of the Continental Shelf', in Nordquist, Myron H., John Norton Moore & Tomas H. Heidar (eds), *Legal and Scientific Aspects of Continentals Shelf Limits*, pp. 215–250, at pp. 225–226.

22   Ulfstein, Geir, 'Institutions and Competences', in Klabbers, Jan, Anne Peters and Geir Ulfstein, *The Constitutionalization of International Law* (Oxford University Press, 2009), pp. 45–80, at p. 48.

23   See for instance the Conferences of the Parties under the Convention on International Trade of Endangered Species (adopted in Washington, D.C., 3 March 1973; entered into force 1 July 1975. Published in *UNTS*, Vol. 993, p. 243), which is empowered to change the list of endangered animals and plants following ratification (Article XI of the Convention). The Conferences of the Parties under the Convention on the Prevention of Marine Pollution by Dumping of Wastes and Other Matters (adopted in London, 29 December 1972; entered into force 30 August 1975. Published in *UNTS*, Vol. 1046, p. 120), which may

implicitly given authority through other treaties,[24] to adopt general harmonization standards. Nor do its functions resemble those of, for instance, the ISA, which under Article 156 of the LOS Convention is established to 'organize and control' activities in the Area, i.e. a type of conservation and practical administration of the natural resources.[25]

Inspiration for standards of good governance may thus be found in the regulations of institutions dealing with international treaty law as a core element of their activity, such as international courts and tribunals. But the normative standards applied in such regimes should by no means be used uncritically or unreservedly as a model in connection with the Commission. First, the Commission deals not only with treaty interpretation, but with complex technical and scientific matters as well. That should have a bearing on what should be required, for instance, in terms of its composition. Second, the Commission is not empowered to make binding decisions, as is generally the case with dispute resolution bodies. The recommendations of the Commission are something of a quasi-legal instrument and bear greater resemblance to 'soft-law' instruments, like some of those emanating from the activities of human rights treaty bodies.[26] Such bodies may therefore also influence the views on

---

change the list of banned substances, is another example (see Article XV of the Convention). Other examples include the International Whaling Commission (IWC), established under Article III of the International Convention for the Regulation of Whaling (adopted in Washington, D.C., 2 December 1946; entered into force 10 November 1948. Published in *UNTS*, Vol. 161, p. 72.), which may amend from time to time the provisions of the Convention's Annex (the 'Schedule') by adopting regulations with respect to the conservation and utilization of whale resources (see Article V of the Convention), and the Codex Alimentarius Commission (CAC), which adopts food-safety standards under the UN Food and Agricultural Organization (FAO). On the CAC, see generally Livermore, Michael, 'Authority and Legitimacy in Global Governance: Deliberation, Institutional Differentiation, and the Codex Alimentarius', in *New York University Law Review*, Vol. 81, 2006, pp. 766–801.

24   For instance the IMO, whose purpose is to develop a regulatory framework for shipping through the enactment of new conventions. See Wolfrum, Rüdiger, 'IMO Interface with the Law of the Sea Convention', in Nordquist, M.H., and J.N. Moore (eds), *Current Maritime Issues and the International Maritime Organization* (Martinus Nijhoff Publishers, 1999), pp. 223–236.

25   Article 157, para. 1, of the LOS Convention.

26   Examples include 'opinions' of the Committee on the Elimination of Racial Discrimination, established under the International Convention on the Elimination of All Forms of Racial Discrimination (adopted in New York, 7 March 1966; entered into force 4 January 1969. Published in *UNTS*, Vol. 660, p. 195), the 'views' of the HRC or the Committee on the Elimination of Discrimination against Women, established under the ICCPR and the

which normative standards should apply in the context of the Commission, for instance, in terms of review mechanisms.

The submission process under Article 76 is non-adversarial, and the Commission's handling of a submission perhaps most of all resembles how an administrative agency is set to administer a general statutory provision in a specific case. The Commission shall exercise legal discretion, that is, discretion bounded by the law, and not be arbitrary, capricious or unrestrained. Although the Commission as an institution seems unique in the context of international law—'a unique [...] scientific-administrative international body'[27]—its functions and competences thus also bear resemblance to bodies under some other regulatory regimes, such as those focusing on technical determinations of compliance (for instance the Compliance Committee, established under the Kyoto Compliance System).[28] Another interesting example is how the European Patent Office (EPO) in its capacity as International Preliminary Examination Authority (IPEA) under Chapter II of the Patent Cooperation Treaty (PCT),[29] on the basis of requests from patent applicants, makes a preliminary and non-binding opinion—an International Preliminary Report on Patentability (IPER or 'IPRP Chapter II')—on whether a claimed invention appears to be novel, to involve an inventive step, and to be industrially applicable as defined in Article 33 of the PCT. This does not mean that the IPEA automatically grants patents to applicants, but the IPRP Chapter II report—the 'recommendation'— provides the applicant with a good basis to evaluate the chances of obtain-

---

Convention on the Elimination of All Forms of Discrimination against Women (adopted in New York, 18 December 1979; entered into force 3 September 1981. Published in *UNTS*, Vol. 1249, p. 13) respectively, or, the 'decisions' of the Committee Against Torture that monitors the Convention against Torture and Other Cruel, Inhuman or Degrading Treatment or Punishment (adopted in New York, 10 December 1984; entered into force 26 June 1987. Published in *UNTS*, Vol. 1465, p. 85). These instruments of human rights treaty bodies stand in contrast to instruments which are 'general' in character, i.e. general statements issued by a treaty body meant to provide guidance on the interpretation of procedural and substantive requirements of the relevant treaty. See generally Ando, Nisuke, 'General Comments/Recommendations', in Wolfrum, Rüdiger (ed.), *The Max Planck Encyclopedia of Public International Law*. Online edition. Available at: <www .mpepil.com> (accessed 1 January 2014).

27   Ulfstein, Geir, 'Treaty Bodies and Regimes', in Hollis, Duncan B. (ed.), *Oxford Guide to Treaties* (Oxford University Press, 2012), pp. 428–447, at p. 436.

28   See Ulfstein, Geir, and Jacob Werksman, 'The Kyoto Compliance System: Towards Hard Enforcement', in Stokke, Olav Schram, Jon Hovi and Geir Ulfstein (eds), *Implementing the Climate Regime: International Compliance* (Earthscan/James and James, 2005), pp. 39–62.

29   Patent Cooperation Treaty, Washington, D.C., 19 June 1970; entered into force 24 January 1978. Published in *UNTS*, Vol. 1160, p. 231.

ing a patent in the procedures before the various designated offices in a later national phase.

The work of the IPEA is a type of international administration, which comes close to how the Commission provides recommendations to coastal states as to whether the requirements of Article 76 are met in a specific case. Thus, in addition to regulations applicable to courts or tribunals, those applicable to other dispute resolutions bodies (such as those under the WTO dispute settlement system) or human rights treaty bodies should influence which normative standards should apply to the Commission's composition and procedures. The Commission exercises a type of global administration, that is, exercise of an authority which is not legislative or primarily adjudicative in character.[30] Thus insights regarding what is normatively legitimate could also be gleaned from the catalogue of procedural standards identified under the field of global administrative law. Global administrative law has developed particularly in response to the mismatch between empowerment of administrative bodies and accountability mechanisms at the international level, and has been described as comprising the

> mechanisms, principles, practices, and supporting social understandings that promote or otherwise affect the accountability of global administrative bodies, in particular by ensuring they meet adequate standards of transparency, participation, reasoned decision, and legality, and by providing effective review of the rules and decisions they make. Global administrative bodies include formal intergovernmental regulatory bodies, informal intergovernmental regulatory networks and coordination arrangements, national regulatory bodies operating with reference to an international intergovernmental regime, hybrid public–private regulatory bodies, and some private regulatory bodies exercising transnational governance functions of particular public significance.[31]

Not all principles pooled together and identified as adequate standards in global administrative law can automatically be transferred to the Commission

---

30   Krisch, Nico, and Benedict Kingsbury, 'Introduction: Global Governance and Global Administrative Law in the International Legal Order', in *The European Journal of International Law*, Vol. 17, 2006, pp. 1–13, at p. 3.

31   Kingsbury, Benedict, Nico Krisch and Richard B. Stewart, 'The Emergence of Global Administrative Law', in *Law and Contemporary Problems*, Vol. 68, 2005, pp. 15–61, at p. 17.

without respecting and being conscious of its distinct characteristics.[32] However, global administrative law does indicate relevant standards of normative legitimacy on issues such as transparency, procedural participation and review.

4.4 Membership and Composition

4.4.1 *Introduction*

The Commission should be composed of individuals who are qualified to perform the Commission's allotted duties under the LOS Convention. Here we must therefore ask whether there is a proper balance between the Commission's function and competences on the one hand, and its composition on the other. For this purpose, the appropriateness of the LOS Convention's requirements related to the formal expertise and professional background of Commission members are examined below. Section 4.4.3 discusses the level of qualification required for service in the Commission, while section 4.4.4 focuses on the issue of representativeness. Some concluding remarks are offered in section 4.4.5.

4.4.2 *Expertise and Professional Background*

According to Article 3 of Annex II to the LOS Convention, one main function of the Commission is to make substantive recommendations to coastal states in accordance with Article 76 regarding the outer limits of the continental shelf beyond 200 nautical miles. Article 76 is a treaty provision. The Commission is thus to make an autonomous interpretation of Article 76 by applying the law of treaties, with emphasis on wording and other means of interpretation according to Articles 31–33 of the Vienna Convention.

The LOS Convention does not require, however, any of the Commission's members to be jurists or otherwise have any formal legal expertise. Quite the contrary: according to Article 2 of Annex II, the Commission is to be composed of geologists, geophysicists and hydrographers, that is, exclusively natural scientists, even though its function is *also* of a legal nature. And if we look at individuals who have been members of the Commission to date, the Convention's formal requirements have been met. As of 1 January 2014, all

---

32   Krisch, Nico, 'The Pluralism of Global Administrative Law', in *The European Journal of International Law*, Vol. 17, 2006, pp. 247–248.

those who have served on the Commission have been geologists, geophysicists or hydrographers.[33]

---

33   At the first election, for a term of five years commencing on 16 June 1997 and ending on 15 June 2002, the following 21 persons were elected (see UN Doc. SPLOS/20—'Report of the sixth Meeting of States Parties'—para. 19): Alexandre Tagore Medeiros de Albuquerque (Brazil), Osvaldo Pedro Aztis (Argentina), Lawrence Folajimi Awosika (Nigeria), Aly I. Beltagy (Egypt), Samuel Sona Betah (Cameroon), Harald Brekke (Norway), Galo Carrera Hurtago (Mexico), André C.W. Chan Chim Yuk (Mauritius), Peter F. Croker (Ireland), Noel Newton St. Claver Francis (Jamaica), Kazuchika Hamuro (Japan), Karl H.F. Hinz (Germany), A. Bakar Jaafar (Malaysia), Mladen Juračić (Croatia), Yuri Borisovitch Kazmin (Russian Federation), Iain C. Lamont (New Zealand), Wenzheng Lu (China), Chisengu Leo M'Dala (Zambia), Yong-Ahn Park (Republic of Korea), Daniel Rio (France) and K.R. Srinivasan (India). At the second election, for a term of five years commencing on 16 June 2002 and ending on 15 June 2007, the following 21 persons were elected (see UN Doc. SPLOS/91 'Report of the twelfth Meeting of States Parties'—para. 100): Noel Newton St. Claver Francis (Jamaica), Lawrence Folajimi Awosika (Nigeria), Indurlall Fagoonee (Mauritius), Yuri Borisovitch Kazmin (Russian Federation), Alexandre Tagore Medeiros de Albuquerque (Brazil), Galo Carrera Hurtado (Mexico), Mihai Silviu German (Romania), Yao Ubuènalè Woeledji (Togo), Osvaldo Pedro Astiz (Argentina), Samuel Sona Betah (Cameroon), Mladen Juračić (Croatia), Naresh Kumar Thakur (India), Peter F. Croker (Ireland), Wenzheng Lu (China), Fernando Manuel Maia Pimentel (Portugal), Kensaku Tamaki (Japan), Hilal Mohamed Sultan Al-Azri (Oman), Yong-Ahn Park (Republic of Korea), Harald Brekke (Norway), Abu Bakar Jaafar (Malaysia), Philip Alexander Symonds (Australia). On the third election, for a term of five years commencing on 16 June 2007 and ending on 15 June 2012, the following 21 persons were elected (see UN Doc. SPLOS/164— 'Report of the seventeenth Meeting of States Parties'—para. 92): Alexandre Tagore Medeiros de Albuquerque (Brazil), Osvaldo Pedro Astiz (Argentina), Lawrence Folajimi Awosika (Nigeria), Harald Brekke (Norway), Galo Carrera Hurtado (Mexico), Francis L. Charles (Trinidad and Tobago), Peter F. Croker (Ireland), Indurlall Fagoonee (Mauritius), Mihai Silviu German (Romania), Abu Bakar Jaafar (Malaysia), George Jaoshvili (Georgia), Emmanuel Kalngui (Cameroon), Yuri Borisovitch Kazmin (Russian Federation), Wenzheng Lu (China), Isaac Owusu Oduro (Ghana), Yong Ahn Park (Republic of Korea), Fernando Manuel Maia Pimentel (Portugal), Sivaramakrishnan Rajan (India), Michael Anselme Marc Rosette (Seychelles), Philip Alexander Symonds (Australia), Kensaku Tamaki (Japan). And at the fourth election, for a term of five years commencing on 16 June 2012 and ending on 15 June 2017, the following 20 persons were elected (see UN Doc. SPLOS/251—'Report of the twenty-second Meeting of States Parties'—para. 91), Lawrence Folajimi Awosika (Nigeria), Galo Carrera Hurtado (Mexico), Francis L. Charles (Trinidad and Tobago), Ivan F. Glumov (Russian Federation), Richard Thomas Haworth (UK), Martin Vang Heinesen (Denmark), George Jaoshvili (Georgia), Emmanuel Kalngui (Cameroon), Wenzheng Lu (China), Mazlan Bin Madon (Malaysia), Estevao Stefane Mahanjane (Mozambique), Jair Alberto Ribas Marques (Brazil), Simon Njuguna (Kenya), Isaac Owusu Oduro (Ghana), Yong Ahn Park (Republic of Korea), Carlos Marcelo Paterlini

An important basic question, however, is whether the requirement that the Commission shall consist solely of natural scientists is appropriate. Does the Commission's composition constitute a legitimacy problem? Some writers have already argued that the Commission's 'geological make-up' is problematic. For instance, Judge Treves of the ITLOS has remarked that the Commission, when it performs 'legal, judicial-like tasks [...] such matters should be treated according to legal procedures and with legal expertise'.[34] Note also the following statement by the ITLOS in its 2012 judgment between Bangladesh and Myanmar concerning the delimitation of the maritime zones in the Bay of Bengal:

> The Tribunal's consideration of whether it is appropriate to interpret article 76 of the Convention requires careful examination of the nature of the questions posed in this case and the functions of the Commission established by that article. It takes note in this regard that, as this article contains elements of law and science, its proper interpretation and application requires both legal and scientific expertise.[35]

As for traditional judicial bodies at the international level, courts and tribunals generally consist of individuals with formal legal expertise. For instance, the Statute of the ICJ states that judges

---

(Argentina), Sivaramakrishnan Rajan (India), Walter R. Roest (the Netherlands), Tetsuro Urabe (Japan). On 19 December 2012, the Meeting of States Parties elected Szymon Uścinowicz (Poland) for the last seat of the Commission. His term of office started on 19 December 2012 and will end on 15 June 2017 (See UN Doc. SPLOS/252—'Election of one member of the Commission on the Limits of the Continental Shelf—Note by the Secretary-General').

34   Treves, Tullio, 'Remarks on Submissions to the Commission on the Limits of the Continental Shelf in Response to Judge Marotta's Report', in *The International Journal of Marine and Coastal Law*, Vol. 21, 2006, pp. 363–367, at p. 367. See also Brown, E.D., *Sea-Bed Energy and Minerals: The International Legal Regime (Volume 1: The Continental Shelf)* (Martinus Nijhoff Publishers, 1992), p. 31, Karagiannis, Symeon, 'Observations sur la Commission des Limites du Plateau Continental', in *Espaces et Ressources Maritimes*, Vol. 8, 1994, pp. 163–194, at pp. 167–168, and Nelson, L.D.M., 'The Continental Shelf: Interplay of Law and Science', in Ando, Nisuke, Edward McWhinney and *Rüdiger* Wolfrum (eds), *Liber Amicorum Judge Shigeru Oda* (Kluwer Law International, 2002), pp. 1235–1253, at p. 1238.

35   Judgment, para. 411.

shall be elected from among persons who possess the qualifications required in their respective countries for appointment to the highest judicial offices, or are jurisconsults of recognized competence in international law.[36]

Article 36, paragraph 3 (*litra* a), of the Statute of the International Criminal Court (ICC) states that judges shall be chosen from among persons who possess the qualifications required in their respective states for appointment to the highest judicial offices.[37] Article 2, paragraph 1, of Annex VI of the LOS Convention requires that the ITLOS shall be composed of a body of 21 judges, elected from among persons enjoying recognized competence in the field of the law of the sea. Also Article 253 of the Consolidated version of the Treaty on the Functioning of the European Union states that judges of the European Court of Justice (ECJ) are to be chosen from legal experts who possess the qualifications required for appointment to the highest judicial offices in their respective countries or who are of recognized competence.[38] The same applies to members of the European Court of Human Rights (ECtHR), who under the Convention for the Protection of Human Rights and Fundamental Freedoms (European Convention on Human Rights; ECHR) are required to have qualifications suitable for high judicial office, or to be jurisconsults of recognized competence.[39]

Some exceptions, however, seem to be provided for by the rules applying to certain arbitration procedures at the international level. For instance, under the Convention on the Settlement of Investment Disputes between States and Nationals of Other States,[40] the International Centre for Settlement of Investment Disputes (ICSID) is provided with facilities for arbitration of international investment disputes. An Arbitral Tribunal shall be set up, and arbitrators may be chosen from the so-called 'Panels of Arbitration' or from outside

---

36   Article 2 of the Statute of the ICJ. The Statute is an integral Annex to the UN Charter, adopted in San Francisco, 26 June 1945; entered into force 24 October 1945. Published in *UNTS*, Vol. 1 (XVI).

37   Rome Statute of the ICC, adopted in Rome, 17 July 1998; entered into force 1 July 2002. Published in *UNTS*, Vol. 2187, p. 3.

38   Adopted 13 December 2007; entered into force 1 December 2009. In *Official Journal of the European Union*, Vol. 51, 2008, p. 47.

39   Article 21, para. 1, of the ECHR. Convention adopted in Rome, 4 November 1950; entered into force 3 September 1953. Published in *UNTS*, Vol. 213, p. 221.

40   Convention on the Settlement of Investment Disputes between States and Nationals of Other States, Washington, D.C., 18 March 1965; entered into force 14 October 1966. Published in *UNTS*, Vol. 575, p. 159.

these panels. Read in context, section 2 of Chapter IV and section 4 of Chapter I of the Convention suggest that there is no *absolute* requirement that the persons so designated shall have competence in law. Article 14 of the Convention, however, indicates that legal competence is strongly preferred:

> Persons designated to serve on the Panels shall be persons of high moral character and recognized competence in the fields of law, commerce, industry *or* finance, who may be relied upon to exercise independent judgment. Competence in the field of law shall be of particular importance in the case of persons on the Panel of Arbitrators. (Emphasis added)

While there is no formal requirement that members of the panels in WTO dispute settlement proceedings have a formal background in law,[41] each member of the AB is required to be a person of legal training:

> The [AB] shall comprise persons of recognized authority, with demonstrated expertise in law, international trade and the subject matter of the covered agreements generally.[42]

Thus we see that members of international institutions tasked with rendering decisions on the basis of law generally have formal legal qualifications. Importantly also, although the law and facts are complicated by nature— there is nothing unique about Article 76 in that sense—the rule is for law-interpreting institutions to be composed of persons with a formal background in law, and who are not necessarily experts in other areas or disciplines.

For instance, the ICJ has received and adjudicated several maritime delimitation disputes.[43] Such disputes are subject to less complicated legal provisions

---

41   Article 8, para. 1, of the Understanding on Rules and Procedures Governing the Settlement of Disputes (Dispute Settlement Understanding). Published in *UNTS*, Vol. 1869, p. 401.

42   Article 17, para. 3, of the Dispute Settlement Understanding.

43   These are the *North Sea Continental Shelf* cases (Federal Republic of Germany/ Denmark/The Netherlands), published in *I.C.J. Reports* 1969, p. 3, the *Tunisia/Libyan Arab Jamahiriya* case, published in *I.C.J. Reports* 1982, p. 18, the *Gulf of Maine* case (United States/Canada), published in *I.C.J. Reports* 1984, p. 246, the *Libya/Malta* case, published in *I.C.J. Reports* 1985, p. 13, the *Greenland/Jan Mayen* case (Norway/Denmark), published in *I.C.J. Reports* 1993, p. 38, the *Qatar/Bahrain* case, published in *I.C.J. Reports* 2001, p. 40, the *Cameroon/Nigeria* case, published in *I.C.J. Reports* 2002, p. 303, the *Nicaragua/Honduras* case, published in *I.C.J. Reports* 2007, p. 659, the *Romania/Ukraine* case, published in *I.C.J. Reports* 2009, p. 650, and the *Nicaragua/Columbia* case, published in *I.C.J. Reports* 2012, p. 624.

under the LOS Convention as compared to Article 76,[44] but also in a maritime delimitation dispute the matter at hand may give rise to highly complex geographical and geological questions. The Statute of the ICJ does not require, however, members of the bench to have special expertise in geography or geology for that reason. If the Court perceives a need for expert assistance, it may, under Article 50 of the Statute, call for qualified experts to provide necessary assistance:

> The Court may, at any time, entrust any individual, body, bureau, commission, or other organisation that it may select, with the task of carrying out an enquiry or giving an expert opinion.

This also applies to other judicial bodies exercising authority under Part XV of the LOS Convention. According to Article 289 of the LOS Convention, in any dispute involving scientific or technical aspects, the body which has been given authority to resolve the dispute may select at least two scientific or technical experts to assist it, at the request of a Party or of its own initiative. Thus, the Article provides for experts to be called in for assistance in order to ensure that the body has the necessary insight and understanding of any scientific or technical factors.

Nor, we may note, is the Commission's composition in line with that of other international legal institutions which adopt decisions on the basis of treaty provisions. The members of human rights treaty bodies are predominantly—but not exclusively—lawyers.[45] The requirement is usually that they shall have good knowledge of human rights, but not necessarily the in-depth and detailed understanding that may be required of lawyers.

The Commission's composition in fact resembles institutions tasked *exclusively* with providing scientific recommendations. One example is the Scientific Committee established within the framework of the ICRW. The Scientific Committee provides information to the IWC on the status of whale stocks, on the basis of which the IWC develops regulations for the control of whaling. The Scientific Committee consists of up to 200 whale biologists.

A further example is the Scientific, Technical and Economic Committee for Fisheries (STECF), established to assist in the implementation of the European

---

44 Respectively Article 15 (the territorial sea), Article 74 (the exclusive economic zone) and Article 83 (the continental shelf).

45 Ulfstein, Geir, 'Individual Complaints', in Keller and Ulfstein (eds), *UN Human Rights Treaty Bodies—Law and Legitimacy*, pp. 73–115, at p. 78.

Commission's Fisheries Policy.[46] The STECF shall, *inter alia*, prepare an annual report on the situation as regards fishery resources relevant to the European Commission, with reference to biological, ecological, technical and economic factors affecting fisheries.[47] STECF members must be scientific experts in the fields of marine biology, marine ecology, fisheries science, nature conservation, population dynamics, statistics, fishing gear technology, aquaculture, and the economics of fisheries and aquaculture.[48]

A third example is the SBSTTA, established pursuant to Article 25 of the CBD. Functions of the SBSTTA include providing scientific and technical assessments of the status of biological diversity, preparing scientific and technical assessments of the effects of measures taken in accordance with the provisions of the CBD, and responding to scientific, technological and methodological questions put to it by the Conferences of the Parties and its subsidiary bodies.[49] The SBSTTA is composed of scientists and experts with competence in the relevant field of expertise.

Finally, perhaps the best example of the marked distinction in terms of the skills required of those who deal with treaty interpretation on the one hand, and those who do not, on the other, is found in the Marrakesh Accords—the agreements reached at the 7th Conference of the Parties to the UN Framework Convention on Climate Change. The Marrakesh Accords established a Compliance Committee, consisting of an Enforcement Branch and a Facilitative Branch. For the Facilitative Branch—responsible for providing 'advice and facilitation to parties in implementing the Protocol, and for promoting compliance with Protocol commitments'[50]—there is no mandatory requirement of legal expertise among the members, only that they have 'recognized competence relating to climate change and in relevant fields

---

46   Commission Decision 93/619/EC of 19 November 1993 relating to the institution of a Scientific, Technical and Economic Committee for Fisheries (in *Official Journal L* 297, 02/12/1993, pp. 25–26), renewed in 2005 by Commission Decision 2005/629/EC of 26 August 2005 (in *Official Journal L 225, 31/08/2005*, pp. 18–22), amended by Commission Decision 2010/74/EU of 4 February 2010 (in *Official Journal L 37, 10/02/2010*, pp. 52–54) and Commission Decision 2012/C 72/06 of 9 March 2012 on appointment of three new members of the Scientific, Technical and Economic Committee for Fisheries (in *Official Journal, L 72, 10/03/12*, p. 26).

47   See Article 2, para. 3, of Commission Decision 2005/629/EC (*ibid.*).

48   *Ibid.*, Article 3.

49   Appendix A to Annex III of Decision VIII/10 of the 8th Conference of the Parties, available at: <www.cbd.int/decision/cop/?id=11024> (accessed 1 January 2014).

50   UN Doc. FCCC/CP/2001/13/Add.3 ('Decision 24/CP.7: Procedures and mechanisms relating to compliance under the Kyoto Protocol, Annex'), Section IV, para. 4.

such as the scientific, technical socio-economic or legal fields'.[51] By contrast, for the Enforcement Branch, which was set up to 'determining cases of non-compliance',[52] members are required to have 'legal experience'.[53]

So is it not problematic that the Commission is not composed of individuals with formal legal expertise? The ILA Committee on the Outer Continental Shelf has argued that the question of how the absence of legal expertise in the Commission is to be judged depends, *inter alia*, on the extent to which procedures involving the Commission might exclude application of Part XV of the LOS Convention to questions concerning the interpretation or application of Article 76:

> If article 76 were to be completely excluded from the procedures of Part XV, the absence of legal expertise in the Commission would seem to be problematic, as there then would be hardly any possibility to submit questions of interpretation raised by a submission to legal scrutiny.[54]

However, I feel that the soundness of this argumentation can be questioned. In effect, the ILA is arguing that as long as the issue of the outer limit can be considered by a dispute resolution body, it is not problematic if the Commission should be mistaken in its treaty interpretation. But whether a court can pass judgment on a question of the outer limit at a later date is not a good argument for accepting a higher risk of miscarriage of legal interpretation in the first place. The Commission is mandated, always and in any case, to adopt recommendations 'in accordance with Article 76', regardless of whether a court may eventually rule on the matter in another setting.

The problem with the ILA's argumentation becomes even more evident if we view the matter from the perspective of the submitting coastal state. On its own, a coastal state does not have the opportunity to instigate proceedings with an international court if it disagrees with the Commission's recommendations. For a coastal state that receives recommendations and finds itself in doubt as to whether the Commission has interpreted Article 76 correctly, it is a rather weak consolation that the question one day—and depending on the lawsuit of another state—may be subject to litigation.

---

51   *Ibid.*, Section II, para. 6.
52   *Ibid.*, Section V, para. 4.
53   *Ibid.*, Section V, para. 3.
54   Report of the Committee on the Outer Continental Shelf of the ILA, Berlin Conference, 2004, p. 4. Available at: <www.ila-hq.org/> (accessed 1 January 2014).

The ILA has also argued that the absence of legal expertise in the Commission is mitigated by the fact that the Commission

> can seek advice in legal matters from the Legal Counsel of the United Nations and that the secretariat of the Commission is in the Division for Ocean Affairs and Law of the Sea of the United Nations Secretariat. This may assist the Commission to decide how to deal with legal issues that it will be confronted with. The Commission may also consider to request the Meeting of States Parties to the Convention for a clarification or recommendation on specific issues.[55]

What kind of assistance may the Commission seek from others in interpreting and applying Article 76? In Rule 57 of the Commission's Rules of Procedure, the Commission—to the extent considered necessary and useful—has allowed itself to consult specialists in *any* field relevant to its work. However, according to Article 3, paragraph 2, of Annex II to the LOS Convention, the Commission may collaborate with competent international organizations only 'for the purpose of exchanging scientific and technical information' which might be of assistance in the discharge of its functions. Explicit mention is made of the Intergovernmental Oceanographic Commission of UNESCO and the International Hydrographic Organization. The Commission may also consult other specialists—but solely for the purpose of 'exchanging scientific and technical information'. Legal expertise does not fit into that category.

But what then about the secretariat of the Commission? According to Article 2, paragraph 5, of Annex II to the LOS Convention, the Commission secretariat shall be provided by the UNSG. Upon the entry into force of the LOS Convention—at its 49th session—the UNGA thus requested the UNSG

> to provide, from within existing resources, such services as may be required for the [...] Commission on the Limits of the Continental Shelf [in particular by preparing] for the meetings of the Commission [...] and providing the necessary services to the Commission in accordance with the Convention.[56]

As set out in the LOS Convention, the functions of the UNSG as regards the work of the Commission are to, first, act as depositary unit and give due publicity to the outer limits of the continental shelf deposited by the coastal state

---

55   *Ibid.*
56   UN Doc. A/RES/49/28 ('Law of the Sea').

in accordance with Article 76, paragraph 9;[57] second, issue a letter to States Parties three months before the date of each election, inviting the submission of nominations in accordance with Article 2, paragraph 2, of Annex II; third, prepare an alphabetical list of all persons thus nominated and submit it to all the States Parties in accordance with Article 2, paragraph 2, of Annex II; and fourth, to convene the meetings of States Parties at the UN Headquarters for the election of the Commission in accordance with Article 2, paragraph 3, of Annex II. There is nothing in the LOS Convention to indicate that the Commission's secretariat has any obligation to provide input on interpreting Article 76.[58]

---

57   See also Article 6, para. 3, of Annex II to the LOS Convention.

58   Nor in the Commission's Rules of Procedure, under which the tasks of UNSG are outlined as follows: 1) according to Rule 16, the UNSG shall perform all work that the Commission may require for the effective performance of its functions. It shall be responsible for making the arrangements related to the sessions of the Commission and meetings of its sub-commissions and any subsidiary bodies which it may establish, and shall provide and direct the staff required for such sessions and meetings; 2) according to Rule 5, the UNSG shall prepare the provisional agenda of each session in consultation with the Chairperson of the Commission. The agenda shall be transmitted to the members of the Commission; 3) according to Rule 17, the UNSG may make oral or written statements at any meeting of the Commission and of its sub-commissions; 4) according to Rule 48, the Commission shall record each submission upon receipt; 5) according to Rule 49, the Commission shall promptly acknowledge by letter to the coastal state the receipt of its submission and attachments and Annexes thereto, specifying the date of receipt; 6) according to Rule 47, if made in an official language other than English, a submission shall be translated by the UNSG into English. In order to enable the UNSG to make public the proposed outer limits pursuant to the submission, the executive summary of the submission shall be translated expeditiously; 7) according to Rule 50, the UNSG shall, through the appropriate channels, promptly notify the Commission and all Members of the UN and States Parties to the Convention, of the receipt of the submission, and make public the executive summary including all charts and coordinates referred to in paragraph 9.1.4 of the Commission's Scientific and Technical Guidelines; 8) under Rule 1 of Annex II to the Rules of Procedure, the UNSG has an obligation to ensure the safe custody of the submission and the attachments and annexes thereto at the UN Headquarters until such time as they are required by the Commission; 9) according to Rule 5, para. 2 (*litra* b), of Annex III, during examination of each submission, the secretariat shall provide logistical and technical support; 10) according to Rule 6, para. 2, of Annex III, when Commission members request clarifications from coastal states, clarifications shall be submitted through the UNSG and, if necessary, the UNSG shall also in this regard provide for translation services, etc.; 11) according to Rule 8, para. 2, of Annex III, the UNSG shall notify the coastal state of the preliminary timetable for the examination of the submission by the sub-commission; 12) according to Rule 10, para. 1, of Annex III, should the sub-commission conclude that there is a need for

The question can be raised, however, whether the Commission has a *right* to obtain legal studies from its secretariat on the interpretation of Article 76, or on other legal matters, such as procedural legal issues. It is DOALOS that is the unit under the UNSG that specifically deals with law of the sea issues.[59] DOALOS is a section of the Office of Legal Affairs of the UN (OLA). According to the UNSG bulletin 'Organization of the [OLA]', one of the core functions of DOALOS is to 'provide substantive servicing [...] to the Commission'.[60] However, the Commission has on several occasions called for legal assistance from another unit of the OLA, the Office of the Legal Council (OLC). First, the Commission requested the OLC to provide a legal opinion as to the applicability of the Convention on the Privileges and Immunities of the United Nations to the members of the Commission.[61] Second, OLC was engaged[62] to give a legal opinion as to the most appropriate procedure in cases where it might be necessary to institute proceedings following an alleged breach of confidential-

---

additional data, information or clarifications, its Chairperson shall request the coastal state to provide such data or information or to make clarifications through the UNSG, which, if necessary, will translate the request and questions; and 13) according to Rule 14 of Annex III, when the recommendations prepared by the sub-commission are submitted to the Chairperson of the Commission, they shall be submitted through the UNSG.

59   UN Doc. A/RES/49/28 ('Law of the Sea').

60   Also according to the Bulletin 'Organization of the [OLA]', the core functions of DOALOS are to: (1) provide advice, studies, assistance and research on the implementation of the LOS Convention, on issues of a general nature and on specific developments relating to the research and legal regime for the oceans; (2) provide substantive servicing to the UNGA on the law of the sea and ocean affairs, to the Meeting of States Parties to the LOS Convention and to the Commission; (3) provide support to the organizations of the UN system to facilitate consistency with the Convention of the instruments and programs in their respective areas of competence; (4) discharge the responsibilities, other than depositary functions, of the UNSG under the Convention; (5) conduct monitoring and research activities and maintaining a comprehensive information system and research library on the Convention and on the law of the sea and ocean affairs; (6) provide training and fellowship and technical assistance in the field of the law of the sea and ocean affairs; and (7) prepare studies on relevant Articles of the Charter for the Repertory of Practice of UN Organs. See UN Doc. ST/SGB/1997/8 ('Organization of the Secretariat of the United Nations').

61   Doc. CLCS/4, para. 20. The question was whether the Commission can be considered to be an 'organ' of the UN to which the provisions of the said Convention applied, and so that members of the Commission might be considered as 'experts on mission for the United Nations' within the meaning of Article VI. OLC referred to precedent in respect of similar treaty organs and concluded that Article VI was applicable to the Commission's members (see Doc. CLCS/5).

62   Doc. CLCS/13.

ity pursuant to Annex II of the Rules of Procedure.[63] Third, the Commission requested the OLC to answer if, under the LOS Convention, it is permissible for a coastal state which has made a submission, in the course of the Commission's examination of that submission, to provide additional material and information relating to the limits of its continental shelf which constitute a significant departure from the original limits and formulae lines given due publicity by the UNSG in accordance with Rule 50 of the Commission's Rules of Procedure, i.e. the executive summary of the submission.[64]

The Commission has, however, never made a formal request to DOALOS, OLC or other units under the UNSG regarding how Article 76 shall be interpreted and applied with respect to individual coastal state submissions. This is consistent with the fact that it is the Commission which under the LOS Convention has the competence to make recommendations to coastal states, not the UNSG. But what is not known is whether the Commission in practice has the habit of requesting DOALOS to investigate complex legal questions that may arise during its examination of the submission. On the one hand such investigations could be considered part of the Commission's 'law source search', and should be accepted. On the other, there is a danger that it is the UNSG that *de facto* determines how Article 76 is to be interpreted—not the Commission's members, who have been nominated and elected by the States Parties.

DOALOS is a well-qualified and strong secretariat, many of whose members without doubt dispose of the requisite knowledge of law of the sea issues

---

63   Doc. CLCS/14, para. 1. The reason for the request was that the LOS Convention is silent on the question of what actions should be taken if a member of the Commission is accused of being involved in activities inconsistent with his or her duties as a member of the Commission. No specific procedures were recommended by the OLC. Thus the Commission should itself take proper measures to investigate any such incidents. However, the OLC underscored that investigations should be conducted in strict confidentiality, to avoid tarnishing the reputation of the member concerned during the process; and, having completed the examination of the case, the investigating body should prepare a report, which also should be forwarded to the Meeting (see Doc CLCS/14, para. 27).

64   The OLC concluded that there was nothing in the LOS Convention to preclude a coastal state from submitting revised particulars of the limits of its continental shelf if the state concerned felt that any of the particulars of the limits in the original submission should be adjusted, or if it had discovered errors or miscalculations that needed to be rectified. The OLC also held that the Convention did not prevent a coastal state from submitting new outer limits if that state had obtained additional scientific and technical data (see Doc. CLCS/46).

and international legal methodology, including Article 76 and continental shelf issues. Therefore, it is not inconceivable that the Commission may at the very least have been tempted to ask for legal advice—for instance in the case of straight bridging lines, that is, in cases where an outer limit established in accordance with Article 76, paragraph 4, has incorporated seabed areas located outside of the continental margin. As noted, however, DOALOS' duties and competences with regard to the Commission are solely technical, logistic and administrative in nature. A high-ranking member of the Commission's secretariat has also confirmed that DOALOS does not contribute to substantive interpretations of Article 76.[65]

One's impression, nevertheless, is of a conspicuous imbalance between the Commission's functions and competences, and its composition. The qualification requirement contained in the LOS Convention pulls exclusively in the direction of a 'technocratic' Commission. However, the Commission's actual work requires it to possess (at the very least some) formal legal expertise. Legal expertise within the Commission would strengthen its normative legitimacy, since other international institutions engaged in treaty interpretation are made up of jurists, or at least have a significant representation of jurists.

To illustrate how the Commission's composition constitutes a real problem—not just a question of principle in light of how other legal institutions are composed—it is sufficient to refer to some of the examples in the previous chapter, where we saw that the Commission often faces difficult questions of legal interpretation, and where legal expertise would definitely have been a key requirement. And to date, there has been only one Commission member with a formal legal background, its former Chairman, Yuri Borisovitch Kazmin, who according to his *curriculum vitae* holds a doctorate in public international law. He also has experience from UNCLOS III.[66]

In my view, it can thus be argued that the Commission should have had a more varied composition in terms of professional expertise. A strong element of scientific competence is clearly important, but the point here, however, is the interplay between science and law in Article 76 and how the LOS Convention *should* have resolved the issue of the Commission's formal composition. Should the current solution apply, but so that the Commission could call for legal expertise in cases where it felt the need? Should the Commission

---

65   Jares, Vladimir, 'The Work of the Commission on the Limits of the Continental Shelf', in Vidas, Davor (ed.), *Law, Technology and Science for Oceans in Globalisation: IUU Fishing, Oil Pollution, Bioprospecting, Outer Continental Shelf*, pp. 449–475, at p. 474.

66   UN Doc. SPLOS/151 ('Curricula vitae of candidates nominated by States Parties for election to the Commission on the Limits of the Continental Shelf—Note by the Secretary-General').

be composed exclusively of lawyers, but with the possibility of calling on scientific expertise if it felt the need? Or should the Commission on a permanent basis have had an interdisciplinary composition, and if so, what of the proportion between scientists and lawyers?

It seems less useful to speculate on which is *more* important—scientific or legal expertise. The Commission's main function—to conduct substantive examinations of coastal states' continental shelf claims and to issue recommendations in accordance with Article 76—requires both scientific and legal acumen. It would be unnecessarily bureaucratic were the Commission to consist of one discipline only, with the possibility of bringing in additional expertise as needed. Therefore, the best solution would be for the Commission to be permanently composed of both scientists and lawyers.

In practice, the time-consuming and complicated analysis of each coastal state's continental shelf claim could indicate a need for a 'geological' majority. For example, each sub-commission might be composed of five geologists and two legal scholars; the Commission in total would consist of six lawyers and fifteen geologists/geophysicists/hydrographers.

4.4.3   *Qualifications*

In addition to the matter of formal legal expertise, it may also be relevant to question whether the LOS Convention ensures that those who serve on the Commission are sufficiently qualified.

The LOS Convention requires not only that members of the Commission shall be geologists, geophysicists or hydrographers, but also that they be 'experts' within their respective disciplines. This resembles the qualification standards applicable to certain other international institutions—for example, members of human rights treaty bodies are to have '*recognized* competence in the field of human rights' (emphasis added).[67] But is the LOS Convention's requirement regarding the skill level of Commission members sufficiently precise and strict?

First, what is required for a geologist, geophysicist or hydrographer to be regarded 'expert' within the context of Article 2 of Annex II of the LOS Convention? The provision states that anyone with a formal education in geology, geophysics or hydrography will not automatically be eligible to sit on the Commission: that person must also be an 'expert' within at least one of the three disciplines. But the LOS Convention does not specify the difference

---

67   Note, however, the Committee on the Elimination of Discrimination against Women, where Article 17, para. 1, requires that members shall be of 'high moral standing and competence'. See Ulfstein, 'Individual Complaints', p. 79.

between someone who is 'merely' a geologist, geophysicist or hydrographer—and therefore not qualified to sit on the Commission—and one who in addition is an 'expert', and is thus qualified. Must, for example, the person have experience of continental shelf issues to be called an 'expert'? Or have published in scholarly journals? The term 'expert' is broad and gives not much more guidance than that the person in question has to be 'something more' than a formally educated geologist, geophysicist or hydrographer. A first objection is thus that further details should have been provided as to who can be regarded as an 'expert' within the meaning of Article 3 of Annex II.

Second, we may ask if the 'expert'—on the basis of a normal linguistic understanding of the word—is a sufficiently strict criterion in light of the important work of the Commission. Here we could note the strict qualification requirements that apply to members of international courts: the judges must not only be lawyers, but also lawyers with an outstanding formal background. Article 2 of the Statute of the ICJ requires that judges 'shall possess the qualifications required in their respective countries for appointment to the highest judicial offices'. Similarly, Article 36, paragraph 3 (*litra* a), of the Statute of the ICC requires that judges shall be persons 'who possess the qualifications required in the respective states for appointment to the highest judicial offices'. And the judges of the ITLOS are, according to Article 2, paragraph 1, of Annex VI of the LOS Convention, to be 'of recognized competence in the field of the law of the sea'.

Should not such qualification requirements apply to members of the Commission as well? It could have been stipulated that they all should be experts of the highest rank, for instance geologists, geophysicists or hydrographers who are recognized as leading experts in their fields and with demonstrated experience in continental shelf issues or issues particularly relevant within the context of Article 76. The problem with the current arrangement—the somewhat imprecise 'expert' requirement—is the risk of electing Commission members who are not really qualified to do a good job. Indeed, perusal of the *curricula vitae* (CVs) of nominated candidates shows that persons of highly varying professional and academic backgrounds have run for seats on the Commission.[68] And a survey of the CVs of current and past

---

68   See UN Docs. SPLOS/17 and SPLOS/17/Add. 1 ('Curricula Vitae of Candidates Nominated
      by States Parties for Election to the Commission on the Limits of the Continental Shelf')
      for the first election in 1997, UN Doc. SPLOS/81 ('Curricula vitae of candidates nominated
      by States Parties for election to the Commission on the Limits of the Continental Shelf—
      Note by the Secretary-General') for the second election in 2002, UN Doc. SPLOS/151
      ('Curricula vitae of candidates nominated by States Parties for election to the Commission

members of the Commission shows the same pattern. Here we can find, for instance, persons with only moderate prior formal experience of continental shelf issues. It can therefore be argued that the level of qualification required by the LOS Convention with respect to Commission members should have been both more specific and stricter.

4.4.4 Geographical Representation

The LOS Convention requires not only that Commission members shall have formal education as geologists, geophysics or hydrographers, but also that they shall come from different parts of the world. Article 76, paragraph 8, of the LOS Convention requires the composition of the Commission to reflect 'equitable geographical representation'. Article 2 of Annex II specifies this, enjoining states to show 'due regard' to the need to ensure equitable geographical representation in electing members to the Commission. According to paragraph 3 of that provision, no less than three members shall be elected from 'each geographical region'. Also, under Rule 42, paragraph 1 (*litra* c), of the Commission's Rules of Procedure, the Commission—'to the extent possible'—shall seek to maintain geographical distribution when the sub-commissions are appointed to undertake review of submissions.

Geographical distribution is also required of other international institutions. According to Article 9 of the Statute of the ICJ, 'representation of the main forms of civilization and of the principle legal systems of the world should be assured'. Likewise, Article 2 of Annex VI of the LOS Convention provides that in the ITLOS 'the representation of the principal legal systems of the world and equitable geographical distribution shall be assured'. Human rights conventions also specify that consideration shall be given to ensuring that membership of treaty bodies is based on geographical representation. For example, Article 31 of the ICCPR states:

> In the election of the [Human Rights] Committee, consideration shall be given to equitable geographical distribution of membership and to the representation of the different forms of civilization and of the principal legal systems.

on the Limits of the Continental Shelf—Note by the Secretary-General') for the third election in 2007 and UN Doc. SPLOS/240 ('Curricula vitae of candidates nominated by States Parties for election to the Commission on the Limits of the Continental Shelf') for the fourth election in 2012. For the CV of the candidate nominated and elected in the late 2012 election, see Annex to UN Doc. SPLOS/252 ('Election of one member of the Commission on the Limits of the Continental Shelf—Note by the Secretary-General').

Generally, membership of human rights treaty bodies reflects Resolution 1985/17 of UN's Economic and Social Council (ECOSOC), according to which due consideration shall be given to equitable geographical distribution and to the representation of different forms of social and legal systems.[69] A requirement of geographical representation also applies to purely scientific institutions, such as the aforementioned STECF. As specified in Article 4, paragraph 2, of the European Commission's decision to establish the STECF,

> [t]he members of the STECF shall be appointed on the basis of their expertise and consistent with a geographical distribution that reflects the diversity of scientific issues and approaches within the Community.[70]

But what exactly is a 'region' within the context of Article 3, paragraph 3, of Annex II to the LOS Convention ('each geographical region')? One interpretation would be that the Commission is to have at least three members from each of the geographical groups negotiated and approved by the UNGA. Article 2 of Annex VI to the LOS Convention—the Statute of the ITLOS—explicitly refers to the 'geographical groups as established by the General Assembly of the United Nations' when members of the ITLOS are to be elected. These regions are Africa, Asia, Eastern Europe, Latin America and the Caribbean, and Western Europe and Others.[71] The allocation of seats to different regions has followed this geographical pattern in the four elections held so far by the Meeting of States Parties to the LOS Convention, which has thus applied 'standard' UN procedure in the distribution of candidates.

For the purpose of the first election in 1997, the Meeting decided that members of the Commission should be elected as follows: five members from Africa, five from Asia, three from Eastern Europe, four members from Latin America/the Caribbean and four members from Western Europe/Other States.[72] However, the Group of Eastern European states decided not to fill the third seat to which it was entitled, and to instead permit that seat to be filled by a member from the Western European and Others group. Thus, after the first election, the Commission had five members from the African states group, five from the Asian states group, two from the Eastern European states group,

---

69   Ulfstein, 'Individual Complaints', pp. 82–83.

70   *Supra* note 46.

71   See Bosch, Miguel Marín, *Votes in the UN General Assembly* (Martinus Nijhoff Publishers, 1998), pp. 15–19.

72   UN Doc. SPLOS/20 ('Report of the sixth Meeting of States Parties'), para. 13.

four from the Latin American and Caribbean states group, and five from the Western European and Others group.[73] In this case, then, each geographical region—as determined by the Meeting of States Parties—was *not* represented with three candidates each, as required by the Convention.

After consultations and in accordance with the understanding reached by the twelfth Meeting of States Parties, for the purpose of conducting the second election, Commission members were elected as follows: four from the group of African states, six from the group of Asian states, three from the group of Eastern European states, four from the group of Latin American and Caribbean states, and four from the group of Western European and Others. As can be seen, the Meeting decided on a somewhat different composition to that of the first election: the Eastern European region was represented by three members, while the group of Western European and Other states was reduced to four members and it was decided that Africa should transfer one seat to the Asian region.[74]

On the basis of informal consultations conducted by the President of the sixteenth Meeting of the States Parties, agreement had been reached regarding the regional allocation of seats for the third election of members to the Commission. On the basis of that agreement, which was adopted by the seventeenth Meeting and before the start of the election process, seats were to be allocated as follows: five members from the group of African states; five from the group of Asian states; three from the group of Eastern European states; four from the group of Latin American and Caribbean states; and four from the group of Western European and Others.[75] Thus, at the 2007 meeting, the States Parties decided to alter the 2002 understanding and remove one seat from Asia and give it back to Africa. The 2007 elections was therefore the first time the Commission achieved the originally intended geographical composition.

At the nineteenth Meeting of States Parties in June 2009, the following arrangement for the fourth election of members to the Commission was envisaged: five from African states; five from Asian states; three from Eastern European states; four from Latin American and Caribbean states; and three from Western European and other states. One 'floating' seat would be elected from the African states, the Asian states or the Western European and other

---

73   *Ibid.*

74   UN Doc. SPLOS/91 ('Report of the twelfth Meeting of States Parties'), para. 97.

75   UN Doc. SPLOS/164 ('Report of the seventeenth Meeting of States Parties'), para. 81.

states.[76] That decision meant that the Western European region risked losing one member to either Africa or Asia.

Thus far, the Commission's composition has reflected the geographical distribution required by the LOS Convention (except for the 'Eastern European' seat transferred to the group of Western Europe and Others at the first election). As of 1 January 2014, members who have served in the Commission have been distributed as follows: 19 from Africa, 22 from Asia, 11 from Eastern Europe,[77] 16 from Latin America and the Caribbean and 16 from the Western Europe and Others group.

TABLE 4.1   *Members of the Commission by geographical region*

	Africa	Asia	Eastern Europe	Latin America/ Caribbean	Western Europe/ Others
1997–2002	5	5	2	4	5
2002–2007	4	6	3	4	4
2007–2012	5	5	3	4	4
2012–2017	5	6	3	4	3
Total number of members	19	22	11	16	16

The requirement concerning geographical representation reflects the desire to ensure confidence in the Commission's overall expertise among states in different parts of the world; confidence in the Commission becomes more likely within a wider geographical ambit. As such, the requirement for geographical distribution is also in line with a 'multilateral' approach to law of the sea issues.

Leaving such perspectives aside, however, we need to ask whether the requirement of geographical representativeness is useful. 'Representative' Commission members are not necessarily the best qualified—nor are the best

---

76   UN Doc. SPLOS/238 ('Election of the members of the Commission on the Limits of the Continental Shelf'), para. 8. See also UN Docs. SPLOS/201 ('Arrangement for the allocation of seats on the International Tribunal for the Law of the Sea and the Commission on the Limits of the Continental Shelf') and SPLOS/203 ('Report of the nineteenth Meeting of States Parties'), paras. 100–102.

77   Including the candidate from Poland elected on 19 December 2012.

qualified individuals necessarily distributed evenly across the globe. Of course, this is not a concern that applies solely to the Commission, since geographical distribution is practised in other international legal institutions as well.

4.4.5 *Conclusions*

The LOS Convention's provision on geographical representativeness is in line with what applies to other international legal institutions. Geographical seat distribution promotes democratic participation in the international community, and probably neither improves nor weakens the performance of the Commission's functions to any great extent.

However, the qualifications requirements that apply to individual members of the Commission should have been both more specified and stricter, for instance in requiring members to be unquestioned global experts as regards continental shelf issues. The publicly available CVs of nominated and elected Commission members indicate highly varying degrees of formal qualification.

The most serious problem with regard to the Commission's membership and composition is that the LOS Convention does not require the Commission to have members with a formal background in law. There is an obvious disparity between the Commission's function and competences on the one hand—to make recommendations (with legal effects) in accordance with Article 76—and the formal background required of Commission members, on the other. The need for legal expertise applies even though questions of the outer limits may be subject to litigation, i.e. at a later stage be subject to examination by trained legal judges in a court or a tribunal. Since the mandate of the Commission is to interpret Article 76 in its application to individual cases, the LOS Convention should have ensured the Commission is able to do precisely that.

A first step would be to emplace formal requirements as to legal background on those serving on the Commission. Given the nature of Article 76, however, there is clearly also a need for geological, geophysical or hydrographical expertise in the Commission, perhaps even to a greater extent than legal expertise.

We must assume that there are few individuals worldwide who possess the unusual cross-skills of geology/geophysics/hydrography *and* international law (as mentioned, one exception is the Commission's former Chairman, Yuri Borisovitch Kazmin). An alternative would thus be to require—in accordance with the statement by the ITLOS in the *Bay of Bengal* case between Bangladesh and Myanmar—that the Commission should have been interdisciplinary in composition, consisting of both scientists *and* lawyers.

4.5   Independence and Impartiality

4.5.1   *Introduction*

Can the Commission—and its individual members—be relied upon to adopt recommendations independently and impartially? What might be sources of potential bias? These are issues of critical importance to the functioning of the Commission. In the following we shall therefore inquire into the extent to which principles of independence and impartiality have been made applicable to the members of the Commission.

In section 4.5.2, the basic legislative considerations for an independent and impartial Commission are presented, followed in section 4.5.3 by an introduction to the regulations on independence and impartiality applicable under the LOS Convention and the Commission's Rules of Procedure. Here we will also take a brief look at rules on independence and impartiality that apply to certain other international legal institutions. The subsequent sections deal with specific issues that challenge independence and impartiality: how Commission members are nominated and elected; how they are financed; their tenure; re-elections; as well as their possibilities for engaging in extra-professional activity. Section 4.5.9 offers some concluding observations.

4.5.2   *Legislative Considerations*

Independence and impartiality are interrelated concepts. To be independent means not to be subject to control, restriction, modification, or limitation from a given outside source.[78] To be impartial means not to favour one party over another, to be disinterested, and not to pre-judge the merits of a case.[79] Only an independent decision-maker can render justice impartially on the basis of the law.

Rules on impartiality and independence rest on the fundamental ethical requirements that a decision-maker shall act impartially and independently of any special interests or political sympathies/antipathies. The ideal on which such rules are based can also be summarized by the injunction not to judge in one's own case: *nemo judex in propia sua causa*. But the rules concerning conflicts of interest serve to protect the individual decision-maker as well: after all, it is easier to vacate one's chair if one has both a right and a duty to do so.

In domestic legal settings, the origin of the principle of an independent and impartial judiciary lies in the theory of separation of powers: that the

---

78   From definition of 'Independent', in *Black's Law Dictionary* (West Publishing, 1979), p. 693.

79   From definition of 'Impartial jury', *ibid.*, p. 678.

legislature, the executive and the judiciary form three separate branches of government that constitute a system of mutual checks and balances aimed at preventing abuse of power. Today, the requirement that members of national judicial institutions shall be independent and impartial also follows from obligations set out in many universal and regional human rights instruments.[80] These guarantee the right to a fair hearing in civil and criminal proceedings before an independent and impartial court or tribunal. These rules, however, apply to national courts, etc., not international institutions.

But the question of the independence of *international* legal institutions and their members is also attracting increased attention. At the international level, however, it is not the separation of powers that has motivated this development. The basic legislative consideration is rather that an international institution—and its individual members—must be independent of states and other international institutions. Special focus at the international level has been directed at the independence and impartiality of judges of courts and

---

80 Notably, Article 14, para. 1, of the ICCPR provides that 'in the determination of any criminal charge against him, or of his rights and obligations in a suit of law, everyone shall be entitled to a fair and public hearing by a competent, independent and impartial tribunal established by law'. The HRC has claimed that the right to be tried by an independent and impartial tribunal is an 'absolute right that may suffer no exception' (see UN Doc. A/48/40—'Report of the Human Rights Committee'—p. 20). Article 8, para. 1, of the American Convention on Human Rights provides that 'every person has the right to a hearing, with due guarantees and within a reasonable time, by a competent, independent, and impartial tribunal, previously established by law, in the substantiation of any accusation of a criminal nature made against him or for the determination of his rights and obligations of a civil, labor, fiscal, or any other nature' (Convention adopted in San José on 21 November 1969; entered into force 18 July 1978. Published in *UNTS*, Vol. 1144, p. 123). Similarly, Article 7, para. 1, of the African Charter provides that 'every individual shall have the right to have his cause heard [...] by an impartial court or tribunal', and furthermore, under Article 26, that the states parties 'shall have the duty to guarantee the independence of the Courts'. And, according to Article 6, para. 1, of the ECHR, 'in the determination of his civil rights and obligations or of any criminal charge against him, everyone is entitled to a fair and public hearing within a reasonable time by an independent and impartial tribunal established by law'. The ECtHR has observed that 'in order to establish whether a [judicial] body can be considered 'independent', regard must be had, *inter alia*, to the manner of appointment of its members and their term of office, to the existence of guarantees against outside pressures and to the question whether the body presents an appearance of independence' (see *Case of Langborger v. Sweden (Application no 11179/84), Judgment, 22 June 1989, Series A, No. 155*, para 32). See also Trechsel, Stefan, *Human Rights in Criminal Proceedings* (Oxford University Press, 2005), pp. 49–50.

tribunals, for instance through the 'Burgh House Principles on the Independence of the International Judiciary'—developed by a study group of the ILA and in association with a project on international courts and tribunals.[81] But there is no reason why members of other international decision-making institutions should be any less independent and impartial as regards national or other influences. Bias may be a threat to the Commission, particularly if it comes from states with direct political and economic interests in the placement of the outer limits of the continental shelf.

4.5.3   Regulations on Independence and Impartiality in the LOS Convention

According to Article 2, paragraph 1, of Annex II to the LOS Convention, the Commission shall be composed of nationals of states that are parties to the LOS Convention. However, the members of the Commission 'serve in their personal capacities'. Each Commission member is thus to act independently

81   See Sands, Philippe, Campbell McLachlan and Ruth Mackenzie, 'The Burgh House Principles on the Independence of the Judiciary', in *The Law and Practice of International Courts and Tribunals*, Vol. 4, 2005, pp. 247–260. The work of the study group responsible for drafting these principles was informed by a preparatory symposium held in Florence in 2002, the proceedings of which were published in *The Law and Practice of International Courts and Tribunals*, Vol. 2, 2003, pp. 1–173. The Burgh House Principles considered the following principles of international law to be of general application to international judges: First, judges must enjoy independence from the parties to cases before them, their own states of nationality or residence, the host countries in which they serve, and the international organizations under the auspices of which the court or tribunal is established. Second, judges must be free from undue influence from any source. Third, judges shall decide cases impartially, on the basis of the facts of the case and the applicable law. Fourth, judges shall avoid any conflict of interest, as well as being placed in a situation which might reasonably be perceived as giving rise to any conflict of interests. Fifth, judges shall refrain from impropriety in their judicial and related activities. Mention should also be made of the opinions of the Consultative Council of European Judges (CCJE), an advisory body of the Council of Europe on issues related to the independence, impartiality and competence of judges. The CCJE has issued one opinion on standards concerning the independence of the judiciary and the irremovability of judges, one opinion on the funding and management of courts and one opinion on ethics and liability of judges. Second, there is the 'Recommendation of the Committee of Ministers of the Council of Europe to Member States on the Independence, Efficiency and Role of Judges'. Third, the Council of Europe has adopted the 'European Charter on the Statute for Judges', including its Explanatory Report. For references to all these documents, see Mahoney, Paul, 'The International Judiciary—Independence and Accountability', in *The Law and Practice of International Courts and Tribunals*, Vol. 7, 2008, pp. 313–349, at p. 314.

and impartially, without the involvement of government officials or any others. Accordingly, the Commission shall not be instructed in its performance.

That the Commission members are to act independently is also specified in the Commission's Rules of Procedure. According to Rule 10, before assuming his or her duties, each member of the Commission shall make the following solemn declaration in the Commission:

> I solemnly declare that I will perform my duties as a member of the Commission on the Limits of the Continental Shelf honourably, faithfully, impartially and conscientiously.

The substantive duty to act independently is then set out in Rule 11:

> In the performance of their duties, members of the Commission shall not seek or receive instructions from any Government or from any other authority external to the Commission. They shall refrain from any action which might reflect negatively on their position as members of the Commission.

Likewise, an internal code of conduct stipulates the duty of members of the Commission to preserve integrity, independence and impartiality:

> While the personal views and convictions of the members of the Commission, including their political and religious convictions, remain inviolable, they shall ensure that those views and convictions do not adversely affect their official duties. Members of the Commission shall conduct themselves at all times in a manner befitting their status. They shall not engage in any activity that is incompatible with the proper discharge of their duties. They shall avoid any action and, in particular, any kind of public pronouncement that may adversely reflect on their status, or on the integrity, independence and impartiality that are required by that status.[82]

Further, Commission members shall avoid any conflict of interest:

> Members of the Commission shall not use their knowledge or official functions for private gain, financial or otherwise, or for the gain of any third party, including family, friends and those they favour. Nor shall they

---

82   Doc. CLCS/47.

use their office for personal reasons to prejudice the positions of those they do not favour.[83]

Also, members of the Commission have a duty to act independently:

> In accordance with rule 11 of the Rules of Procedure, members of the Commission shall not seek or receive instructions from any Government or from any other authority external to the Commission. They shall exercise the utmost discretion in regard to all matters of official business. They shall not communicate to any Government, entity, person or any other source any information known to them by reason of their official position that they know or ought to have known has not been made public, except as appropriate in the normal course of their duties or by the authorization of the Commission. These obligations do not cease upon the cessation of their official functions.[84]

Special regulations on independence and impartiality for the Commission come into force when the Commission appoints a sub-commission to prepare draft recommendations which the Commission later shall consider in plenary session. Article 5 of Annex II to the LOS Convention specifies:

> Nationals of the coastal State making the submission who are members of the Commission and any Commission member who has assisted a coastal State by providing scientific and technical advice with respect to the delineation shall not be a member of the sub-commission dealing with that submission but has the right to participate as a member in the proceedings of the Commission concerning the said submission.

A member may thus automatically be rendered legally incompetent, whether the individual in question actually has any interest in the outcome of the proceedings or not. But when the plenary Commission is to vote on the recommendations prepared by the sub-commission, then the excluded member will take part as usual. So, even though a Commission member must withdraw to the corridor while the sub-commission debates and adopts draft recommendations, that member may participate with undiminished voting rights when the final recommendations are adopted.

---

83   *Ibid.*
84   *Ibid.*

Moreover, a general rule of independence applies to the appointment of a sub-commission. Rule 42, paragraph 1 (*litra* a), of the Rules of Procedure enjoins the Commission to identify

> any members of the Commission who may, for other reasons, be perceived to have a conflict of interest regarding the submission, e.g., members who are nationals of a State which may have a dispute or unresolved border with the coastal State.

Presumably, the person in question would not be nominated for membership of the particular sub-commission. But Rule 42, paragraph 1 (*litra* c), of the Rules of Procedure does not provide that such a member will be automatically disqualified. The Commission shall 'identify' the member, and then consider whether or not to nominate him.

Similar rules on independence and impartiality are provided for international judges, such as those of the ITLOS. According to Article 2, paragraph 1, of Annex VI to the LOS Convention, the ITLOS shall be composed of 'independent' judges, elected from among persons enjoying the highest reputation for fairness and integrity. According to Article 10, every member of the Tribunal shall, before taking up his duties, make a solemn declaration in open session that he will exercise his powers impartially and conscientiously. Correspondingly, Article 2 of the Statute of the ICJ provides that '[t]he Court shall be composed of a body of independent judges'. Moreover, Article 20 of the Statute determines that every member of the Court shall, before taking up his duties, make a solemn declaration in open court that he will exercise his powers impartially and conscientiously. Similar provisions apply to judges of the ICC. Article 40 of the Statute of the ICC provides that judges 'shall be independent in the performance of their functions'. According to Article 45— before taking up duties—each judge shall also make a solemn undertaking in open court to exercise his or her respective functions impartially and conscientiously. Further, Article 21, paragraphs 2 and 3, of the ECHR stipulate that judges of the ECtHR shall sit on the Court in their individual capacity; during their term of office they shall not engage in any activity incompatible with their independence and impartiality. Also judges of the ECtHR must, before taking up office, take an oath or solemnly declare to exercise the functions as a judge independently and impartially.[85]

General regulations on independence and impartiality apply also to members of human rights treaty bodies. Articles 28 and 29 of the ICCPR require,

---

85   See Rule 3 of the Rules of the ECtHR.

first, that members of the HRC shall serve in their personal capacity; and second, that they shall, before taking up their duties, make a solemn declaration in open committee that they will perform their functions impartially and conscientiously. Article 8 of the International Convention on the Elimination of All Forms of Racial Discrimination states that members of the Committee on the Elimination of Racial Discrimination shall serve in their personal capacities. Members of the Enforcement Branch, as well as other members of the Compliance Committee under the Kyoto Compliance System, are to 'serve in their individual capacities'.[86] Also WTO panellists shall 'serve in their individual capacities and not as government representatives, nor as representatives of any organization';[87] also members of the AB shall be 'unaffiliated with any government'.[88]

4.5.4   *Nomination*
The current process of selection to the Commission begins with the nomination of candidates, followed by an election by the Meeting of States Parties to the LOS Convention. A sound nomination process is vital for obtaining the best-qualified candidates to serve on the Commission. But the nomination process is also the first source of threat to the Commission's independence and impartiality.[89]

Article 2, paragraph 2, of Annex II to the LOS Convention determines that only States Parties may nominate members to the Commission. The UNSG circulates a letter in the UN system at least three months prior to each election, and so that the states have at least three months to nominate candidates. NGOs, international organizations or individuals may not nominate candidates.

The fact that states have the sole authority to nominate candidates to the Commission is not unique to the LOS Convention. It is the case for all human rights treaty bodies, like the HRC,[90] the Committee on the Elimination of

---

86   UN Doc. FCCC/CP/2001/13/Add.3 ('Decision 24/CP.7: Procedures and mechanisms relating to compliance under the Kyoto Protocol, Annex'), Section II, para. 6.

87   Article 8, para. 9, of the Dispute Settlement Understanding.

88   Article 17, para. 3, of the Dispute Settlement Understanding.

89   At least, the process of appointing international judges has been presented as constituting a source of threat to judicial independence. See the report 'Judicial Independence: Law and Practice of Appointments to the European Court of Human Rights', prepared by Limbach, Jutta, Pedro Cruz Villalón, Roger Errera, Anthony Lester, Tamara Morshchakova, Stephen Sedley and Andrzej Zoll. Available at: <www.interights.org/jud-ind-en/index.html> (accessed 1 January 2014).

90   Article 29 of the ICCPR.

Discrimination against Women,[91] the Committee against Torture[92] and the Committee on the Rights of the Child.[93] It also seems to be the general rule that only states may nominate candidates to international courts and tribunals.[94]

However, some treaties allow others in addition to their member states to nominate candidates for treaty bodies. This applies, for example, under the Convention on Access to Information, Public Participation in Decision-Making and Access to Justice in Environmental Matters (the Aarhus Convention),[95] in which nominations for membership of the Compliance Committee may also be initiated by 'non-governmental organizations falling within the scope of article 10, paragraph 5, of the Convention': that is, non-governmental organizations qualified in the fields to which the Aarhus Convention relates.[96]

According to Article 2, paragraph 2, of Annex II to the LOS Convention, the submission of nominations shall be made after 'appropriate regional consultations'. This rule aims to ensure that appropriate candidates have nomination support of more than one state within the same geographical region. It is, however, difficult to check whether regional consultations have actually taken place. And judging from the number of 'joint nominations' to the Commission so far, the rule seems to have minimal impact on state nominating processes.

At the first election of Commission members, only one member was nominated by more than one state. The Norwegian Harald Brekke was nominated by Iceland and Norway; the other 24 were nominated by just one state.[97] At the second election, a single candidate was again nominated by more than one state and again it was Harald Brekke, this time by Iceland, Norway, Sweden and

---

91   Article 17 of the Convention on the Elimination of All Forms of Discrimination against Women.

92   Article 17 of the Convention against Torture and Other Cruel, Inhuman or Degrading Treatment or Punishment.

93   Article 43 of the Convention on the Rights of the Child (adopted in New York, 20 November 1989; entered into force 2 September 1990. Published in *UNTS*, Vol. 1577, p. 3).

94   See for example Article 4 of Annex VI to the LOS Convention, Article 4 of the Statute of the ICJ, Article 4 (*litra* a) of the Statute of the ICC and Article 22 of the ECHR.

95   Convention on Access to Information, Public Participation in Decision-Making and Access to Justice in Environmental Matters. Adopted in Aarhus, 25 June 1998; entered into force 30 October 2001. Published in *UNTS*, Vol. 2161, p. 447.

96   UN Doc. ECE/MP.PP/2/Add.8 ('Meeting of the Parties to the Convention on Access to Information, Public Participation in Decision-making and Access to Justice in Environmental Matters: Report of the First Meeting of the Parties'), Annex to Decision 1/7, para. 4.

97   UN Doc. SPLOS/16 ('List of Candidates Nominated by States Parties for Election to the Commission on the Limits of the Continental Shelf English').

Finland.[98] At the third election in 2007, Brekke was nominated by Norway, Iceland, Sweden, Finland and Denmark.[99] In addition, Philip Alexander Symmonds was nominated by Australia, Canada and New Zealand.[100] At the most recent elections in 2012, the Nordic countries had nominated Martin Heinesen Vang of Denmark, but it was still a case of 'joint nomination' only for this candidate and for Symmonds, who was nominated by Australia, Canada and New Zealand.[101]

Article 2 of Annex II to the LOS Convention sets no limit on the number of Commission members each state may nominate. Some human rights treaty bodies have no maximum limit either.[102] Maximum limits on the number of nominees apply to other human rights treaty bodies, however, including the HRC (maximum two nominations)[103] and the Committee on the Rights of the Child (maximum one nomination).[104] Also for many international courts and tribunals, the rule seems to be a limit on the number of nominations from each state. For instance, Annex VI of the LOS Convention provides that each State Party may only nominate two candidates for a seat in the ITLOS.[105] The Statute of the ICJ also applies restrictions, in that no geographical group may nominate more than four persons, not more than two of whom shall be of their own nationality.[106]

It can be argued that the LOS Convention's arrangement on this point promotes independence between the state and individual nominees. However, practice has shown that those states that do nominate do not take the opportunity to nominate more than one candidate. Quite the contrary: the number of nominees is very low. To the 21 seats in the Commission, only 25 candidates were nominated to stand at the first election in 1997.[107] Twenty-four were nom-

---

98   UN Doc. SPLOS/80 ('List of candidates nominated by States Parties for election to the Commission on the Limits of the Continental Shelf -Note by the Secretary-General').

99   UN Doc. SPLOS/150 ('List of candidates nominated by States parties for election to the Commission on the Limits of the Continental Shelf').

100   *Ibid.*

101   UN Doc. SPLOS/239 ('List of candidates nominated by States parties for election to the Commission on the Limits of the Continental Shelf—Note by the Secretary-General').

102   Ulfstein, 'Individual Complaints', p. 84.

103   Article 29, para. 2, of the ICCPR.

104   Article 43, para. 3, of the Convention on the Rights of Child.

105   Article 4 of Annex VI to the LOS Convention.

106   Article 5, para. 2, of the ICJ Statute.

107   See UN Doc. SPLOS/16 ('List of Candidates Nominated by States Parties for Election to the Commission on the Limits of the Continental Shelf English'). Jares claims that the number of nominees was 28. See Jares, Vladimir, 'The Work of the Commission on the Limits

inated for the election in 2002; then 26 for the 2007 elections, and 24 for the most recent elections in June 2012. And only one person was nominated to the final seat in the Commission, the election to which took place on 19 December 2012.[108] So, in all elections so far, there have been relatively few candidates to choose from. It would have been desirable to have more candidates who were qualified, precisely so that elections of the members of the Commission could be real ones, not simply a formality. Therefore, a better rule than that each state *can* nominate as many as it wishes, might have been that every state has an *obligation* to nominate *at least* one candidate. A noteworthy example along these lines is the Council of Europe that has sought to strengthen transparency, reliability and legitimacy surrounding the appointment of judges to the ECtHR by verifying that states put forward a list of three valid and qualified candidates.[109]

Furthermore, the nomination process at the national level is veiled in a certain degree of mystery. It is not known whether states internally call for applicants and then start the recruitment processes for the selection of the best candidate. The procedure appears to be that a state approaches a potential candidate, someone thought to be suitable, and encourages this person to run for election. The national nominating processes can thus be criticized for being closed. Where there is little or no involvement of civil society in finding suitable geologists, geophysicists or hydrographers, there is the risk that well-qualified candidates will not come into consideration at all.

The procedures for the nomination of candidates are thus not in conformity with, for instance, the aforementioned Burgh House Principles, according to which procedures for the nomination of judges are to be transparent and provide appropriate safeguards against nominations motivated by improper considerations.[110] Furthermore, the Burgh House Principles encourage international organizations or other bodies responsible for the nomination, election and appointment to publicize information on the appointment process and the candidates running for judicial office, in due time and in an effective manner.[111]

---

of the Continental Shelf', in Vidas (ed.), *Law, Technology and Science for Oceans in Globalisation*, at p. 451.

108   UN Doc. SPLOS/252 ('Election of one member of the Commission on the Limits of the Continental Shelf—Note by the Secretary-General').

109   See draft report of the Assembly's Committee on Legal Affairs and Human Rights on 'Nomination of candidates and election of judges to the European Court of Human Rights' (Doc. AS/JUR (2008)34 of 3 September 2008, para. 8).

110   The Burgh House Principles, para. 2.3.

111   *Ibid.*, para. 2.4.

It could also be argued that the nominations process ought to follow a completely different procedure—for example, by issuing an international call, reaching out to all potential individuals. State interests would still be protected through the election. At least, the number of nominations thus far seems to indicate a need to improve the announcement procedures, and the nomination procedure in general.

That there are so few nominees may also create a dilemma for member states, in the sense that a state may feel 'pressured' to elect a candidate it is not completely satisfied with. There may be reason to believe that this has actually happened, most recently in the June 2012 election of Commission members. For the 20th seat on the Commission, there was only one candidate: at a late point, the representatives of Vietnam and Spain announced the withdrawal of their candidates from the race, leaving a Pakistani as the sole candidate for the final round. He was subsequently elected by 139 votes. However, the member states had no real choice. Moreover, to the election of the 21st seat in December 2012, there was also only one nominee.[112]

4.5.5   *Elections*

In addition to the nomination process, it is essential to examine the election procedures for Commission members. According to Article 2, paragraph 3, of Annex II to the LOS Convention, it is the States Parties that shall elect the members of the Commission at a meeting convened by the UNSG at UN Headquarters.[113] To date, there have been four elections, held at five-year intervals: in 1997,[114] 2002,[115] 2007[116] and in 2012.[117]

That Commission members are chosen by election might seem controversial, since such 'hiring' procedures at the national level are usually reserved for purely political institutions. At the international level, however, membership

---

112   UN Doc. SPLOS/252 ('Election of one member of the Commission on the Limits of the Continental Shelf—Note by the Secretary-General').

113   See also Rule 71 of the Rules of Procedure for the Meeting of States Parties to the LOS Convention (UN Doc. SPLOS/2/Rev.4—'Rules of Procedure for Meetings of States Parties').

114   UN Doc. SPLOS/15 ('Election of the Members of the Commission on the Limits of the Continental Shelf').

115   UN Doc. SPLOS/79 ('Election of the members of the Commission on the Limits of the Continental Shelf—Note by the Secretary-General').

116   UN Doc. SPLOS/149 ('Election of the members of the Commission on the Limits of the Continental Shelf—Note by the Secretary-General').

117   UN Doc. SPLOS/238 ('Election of the members of the Commission on the Limits of the Continental Shelf').

of legal institutions is—as a main rule—determined by election. Members of WTO panels and the AB are elected,[118] as are the members of the Compliance Committee under the Kyoto Compliance System[119] and members of the Compliance Committee of the Aarhus Convention.[120] Seats on international courts and tribunals are also filled through elections.

That it is the *States Parties* that elect Commission members is also in line with how the seats of treaty bodies and international judicial institutions are filled. Members of the Committee on Migrant Workers, established under the International Convention on the Protection of the Rights of All Migrant Workers and Members of their Families,[121] are elected by member states in accordance with Article 72. Members of the HRC, established under the ICCPR, are elected by member states in accordance with Articles 28 to 39 of the Covenant. The same applies to the other treaty bodies that monitor implementation of the core human rights conventions.[122] States Parties also elect members of the Compliance Committee under the Aarhus Convention,[123] and members of the Compliance Committee of the Kyoto Protocol are also elected by member states.[124] Judges of the ITLOS are elected by the States Parties;[125] likewise in the context of the ICJ,[126] the ICC,[127] and the ECtHR.[128]

---

118 Articles 6 and 17, para. 1, of the Dispute Settlement Understanding.

119 See Ulfstein and Werksman, 'The Kyoto Compliance System: Towards Hard Enforcement', in Stokke, Hovi and Ulfstein (eds), *Implementing the Climate Regime: International Compliance*, pp. 39–62, at p. 47.

120 See UN Doc. ECE/MP.PP/2/Add.8 ('Meeting of the Parties to the Convention on Access to Information, Public Participation in Decision-making and Access to Justice in Environmental Matters: Report of the First Meeting of the Parties').

121 Convention adopted in New York, 18 December 1990; entered into force 1 July 2003. Published in *UNTS*, Vol. 2220, p. 3.

122 Ulfstein, 'Individual Complaints', pp. 85–86.

123 UN Doc. ECE/MP.PP/2/Add.8 ('Meeting of the Parties to the Convention on Access to Information, Public Participation in Decision-making and Access to Justice in Environmental Matters: Report of the First Meeting of the Parties'), Annex to Decision 1/7, para. 7.

124 UN Doc. FCCC/CP/2001/13/Add.3 ('Decision 24/CP.7: Procedures and mechanisms relating to compliance under the Kyoto Protocol, Annex'), Section II, para. 3.

125 Article 4 of Annex VI to the LOS Convention.

126 Article 4 of the ICJ Statute: 'The members of the Court shall be elected by the General Assembly and by the Security Council [...]'.

127 Article 36, para. 6 (*litra* a), of the ICC Statute: 'The judges shall be elected by secret ballot at a meeting of the Assembly of States Parties [...]'.

128 Article 22 of the ECHR: 'The judges shall be elected by the Parliamentary Assembly with respect to each High Contracting Party [...]'.

The method by which the State Parties elect Commission members can be considered 'democratic' in the sense that all states stand on an equal footing in terms of number of votes. In addition, the LOS Convention sets formal pre-requisites for a valid election: two-thirds of the States Parties shall constitute a quorum; and the persons elected to the Commission shall be those nominees who obtain a two-thirds majority of the votes of the representatives of States Parties present and voting.

Nonetheless, elections as a method of recruitment open the possibility that non-professional factors might be taken into account. Ideally, the main objective is not only to elect members of the Commission who are 'experts in the fields of geology, geophysics or hydrography'. That is the minimum requirement. It is also crucial to elect the *best* candidates from among the nominees.

The first aspect to consider in this context is whether the States Parties have an opportunity to familiarize themselves with the individual qualifications of nominees prior to each election. For instance, Article 36, paragraph 4 (*litra* a), of the Statute of the ICC provides that nominations of candidates for election to the Court shall be accompanied by a statement which in detail specifies how the candidate fulfils the requirements of paragraph 3: i.e. that they possess the qualifications required in their respective states for appointment to the highest judicial offices. By contrast, the LOS Convention has no such provision for the Commission. It is only required that the UNSG sets up an alphabetical list of all persons nominated, which is then presented to the States Parties.[129] This has been the procedure in connection with each election: in 1997,[130] in 2002,[131] in 2007[132] and in 2012.[133] Moreover, prior to each election to the Commission, the UNSG has provided member states with the *curricula vitae* of nominated candidates.[134] CVs are also available for perusal at the DOALOS website. This

---

129   Article 2, para. 2, of Annex II to the LOS Convention.

130   UN Doc. SPLOS/16 ('List of Candidates Nominated by States Parties for Election to the Commission on the Limits of the Continental Shelf English').

131   UN Doc. SPLOS/80 ('List of candidates nominated by States Parties for election to the Commission on the Limits of the Continental Shelf -Note by the Secretary-General').

132   UN Doc. SPLOS/150 ('List of candidates nominated by States parties for election to the Commission on the Limits of the Continental Shelf').

133   UN Doc. SPLOS/239/Add.1 ('List of candidates nominated by States parties for election to the Commission on the Limits of the Continental Shelf—Note by the Secretary-General: Addendum').

134   See UN Docs. SPLOS/17 and SPLOS/17/Add. 1 ('Curricula Vitae of Candidates Nominated by States Parties for Election to the Commission on the Limits of the Continental Shelf') for the first election, UN Doc. SPLOS/81 ('Curricula vitae of candidates nominated by States Parties for election to the Commission on the Limits of the Continental Shelf—

helps to ensure that member states can familiarize themselves with the background of individual candidates.

Surveying the list of the CVs circulated in connection with the 2012 election, we can note that elements such as academic background, place of employment, previous work experience, etc., are included for each of the nominees. However, there is no standard format. The CV of one candidate included only position, education and work experience, while the CV of another described present position, date of birth, language knowledge, academic background, professional qualifications in ocean sciences, appointments and distinguished posts, membership of national maritime forums, LOS Convention-related works, other professional activities, awards and achievements, and so on.

Thus, while some CVs are very brief, others can be highly detailed. It would be preferable to have a standardized template. For example, there could be a separate category for 'publications', which would make it easier to check the nominees' qualifications. For instance, among the CVs made available for the 2012 election, that of Lawrence Folajimi Awosika (Nigeria) has a multi-page publication list, whereas for certain other candidates there is no reference to a single scientific publication. It would definitely be advantageous to know whether a nominee has published any relevant work.

Given the original languages of the LOS Convention, of which the Arabic, Chinese, English, French, Russian and Spanish texts are equally authentic,[135] it would also be relevant for states to acquire an overview of the language qualifications of each nominee. Thus, although a traditional résumé or CV can give information about each candidate, the model as practised by UNSG is inadequate precisely because the nominating states/the nominees are basically free to present their backgrounds and qualifications as they wish.

Requirements on standardized CV forms could, for example, have been regulated by the model adopted by the Council of Europe for the procedure for examining candidatures for the election of judges to the ECtHR.[136] In order to

---

Note by the Secretary-General') for the second election in 2002, UN Doc. SPLOS/151 ('Curricula vitae of candidates nominated by States Parties for election to the Commission on the Limits of the Continental Shelf—Note by the Secretary-General') for the third election in 2007 and UN Doc. SPLOS/240 ('Curricula vitae of candidates nominated by States Parties for election to the Commission on the Limits of the Continental Shelf') for the fourth election in 2012. For the CV of the candidate nominated and elected in the late 2012 elections, see Annex to UN Doc. SPLOS/252 ('Election of one member of the Commission on the Limits of the Continental Shelf—Note by the Secretary-General').

135   Article 320 of the LOS Convention.

136   Parliamentary Assembly Resolution 1082 (1996). Available at <www.assembly.coe.int/Main .asp?link=/Documents/AdoptedText/ta96/ERES1082.htm> (accessed 1 January 2014).

strengthen openness, reliability and legitimacy, and to ensure members of the Parliamentary Assembly of the Council of Europe have comparable information at their disposal when electing judges to the Court, candidates are invited to submit a CV, which is then subject to standard editing. The document is to include: (1) 'personal details' (including full name, sex, date, place of birth and nationality); (2) 'education and academic and other qualifications'; (3) 'professional activities' (details of judicial activities, details of non-judicial legal activities, details of all non-legal professional activities); (4) 'activities and experience in the field of human rights'; (5) 'political activities' (posts held in a political party, duration and membership of parliament); (6) 'other activities' (field, duration and functions); (7) 'publications and other works' (indicating the total number of books and articles published but so that only the most important ones, and maximum twelve, are specified); (8)'languages'; and (9) 'other relevant information'.[137]

It might also be questioned whether a CV provides sufficient basic material for the States Parties to elect the members of the Commission. Any CV—standardized or not—can provide only limited information of relevance to determining whether a candidate is suitable for a seat on the Commission. In fact, there do exist more sophisticated international selection procedures. Again we can turn to the procedures for electing members to the ECtHR. Under the ECHR, the 47 judges of the Court

> shall be elected by the Parliamentary Assembly with respect to each High Contracting Party by a majority of votes cast from a list of three candidates nominated by the High Contracting Party.[138]

The Parliamentary Assembly invites candidates to participate in personal interviews, conducted by a sub-committee of the Assembly's Committee on Legal Affairs and Human Rights. The sub-committee sends a recommendation to the Bureau of the Assembly, which the Bureau then forwards to the Assembly. The Assembly proceeds to elect judges to the Court during its part-sessions. The candidate who obtains an absolute majority of votes cast is elected. If no candidate obtains an absolute majority, a second ballot is held, and the candidate who obtains a relative majority of votes cast is declared elected.[139]

---

137   *Ibid.*, Appendix.
138   Article 22 of the ECHR.
139   See Appendix to Resolution 1432 (2005), reproduced in the Rules of Procedure of the Assembly, January 2011, p. 156. Available at: <www.assembly.coe.int/Main.asp?link=/ Documents/AdoptedText/ta05/ERES1432.htm> (accessed 1 January 2014).

Or take the method of election of judges to the ICC. At its Tenth session, the Assembly of States Parties to the ICC decided to establish an Advisory Committee on Nominations as provided for in Article 36, paragraph 4 (*litra* c), of the Court's Statutes. The Assembly noted that the current procedure for the nomination and election of judges did not include the intervention of any evaluating independent body that would check whether the candidate fulfilled the set requirements.[140] It was thus argued that the establishment of an Advisory Committee would introduce an independent organism into the structure of the Assembly to facilitate the election of the best qualified judges.[141] The Committee was not intended to duplicate the Assembly in its role of election, but the Committee would enjoy legitimacy which was 'not to be found in any other organism with similar functions'.[142]

The Assembly recommended that an Advisory Committee on Nominations of Judges of the ICC be established. It would be composed of nine members, nationals of States Parties, who would be mandated to facilitate that the highest-qualified individuals were appointed as judges of the Court. Its assessment of candidates would be based strictly on the requirements of Article 36, paragraph 3 (*litras* a, b and c), of the Court's Statutes.[143] The establishment of the Advisory Committee on Nominations can be considered an important initiative aimed at improving the election process of the ICC. Despite the differences in functions between the ICC and the Commission, it can be argued that something similar should be used as inspiration for the process of selecting Commission members, so that states will vote only for candidates who meet the highest standards of expertise.

The election of the members of the Commission is secret, although secrecy is not prescribed by the LOS Convention.[144] The principle of secret voting has both advantages and disadvantages. One of the advantages is that states can vote freely and without being subject to undue influence, that is, without being subjected to coercion or pressure. Another advantage is that the members of the Commission will not know which states did or did not vote for them. Secret elections are common in other international institutions. For instance, ballots

---

140   Doc. ICC-ASP/10/36 ('Report of the Bureau on the establishment of an Advisory Committee on nominations of judges of the International Criminal Court'), para. 9. Available at: <www.2.icc-cpi.int/Menus/ASP/> (accessed 1 January 2014).

141   *Ibid.*, para. 10.

142   *Ibid.*, para. 10.

143   *Ibid.*, Annex, paras. 5 and 7.

144   UN Doc. SPLOS/164 ('Report of the seventeenth Meeting of States Parties'), para. 83.

for membership in the HRC and other human rights treaty bodies are secret.[145] Also the members of the ITLOS are elected by secret ballot.[146]

On the other hand, secret elections make it impossible to reveal why the elected members of the Commission were actually elected, and what may have lain behind. This could prompt speculations that the election was influenced by factors other than the qualifications of the nominees—such as political favours or trade-offs. It has been argued that a significant element of power politics underlies international elections within the UN system.[147] Most states have 'allies' in some form, or other means of available pressure that can have an impact close to the ballot box. For human rights treaty bodies, it has been argued that the electoral process is 'haphazard and takes limited account of qualifications'.[148] And for international courts, it has even been claimed that the defeat of candidates has been the consequence of previous rulings by the relevant judge.[149]

4.5.6   Financing and Resources

According to the Consultative Council of European Judges (CCJE), 'the funding of courts is closely linked to the issue of independence of judges in that it determines the conditions in which the courts perform their functions'.[150] Similarly, we should ask whether the arrangements for financing and resources place the Commission and its members in an uncomfortable position of dependency towards those who finance its activity.

Article 2, paragraph 5, of Annex II to the LOS Convention stipulates that it is the state that submitted the nomination of a member of the Commission which shall cover the expenses of that member while he or she is in performance of Commission duties.[151] This is a different arrangement than what

---

145   Ulfstein, 'Individual Complaints', p. 86.
146   Article 4, para. 4, of Annex VI to the LOS Convention.
147   Malone, David M., 'Eyes on the Prize: The Quest for Non-permanent Seats on the UN Security Council', in *Global Governance*, Vol. 6, 2000, pp. 3–23, at p. 18.
148   Crawford, James, 'The UN Human Rights Treaty System: A System in Crisis?', in Alston, Philip, and James Crawford (eds), *The Future of UN Human Rights Treaty Monitoring* (Cambridge University Press, 2009), pp. 1–15, at p. 9.
149   Some have seen the defeat of the Australian candidate to succeed Judge Sir Percy Spender on the ICJ in the 1960s as a reprisal for Spender's position in the *South West Africa Cases*. See Mahoney, 'The International Judiciary—Independence and Accountability', at p. 325.
150   CCJE Opinion No 2, 2001, para. 2. Doc. referred to by Mahoney, 'The International Judiciary—Independence and Accountability', at p. 314.
151   The LOS Convention does not resolve the question of which state(s) shall defray the expenses of a member who has been jointly nominated.

applies to human rights treaty bodies. For instance, Article 42, paragraph 9, of the ICCPR provides that member states shall share equally all the expenses of the members of the HRC in accordance with estimates to be provided by the UNSG. And Article 17, paragraph 7, of the Convention against Torture and Other Cruel, Inhuman or Degrading Treatment or Punishment specifies that member states shall be responsible for the expenses of the members of the Committee against Torture.

The arrangement provided for the Commission also differs from what applies to courts and tribunals. For instance, Article 19 of Annex VI to the LOS Convention provides that the ITLOS' expenses are to be borne by the States Parties and by the ISA on such terms and in such a manner as shall be decided at Meetings of the States Parties. Thus individual judges are not to be compensated directly by the nominating States Parties. Similarly, according to Article 49 of the Statute of the ICC, judges shall receive such salaries, allowances and expenses as may be decided upon by the Assembly of States Parties—not by the nominating states.

It is problematic that the state submitting the nomination of a particular member to the Commission also shall cover the expenses of that member while in performance of Commission duties. First, it makes it difficult for other states to find out the size of these 'expenses'. Why is it the nominating states that shall determine the compensation, with no overreaching guidance from the Meeting of States Parties? A solution such as that prescribed for the ITLOS would help ensure equal treatment. And the minutes of the Meetings of States Parties would provide a control mechanism, as is the case with resolutions of the UNGA in relation to wages for judges of the ICJ.[152]

Second, if the Commission itself covered the costs of its members, it would help 'neutralize' payments by member states by filtering them through a common budget. That a member is nominated for a seat, elected and compensated by a state is one thing. But that the same person takes part in decision-making in matters concerning the rights and duties of that state is likely to undermine the impression of the decision-maker's impartiality and neutrality; hence it impacts on legitimacy. Take, for instance, national legal administrative bodies: any financial ties linking the party or others with a legal interest in the outcome of the case, and the person making the decision, are banned outright.

---

152   UN Doc. A/RES/61/262 ('Conditions of service and compensation for officials other than Secretariat officials: members of the International Court of Justice and judges and ad litem judges of the International Tribunal for the Former Yugoslavia and the International Criminal Tribunal for Rwanda').

It can be argued that the voluntary trust fund set up to cover the costs of participation for Commission members from developing states in the meetings of the Commission has helped remove part of the financial link between state and members of the Commission, at least for Commission members who are reimbursed by this fund.[153] But this arrangement—which by the way is also at the mercy of the rich states' benevolence—has not been established to improve the independence and impartiality of the members of the Commission, only to assist developing states that have weaker financial capacities. And what about other members of the Commission, who are still being reimbursed directly by their nominating states? Are there equally good grounds to believe that members whose costs are met by their respective governments will themselves remain impartial to submissions from those same governments? If, instead, the Meeting of States Parties or the Commission itself covered members' costs, it would strengthen the impression that all members of the Commission are independent, not only those whose costs are reimbursed by the voluntary fund.[154]

It is interesting to note that the Commission itself has proposed improvements to this end. At its Seventeenth session, the Commission adopted a draft decision in which it proposed that the States Parties to the LOS Convention approached the UNGA, with a view of adopting a resolution that

> the members of the Commission receive emoluments and expenses while they are performing Commission duties concerning the consideration of submissions made by coastal States on the outer limits of the continental shelf under article 76, and that such emoluments and expenses be defrayed through the regular budget of the United Nations.[155]

A problem here, however, might be the competence—or at least willingness—of the UNGA to circumvent the provisions set out in the LOS Convention. The OLC has previously argued that inclusion of expenses of a treaty body into the common budget of the UN must be considered in light of the treaty which established the body in question:

---

153   UN Doc. SPLOS/58 ('Decision regarding the establishment of a voluntary trust fund for the purpose of the Commission on the Limits of the Continental Shelf').

154   See Cavnar, 'Accountability and the Commission on the Limits of the Continental Shelf: Deciding Who Owns the Ocean Floor', pp. 428–429, and Suarez, *The Outer Limits of the Continental Shelf: Legal Aspects of their Establishment*, pp. 91–92.

155   Doc. CLCS/50, Annex.

> Treaty organs must function in accordance with the provisions of the treaties which create them and give them tasks to perform [...]. General Assembly resolutions cannot amend treaties, and until the treaties are formally amended by one of the recognized procedures, resolutions which conflicts with them have no legal effect in respect of the treaty organs concerned.[156]

As noted, the LOS Convention provides that the expenses of the Commission's members shall be covered by the states that nominated them. Thus, would not a resolution of the UNGA which transmits these expenses to the UN common budget conflict with the Convention? We might only speculate if the UNGA would have adopted a resolution interfering with the LOS Convention to this extent. An amendment of the Convention is nevertheless also a formal possibility.[157]

4.5.7   Tenure

Another aspect relating to Commission members' independence and impartiality is the terms of service and possibilities of re-elections. Article 2, paragraph 3, of Annex II to the LOS Convention specifies:

> The members of the Commission shall be elected for a term of five years. They shall be eligible for re-election.

The LOS Convention sets no limits on the length of time a Commission member can serve. What this arrangement resembles most of all is the four-year term of office of members of human rights treaty bodies—which can be renewed any number of times.[158] By contrast, judges of the ICC are elected for a nine-year term, with no re-election;[159] the same applies to judges of the ECtHR. However, members of the ICJ serve nine-year terms *and* may be re-elected.[160] As per Article 5 of Annex VI to the LOS Convention, the same arrangement holds for members of the ITLOS.

---

156 *Repertory of Practice of United Nations Organs*, Vol. I, 1970–1978, para. 9.
157 See Articles 312–313 of the LOS Convention. See also Suarez, *The Outer Limits of the Continental Shelf: Legal Aspects of their Establishment*, pp. 92–93.
158 Exceptions apply for the Committee on the Rights of Persons with Disabilities and the Committee on Enforced Disappearances. See Ulfstein, 'Individual Complaints', p. 81.
159 Article 36, para. 9 (*litra* a), of the ICC Statute.
160 Article 13 of the Statute of the ICJ.

Allowing members of the Commission to serve for several consecutive periods helps to ensure continuity in the work of the Commission. On the other hand, having a limited term of office prompts battles for re-election which may politicize the process, and possibly lead to outside pressure for the Commissioner in question. It may also be that systems permitting re-election in lieu of longer terms 'carry the suspicion of throwing candidates for re-appointment at the mercy of their national (and other appointing) Governments during their term of office'.[161] In connection with the ICJ, its former president, Judge Elias, has argued that

> three-yearly elections often involve a good deal of horse-trading at the best of times; henceforth, this has become accentuated, leading to a situation in which candidates had been and would in future be likely to be elected more on a consideration as to how they might vote on certain delicate issues coming before the Court than on whether they would or could render objectively valid judicial opinions in all cases and at all times.[162]

In my opinion, a better alternative for the Commission would be to have an extended term of office, with no re-election. This argument is underpinned by the fact that several members of the Commission have served for a very long time. The Norwegian Harald Brekke and the Russian Yuri Borisovitch Kazmin are notable examples: both served for three consecutive periods from 1997 to 2012, being re-elected twice.

4.5.8 Extra-Professional Activity

Another problematic aspect concerning the independence and impartiality of Commission members relates to the fact that these posts are not permanent, full-time jobs, and members may have or take up other professional positions while serving on the Commission. It can be argued that Commission posts should be full-time positions, as that would make members of the Commission less exposed to outside pressure.

Judges in international courts generally have full-time positions. According to Article 21, paragraph 3, of the ECHR, for example, during their term of office

---

161   Mahoney, 'The International Judiciary—Independence and Accountability', at p. 325.
162   Quote from Aznar-Gómez, Mariano J., 'Organization of the Court', in Zimmermann, Andreas, Christian Tomuschat and Karin Oellers-Frahm (eds), *The Statute of the International Court of Justice: A Commentary* (Oxford University Press, 2006), pp. 205–218, at pp. 209–210.

the judges [of the ECtHR] shall not engage in any activity which is incompatible with their independence, impartiality or with the demands of a *full-time office* [...]. (Emphasis added)

Similar rules apply to the judges of the ICC. Article 40, paragraph 3, of the Statute of the Court states:

Judges are required to serve on a full-time basis at the seat of the Court [...].

For international judges, certain types of other activities—including political or administrative positions—are commonly not allowed in addition to the court position. This is the case for the judges of the ITLOS; as specified in Article 7 of Annex VI to the LOS Convention:

No member of the Tribunal may exercise any political or administrative function, or associate actively with or be financially interested in any of the operations of any enterprise concerned with the exploration for or exploitation of the resources of the sea or the seabed or other commercial use of the sea or the seabed [...]. No member of the Tribunal may act as agent, counsel or advocate in any case [...]. Any doubt on these points shall be resolved by decision of the majority of the other members of the Tribunal present.

Similarly, Article 16 of the ICJ Statute:

No member of the Court may exercise any political or administrative function, or engage in any other occupation of a professional nature (...).

Such rules apply also to judges of the ICC. According to Article 40, paragraph 2, of the Statute of the Court,

Judges shall not engage in any activity which is likely to interfere with their judicial functions or to affect confidence in their independence.[163]

---

163   That extra-judicial activity may challenge the judge's independence and impartiality was also expressed in the aforementioned Burgh House Principles. Para. 8 provides that 'judges shall not engage in any extra-judicial activity that is incompatible with their judicial function or the efficient and timely functioning of the court of which they are members, or that may affect or may reasonably appear to affect their independence or

In the Commission, however, there is no explicit ban on extra-professional activity. Nothing in the LOS Convention—besides the general requirement that members of the Commission shall serve in their 'personal capacity'—precludes Commission members from holding paid or unpaid positions elsewhere.

In a comparative perspective, the situation for the Commission is arguably much the same as it is for human rights treaty bodies, where rules like those applicable to international courts do not exist. It has been argued, however, that such rules could be developed for individuals holding decision-making positions in governments or in any other organization which might give rise to a conflict of interest, for instance along the lines as those established by the Human Rights Council.[164] Here it should be mentioned that the vague requirements of impartiality and independence in the Commission's Rules of Procedure and the internal code of conduct of the Commission have not prevented members of the Commission from somewhat 'suspicious' affiliations with governments and companies. For instance, a Norwegian—who served on the Commission for three consecutive periods from 1997 to 2012—had (at least until the election in 2007) a position as Senior Geologist and Project Coordinator in the Exploration Department in the Norwegian Petroleum Directorate, as well as being technical advisor to the Norwegian government and member of the national committee on the delineation of the Norwegian continental shelf.[165] He attended the session in which the plenary Commission considered and adopted by consensus the 'Recommendations of the Commission on the Limits of the Continental Shelf in regard to the submission made by Norway in respect of areas in the Arctic Ocean, the Barents Sea and the Norwegian Sea on 27 November 2006'.[166]

Also, a Russian—who served in the Commission for three consecutive periods from 1997 to 2012 (and served as its Chairman for five years, 1997–2002)—

---

impartiality'. Furthermore, it is stated that 'judges shall not exercise any political function' and that '[e]ach court should establish an appropriate mechanism to give guidance to judges in relation to extra-judicial activities, and to ensure that appropriate means exist for parties to proceedings to raise any concerns'. Moreover, judges are not to sit in any case in the outcome of which they hold any material personal, professional or financial interest, nor in any case in the outcome of which other persons or entities closely related to them hold a material personal, professional or financial interest (para. 11).

164   Ulfstein, 'Individual Complaints', p. 81.
165   See UN Doc. SPLOS/151 ('Curricula vitae of candidates nominated by States Parties for election to the Commission on the Limits of the Continental Shelf—Note by the Secretary-General'), p. 21.
166   See Doc. CLCS/62, paras. 2 and 19.

had, while serving on the Commission, work for the for the Russian government in various positions, in addition to private engagements.[167] From 2004 (and at least until 2007) he served as adviser to the Director of the Russian Federal Mineral Resources Agency on legal, scientific and geological matters concerning marine research, prospecting and exploration. From 2001 to 2004 he served as consultant to the Ministry of Natural Resources of the Russian Federation, advising on legal, scientific and technical matters concerning marine research, prospecting and exploration. From 1992 to 2001 he served as counsellor to the Ministry of Natural Resources of the Russian Federation. And, from 2004 (and at least until 2007), he was chief geologist for Sevmorneftegaz—at that time, Gazprom's offshore division, dealing with petroleum prospecting and exploration, *inter alia*, in the Barents Sea. He attended the session at which the plenary Commission considered and adopted the Recommendations of the Commission in regard to the submission of the Russian Federation.[168]

It must be strongly emphasized that there is *nothing* to indicate that either of them has been involved in any formal irregularities. At issue is not, however, whether or not these individuals have done anything wrong or not, but whether the outside world can have confidence in the Commission's members, or if circumstances like these might impair their trust. Being an employee of a state or an oil company can undoubtedly create certain ties to the relevant state or company which are hardly reconcilable with service on the Commission. In light of the more stringent rules that apply to international courts and tribunals, it can therefore be argued that also the LOS Convention should have had more stringent and more specific rules regarding involvement in other activities while serving on the Commission. At the very least, there should be regulations prohibiting Commission members from maintaining affiliations with governed entities, institutions or companies where the question of the outer limits of the continental shelf is of factual relevance—notably, oil companies and states.

An important aspect of the principle of independence also relates to a general duty of loyalty. Commission members should have a common duty to devote themselves to the work of the Commission without being hampered by other tasks. In principle, the precise type of the extra-professional activity in question is not relevant: *all* extra-professional activity can cause problems with the pace and effectiveness of the Commission's work. The Commission's heavy workload has given rise to much debate.[169] At the

---

167   See UN Doc. SPLOS/151, p. 70.
168   See Doc. CLCS/34, para. 2.
169   See for instance Doc. CLCS/50, Annex.

twenty-second Meeting of States Parties to the LOS Convention, one state representative voiced concerns because the workload had 'increased beyond imaginable and expected levels'.[170] In order to clear the backlog, one suggestion was that states should investigate the possibility of funding the current members to stay full-time at UN Headquarters in New York.[171] It is also worth noting Rule 2 of the Commission's Rules of Procedure in this context, according to which the Commission

> shall hold sessions at least once a year and *as often as is required for the effective performance of its functions* under the Convention, in particular, to consider submissions by coastal States and to make recommendations thereon. (Emphasis added)

4.5.9 *Conclusions*

Quite possibly, the Commission's members are in fact largely independent and impartial. However, the *regulations* intended to ensure this suffer from certain shortcomings; there is also room for improvement to secure the guarantees of independence and impartiality in accordance with practice in some other international treaty regimes.

The nomination process of the members of the Commission should be more open, not least by enabling adequate publicity for vacancies on the Commission. Also, states should have the duty to nominate more than one candidate for election, in order to weaken the relationship between individual nominees and the particular state. The Meeting of States Parties should also seek to de-politicize the election process—for instance, by establishing an appointment committee of experts which, prior to each election, submits an independent recommendation as to which candidates are deemed best qualified to serve on the Commission. Furthermore, there is the question of independence regarding financial matters. If the Meeting of States Parties, through the Commission, were to cover members' costs, that would help to neutralize payments by filtering them through a common budget. Also, it has been argued that an extended term of office would be advantageous for enhancing the independence and impartiality of the members of the Commission: a single and non-renewable long term of service, instead of a system of unlimited re-election that may contribute to politicize elections. Finally, that Commission members may hold paid or unpaid positions elsewhere, as at present, is likely

---

170 UN Doc. SPLOS/251 ('Report of the twenty-second Meeting of States Parties').
171 *Ibid.*

to compromise the impression of members of the Commission as independent and impartial.

4.6   Procedures

4.6.1   *Introduction*

The following section focuses on the Commission's procedures. The legal literature argues that certain procedural guarantees, like participation and the right to be heard, constitute factors which may induce legitimacy for international regimes.[172] The basic assumption is thus—as noted in the introduction to this chapter—that the procedures of the Commission should satisfy certain minimum procedural criteria, as reflected in the principle of 'due process of law'.[173]

But what normative frameworks should guide the activity of the Commission—that is, which international bodies offer the most suitable comparison? In regard to composition and independence/impartiality, traditional international dispute-resolution bodies were used to constitute the comparative perspective. With regard to the Commission's procedures, however, insights should be drawn more from the field of global administrative law, as the Commission's way of processing submissions largely resembles a type of administration, and is a non-adversarial process. Global administrative law has identified the spread of procedural standards that long have been taken for granted in domestic legal settings to international administrative institutions. Some of these may be relevant for evaluating the standards that should apply to the Commission as well.

The rules on admissibility of facts and evidence are discussed in section 4.6.2 below before coastal state participation and the right to be heard (section 4.6.3). Section 4.6.4 takes up transparency and openness, an aspect of particular importance and interest to all states. Reason-giving is evaluated in section 4.6.5, while section 4.6.6 discusses the possible need for a review mechanism in the Article 76 implementation process. Concluding remarks are offered in section 4.6.7.

---

172   Bodansky, 'Legitimacy', p. 717. See also Keller and Ulfstein, 'Introduction', p. 8.
173   Further on the principle of 'due process', see Orth, John V., *Due Process of Law: A Brief History* (University Press of Kansas, 2003).

4.6.2 *Admissibility of Facts and Evidence*

4.6.2.1 Introduction

The extent of coastal-state entitlement to the continental shelf beyond 200 nautical miles depends on the physical properties of the seabed, not a simple criterion such as pure distance from the baselines. Accordingly, the production and assessment of evidence are crucial, and should be organized so as to enable the Commission to adopt recommendations on the basis of all the necessary factual information. However, the LOS Convention's system for determination of the facts gives rise to fundamental questions of legitimacy. Basically, are rules that limit the rights and responsibility to provide 'the facts of the matter' to the coastal state acceptable according to standards of good decision-making?

4.6.2.2 Fact-Finding and Evidence under Article 76

Under the LOS Convention, only the coastal state may provide the Commission with scientific data and information on the limits of its continental shelf beyond 200 nautical miles. According to Article 76, paragraph 8, information on the limits of the continental shelf beyond 200 nautical miles shall be submitted by 'the coastal State' to the Commission. In Article 4 of Annex II this rule is restated:

> Where a coastal intends to establish the outer limits of its continental shelf, the coastal State shall submit particulars of such limits to the Commission along with supporting scientific and technical data.

Article 3 of Annex II provides that the Commission shall consider the data and other material submitted by the coastal state, and make recommendations in accordance with Article 76. Thus, the object of proof—what needs to be proven—is the physical circumstances on the seabed, and the means of such proof is the submission prepared by the coastal state in question. Indeed, according to the LOS Convention, the submission of the coastal state represents the sole means of proof on which the Commission is to rely in its application of Article 76.

That it is only the coastal state that may provide the Commission with information concerning the continental shelf's extent beyond 200 nautical miles also follows indirectly from Article 77, paragraph 2, of the LOS Convention. Under paragraph 2, the coastal state exercises sovereign rights over the continental shelf for the purpose of exploring it and exploiting its resources. That means that others than the coastal state do not have a right to examine the properties of the seabed, unless surveys conducted as part of marine scientific research on the continental shelf should reveal such information[174]—but marine scientific research is to be conducted only with the express consent of and under the conditions stipulated by the coastal state.[175] And the fact that other states, as a main rule, have the right to engage in scientific exploration of the ocean floor—possibly thereby acquiring knowledge of the extent of the continental shelf beyond 200 nautical miles—does not thereby entitle them to affect the content of the coastal state's submission.

That the Commission shall base its recommendations solely on information provided by the coastal state represents a form of 'indirect' fact-finding. It is up to the coastal state to survey the seabed and provide documentation. There is no intervention or engagement by the Commission in the production of evidence. There is also no independent fact-finding body, and the Commission has no investigatory capacities, other than that it may consult other experts with a view to exchanging scientific and technical information which might be of assistance in discharging the Commission's responsibilities.[176] Thus the coastal state has total control over which factual material is submitted. This also means that any supplementary information has to come from the coastal state itself, as was the case with the Russian submission in 2001. For the central Arctic Ocean, the Commission requested that Russia submitted more information, to enable a new evaluation.[177]

On the one hand, these rules are in accordance with the principle *actori incumbit probatio* in international litigation, i.e. that the party which alleges a fact—in this case the coastal state—bears the burden of proof.[178] But the

---

174 Article 246 of the LOS Convention.

175 Article 245 of the LOS Convention.

176 Article 3, para. 2, of Annex II to the LOS Convention.

177 UN Doc. A/57/57/Add.1 ('Oceans and the Law of the Sea: Report of the Secretary-General'), paras. 40–41. For a note on the reaction of the Russian submission, see Macnab, Ron, and L. Parsons, 'Continental Shelf Submissions: The Record to Date', in *The International Journal of Marine and Coastal Law*, Vol. 21, 2006, pp. 309–322, at pp. 311–313.

178 The rule of the claimant's duty was highlighted by the ICJ in the *Corfu Channel* case. The ICJ did not agree that the burden of proof would shift from (the claimant state) UK to (the respondent state) Albania, on the basis that an act contrary to international law had occurred in the territorial waters of Albania: 'It is true, as international practice shows, that a State on whose territory or in whose waters an act contrary to international law has occurred, may be called upon to give an explanation. It is also true that that State cannot evade such a request by limiting itself to a reply that it is ignorant of the circumstances of the act and of its authors. The State may, up to a certain point, be bound to supply particulars of the use made by it of the means of information and inquiry at its disposal. But it cannot be concluded from the mere fact of the control exercised by a State over its territory and waters that that State necessarily knew, or ought to have known, of any unlawful

Article 76 process is not an adversarial one. The rules and principles that apply in inter-state litigation should not automatically be considered appropriate for the Article 76 implementation process. Other states do not participate with regard to the establishment of the outer limits of the continental shelf under the LOS Convention, as they do in adversarial proceedings before a court or tribunal; and a court or tribunal may request a second opinion from the other party. In the Article 76 implementation process, there is the risk that the coastal state might be tempted to hide or suppress facts which are to the disadvantage of its own continental shelf claim, so that the submission might not include *all* relevant 'evidence' related to a particular seabed area.

---

act perpetrated therein, nor yet that it necessarily knew, or should have known, the authors. This fact, by itself and apart from other circumstances, neither involves *prima facie* responsibility nor shifts the burden of proof' (see *I.C.J. Reports* 1949, p. 4, at p. 18). Although the issue of burden of proof was controversial among the members of the Court, the approach of the ICJ demonstrates that there shouldn't be any deviation from the principle *actori incumbit probatio* unless there are good reasons for it. In saying that failure of Albania to carry out an international obligation must be proven, also the views of the judges who disagreed with the finding of the majority of the Court on the issue of the knowledge of Albania of the mine-laying, emphasized the rule that the burden of proof rests with the plaintiff (see for instance dissenting opinion of Judge Winiarski in the *Corfu Channel* case, *ibid.*, pp. 49–57, and the dissenting opinion of Judge Krylov, in the *Corfu Channel* case, *ibid.*, pp. 68–77). This was also the approach in the *Temple of Preah Vihear* case between Cambodia and Thailand, in which the ICJ stated that the rule to be applied for the distribution of the burden of proof is that each party shall prove claims put forward by it: 'As concerns the burden of proof, it must be pointed out that though, from the formal standpoint, Cambodia is the plaintiff, having instituted the proceedings, Thailand also is a claimant because of the claim which was presented by her in the second Submission of the Counter-Memorial and which relates to the sovereignty over the same piece of territory. Both Cambodia and Thailand base their respective claims on a series of facts and contentions which are asserted or put forward by one Party or the other. The burden of proof in respect of these will of course lie on the Party asserting or putting them forward' (see *I.C.J. Reports* 1962, p. 6, at pp. 15–16). Also in the *Western Sahara* case, the dissenting Judge De Castro championed the principle of the claimant's duty: 'Morocco's assertion of rights of sovereignty over Western Sahara called for the examination, as a question of fact, of the way in which those rights had been acquired and whether they still subsisted at the time of colonization. It was thus for Morocco as the claimant to prove to the satisfaction of the Court when and how the Moroccan Empire had acquired Western Sahara' (see *I.C.J. Reports* 1975, p. 12). See generally Highet, Keith, 'Evidence, the Chamber and the ELSI Case', in Lillich, Richard (ed.), *Fact-Finding by International Tribunals* (Transnational Publishers, 1992), pp. 33–79, at p. 46.

4.6.2.3   Other States' Submissions

The scope of this problem has been highlighted in practice. For instance, the USA—as of 1 January 2014 *not* a party to the LOS Convention, it should be noted—commented extensively on both Russia's and Brazil's continental shelf claims. After an overview map of Russia's submission to the Commission was circulated to all UN member states, the USA responded with a position paper claiming that the Russian submission had 'major flaws as it relates to the continental shelf claim in the Arctic'.[179] The USA held, *inter alia*, that Russia had not provided information sufficient for determining the position of the 2,500 metre isobaths and the foot of the continental slope:

> Critical to the Russian submission relating to the Arctic Ocean are the positions of the 2,500 meter isobaths and the foot of the continental slope. The positions of these lines in the Russian presentation could not be examined for accuracy and completeness, because they are not included in the executive summary. Independent estimates of the position of the 2,500 meter isobaths and the foot of the continental shelf can be obtained from the data base used to prepare the International Bathymetric Chart of the Arctic Ocean (IBCOA). This chart, sponsored by the International Arctic Science Committee, the Intergovernmental Oceanographic Commission and the International Hydrographic Organization, was first published in 2000 and is periodically updated. Objective evaluation of the Russian claim will require that the positions of the 2,500 meter isobaths and base of continental slope in the Russian claim be compared with their positions on the new chart and its data base.[180]

The USA was also critical to Russia's claim to the Alpha-Mendeleev Ridge, as Article 76, paragraph 3, of the LOS Convention states that the continental margin 'does not include the deep ocean floor with its oceanic ridges or the subsoil thereof':

> Mounting geologic and physical evidence indicates that the Alpha-Mendeleev Ridge System is the surface expression of a single continuous geologic feature that formed on oceanic crust of the Arctic Ocean basin

---

179   US position paper made available at the website of the Commission: <www.un.org/Depts/los/clcs_new/submissions_files/rus01/CLCS_01_2001_LOS__USAtext.pdf> (accessed 1 January 2014).

180   *Ibid.*, para. 5.

by volcanism over a 'hot spot.' (A 'hotspot' is a magma source rooted in the Earth's mantle that is persistent for at least a few tens of millions of years and intermittently produces volcanoes on the overlying earth's crust as it drifts across the hot spot during continental drift.) The Alpha-Mendeleev hot spot was formed by magma that was funneled from a hot spot to the spreading axis that created the Amerasia Basin of the Arctic Ocean 130 to 120 million years ago, and built a volcanic ridge about 35 km thick on the newly formed oceanic crust. Both aeromagnetic and bathymetric data show that the ridge extends entirely across the Arctic Ocean, and that its characteristic aeromagnetic expression ends at the continental margins at both ends and is absent from the adjacent continental shelves [...]. The lpha-Mendeleev Ridge System is therefore a volcanic feature of oceanic origin that was formed on, and occurs only within the area of, the oceanic crust that underlies the Amerasia Subbasin of the deep Arctic Ocean Basin. It is not part of any State's continental shelf.[181]

Referring to several other issues, the USA concluded that there 'are substantial differences between the Russian submission on the one hand and others in the relevant scientific community on the other hand, regarding key aspects of the proposed submission, based on reports in the open, peer-reviewed scientific literature'.[182] The USA urged 'further consideration and broad debate before any recommendation is made by the Commission'.[183]

Also in the response of Brazil's 2004 shelf claim, the USA took issue over a specific aspect—here, the thickness of the sediment associated with the Vitoria-Trinidade feature:

> The United States has reviewed the executive summary of the Brazilian submission to the Commission on the Limits of the Continental Shelf (Commission) of May 17, 2004, and has several comments [...]. With respect to sediment thickness, the United States examined those portions of the line in figure 2 that were derived by applying Article 76, paragraph 4(a)(i) (the 'sediment thickness line'). The United States compared this sediment thickness line with publicly available data, for example, from the Deep Sea Drilling Project, from published journal articles, and from the database called Total Sediment Thickness of the World's Oceans and Marginal Seas, prepared by the National Geophysical Data Center

---

181   *Ibid.*, para. 7.
182   *Ibid.*, para. 11.
183   *Ibid.*, para. 5.

of the U.S. Department of Commerce, National Oceanic & Atmospheric Administration (NGDC). In several places, the United States observed that there are differences between the sediment thickness as presented in the Brazilian summary and the sediment thickness derived from publicly available sources. While the United States recognizes that exploration seismic surveys conducted in this part of the margin may have produced data that is more refined than that contained in the NGDC database, the United States suggests that the Commission may want to examine Brazil's sediment thickness data carefully. With respect to points 65 to 69, the United States also notes that the zigzag pattern appears to be erratic compared to other parts of the sediment thickness line and may bear additional scrutiny.[184]

The Commission, however, pointed out that the right of other states to respond to other states' submissions applies only in matters concerning disputes between states with opposite or adjacent coasts or in other cases of unresolved land or maritime disputes:

> In regard to the letter of the United States, the Commission noted that both annex II to the Convention and the rules of procedure of the Commission provided for only one role to be played by other States in regard to the consideration of the data and other material submitted by coastal States concerning the outer limits of the continental shelf beyond 200 nautical miles. Only in the case of a dispute between States with opposite or adjacent coasts or in other cases of unresolved land or maritime disputes would the Commission be required to consider communications from States other than the submitting one. Consequently, the Commission concluded that the content of the letter from the United States should not be taken into consideration by the Commission. The Commission also instructed the Subcommission to disregard the comments contained in that letter during its examination of the Brazilian submission.[185]

The USA disagreed with the Commission's reading of the Rules of Procedure, referring to Rule 2 (*litra* a) of Annex III, under which representatives of the

---

184   US reactions to the Brazilian submission are available at the website of the Commission: <www.un.org/Depts/los/clcs_new/submissions_files/bra04/clcs_02_2004_los_usatext .pdf> (accessed 1 January 2014).

185   Doc. CLCS/42, para. 17.

coastal state are to make a presentation on 'comments on any *note verbale* from other States regarding the data reflected in the executive summary including all charts and coordinates made public by the Secretary-General in accordance with rule 50'. The USA interpreted the Rules of Procedure so that

> other States shall have the opportunity to comment on the 'data reflected in the executive summary', that the Commission would hear the coastal State's response to these comments, and necessarily, that the Commission would consider both the comments and the coastal state's response. These comments are clearly not to be limited to information relating to disputes, for paragraph II. (2)(b) of Annex III separately provides for 'consideration of any information regarding any disputes related to the submission'. Accordingly, we believe that the Rules of Procedure in fact require the Commission and Sub Commission to consider comments 'from other States regarding the data reflected in the executive summary,' not only comments related to disputes between States with opposite or adjacent coasts or other disputes.[186]

Furthermore, the USA held, even if the Commission were to conclude that the Commission's Rules did not require it to consider communications from states other than the submitting one or ones involved in unresolved disputes, there was nothing in the LOS Convention or the Rules of Procedure that prohibited the Commission from doing so. The information submitted by the USA did not belong to any other category than scientific literature. And if the Commission can review scientific literature, why should it not also be able to accommodate opinions coming from other states, the USA asked. The USA thus disagreed with the Commission's decision to disregard its comments on Brazil's submission and requested that it reconsider its conclusion.[187]

Article 3 of Annex II to the LOS Convention, however, indicates that the Commission was correct, *lex lata*. The Commission shall adopt recommendations on the basis of information submitted by the 'coastal State'. Allowing other entities—whether third states, non-members, private actors, an IO, etc.—to submit 'evidence' would thus presume a very liberal reading of the law.

---

186 Information available at the website of the Commission: <www.un.org/Depts/los/clcs_new/submissions_files/bra04/clcs_2004_los_usatext_2.pdf> (accessed 1 January 2014).
187 *Ibid.*

4.6.2.4   Fact-Finding in Other Regimes

In fact, the LOS Convention is out of step with how various other treaty regimes go about the production of evidence. Let us first look at the *sources* of information. Under the Kyoto Compliance System, for instance, the Enforcement Branch is not restricted to relying solely on information provided by the state directly affected. Also IOs and NGOs may submit factual and technical information to both the Enforcement Branch and the Facilitative Branch. Relevant information may also include reports from expert review teams or reports of the Conferences of the Parties.[188]

Also when a human rights treaty body examines the periodic reports required of each state party, the treaty body may receive information from a range of other sources as well—from civil society organizations, national-level human rights institutions, UN entities, IOs and academic institutions.[189]

The contrast is perhaps greatest to the more traditional systems of dispute resolution. In the WTO system, for instance, other states have the right to make written submissions as third parties. According to Article 10, paragraph 2, of the Dispute Settlement Understanding,

> [a]ny Member having a substantial interest in a matter before a panel and having notified its interest to the DSB (referred to in this Understanding as a 'third party') shall have an opportunity to be heard by the panel and to make written submissions to the panel. These submissions shall also be given to the parties to the dispute and shall be reflected in the panel report.[190]

Also—as determined by the AB's ruling in *United States—Import Prohibition of Certain Shrimp and Shrimp Products*—WTO panels may accept and consider information under Articles 12 and 13 of the Dispute Settlement Understanding. The AB reversed the panel's original refusal and held:

> The thrust of Articles 12 and 13, taken together, is that the DSU accords to a panel established by the [Dispute Settlement Body], and engaged in a dispute settlement proceeding, ample and extensive authority to undertake and to control the process by which it informs itself both of

---

188   UN Doc. FCCC/CP/2001/13/Add.3 ('Decision 24/CP.7: Procedures and mechanisms relating to compliance under the Kyoto Protocol, Annex'), Section VIII, para. 3.

189   UN Doc. A/CONF.157/24 ('Report of the World Conference on Human Rights').

190   See also Article 17, para. 4, of the Dispute Settlement Understanding.

the relevant facts of the dispute and of the legal norms and principles applicable to such facts.[191]

Relying on Article 17, paragraph 9, of the Dispute Settlement Understanding, the AB in *European Communities—Trade Description of Sardines* also accepted information from a WTO member that was not party to the case:

> [W]e find that we are entitled to accept the amicus curiae brief submitted by Morocco, and to consider it. We wish to emphasize, however, that, in accepting the brief filed by Morocco in this appeal, we are not suggesting that each time a Member files such a brief we are required to accept and consider it. To the contrary, acceptance of any amicus curiae brief is a matter of discretion, which we must exercise on a case-by-case basis. We recall our statement that: The procedural rules of WTO dispute settlement are designed to promote [...] the fair, prompt and effective resolution of trade disputes [...]. Therefore, we could exercise our discretion to reject an amicus curiae brief if, by accepting it, this would interfere with the 'fair, prompt and effective resolution of trade disputes.' This could arise, for example, if a WTO Member were to seek to submit an amicus curiae brief at a very late stage in the appellate proceedings, with the result that accepting the brief would impose an undue burden on other participants.[192]

The same applies to the proceedings of the ICJ. While the Statute of the ICJ or the ICJ Rules make no express provision for others than the involved parties to bring information before the Court that is relevant to the dispute, Article 34, paragraph 2, of the Statute of the ICJ states that the Court

> may request of public international organizations information relevant to cases before it, and shall receive such information presented by such organizations on their own initiative.[193]

---

191   *United States—Import Prohibition of Certain Shrimp and Shrimp Products*, para. 106.

192   *European Communities—Trade Description of Sardines*, para. 167.

193   Notably, in the *Aerial Incident* cases, the ICJ invited the International Civil Aviation Organization (ICAO) to supply information regarding ICAO proceedings (*I.C.J. Reports* 1959, p. 127).

And in advisory proceedings, the Statute of the ICJ allows others to submit evidence or send unsolicited submissions to the Court. According to Article 66, paragraph 2, the ICJ shall

> notify any State entitled to appear before the Court or international organization considered by the Court, or, should it not be sitting, by the President, as likely able to furnish information on the question, that the Court will be prepared to receive, within a time limit to be fixed by the President, written statements, or to hear, at a public sitting to be held for the purpose, oral statements relating to the question.[194]

Second, the negative aspect of one-sided fact-finding—that only the coastal state may present 'evidence' to the Commission—is accentuated by the fact that the Commission has no opportunity to instigate its own evidence-gathering in the preparation of recommendations. As noted, the Commission may request the coastal state to provide additional information[195] or it can collaborate with relevant international organizations with a view to exchanging scientific and technical information that may be useful in its work.[196] However, there will be no further scrutiny of the facts, for instance by dispatching experts on fact-finding missions. Thus, the Commission has only limited means available for ascertaining whether the information submitted is a faithful representation of actual conditions on the seabed.

Also in this context, the regulations of the LOS Convention differ from those of certain other treaty regimes. For instance, the Scientific Committee under the ICRW—charged with obtaining information on the stock of whales and with monitoring the extent of whaling operations by States Parties—does not rely solely on what individual states present to it. The Scientific Committee is responsible for conveying the information to the Convention's treaty body,

---

194 Also, Article 36, para. 2, of the ECHR determines: 'The President of the Court may, in the interest of the proper administration of justice, invite any High Contracting Party which is not a party to the proceedings or any person concerned who is not the applicant to submit written comments or take part in hearings'. Accordingly, Rule 44 of the Rules of the ECtHR—titled 'Third-party intervention'—provides guidance concerning practical aspects of such intervention. In particular NGOs have made extensive use of this provision to make submissions in cases before the ECtHR, and the Court has also made reference to such submissions in its judgments. See Razzaque, Jona, 'Changing Role of Friends of the Court in the International Courts and Tribunals', in *Non-State Actors and International Law*, Vol. 1, 2001, pp. 169–200.

195 Article 10 of Annex IV of the Rules of Procedure.

196 Article 3, para. 2, of Annex II to the LOS Convention.

the IWC. The initial decision-making procedure of the ICRW gave rise to con-troversy because decision-making was based on information provided by individual states, which could, it was argued, undermine and even 'paralyse the promulgation of regulatory measures by the [IWC]'.[197] The IWC has since taken steps to promote objectivity in fact-finding and surveillance. An interna-tional inspection and observation plan has been drafted by the IWC through a revision of the 1992 Management Procedures.[198] Other steps include putting data collection on a more 'multinational' footing, rather than relying on indi-vidual states with vested interests.[199]

Also human rights treaty bodies have at their disposal sophisticated mech-anisms enabling fact-finding. It has been argued that relying solely on state reports would risk reducing 'the treaty body [...] to a mere rubberstamp, and the exercise watered down to a formalistic one in which the only ques-tion is *if* the state reported and whether its report complied with the report-ing guidelines' (emphasis added).[200] With several human rights conventions there are optional protocols that give their respective treaty bodies the pos-sibility of obtaining information by undertaking investigations—fact-finding missions—in member states, in case of indications of violations of human rights conventions.[201] Thus, the importance of comprehensive and objective

---

197   Rose, Gregory, and Saundra Crane, 'The Evolution of International Whaling Law', in
      Sands, Philippe (ed.), *Greening International Law* (The New Press, 1994), pp. 159–179, at
      p. 165.
198   Vice, Daniel, 'Implementation of Biodiversity Treaties: Monitoring, Fact-Finding, and
      Dispute Resolution', in Szasz, Paul C. (ed.), *Administrative and Expert Monitoring of
      International Treaties* (Transnational Publishers, 1999), pp. 135–163, at p. 143.
199   *Ibid.*
200   Viljoen, Frans, 'Fact-Finding by UN Human Rights Complaints Bodies—Analysis and
      Suggested Reforms', in *Max Planck Yearbook of United Nations Law*, Vol. 8, 2004,
      pp. 49–100, at p. 59.
201   See the Optional Protocol to the Convention against Torture and other Cruel, Inhuman
      or Degrading Treatment or Punishment (adopted on 18 December 2002; entered into
      force on 22 June 2006. Published in *UNTS*, Vol. 2375, p. 237), the Optional Protocol to the
      International Covenant on Economic, Social and Cultural Rights (adopted on 10 December
      2008; entered into force 5 May 2013. In UN Doc. A/63/435; 'Report of the Human Rights
      Council'), the Optional Protocol to the Convention on the Elimination of Discrimination
      against Women (adopted on 6 October 1999; entered into force 22 December 2000.
      Published in *UNTS*, Vol. 2131, p. 83), the Optional Protocol to the Convention on the Rights
      of Persons with Disabilities (adopted on 13 December 2006; entered into force 3 May
      2008. In UN Doc. A/61/611; 'Final report of the Ad Hoc Committee on a Comprehensive
      and Integral International Convention on the Protection and Promotion of the Rights
      and Dignity of Persons with Disabilities') and the Optional Protocol to the Convention

fact-finding is given priority not only in the field of international peace and security,[202] but also in regard to the protection of human rights.

A further example is the complaints procedures in the application of international labour standards under Articles 26 to 34 of the Constitution of the International Labour Organization.[203] According to Article 26 of the Constitution

> [a]ny of the Members shall have the right to file a complaint with the International Labour Office if it is not satisfied that any other Member is securing the effective observance of any Convention which both have ratified in accordance with the foregoing articles [...]. The Governing Body may appoint a Commission of Inquiry to consider the complaint and to report thereon.

Appointing a Commission of Inquiry is thus a specific investigative procedure initiated by the Governing Body of the International Labour Organization (ILO), established to facilitate the full investigation of a complaint, ascertaining all the facts of the case and then making recommendations on measures to be taken.

Bearing in mind the differences in functions and competences, it is also worth mentioning that in more traditional procedures for dispute settlement, more flexible regimes for methods of fact-finding apply, compared to those available to the Commission. For instance, in the *European Communities— Measures Concerning Meat and Meat Products (Hormones)* case, the EU had challenged the WTO panel's selection and use of experts. To this, the AB stated that a panel has the discretion to decide whether to seek advice from individual

---

on the Rights of the Child on a Communications Procedure (adopted 19 December 2011; in accordance with Article 19, para. 1, it will enter into force on 14 April 2014. In UN Doc. A/RES/66/138; 'Optional Protocol to the Convention on the Rights of the Child on a Communications Procedure').

202 UN Doc. A/RES/46/59 ('Declaration on Fact-finding by the United Nations in the Field of the Maintenance of International Peace and Security'), which states: 'In performing their functions in relation to the maintenance of international peace and security, the competent organs of the United Nations should endeavour to have full knowledge of all relevant facts. To this end they should consider undertaking fact-finding activities.' The Resolution allows UN representatives to be dispatched on fact-finding missions, which 'should be comprehensive, objective, impartial and timely'. *Ibid.*

203 Adopted in Paris on 1 April 1919; entered into force on 28 June 1919. Available at: <www .unhcr.org/refworld/docid/3ddb5391a.html> (accessed 1 January 2014).

scientific experts or from a group of such experts, and that it may establish *ad hoc* rules for such consultations:

> Both Article 11.2 of the SPS Agreement and Article 13 of the DSU enable panels to seek information and advice as they deem appropriate in a particular case [...]. We find that in disputes involving scientific or technical issues, neither Article 11.2 of the SPS Agreement, nor Article 13 of the DSU prevents panels from consulting with individual experts. Rather, both the SPS Agreement and the DSU leave to the sound discretion of a panel the determination of whether the establishment of an expert review group is necessary or appropriate. The rules and procedures set forth in Appendix 4 of the DSU apply in situations in which expert review groups have been established. However, this is not the situation in this particular case. Consequently, once the panel has decided to request the opinion of individual scientific experts, there is no legal obstacle to the panel drawing up, in consultation with the parties to the dispute, ad hoc rules for those particular proceedings.[204]

This was confirmed in *United States—Import Prohibition of Certain Shrimp and Shrimp Products*. The panel had received information from three NGOs, but the complaining parties requested it not to consider the contents of the briefs submitted. The USA, however, stepped forward and urged the panel to take into account any relevant information. The panel found that

> [a]ccepting non-requested information from non-governmental sources would be, in our opinion, incompatible with the provisions of the DSU as currently applied. We therefore informed the parties that we did not intend to take these documents into consideration.[205]

The AB nevertheless concluded that the panel was incorrect in its legal interpretation of Article 13 of the Dispute Settlement Understanding, and held that accepting non-requested information from non-governmental sources was not incompatible with the provisions of the Dispute Settlement Understanding. The AB began its analysis by emphasizing the 'comprehensive nature' of a panel's authority to seek information in the context of a dispute:

---

204   *EC—Measures Concerning Meat and Meat Products (Hormones)*, para. 148.
205   *United States—Import Prohibition of Certain Shrimp and Shrimp Products*, para. 99.

The comprehensive nature of the authority of a panel to 'seek' information and technical advice from 'any individual or body' it may consider
appropriate, or from 'any relevant source', should be underscored. This
authority embraces more than merely the choice and evaluation of the
source of the information or advice which it may seek. A panel's authority
includes the authority to decide not to seek such information or advice
at all. We consider that a panel also has the authority to accept or reject
any information or advice which it may have sought and received, or to
make some other appropriate disposition thereof. It is particularly within
the province and the authority of a panel to determine the need for information and advice in a specific case, to ascertain the acceptability and
relevancy of information or advice received, and to decide what weight
to ascribe to that information or advice or to conclude that no weight at
all should be given to what has been received.[206]

Further:

The thrust of Articles 12 and 13, taken together, is that the DSU accords
to a panel established by the DSB, and engaged in a dispute settlement
proceeding, ample and extensive authority to undertake and to control
the process by which it informs itself both of the relevant facts of the dispute and of the legal norms and principles applicable to such facts. That
authority, and the breadth thereof, is indispensably necessary to enable
a panel to discharge its duty imposed by Article 11 of the DSU to 'make
an objective assessment of the matter before it, including an objective
assessment of the facts of the case and the applicability of and conformity with the relevant covered agreements [...]'.[207]

The AB subsequently held that the word 'seek' in the phrase 'seek information'
should not be given a 'formal and technical' understanding. Given the breadth
of a panel's general mandate to seek information, the distinction between
'requested' and 'non-requested' information vanished.[208]

Thus, at least within the WTO dispute settlement system, there seems to be
a trend towards wider and more comprehensive rules concerning the admissibility of facts and evidence. Panels may seek to elucidate a matter by calling for or receiving information from governmental authorities and private or

---

206   *Ibid.,* para. 104
207   *Ibid.,* para. 106.
208   *Ibid.,* paras. 107–110.

other public parties. It has been argued that opening the door to others than the immediately affected states ensures the best possible elucidation of a matter, while also enhancing the legitimacy of the system by introducing greater fairness.[209]

In the procedures available to international courts and tribunals, there are also 'inquisitorial' elements to a much greater extent than as regards the Commission. Article 77 of the Rules of the ITLOS provides that the Tribunal may at any time call upon the parties to produce such evidence or to give such explanations as it may consider necessary for the elucidation of any aspect of the matters in issue, or may itself seek other information for this purpose.[210]

Nor is the ICJ restricted to asking the parties to clarify the facts of the matter:[211] the Court may undertake its own on-site investigations,[212] or give 'the task of carrying out an enquiry or giving an expert opinion' to others.[213] In the course of a hearing, the ICJ may summon witnesses and experts at its own initiative;[214] the Court may also approach IOs for such information as it deems relevant to the case.[215] We may note that the ICJ stated in *Nicaragua*:

> As to the facts of the case, in principle the Court is not bound to confine its consideration to the material formally submitted to it by the parties.[216]

Thus we see that both international courts and several other treaty bodies are at liberty to draw on a wider range of methods concerning the determination of facts and production of evidence. This issue is problematic, and not only in terms of normative legitimacy. In a case concerning the application of Article 76, there is then also a wide gap between a court's possibility to verify and seek information on the one hand, and the Commission's possibility on the other. If a dispute concerning the establishment of the outer limits of the continental shelf becomes subject to international litigation, this will imply vastly divergent fact-finding procedures.

---

209   Cass, *The Constitutionalization of the World Trade Organization: Legitimacy, Democracy, and Community in the International Trading System*, pp. 196–197.

210   See Rules of the Tribunal, as amended. In *International Tribunal for the Law of the Sea: Basic Texts* (Martinus Nijhoff Publishers/Brill Publishers, 2004).

211   ICJ Statute, Article 49.

212   *Ibid.*, Article 44.

213   *Ibid.*, Article 50.

214   *Ibid.*

215   *Ibid.*

216   *I.C.J. Reports* 1986, p. 4, at p. 25 (para. 30).

Interesting to note in this connection is how international courts tend to deal with different types of proof in proceedings. For instance, the ICJ has handled a number of fact-intensive cases where the question of 'what really happened' constituted a major part of the proceedings.[217] In *Armed Activities on the Territory of the Congo*, the ICJ differentiated between *types* of evidence, as to which information the Court felt could be considered objective and reliable. The case concerned the allegation of the Democratic Republic of the Congo (DRC) that Uganda, by occupying DRC territory and supporting insurrection, had violated the ban on the use of force and the principle of non-intervention in international law. The ICJ relied largely on evidence procured from official UN reports and the findings of the 'Porter Commission', an independent tribunal of inquiry established by the Ugandan government in 2001. The Court held that the methods of inquiry had followed broadly accepted standards and included testimonies of Ugandan officials that contained statements against interest.[218] However, the ICJ stated that it would

> treat with caution evidentiary materials specially prepared for this case and also materials emanating from a single source.[219]

The ICJ's practice thus suggests that the Court would have taken pains to illuminate a case over Article 76 as much as possible, and also that it would have aimed for neutral and broad fact-finding. This would probably imply that the coastal state would not be the sole party allowed to submit information.[220]

---

217   See further Bothe, Michael, 'Fact-Finding as a Means of Ensuring Respect for International Humanitarian Law', in Epping, Volker, and Wolff Heinstel von Heinegg (eds), *International Humanitarian Law Facing New Challenges* (Springer, 2007), pp. 249–267.

218   *I.C.J. Reports* 2005, p. 168, at p. 201 (para. 61). See also *I.C.J. Reports* 1986, p. 4, at p. 41 (para. 64).

219   *I.C.J. Reports* 2005, p. 168, at p. 201 (para. 61).

220   The 2012 *Bay of Bengal* case between Bangladesh and Myanmar is—regrettably—less instructive in this regard. The ITLOS stated that '[w]ith respect to the question of the Parties' entitlements to the continental shelf beyond 200 nm, Bangladesh has made considerable efforts to describe the geological evolution of the Bay of Bengal and its geophysical characteristics known as the Bengal depositional system' (Judgment, para. 424). However, the facts of the matter did not play a prominent role as 'Myanmar [did] not dispute Bangladesh's description of the area in question and the scientific evidence presented to support it. What Myanmar does contest, however, is the relevance of these facts and evidence to the present case. The disagreement between the Parties in this regard essentially relates to the question of the interpretation of article 76 of the convention, in particular the meaning of 'natural prolongation' in paragraph 1 of that article' (Judgment, para. 425).

4.6.2.5   Preliminary Conclusions

Summing up then, in the current Article 76 implementation process, it is only the coastal state that may contribute to shed light on the case. *Lex ferenda*, this is a weak procedure, also because the Commission has no inquiry mechanisms at its disposal. True, the Commission may request the coastal state to provide additional or clarifying information—but that is still information that is produced by the coastal state: the same party that is seeking to extend its jurisdiction over the continental shelf. The inadequacy of these regulations should also be evident when we consider the following point: Whereas a decision by, say, the ICJ concerning Article 76 has no binding force except between the parties, the outer limits established by the coastal state on the basis of the Commission's recommendations are 'final and binding' on *all* parties to the LOS Convention. It could therefore be argued that other states have at least as much interest in contributing to fact-finding and the production of evidence when the Commission deals with a continental shelf claim, as when that claim is being litigated by an international court.

4.6.3   *Participatory Rights of the Coastal State*

4.6.3.1   Introduction

One fundamental requirement of procedural fairness and good administration is procedural participation, including the principle of the right to be heard. Basically, this means that a subject of law should be given the opportunity to be heard before a decision that could affect that subject is made. Participation from the coastal state promotes administrative embeddedness, first and foremost; it is reasonable that the coastal state should have the right to be heard before the Commission adopts its recommendations. But the principle of the right to be heard also ensures wider information on the case, and will increase the chances of substantively correct recommendations. In addition, procedural participation serves to make the authorities more accountable to those affected by the decisions.[221]

In the following we critically examine how satisfactory are the coastal state's participatory rights in the Article 76 implementation process. Here we will ask, for example, whether the coastal state at a proper time and in a proper way is informed during procedures; if the coastal state may take part at relevant stages of the proceedings; if interim findings and conclusions are communicated to the coastal state and it is given an opportunity to respond; if the coastal state is allowed to make its case before final recommendations are adopted; and if

---

221   Bodansky, 'Legitimacy', p. 717.

the coastal state has an opportunity to be heard when the Commission has delivered its recommendations.

4.6.3.2   Participatory Rights in International Law

Procedural participation and the principle of the right to be heard are central to most domestic legal procedural systems based on a fair hearing, at least in Western legal regimes. They lie at the core of, for instance, the procedural system of English courts and administrative government authorities.[222] In the USA, the principle of the right to be heard has been described as the 'oldest established principle in Anglo-American administrative law',[223] and defined as the 'opportunity to be heard at a meaningful time and in a meaningful manner'.[224]

Participatory rights and the principle of the right to be heard have spread and become embodied in key human rights treaties, requiring national states to put minimum procedural arrangements in place.[225] Such principles have also been highlighted in cases where *international* institutions have failed to provide fair procedures standards for individuals. For instance, the Administrative Tribunal of the International Monetary Fund (IMF) has argued that the right to be heard is a general principle of international administrative law

> so widely accepted and well-established in different legal systems that [it is] regarded as generally applicable to all decisions taken by international organizations, including the Fund.[226]

Traditional civil or criminal trial—with its manifold safeguards, designed for instance to protect individuals in custody or labour rights—cannot, however,

---

222   See generally Clark, D.H., *Natural Justice: Substance and Shadow* (Stevens, 1975).

223   The right to a fair hearing is protected by the Fifth Amendment to the US Constitution, under which it is required that administrative government authorities and courts adhere to the general principle of 'due process of law'. See Wade, William, *Administrative Law* (Oxford University Press, 1982), pp. 447–452.

224   Joshua, Julian, 'The Right to be Heard in EEC Competition Procedures', in *Fordham International Law Journal*, Vol. 15, 1991, pp. 16–91, at p. 25.

225   Notably, under Article 6, para. 1, of the ECHR, everyone is entitled to a 'fair trial' in civil and criminal cases alike.

226   Judgment No. 2010–4 of the Administrative Tribunal of the IMF, para. 100. Available at <www.imf.org/external/imfat/pdf/j2010_4.pdf> (accessed 1 January 2014). Having reviewed the IMF's procedural history with regard to the decision to place an employee on paid leave, the Tribunal concluded that the IMF had failed to ensure the protection of due process rights.

automatically be taken as an appropriate model for a procedure like that under Article 76. But it is important to note that participatory rights and the right to be heard are also granted national governments in global decision-making processes. In view of the concerns regarding France's non-appearance at the judgment in the *Nuclear Tests* case, the ICJ emphasized that

> as a judicial body the Court is conscious of the importance of the prin-
> ciple expressed in the maxim *audi alteram partem* [...].[227]

The statement indicates that the right to be heard is a substantive principle of law which is important and which the Court felt committed to take into consideration. In addition, several specific provisions of the Court's rules are intended to safeguard participatory rights and the right to be heard.[228] Similarly, procedural participation is enshrined in the rules applying to the proceedings of other judicial bodies such as the ITLOS,[229] and in the dispute settlement system of the WTO.[230] According to the procedures and mechanisms relating to the Kyoto Compliance System, the affected party has an opportunity to attend various stages of the process and to demand a hearing; time limits are set for impending decisions; and the affected state party is notified of findings and conclusions during the proceedings.[231]

Particularly important as regards the Commission, procedural participation and the right to be heard have also been highlighted as doctrinal features of

---

227 *I.C.J. Reports* 1974, p. 457, at p. 469 (para. 34). See also *I.C.J. Reports* 1974, p. 253, at p. 265 (para. 33).

228 For instance, under Article 31 of the Rules of the Court, the President shall ascertain the views of the parties with regard to questions of procedure; Article 44 concerning the extension of a time limit provides that a party shall be given an opportunity to state its views; Article 56 requires the consent of the parties to produce new evidence after the closure of the written proceedings; Article 72 provides for the right to respond to additional evidence produced at the request of the Court; and Article 76, para. 3, provides that the Court shall afford the parties an opportunity of presenting their observations on the revocation or modification of interim measures.

229 For instance, Article 45 of the ITLOS' Rules of Procedure provides that in every case submitted to the Tribunal, the President shall ascertain the views of the parties with regard to questions of procedure. Under Article 73, para. 2, the Tribunal shall, *inter alia*, determine the order in which the parties will be heard and the method of handling the evidence and examining any witnesses and experts, only after ascertaining the views of the parties.

230 See for instance Appendix 3—Working Procedures—to the Dispute Settlement Understanding.

231 UN Doc. FCCC/CP/2001/13/Add.3 ('Decision 24/CP.7: Procedures and mechanisms relating to compliance under the Kyoto Protocol, Annex'), Section VIII, para. 3.

global administrative law and as basic principles increasingly applied in global administrative governance affecting individual states.[232] For instance, the Financial Action Task Force—an inter-governmental body for developing and promoting policies to combat money laundering and terrorist financing—has made attempts to consult with states before taking measures against them.[233] And under the PCT, rather extensive rights are established for the applicant of a patent to communicate with the authority conducting an international search; the IPEA.[234]

4.6.3.3 Participatory Rights in the Article 76-Process

The LOS Convention basically provides three opportunities for the coastal state to participate and be heard in the proceedings for setting the outer limits of the continental shelf beyond 200 nautical miles. First, the coastal state has the opportunity to 'speak out' through its submission, which constitutes the very premise of the Commission's involvement. Second, according to Article 5 of Annex II to the LOS Convention, a coastal state having made a submission to the Commission may send its representatives to participate in the 'relevant proceedings' of the Commission, however, without voting rights. Third, according to Article 8 of Annex II to the LOS Convention,

> [i]n the case of disagreement by the coastal State with the recommendations of the Commission, the coastal State shall, within a reasonable time, make a revised or new submission to the Commission.

4.6.3.3.1 *Submission*

While a submission—according to Rule 47, paragraph 1, of the Commission's Rules of Procedure—shall conform to certain formal requirements, no limitations are specified as to the character of the information the coastal state is to include in its continental shelf submission to the Commission. The Commission's Scientific and Technical Guidelines indicate the kind of information the Commission expects the coastal state to include in its submission—but

---

232 See generally Krisch, Nico, and Benedict Kingsbury, 'Introduction: Global Governance and Global Administrative Law in the International Legal Order', pp. 1–13.

233 Kingsbury, Krisch and Stewart, 'The Emergence of Global Administrative Law', at p. 47.

234 See Rule 66.2 of the Regulations under the PCT, which provides that if the IPEA considers that its international preliminary examination report shall be negative in respect of a patent claim, the Authority shall enter into dialogue with the applicant (Regulations to the PCT, adopted on June 19, 1970, as amended. Available at the website of the World Intellectual Property Organization (WIPO): <www.wipo.int/pct/en/texts/> (accessed 1 January 2014).

the coastal state is not bound by these Guidelines. Nor are there any limits on the size of the coastal state's submission, which basically gives the coastal state an unrestricted opportunity to present its continental shelf claim.

4.6.3.3.2 *Proceedings*

As noted, Annex II of the LOS Convention explicitly states that the coastal state may send its representatives to participate (without voting rights) in the 'relevant' proceedings of the Commission. Just which proceedings these 'relevant' ones are, however, is not specified in the Convention.

More detailed regulations on the coastal state's right to participate and be heard during proceedings are provided for by the Commission's Rules of Procedure, according to which the Commission shall keep the coastal state briefed on how the case is progressing. The first briefing—actually more of a formal detail—takes place when the submission has been received and recorded. According to Rule 49 of the Rules of Procedure,

> [t]he Secretary-General shall promptly acknowledge by letter to the coastal State the receipt of its submission and attachments and annexes thereto, specifying the date of receipt.

These rules are similar to those that apply, for instance, under the PCT, when a claim for a patent is filed with the receiving office and transmitted to the International Bureau and the competent International Searching Authority.[235] Rules 24 and 25 of the Regulations to the PCT specify that the International Bureau and the International Searching Authority shall promptly notify the applicant of the fact and the date of receipt of the record copy, identify the application by its number, etc.

The Commission's next briefing comes during the sub-commission's preparatory examination of the submission. At this juncture—according to Rule 8, paragraph 2, of Annex III to the Rules of Procedure—the Commission or sub-commission shall notify and inform the coastal state of a preliminary timetable for the handling of the submission.

Apart from this, however, no obligation rests on the Commission to notify the coastal state during proceedings—even though several years may pass before the sub-commission finalizes its work and submits its 'preliminary recommendations' to the plenary Commission. The complex and extensive

---

235   See Articles 10 and 12 of the PCT.

submission of Australia took the Commission almost four years to finalize,[236] and a survey of recommendations adopted by 1 January 2014 reveals an average submission processing time of approximately three years.[237] Since many years usually pass between the initial examination and the sub-commission's presentation at an advanced stage in the process (see below), it can be argued that the duty to notify is rather marginal relative to the length of proceedings.

Moreover, there is no deadline prescribed for the Commission as to the permitted processing time of a submission. An International Search subject to the PCT—culminating in an international search report—is to be carried out within a prescribed time limit, according to Article 18 of the PCT. According to Rule 42 of the Regulations to the PCT, the limit for the International Search shall be three months from the receipt of a claim copy, or nine months from the priority date, whichever time limit expires later. If the Commission had similar short deadlines, then it would perhaps not be unreasonable for the coastal state to wait through the whole process time, without further notification. However, since processing time under the LOS Convention is unspecified—and in practice lasts several years—it can be argued that there should have been more specified regulations with regard to notifications.

The lack of obligation to inform and notify the coastal state during the process is largely mitigated by the fact that the Commission is to invite the coastal state to participate in the proceedings at various stages. Rule 52 of the Rules of Procedure provides:

> The Commission shall, through the Secretary-General, notify the coastal State which has made a submission, no later than sixty days prior to the opening date of the session, of the date and place at which its submission will be first considered. The coastal State shall, in accordance with article 5 of Annex II to the Convention, be invited to send its representatives to participate, without the right to vote, in the relevant proceedings of the Commission pursuant to section VI of annex III to these Rules.

Article 15 of Annex III to the Rules of Procedure details the stages of the deliberations:

---

236   The date of submission was 15 November 2004 (see Doc. CLCS/44, para. 4). The Commission's recommendations were adopted 9 April 2008 (see Doc. CLCS/58, para. 11).

237   The Commission lists both the date of each submission and the date of the adoption of recommendations. See <www.un.org/Depts/los/clcs_new/commission_submissions .htm> (accessed 1 January 2014).

Representatives of the submitting coastal State can participate in the relevant proceedings of the Commission, in accordance with rule 52. For this purpose, the Commission, taking into consideration the particulars of each submission, will identify the proceedings deemed relevant for the participation of the representatives of the submitting coastal State.

Article 15 further provides that there are three proceedings deemed relevant for all submissions. First, the meeting at which the coastal state is given the opportunity to present its submission to the Commission for the first time in accordance with Rule 2 (*litra* a) of Annex III.[238] Second, the meetings at which the sub-commission invites the representatives of the coastal state for consultation are regarded as relevant proceedings in which the coastal state may participate. Third, relevant proceedings also include meetings at which the representatives of the coastal state wish to provide additional clarification to the sub-commission on any matters related to the submission.

Thus, representatives of the coastal state may attend and put their case at the following junctures in the proceedings: First, when the work of the Commission in connection with a submission is being planned and scheduled.[239] Second, when the sub-commission is conducting its preparatory examination of the submission, the Commission may, pursuant to Rule 6 of Annex III, request clarification from the representatives of the coastal state on any matters to be clarified if necessary.[240] Third, the coastal state will have the possibility of being heard at any stage during the main examination of the sub-

---

238   Pursuant to Rule 2 (*litra* a)—after a period of at least three months following the date of publication in accordance with Rule 51, para. 1—the Commission shall convene a session, of which one item on the provisional agenda shall be a presentation of the submission by the coastal state's representatives. The coastal state shall here be given the opportunity to present charts indicating the proposed outer limits and the provisions of Article 76 which have been invoked. The coastal state shall identify names of members of the Commission who have assisted in providing scientific and technical advice with respect to the delineation, information regarding any disputes related to the submission shall be disclosed, and also, the presentation shall include comments on any *note verbale* from other states regarding the data reflected in the executive summary as made public by the UNSG in accordance with Rule 50 of the Rules of Procedure.

239   According to Rule 2 (*litra* a) of Annex III, the coastal state shall then be given an opportunity to present its submission directly to the Commission's members.

240   Rule 6, para. 3, specifies that the 'coastal State may provide additional clarification to the subcommission on any matters relating to the submission'. Furthermore, '[c]larifications can be provided in the form of presentations and/or additional materials submitted through the Secretariat'.

mission, if the sub-commission feels the need for additional data, information or clarifications.[241] Fourth, according to Rule 10, paragraph 3, of Annex III, at an advanced stage during the examination of the submission, the coastal state is to be informed of the sub-commission's interim findings and conclusions.[242] Fifth, when the sub-commission has submitted its recommendations to the plenary Commission in accordance with Rule 14 of Annex III, the coastal state

> may make a presentation on any matter related to its submission to the plenary of the Commission, if it so chooses. For that presentation, the coastal State may be allowed up to half a day. The coastal State and the Commission shall not engage in discussion on the submission or its recommendations at that meeting. After the presentation made by the coastal State, the Commission shall consider the recommendations in private, without the participation of the representatives of the coastal State.[243]

This meeting is to take place after the sub-commission has presented its recommendations to the Commission, but before the Commission considers and adopts the final recommendations. The coastal state will therefore have a right to present any matter related to its submission to the plenary Commission *before* the final recommendations are adopted.

In my view, the Commission's Rules of Procedure give the coastal state adequate rights and possibilities to participate at different stages of the

---

241 The sub-commission's Chairperson shall then request the coastal state to provide such data or information or to make clarifications, subject to time limitations agreed upon between the coastal state and the sub-commission. See Rule 10, para. 1, of Annex III to the Rules of Procedure.

242 The sub-commission shall invite the delegation of the coastal state to one or several meetings at which the sub-commission shall provide a comprehensive presentation of its views and general conclusions arising from the examination of parts or the entire submission. And at such meetings, the coastal state shall—according to para. 4—have the opportunity to 'respond to the presentations of the subcommission during the same session, and/or at a later stage, in a format and schedule determined by agreement between the delegation and the subcommission. Printed and electronic copies of the written materials presented by the subcommission and the delegation of the coastal State shall be made available to one another through the Secretariat'. Only after the meeting(s) with the delegation of the coastal state, the sub-commission shall proceed to prepare its draft recommendations to be submitted to the plenary Commission for its consideration. See Rule 10, para. 5, of Annex III of the Rules of Procedure.

243 See Rule 15 (1*bis*) of Annex III to the Rules of Procedure.

proceedings. There are also indications that sub-commissions have extensive consultations with the coastal state during the proceedings if there are matters that need additional attention.[244]

However, at the end of the day, there is the matter of legal consideration here. In not providing the coastal states access to *all* meetings, it can still be questioned whether the Commission's practice and Rules of Procedure are fully in harmony with the aforementioned requirement in Article 5 of Annex II to the LOS Convention, under which the coastal state is entitled to participate in the 'relevant' proceedings of the Commission without the right to vote. Notably, the issue became subject to internal discussions in the Commission already regarding the first submission handled by the Commission; that of the Russian Federation. When the Commission during its Eleventh Session was set to deliberate on the draft recommendations from the sub-commission regarding the Russian submission, one member of the Commission—the Russian-nominated member Mr Kazmin—expressed the view that the coastal state, pursuant to Article 5 of Annex II to the Convention, had a right to participate in the proceedings, without the right to vote. Mr Kazmin emphasized that the discussion of the recommendations was part of the 'relevant proceedings' referred to in Article 5 and that the delegation of Russia thus should be present at the meetings of the Commission when the recommendations regarding its submission were considered and adopted. The Chairman of the Commission pointed out, however, that the Commission would only address the issue if and when a formal communication was actually received.

Then, on 26 June 2002, the Chairman received a letter from the permanent representative of Russia to the UN stating that a delegation of Russia was present in New York in order to make a presentation on the submission for the benefit of new members of the Commission or to answer any additional questions regarding the submission the Commission might have. A renewed discussion regarding the participation of representatives of the coastal state in the proceedings took place, in which Mr Kazmin restated his arguments concerning the right of the representatives of the coastal state to participate in the proceedings.

A different opinion, however, was expressed by the Chairman: the Rules of Procedure drew on the provision of Article 5 of Annex II and the Commission should continue to be guided in its work by those Rules. Therefore, at the final stage, the Commission should consider and adopt the recommendations at a private meeting. The differing views were impossible to reconcile and the

---

244   Doc. CLCS/34, para. 23.

Chairman thus suggested putting the matter to a vote in which the members would respond to the following question:

> Do you agree that the Commission may discuss the recommendations of the sub-commission and the Commission in a closed meeting, and consider those proceedings as 'not relevant' for the purposes of inviting the coastal state pursuant to Article 5 of Annex II to the Convention and Rule 51 of the Rules of Procedure of the Commission?

Several members pointed to the sensitive nature of the matter and the Commission thus proceeded to a secret ballot. Out of 18 present and voting members, 15 voted yes, 3 no, with no invalid ballots. For a two-thirds majority, 12 votes were required. Mr Kazmin stated that although he accepted the results of the vote he continued to maintain, and wished to put on record, that the decision was contrary to the provision of Article 5 of Annex II to the Convention.[245]

4.6.3.3.3 *Returning Submissions*

The coastal state's right to file a new continental shelf claim under Article 8 of Annex II to the LOS Convention gives the coastal state an opportunity to address and oppose the substantive elements of the Commission's recommendations *after* they have been adopted. Similar regulations are found in the system under the PCT—for instance, if the IPEA considers that the international preliminary examination report should be negative in respect of a patent claim because the invention in question does not meet the three criteria of novelty, inventive step or industrial applicability. In such case, the IPEA shall notify the applicant in writing, inviting the applicant to submit a written reply.[246] The applicant may respond to the invitation from the IPEA by making amendments or—if he or she disagrees with the opinion of the Authority—by submitting arguments, as the case may be, or do both.[247]

The coastal state's right to be heard after the Commission has delivered its recommendations promotes the coastal state's participatory rights. Indeed, the coastal state is given the opportunity to present a completely new and revised submission, which the Commission then must assess through its regular procedures. The coastal state's right to be heard in this regard is also enhanced by the generous time limit allocated to new and revised submissions. The IPEA,

---

245   Doc. CLCS/34, paras. 18–25.
246   Rule 66.2 (*litra* a), of the Regulations under the PCT.
247   Rule 66.3 of the Regulations under the PCT.

according to Rule 66.2 (*litra* d) of the Regulations under the PCT, must fix a time limit for the reply, which shall be 'reasonable under the circumstances' but shall 'not be more than three months after the said date'. By contrast, Article 8 of Annex II to the LOS Convention merely states that the coastal state shall make a new or revised submission within 'reasonable time'. Thus the deadline running from the time at which the coastal state receives the Commission's recommendations seems to be a very 'relaxed' one, which in fact might undermine the deadline prescribed by Article 4 of Annex II: as soon as possible and at the latest within 10 years.

As of 1 January 2014, the Commission has received only two revised submission in accordance with Article 8 of Annex II. Barbados made its original submission to the Commission on 8 May 2008.[248] On 15 April 2010, the Commission adopted its recommendations.[249] Pursuant to the receipt of recommendations from the Commission, however, the Government of Barbados sought clarification concerning 'Gardiner Point 12 (GP12)' in its submission. Following exchange of correspondence between Barbados and the Commission, the Commission advised that '[…] the most appropriate way to address this matter would be for the Government of Barbados to make a revised submission'.[250] One year and three months after having received the original recommendations, on 25 July 2011, Barbados transmitted to the Commission a revised submission on the limits of its continental shelf beyond 200 nautical miles.[251]

Also the Russian Federation has made a revised submission to the Commission. Russia made its original submission to the Commission on 20 December 2001.[252] On 27 June 2002, the Commission adopted recommendations in regard to that submission, in which it requested Russia to submit more information, *inter alia*, with regard to the continental shelf areas beyond 200 nautical miles in the Okhotsk Sea.[253] Then, more than ten years later, on 28 February 2013, Russia submitted to the Commission a partial revised submission in respect of that sea area.[254]

Sparse practice to date offers little guidance to the interpretation of the phrasing 'reasonable time'. Since Barbados took issue over only one minor

---

248   Doc. CLCS/60, para. 3.
249   Doc. CLCS/66, para. 11.
250   Executive summary of the revised submission by Barbados, p. 2. Available at the website of the Commission: <www.un.org/Depts/los/clcs_new/submissions_files/brb_10rev2011/ Revised%20Executive%20Summary.pdf> (accessed 1 January 2014).
251   Doc. CLCS/72, para. 49.
252   Doc. CLCS/32.
253   Doc. CLCS/34.
254   Doc. CLCS/80.

aspect of the Commission's recommendations, it can be argued that the revised submission was not put forward within 'reasonable time'. Even more so with regard to Russia, where it indeed can be questioned whether a revised submission lodged more than ten years after the original was put forward within the time limit under Article 8. One the other hand, the wording is vague and should perhaps be interpreted to the advantage of the coastal state. Under all circumstances, the rule contained in Article 8 serves to improve the coastal state's chances to be heard.

4.6.3.4   Preliminary Conclusions

The LOS Convention uses a relatively 'simple' system as regards the right of the coastal state to be heard and participate during the Commission's examination. The coastal state makes its submission; it has a right to participate in the 'relevant proceedings without the right to vote'; and it may make a resubmission if it disagrees with the recommendations. The Commission's Rules of Procedure, however, have developed these rudimentary participation rights to a far higher level of sophistication. Thus the coastal state's participation is in practice far more prominent and detailed than what is provided for in the LOS Convention.

But although the coastal state has a right to be present and make its case at separate stages of the review of its submission, we should note that government representatives may not be dispatched to observe during other parts of the Commission's procedure than those specifically designated as 'relevant' by the Commission itself. Pursuant to Rule 23 of the Rules of Procedure—unless the Commission decides otherwise—the meetings of the Commission and the sub-commissions are to be held in private. At this point then, the Commission's rules seem to differ from those applying to certain other treaty regimes. For instance, under the procedures relating to compliance under the Kyoto Protocol,

> [t]he Party concerned shall be entitled to designate one or more persons to represent it during the *consideration* of the question of implementation by the relevant branch.[255] (Emphasis added)

Accordingly, the party shall not be present during the actual deliberations—but it may be present during the 'consideration' of the question of implementation. The main rule under the compliance system of the Kyoto Protocol is thus

---

255   UN Doc. FCCC/CP/2001/13/Add.3 ('Decision 24/CP.7: Procedures and mechanisms relating to compliance under the Kyoto Protocol, Annex'), Section VIII, para. 2.

that the directly affected party has the opportunity to observe the discussions in their entirety, withdrawing only when deliberations start. The Commission's rules do not provide for the same openness for the submitting coastal state. The system developed by the Commission is basically reversed, in that Rule 15 of Annex III to the Rules of Procedure explicitly mentions only those meetings at which the coastal state has a right to attend.

Second, perhaps the most problematic aspect is that the coastal state is not involved more frequently during proceedings which take several years. It would help to increase participation if the coastal state could attend meetings when the sub-commission is approximately halfway through its examination. There is a long interval between the coastal state's appearance after the initial examination and the meeting at which the coastal state is informed of the sub-commission's interim findings and conclusion.[256] Given the length of the proceedings from initiation to conclusion, it could be argued that this is an unsatisfactory element as regards the coastal state's right to participate and be heard under the Article 76 implementation process.

The procedures of the Commission dealing with the participatory rights of the coastal state nevertheless contain elements largely found also in other administrative treaty regimes, such as under the PCT. Importantly, in the last phase during the Commission's examination, the coastal state is given an opportunity to comment *before* the plenary Commission adopts its recommendations. And, if it disagrees with the recommendations, the coastal state may file a new and revised submission. On the whole, then, the procedures concerning the participatory rights of the coastal state can be said to lie within the margins of permissible norms; nonetheless, some improvements—especially as to the frequency of coastal state ability to participate—would be desirable, and could strengthen the legitimacy of the Commission's procedures.

4.6.4   *Transparency*
4.6.4.1   Introduction
With regard to the admissibility of facts and evidence, it has been argued that Article 76 has an insufficient and poor normative construction: only the coastal state is involved in presenting the case, whereas the resulting establishment of the continental shelf's outer limits beyond 200 nautical miles has legal and practical implications for other states as well, to wit, their access to and benefit from resources located on the 'outer' continental shelf.

---

256   That is, the meeting at an advanced stage provided for in Rule 15, para. 1*bis*, of Annex III to the Rules of Procedure.

Another crucial matter involving the interest of third parties—and the outside world in general—is transparency. Generally, transparency and access to information promote accountability in making decisions and proceedings available to public and peer scrutiny.[257] For the purposes here, transparency relates to the extent to which others than the coastal state may familiarize themselves with first, how the Commission exercises its functions, and, second, the Commission's recommendations. Transparency can therefore be said to have both an internal and external dimension. Internal transparency is about giving the States Parties access to the Commission's proceedings and documents, including its recommendations. External transparency, in contrast, is about giving non-members, NGOs and the general public at large, access to the Commission's proceedings and documents.

At several stages of the Commission's submission review, decisional transparency and access to information can be of considerable importance. First, others than the coastal states might have an interest in the information on which the Commission is to base its recommendations—that is, the coastal state's submission. Second, others than the coastal state might wish to be informed about the proceedings of the Commission, for instance by having access to or attending Commission meetings. Third, after the Commission has adopted a recommendation, others might be interested in being able to check whether the recommendation has been adopted in accordance with Article 76. Ultimately, others may wish to check whether the coastal state in fact establishes the outer limits 'on the basis of' the Commission's recommendations. In the following, the main question is thus whether the LOS Convention—supplemented by the Rules of Procedure—provides for regulations that ensure internal and external transparency to this end.[258]

4.6.4.2   Transparency in Global Administrative Law
In domestic administrative decision-making, procedural transparency is a classical component of due process. However, decisional transparency and access to information also are principles that are increasingly being applied in global

---

257   Kingsbury, Krisch and Stewart, 'The Emergence of Global Administrative Law', p. 38.

258   In regard to the Commission and the Article 76 process, the issue of transparency has so far been discussed briefly in legal literature. See, however, Oxman, Bernhard, 'The Territorial Temptation: A Siren Song at Sea', in *American Journal of International Law*, Vol. 100, 2006, pp. 830–851, at pp. 838–839; Elferink, 'Openness and Article 76 of the Law of the Sea Convention: The Process Does Not Need to Be Adjusted'; Mcnab, 'The Case for Transparency in the Delimitation of the Outer Continental Shelf in Accordance with UNCLOS Article 76'; and Cavnar, 'Accountability and the Commission on the Limits of the Continental Shelf: Deciding Who Owns the Ocean Floor'.

administrative governance as well.[259] A first notable example is the Aarhus Convention. According to its Article 3, paragraph 7, states shall promote the application of the principles of the Convention in international decision-making processes and within the framework of international organizations in matters relating to the environment. The Aarhus Convention thus aims to guarantee citizens' participation in both national and international decision-making processes, and is so far the most ambitious attempt at implementing principle 10 of the 1992 Rio Declaration on Environment and Development.[260] A second example is the system of notice and comment procedures and open procedures of consultation with NGOs in the Organisation for Economic Co-operation and Development (OECD).[261] A third example is the action taken by the World Bank in response to the criticism of its 'closed door' policy.[262] A fourth example is in the field of standard-setting, for instance, the procedures of the CAC which, *inter alia,* has sought to include NGOs representing affected social and economic interests in its work.[263] A fifth example is the debate of due process related to transparency highlighted regarding the dispute settlement mechanisms under the WTO regime. The WTO (and its predecessor GATT) had traditionally been characterized by closed procedures.[264] The WTO has, however, made efforts to improve transparency; and using the

259   Kingsbury, Krisch and Stewart, 'The Emergence of Global Administrative Law, p. 37.
260   Reprinted in *ILM*, Vol. 31, p. 876. Principle 10 provides that 'environmental issues are best handled with the participation of all concerned citizens, at the relevant level. At the national level, each individual shall have appropriate access to information concerning the environment that is held by public authorities [...] and the opportunity to participate in decision-making processes. States shall facilitate and encourage public awareness and participation by making information widely available. Effective access to judicial and administrative proceedings, including redress and remedy, shall be provided'.
261   Salzman, James, 'Decentralized Administrative Law in the Organization for Economic Cooperation and Development', in *Law and Contemporary Problems*, Vol. 68, 2005, pp. 189–224, at pp. 216–217.
262   See report by Darbishire, Helen, 'Proactive Transparency: The future of the right to information? A review of standards, challenges, and opportunities', in *Governance Working Paper Series of the World Bank Institute*. Available at: <www.siteresources.worldbank.org/WBI/Resources/213798-1259011531325/6598384-1268250334206/Darbishire_Proactive_Transparency.pdf> (accessed 1 January 2014).
263   See briefing paper by Suppan, Steve, 'Consumers International's Decision-Making in the Global Market'. *Institute for Agriculture and Trade Policy*. Available at: <www.ecolomics-international.org/caa_ci_dec_mkg_in_gl_market_codex_briefing_paper_steve_suppan_iatp_04.pdf> (accessed 1 January 2014).
264   Cass, *The Constitutionalization of the World Trade Organization: Legitimacy, Democracy, and Community in the International Trading System*, p. 222.

WTO as an example, Peters argues that 'there is a clear tendency towards transparency in global and supra-state regional governance'.[265] Accordingly also in global administrative law, decisional transparency has been highlighted as a key legal principle for promoting due process, and it has been remarked that '[v]ersions of such a principle are increasingly applied in global administrative governance'.[266]

4.6.4.3   Transparency in the Article 76-Process

Turning to the extent to which internal and external transparency is implemented in the Article 76 implementation process, we start the examination from the point at which the coastal state prepares and makes its submission and continue from there to the period when the submission is being processed by the Commission. Finally, we examine the period after the Commission has adopted its recommendations.

4.6.4.3.1   *Submissions*

The LOS Convention does not require the Commission (or the coastal state) to make public any documentation contained in the coastal state's continental shelf submission. In the legal literature it has been argued that the Commission's Scientific and Technical Guidelines provide sufficient indications as to the type of information the coastal state includes in its submission. Other states and the public should therefore have a good idea of what the coastal state has in fact submitted.[267]

As indicated in the previous chapter, access to information regarding coastal state submissions has to some extent been ensured through the Commission's Rules of Procedure. Rule 50 of the Rules of Procedure stipulates:

> The Secretary-General shall, through the appropriate channels, promptly notify the Commission and all States Members of the United Nations, including States Parties to the Convention, of the receipt of the submission, and make public the executive summary including all charts and coordinates referred to in paragraph 9.1.4 of the Guidelines and contained in that summary, upon completion of the translation of the executive summary referred to in rule 47, paragraph 3.

---

265   Peters, Anne, 'Dual Democracy', in Klabbers, Peters and Ulfstein, *The Constitutionalization of International Law*, pp. 261–341, at p. 329.

266   Kingsbury, Krisch and Stewart, 'The Emergence of Global Administrative Law', p. 37.

267   Elferink, 'Openness and Article 76 of the Law of the Sea Convention: The Process Does Not Need to Be Adjusted', p. 39.

Accordingly, the UNSG is to make public an 'executive summary' of the coastal state's submission. Further, according to Rule 1, paragraph 1, of Annex III to the Rules of Procedure, any submission made by a coastal state is to contain not only a main analytical and descriptive part—as well as a part containing all data referred to in this part—but also an executive summary. This executive summary shall be a separate body of documentation that must be prepared by the coastal state.[268]

It follows from Rule 50 of the Rules of Procedure that, *inter alia*, the coordinates of the outer limits are to be included in the executive summary issued by the UNSG. This ensures openness about what is arguably the most important point in the coastal state's submission. There are, however, two points worthy of attention here.

First, the Commission is seemingly not permitted to disclose these coordinates if the coastal state invokes the far-reaching rules on confidentiality in Annex II of the Rules of Procedure, under which the coastal state making a submission may classify as confidential 'any data and other material not otherwise publicly available'.[269]

Second, it is a matter of principle why only a 'summary' of the coastal state's continental shelf submission is to be made public. The elements which, according to the Commission's Scientific and Technical Guidelines, the summary should contain (coordinates of the outer limits, applied baselines, invoked rules of Article 76, unresolved maritime disputes and the names of the members of the Commission that the coastal state has had consultations with) are indeed useful information. But the main scientific and technical part of a coastal state's submission will also contain information of possible interest to other states—like the techniques used by the coastal state to locate the foot of the slope or the 2,500 metre isobath.

Responses from states also indicate that efforts made by the Commission to improve transparency regarding submissions are not sufficient to meet the

---

268 Rule 50 and Rule 1, para. 1, of Annex III refer to para. 9.1.4 of the Commission's Scientific and Technical Guidelines. According to paragraph 9.1.4, the coastal state's executive summary must include maps and coordinates showing the position of the outer limits, relevant applied baselines, which provisions under Article 76 that have been invoked, the name of any Commission member which the coastal state has consulted during the preparation of the submission, and information on any outstanding jurisdictional disputes. Beyond this, the coastal state's submission shall otherwise be considered from day one in accordance with the rules on confidentiality contained in Annex II of the Rules of Procedure. Rule 2 of Annex II allows the coastal state to designate as confidential 'any data and other material, not otherwise publicly available'.

269 Rule 2, para. 1, of Annex II to the Rules of Procedure.

public demand for openness. When Russia made the first continental shelf claim in 2001, Rule 49 (the current Rule 50) of the Rules of Procedure had the following phrasing:

> The Secretary-General shall, through the appropriate channels, promptly notify the Commission and all Members of the United Nations, including States Parties, of the receipt of a submission, and make public the proposed outer limits of the continental shelf pursuant to the submission.[270]

Thus, in 2001 only 'the proposed outer limits of the continental shelf pursuant to the submission' were to be made public. Russia complied with the regulation and made public an overview map showing the continental shelf beyond 200 nautical miles, also in the Arctic Ocean.[271] Several states responded to the Russian submission, requesting further information. Canada claimed:

> The Permanent Mission of Canada to the United Nations [...] is not in a position to determine whether it agrees with the Russian Federation's Arctic continental shelf submission without the provision of further supporting data to analyse [...].[272]

And Denmark noted:

> Denmark is not able to form an opinion on the Russian submission. A qualified assessment would require more specific data.[273]

But even after the current Rule 50 came into effect—with explicit reference to paragraph 9.1.4 of the Scientific and Technical Guidelines, and demands for more detailed executive summaries— coastal states have continued to complain about sparse information. For instance, reacting to the submission by Myanmar in 2008, Sri Lanka noted that the

---

270   Doc. CLCS/3/Rev.3.

271   Map available at the website of the Commission: <www.un.org/Depts/los/clcs_new/submissions_files/rus01/RUS_CLCS_01_2001_LOS_2.jpg> (accessed 1 January 2014).

272   Reaction of Canada to the submission made by Russia, available at: <www.un.org/Depts/los/clcs_new/submissions_files/rus01/CLCS_01_2001_LOS__CANtext.pdf> (accessed 1 January 2014).

273   Reaction of Denmark to the submission made by Russia, available at: <www.un.org/Depts/los/clcs_new/submissions_files/rus01/CLCS_01_2001_LOS__JPNtext.pdf> (accessed 1 January 2014).

contents of the Executive Summary do not enable Sri Lanka to make an informed judgment on Myanmar's interpretation and application of [the Statement of Understanding concerning a specific method to be used in establishing the outer edge of the continental margin in the Bay of Bengal, incorporated in annex II of the Final Act of UNCLOS III].[274]

It thus seems that at least states which have outstanding jurisdiction and border disputes with the submitting coastal state are not satisfied with how the issue of transparency regarding submissions has been dealt with, including the legislative initiatives taken by the Commission through its Rules of Procedure.

Moreover, it can be argued, these states' concerns are legitimate. This is because there is nothing in the LOS Convention to prevent a coastal state from making a submission to the Commission *before* maritime border problems and other potential jurisdictional disputes have been resolved.[275] The Commission may therefore peruse information and data concerning a portion of seabed which eventually *may or may not* end up in the continental shelf of the coastal state making the submission, depending on the outcome of the pending delimitation.

For instance, this was the situation with Norway's submission in respect of the 'Loophole' in the Barents Sea. Dealing with this submission, the Commission had to decide whether the Loophole was legally continental shelf, even though the seabed in question was at the time of the submission subject to pending maritime delimitation between Norway and Russia. The continental shelf beyond 200 nautical miles in the Barents Sea—the Loophole—was at the time therefore as much 'Russian' as it was 'Norwegian'.[276] Yet, under the

---

274   Reaction of Sri Lanka to the submission made by the Union of Myanmar, available at the website of the Commission: <www.un.org/Depts/los/clcs_new/submissions_files/ mmr08/clcs16_2008_mmr_lka_e.pdf> (accessed 1 January 2014).

275   In fact, the coastal state will often be obliged to do so because of the 10-year time limit in Article 4 of Annex II to the LOS Convention. And the Commission is not compelled to delay its examination of a submission until any possible dispute has been settled. It has been argued that under the LOS Convention, this is also the procedure that should be followed: First, the Commission shall be involved to determine what legally is 'continental shelf' beyond 200 nautical miles. Second, the continental shelf can be delimited. See Kunoy, Bjørn, 'The Admissibility of a Plea to an International Adjudicative Forum to Delimit the Outer Continental Shelf Prior to the Adoption of Final Recommendations by the Commission on the Limits of the Continental Shelf', in *The International Journal of Marine and Coastal Law*, Vol. 25, 2010, pp. 237–270, at p. 270.

276   Jensen, 'Towards Setting the Outer Limits of the Continental Shelf in the Arctic', in Vidas (ed.), *Law, Technology and Science for Oceans in Globalisation*, pp. 519–538.

LOS Convention, Russia had no opportunity to familiarize itself with the content of the Norwegian continental shelf submission. According to the Rules of Procedure, only an executive summary should be made public.

In one way, however, it could be argued that the interests of neighbouring states are better served in these cases. As noted in the previous chapter, Rule 5 (*litra* a) of Annex I to the Rules of Procedure now provides that the Commission shall accept a shelf submission involving outstanding territorial or maritime delimitation issues only with the express consent of all implicated states.[277] And both Article 76 and Annex II of the LOS Convention serve as a guarantee to other states that delimitations will remain unaffected by the Commission's work.[278] Rules regarding veto and non-prejudice should not, however, obscure the fact that, under the current regulations, states and other actors have only the possibility to familiarize themselves with an executive summary of the coastal state's submission—an arrangement criticized by states which find themselves unable to make informed judgments on the coastal states' interpretation and application of Article 76.

In terms of public transparency regarding submissions, the Commission's practice should nevertheless be praised in certain areas. Only a few days after a submission is received, the Commission posts an acknowledgement thereto on its website. The Commission also publicizes when the submission is to be considered for the first time. A communication is circulated to all member states of the UN, as well as States Parties to the LOS Convention. Further, the Commission's website provides a structured overview with respect to the date of receipt of each and every submission, as well as information on the establishment of the sub-commission for a particular submission. Thus, even though the LOS Convention has no regulations to secure transparency in this regard, the Commission is far from operating in complete secrecy at this first stage of the process.

---

277 Rule 5 (*litra* a) of Annex I: 'In cases where a land or maritime dispute exists, the Commission shall not consider and qualify a submission made by any of the States concerned in the dispute. However, the Commission may consider one or more submissions in the areas under dispute with prior consent given by all States that are parties to such a dispute'.

278 Article 76, para. 10, of the LOS Convention reads: 'The provisions of article 76 are without prejudice to the question of delimitation of the continental shelf between States with opposite or adjacent coasts'. The differently worded rule in Article 9 of Annex II to the LOS Convention provides: 'The actions of the Commission shall not prejudice matters relating to delimitation of boundaries between States with opposite or adjacent coasts'.

4.6.4.3.2   *Submission Review*
(a)   Meetings

The LOS Convention has no rules to ensure internal or external transparency while the Commission is processing a submission. In essence, there is no right of access to meetings for anyone except the Commission's members (and, as noted, the coastal state at certain scheduled meetings). Other States Parties, non-member states, NGOs and the general public therefore have no right to be present during the Commission's examination of a submission. Similarly, Rule 23 of the Rules of Procedure of the Commission provides that the meetings of the Commission shall be held in private:

> The meetings of the Commission, its subcommissions and subsidiary bodies shall be held in private, unless the Commission decides otherwise.[279]

And according to Rule 4, paragraph 1, of Annex II to the Rules of Procedure,

> [t]he deliberations of the Commission and subcommissions on all submissions made in accordance with article 76, paragraph 8, of the Convention shall take place in private and remain confidential.

Thus we see that only members of the Commission are allowed to take part in meetings and during deliberations on submissions.[280] The UNSG and the staff of DOALOS as may be required can be present, but no others, except by permission.[281]

It is worth noting that the LOS Convention—followed by the aforementioned Rules of Procedure—prescribes a process that is closed from day one, not only from the point at which the Commission's members convene to deliberate. This arrangement has been criticized. Judge Treves has argued that also an international court or tribunal deliberates behind closed doors, but that before the court or tribunal withdraws to deliberate, the doors are kept wide open.[282] Similarly, access to proceedings is generous in the WTO dispute settlement system, at both the panel and the AB level. In the paral-

---

279   Similarly, according to Rule 44 *bis,* para. 4, of the Rules of Procedure, '[t]he sessions of the subcommission shall be held in private'.
280   And possibly specialists appointed in accordance with Rule 57 of the Rules of Procedure.
281   Rule 4, para. 2, of Annex II to the Rules of Procedure.
282   Treves, 'Remarks on Submissions to the Commission on the Limits of the Continental Shelf in Response to Judge Marotta's Report', p. 367.

lel disputes *US—Continued Suspension of Obligations (Hormones)*[283] and *Canada—Continued Suspension of Obligations in the EC—Hormones Dispute* in 2005,[284] the WTO panels for the first time determined that the public would be allowed to observe hearings together with the parties, 'thereby ending the consistent practice of sixty years of GATT/WTO dispute settlement hearings behind closed doors'.[285] And at the AB level, transparency was promoted in the context of the merged appeals of these cases when it reached the AB in 2008 by means of open hearings. A legal obstacle to open hearings was found in Article 17, paragraph 10, of the Dispute Settlement Understanding, according to which the 'proceedings of the Appellate Body shall be confidential' and the 'reports of the Appellate Body shall be drafted without the presence of the parties to the dispute and in the light of the information provided and the statements made'. The wording 'proceedings' (compare 'deliberations' under Article 14) indicates that it would be difficult for the AB to open hearings to other states and to the general public. And already in *Canada—Measures Affecting the Export of Civilian Aircraft*, the AB had interpreted the term

---

283   Panel Report, *United States—Continued Suspension of Obligations in the EC—Hormones Dispute*. Published in *DSR* (2008), Vol. XI, p. 3891.

284   Panel Report, *Canada—Continued Suspension of Obligations in the EC—Hormones Dispute*. Published in *DSR* (2008), Vol. XVII, p. 6717.

285   The EC, the USA and Canada had jointly requested that a panel should open its hearings to the public. The panels thus had to determine whether Article 14 of the Dispute Settlement Understanding—titled 'Confidentiality'—prohibited open hearings by providing that panel 'deliberations' shall be conducted in confidentiality. After 'careful consideration of the existing provisions of the DSU', the term 'deliberations' was, however, interpreted only to include the part of the process where the final decision was made (see communication from the Chairman of the panels in Doc. WT/DS321/8). When Article 14, para. 2, of the Dispute Settlement Understanding provides that the 'reports of panels shall be drafted without the presence of the parties to the dispute in the light of the information provided and the statements made', this provision therefore did not apply to the formal proceedings, i.e. the proceedings prior to the 'deliberations'. With this decision, it was put an end to decades of dispute settlement proceedings behind closed doors in the GATT/WTO system. For the first time, the public and other WTO members could then attend the panel hearings through videolink from an adjacent room. According to Ehring, the experience with open hearings was 'favourably received by many government and non-government actors' and 'it confirmed that the WTO could operate such hearings without big difficulties'. See Ehring, Lothar, 'Public Access to Dispute Settlement Hearings in the World Trade Organization', in *Journal of International Economic Law*, Vol. 11, 2008, pp. 1021–1034, at p. 1022.

'proceedings' in Article 17, paragraph 10, to include the oral hearing.[286] The AB nevertheless differentiated the interpretation, ignoring strong opposition by states such as Brazil, China, and Mexico, and agreed with the EC, the USA and Canada in their interpretation that parties had the possibility to circumvent the provision on confidentiality for themselves and their statements during AB hearings. The AB based its interpretation on a contextual reading of Article 17, paragraph 10, and also on the fact that complete secrecy would be impossible since AB reports would be made public at a later time. The AB also argued that when the WTO panels had the opportunity to hold open consultations, this should also apply to appeal proceedings.[287]

It can be argued, however, that the regulations pertaining to courts and other international dispute resolution bodies should not serve as a normative standard for the Commission's regulations on this point. The need for transparency is, in my opinion, more pressing in international litigation, where there is a general principle of oral proceedings. The Commission's meetings are of a different character, dedicated exclusively to the written materials submitted by the coastal state. In this, it is assumed, the sharp distinction between the Commission's 'meetings' and 'deliberations' more or less disappears. The Commission's proceedings thus perhaps more bear resemblance to, for instance, the practice of human rights treaty bodies, where examination of individual complaints takes place in closed sessions.[288] Also the examination of a patent claim under the PCT is a closed procedure, notably when the IPEA exercises its investigations of a patent.

While not all of the Commission's meetings should be open, it might be advantageous to practise a public meeting policy to some extent. Perhaps some of the Commission's meetings could be public, for instance the meeting to which the coastal state at an advanced stage is invited to comment on the sub-commission's draft recommendations, prior to the plenary Commission adopting final recommendations. Scientists, legal scholars or neighbouring coastal states are among those who could have considerable interest in such transparency. And then the proceedings would bear more resemblance to, for instance, the procedures and mechanisms relating to compliance under the Kyoto Protocol, which allows public participation only to some extent. When

---

286   Appellate Body Report, *Canada—Measures Affecting the Export of Civilian Aircraft*. Published in *DSR* (1999), Vol. III, p. 1377. See paras. 141–147.

287   See report written by Ahlborn, Christiane, and James Headen Pfitzer of the Centre for International Environmental Law (CIEL): *Transparency and Public Participation in WTO Dispute Settlement*, pp. 22–23. Available at: <www.ciel.org> (accessed 1 January 2014).

288   Ulfstein, 'Individual Complaints', p. 91.

the Enforcement Branch examines an instance of non-compliance, the party concerned may request a hearing. As a main rule, this hearing shall be public, even though the remaining meetings of the Branch are not public:

> If so requested in writing by the Party concerned within ten weeks from the date of receipt of the notification under section VII, paragraph 4, the enforcement branch shall hold a hearing at which the Party concerned shall have the opportunity to present its views [...]. Such a hearing shall be held in public, unless the enforcement branch decides, of its own accord or at the request of the Party concerned, that part or all of the hearing shall take place in private.[289]

(b)   Documents

Of importance to whether the Commission's proceedings can be characterized as sufficiently transparent, also the extent to which *written* materials are available for public scrutiny is of relevance. Is the Commission's decision-making process well documented? And if so, have other states or the general public access to the relevant documentation?

Under the LOS Convention there is no obligation for the Commission to keep records of its proceedings. No such provisions exist in the Rules of Procedure either. And Rule 4, paragraph 3, of Annex II provides that if any such records do exist, none of them shall be disclosed to states or the general public:[290]

> Any records of the Commission and subcommission deliberations on all submissions shall contain only the title or nature of the subjects or matters discussed and the results of any vote taken. They shall not contain any details of the discussions or the views expressed, provided, however, that any member is entitled to require that a statement made by him be inserted in the records.

It can also be questioned whether the availability of the 'statements' by the Chairman of the Commission has any value for others in terms of increased transparency and openness. The Commission makes public 'Statements by the Chairman of the Commission' on its website, and since 2011, statements

---

289   UN Doc. FCCC/CP/2001/13/Add.3 ('Decision 24/CP.7: Procedures and mechanisms relating to compliance under the Kyoto Protocol, Annex'), Section IX, para. 2.

290   See also Rule 44 *bis,* para. 3, and Rule 5, para. 2 (*litra* b), of Annex III to the Rules of Procedure.

by the Chairman under the title 'Progress of work in the Commission on the Limits of the Continental Shelf'.[291] This appears to be a written summary of the Commission's previous session. Such statements are published sequentially and relatively quickly after a session has ended, that is, usually in April/May and September/October each year.

For instance, the statement by the Chairman of the Commission in relation to the 27th session was issued on 11 May 2011, less than a month after the closing of that session.[292] The Chairman presented each submission dealt with, the progress of each, and, moreover, if the Commission had adopted any recommendations. For instance, item 4 of the statement was titled 'Submission made by Indonesia in respect of North West of Sumatra Island'. The Commission noted that recommendations were adopted, and by which vote count:

> At the twenty-seventh session, after a thorough examination of the recommendations and of outstanding issues, on 28 March 2011 the Commission adopted the 'Recommendations of the Commission on the Limits of the Continental Shelf in regard to the submission made by Indonesia in respect of the area North West of Sumatra on 16 June 2008' by 11 votes to 2, with 2 abstentions. Pursuant to article 6, paragraph 3, of annex II to the Convention, the recommendations, including a summary thereof, were submitted in writing to the coastal State and to the Secretary General.[293]

But the Chairman's summary of each session tends to be very descriptive. It is not clear from the published documentation why, for instance in relation to the aforementioned Indonesian submission, it was impossible for the Commission to achieve consensus in accordance with Rule 13 of the Rules of Procedure. Thus, even though the Commission in practice has attempted to improve written transparency with regard to the drafting process, there is still no access to relevant documents—drafts of recommendations, Commission debates, etc.—and therefore not much better possibilities for verifying the quality of the Commission's work.

---

291   See Docs. CLCS/1, CLCS/4, CLCS/7, CLCS/9, CLCS/12, CLCS/18, CLCS/21, CLCS/25, CLCS/29, CLCS/32, CLCS/34, CLCS/36, CLCS/39, CLCS/42, CLCS/44, CLCS/48, CLCS/48/Corr.1, CLCS/50, CLCS/52, CLCS/54, CLCS/56, CLCS/58, CLCS/60, CLCS/62, CLCS/64, CLCS/66, CLCS/68, CLCS/70 and CLCS/70/Corr.1.

292   Doc. CLCS/70.

293   *Ibid.*

Some of the same concerns have been emphasized in regard to certain human rights treaty bodies as well.[294] And under the procedures and mechanisms related to compliance under the Kyoto Protocol, there seems to be no obligation for the Enforcement Branch or Facilitative Branch to make public the written material from the decisional process other than 'information considered by the branch'.[295]

Nevertheless, in my opinion, it would be advantageous for other states and the general public to have knowledge of specific documents from the Commission's drafting process—notably the draft recommendations. Therefore, perhaps something may be learnt from the regulations pertaining to international institutions not directly comparable to the Commission.

For instance, there has been a trend towards widening document review in the WTO decision-making process. With certain limited exceptions, all official WTO documents are now public.[296] Inspiration might also be provided from regimes of treaty bodies with a more 'political' mandate than that of the Commission, for instance, the regulations pertaining to the World Heritage Committee. Under Section IX of its Rules of Procedure,[297] there is first Rule 46, according to which, at the closure of each session, the Committee shall adopt a report of the session comprising a list of decisions to be published within the month following the closure of that session. The Secretariat is to prepare a 'summary record' of all interventions made during plenary sessions of the Committee. This summary shall be submitted to the Committee members as soon as possible; and the representatives of organizations attending in an advisory capacity, individuals invited for consultations and observers shall have the opportunity to submit corrections to their own statements. Further, Rule 47, paragraph 2, provides that a 'final version of the Summary Record' is to be published as an information document within three months following the closure of the session. And according to Rule 48, reports of the sessions, the Summary Record (and all final documents) shall be transmitted to, *inter alia*, the states members of the Committee and all other organizations invited to the session.

---

294 Keller, Helen, and Leena Grover, 'General Comments of the Human Rights Committee and their legitimacy', in Keller and Ulfstein (eds), *UN Human Rights Treaty Bodies—Law and Legitimacy*, pp. 116–198, at pp. 183–185.

295 UN Doc. FCCC/CP/2001/13/Add.3 ('Decision 24/CP.7: Procedures and mechanisms relating to compliance under the Kyoto Protocol, Annex'), Section VIII, para. 6.

296 Bonzon, Yves, 'Institutionalizing Public Participation in WTO Decision Making: Some Conceptual Hurdles and Avenues', in *Journal of International Economic Law*, Vol. 11, 2008, pp. 751–777, at p. 757.

297 Doc. WHC.2–2011/5 ('Rules of Procedure of the Intergovernmental Committee for the Protection of the World Cultural and Natural Heritage').

And finally, Rule 49 stipulates that the Committee must submit a report of its activities at each General Assembly of States Parties and at each of the ordinary sessions of the General Conference of UNESCO, with copies to be sent to all States Parties to the World Heritage Convention.

4.6.4.3.3   *Recommendations*

When the Commission has adopted recommendations, States Parties, non-members and the general public might wish access to these recommendations for at least two reasons. First, did the Commission adopt recommendations in accordance with Article 76 of the LOS Convention? Second, where is the coastal state to establish the outer limits, in order for these limits to be established 'on the basis of' the Commission's recommendations? If the outside world is to satisfy itself regarding these questions, publication of the Commission's recommendations is necessary.

The LOS Convention, however, does not require the Commission's recommendations to be made public. Without any further specification, Article 76, paragraph 8, of the Convention merely states:

> The Commission shall make recommendations to coastal States [. . .].

Read in conjunction with Article 6, paragraph 3, of Annex II, it is clear that the Commission has an obligation to communicate its recommendations only to the coastal state and the UNSG:

> The recommendations of the Commission shall be submitted in writing to the coastal State which made the submission and to the [UNSG].

Thus, the Commission is not obliged to make its recommendations available to others. Nor does a coastal state relying on the Convention's text have any obligation to make public any parts of the recommendations: the Commission's recommendations will be revealed only to the UNSG and the submitting coastal state. Others are therefore granted no opportunity to apprise themselves of the content of a recommendation. Statements issued by the Chairman of the Commission, and a brief press release posted on the Commission's website, inform other states and the general public when recommendations have been adopted, but their real substance remains undisclosed.

Was it in fact the intention of the drafters to keep the recommendations secret from anyone but the coastal state and the UNSG? The fact that the LOS Convention contains no provisions regarding transparency might indicate that. On the other hand, there is no explicit prohibition in the LOS Convention against making the Commission's recommendations public. Perhaps the drafters did not see any need to include provisions on transparency in the LOS Convention, possibly because they never envisioned that the recommendations would be of significance to others than the coastal state. From an accountability perspective, however, it seems obvious that other states and the general public do have a significant interest in familiarizing themselves with the recommendations. As explained, the recommendations have legal effects with regard to the determination of the outer limits in specific cases, and general significance regarding the interpretation of Article 76. That the recommendations are not binding *strictu sensu* appears less important.

In a comparative perspective we may, for example, note the individual complaints of the HRC—adopted in the procedures under the first Optional Protocol to the ICCPR. These are posted, in six languages, on the Committee's website as part of the Committee's jurisprudence.[298] Transparency is exercised, even though publication may not necessarily be in the victim's best interest.

For another example, take the Regulations under the PCT. Rule 44*ter* of the Regulations stipulates, as the main rule, that the written opinion of the International Searching Authority and the international preliminary report on patentability shall remain confidential until 30 months from the priority date. But there have been recent initiatives in the World Intellectual Property Organization (WIPO) to change these regulations to make the written opinion available to the public sooner, in order to promote transparency within the PCT process.[299]

Not making public the recommendations is—almost needless to say— also a remarkable normative construction when compared to legal instruments which are binding. In the procedures relating to compliance under the Kyoto Protocol, the secretariat shall make final decisions of the Compliance Committee available to other parties and to the public.[300] Judgments of

---

298   See <www2.ohchr.org/english/bodies/hrc/HRCommitteeCaseLaw.htm> (accessed 1 January 2014).

299   Doc. PCT/WG/5/18 ('Document submitted by the United Kingdom and the United States of America').

300   UN Doc. FCCC/CP/2001/13/Add.3 ('Decision 24/CP.7: Procedures and mechanisms relating to compliance under the Kyoto Protocol, Annex'), Section VIII, para. 7.

international courts and tribunals—of the ICJ,[301] the ITLOS[302] and the ECtHR[303]—are available for the public to review. Also decisions emanating from the dispute settlement system of the WTO are made public on the WTO website, circulated to all members and published in the series 'Dispute Settlement Reports' (DSR).[304]

Important improvements as regards transparency have, however, been adopted by the Commission. Coastal states seem to accept Rule 11, paragraph 3, of Annex III to the Commission's Rules of Procedure, under which a 'summary' of the recommendations is to be made public upon approval of the recommendations:

> The recommendations prepared by the subcommission shall include a summary thereof, and such summary shall not contain information which might be of a confidential nature and/or which might violate the proprietary rights of the coastal State over the data and information

---

301 Article 58 of the Statute of ICJ also provides that the judgments of ICJ shall be read in 'open court' (this obligation is restated in Article 94, para. 2, of the Rules of the Court). Under Article 95, para. 3, of the Rules of the ICJ, copies of the judgment shall not only be sent to the UNSG, but to all members of the UN and other states entitled to appear before the Court. All judgments (and Advisory Opinions and Orders) are reprinted on the Court's website and later published (in both English and French) in the series *I.C.J. Reports*. Similar rules apply to the ICC under Article 50, para. 1, of the Rome Statute, which provides that the judgments of the Court, as well as other decisions resolving fundamental issues before the Court, 'shall be published' in all official languages of the Court.

302 Notably, Article 30 of Annex VI to the LOS Convention provides that judgments of the ITLOS 'shall be read in open court' (this obligation is restated in Article 124, para. 2, of the Rules of the ITLOS). Article 125, para. 3, of the Rules of the ITLOS further specifies that copies of the judgment shall be sent, *inter alia*, to States Parties to the LOS Convention. Thus, the ITLOS has an active duty to inform all States Parties when a verdict is delivered. Reports of the ITLOS' judgments (in addition to Advisory Opinions and Orders) are also reprinted on the internet and then published (in both English and French) in a bilingual series of annual publications since 1997.

303 Article 44, para. 3, of the ECHR determines that the 'final judgment [of the ECtHR] shall be published'. Article 24, para. 3, of the Statute of the Inter-American Court on Human Rights provides that decisions, judgments and opinions of the Court shall be delivered in a public session. They are to be published, along with judges' individual votes and opinions (Statutes adopted 1 October 1979; entered into force 1 November 1979. Published in *OAS Official Records* (OEA/Ser.P/IX.0.2/80), Vol. 1, p. 88.

304 See generally Ehring, 'Public Access to Dispute Settlement Hearings in the World Trade Organization'.

provided in the submission. The [UNSG] shall make public the summary of the recommendations upon their approval by the Commission.

As of 1 January 2014, the Commission had published 17 of 18 summaries of final recommendations on its website. However, in relation to the Russian submission of 2001, only a short summary of the Commission's recommendations is contained in the report of the UNSG to the 57th session of the UNGA.[305] We have previously also noted that although the Commission adopted its recommendations on the Brazilian submission already in 2004, no summary of these was published on the Commission's website until late 2013; for almost ten years, only a short, descriptive notification in the statement by the Chairman of the Commission was to be found on the website of the Commission.[306]

Perhaps some coastal states—here, Russia and Brazil—choose to rely solely on the provisions of the LOS Convention and therefore have hesitated to allow publication of more than a brief description. But the consequences with respect to transparency are not insignificant. For instance, the summary of the recommendations to Norway is a 33-page document containing a relatively detailed area-by-area overview, which indicates quite clearly whether or not the Commission has endorsed or rejected Norway's proposal for the placement of the outer limits.[307] Note also the following formulation in the Norwegian summary:

This Summary is Annex VI of the Recommendations [...].[308]

Is it not so that the recommendations to Russia and Brazil also contain an 'Annex VI', prepared by the sub-commission in order for it to be made public as the 'summary' under Rule 11? If so, it cannot be the additional work entailed in drafting a summary that explains why Brazil and Russia would not have permitted the Commission to post their summaries on an equal footing with those of other coastal states.

Although a summary of the recommendations provides much more information than the regular statements of the Chairman, a summary is still little

---

305   UN Doc. A/57/57/Add.1 ('Oceans and the Law of the Sea: Report of the Secretary-General'), paras. 38–41.
306   Doc. CLCS/54, para. 22.
307   Summary of the recommendations of the Commission in regard to the submission made by Norway is available at the website of the Commission: <www.un.org/Depts/los/clcs_new/submissions_files/nor06/nor_rec_summ.pdf> (accessed 1 January 2014).
308   Ibid., para. 5.

more than a glimpse. Ultimately, however, the outside world does have an opportunity to see the entire recommendations of the Commission. Rule 54, paragraph 3, of the Rules of Procedure provides that when the coastal state has established the outer limits and submitted these to the UNSG, the UNSG shall give due publicity, not only to the outer limits established by the coastal state, but also the recommendations of the Commission:

> Upon giving due publicity to the charts and relevant information, includ-ing geodetic data, permanently describing the outer limits of the conti-nental shelf deposited by the coastal State in accordance with article 76, paragraph 9, of the Convention, the [UNSG] shall also give due publicity to the recommendations of the Commission which in the view of the Commission are related to those limits.

Since Australia, Ireland, Mexico and the Philippines established the outer limits of their continental shelf and submitted these limits to the UNSG in accordance with Article 76, paragraph 9, of the LOS Convention, the respec-tive recommendations of these states have been posted on the Commission's website.

The Commission's commendable initiative towards greater openness, how-ever, has continued to experience certain setbacks. In the published recom-mendations related to Mexico's submission, many pages have been replaced with the clause stating: 'not made available at the request of the coastal State'.[309] *Lex lata* there is little to be done to affect Mexico's stance. There is, as noted, no requirement for publication under the LOS Convention, and the coastal state may opt to invoke the wide-ranging rules on confidentiality in the Commission's Rules of Procedure.[310] Thus what this underscores is that, despite the Commission's initiative towards greater transparency, the regu-lations are not sufficient to ensure full disclosure of recommendations to a coastal state that demands full or partial secrecy. And it will be particularly interesting to see whether states that as yet have not been willing to accept

---

309 This concerns bathymetric profiles on the Campeche Escarpment (Figure 2 in the recom-mendations), the foot of the slope on the Campeche Escarpment (Figure 4), bathymetric profiles off the Coast of Tamaulipas (Figure 5), foot of the slope off the Coast of Tamaulipas (Figure 7), seismic lines used for sediment thickness determinations (Figure 9) and seismic lines submitted to support the continuity of sediments across the continental margin (Figure 10). See recommendations to Mexico, available at the website of the Commission: <www.un.org/Depts/los/clcs_new/submissions_files/mex07/mex_rec.pdf> (accessed 1 January 2014).

310 See Annex II of the Rules of Procedure.

publication of even the summaries of their submissions will accept Rule 54, paragraph 3, under which the UNSG is to publish the recommendations in their entirety.

4.6.4.4   Preliminary Conclusions

It might be that the drafting of Article 76 and Annex II to the LOS Convention has been influenced quite significantly by the infamous dictum of the ICJ in the *Anglo-Norwegian Fisheries Case*, concerning the legality of Norway's straight baselines:

> [T]he act of delimitation is necessarily a unilateral act, because only the coastal State is competent to undertake it [...].[311]

That view seems founded on the idea that establishing outer limits under the law of the sea—whether related to the territorial sea, the contiguous zone, the exclusive economic zone, other functional maritime zones or the continental shelf—is to be done exclusively by the coastal state which claims the maritime zones. Clearly, that point is still relevant, as also all maritime zones under the LOS Convention are established unilaterally.

However, the new perspective brought by Article 76—and which under the LOS Convention makes a distinction between the establishment of the outer limits of the continental shelf beyond 200 nautical miles and the establishment of the outer limits of other maritime zones—is the involvement of the Commission. Thus, although the outer limits formally and technically are still established by the coastal state alone, other states and the general public have a legitimate interest in acquainting themselves with the process leading up to it, including the Commission's proceedings and decisions. We should therefore guard against confusing the issue of transparency and openness, in my view, with the question of *who* ultimately has the right and obligation to establish those limits.[312]

As we have seen, there is relatively low transparency related to all stages of the Commission's proceedings. The LOS Convention has no rules to the effect that documents submitted to the Commission (coastal state submissions), documents relating to the proceedings of the Commission, or documents sent from the Commission (its recommendations) shall be made available to others than the coastal state, the Commission's own members or the UNSG. Nor have

---

311   *I.C.J. Reports* 1951, p. 116, at p. 132.

312   See opposite with Elferink, 'Openness and Article 76 of the Law of the Sea Convention: The Process Does Not Need to Be Adjusted', p. 38.

other states, potentially interested NGOs, legal scholars or the general public access to meetings of the Commission. Thus the LOS Convention provides for no mechanisms enabling outsiders to scrutinize and assess the Commission's exercise of its functions.

Criticism of this closed system is to some extent mitigated by the fact that the Commission has, through its Rules of Procedure, taken steps that expand the possibilities for scrutiny. As we have noted, a summary of the coastal state's submission is made public, a summary of the recommendations is made public, and the recommendations are reproduced in their entirety on the Commission's website once the coastal state has established the limits nationally and deposited charts and other information with the UNSG in accordance with the LOS Convention. This has served to improve transparency in that the vast majority of states agree to have these documents reproduced on the Commission's website. Some coastal states seem, however, reluctant to follow the Commission's regulations on publication.

It has been concluded that the meetings of the Commission—where it is hard to distinguish between 'proceedings' and 'deliberations'—should be kept closed as the main rule. A 'closed door' policy may give the Commission the chance to work in peace, perhaps also more effectively. But why cannot representatives of other states, interested NGOs, scientists and the general public, for instance, be allowed to attend one public hearing at an advanced stage of the Commission's examination? It would bring the rules regarding transparency and openness of the Commission's procedures more into line with other decision-making processes and the general requirements of due process.

4.6.5   Statement of Reasons
4.6.5.1   Introduction
The Commission does not have a statutory obligation to provide reasons for its recommendations. The LOS Convention merely states that the Commission shall make recommendations, and subsequently submit them in writing to the coastal state.[313] We must ask: Should the Commission be obliged to provide reasons for its recommendations? And if so, what should such an obligation require as to form and content? Should the Commission, for instance, be obliged to disclose any debate concerning choices arising from conflicting argumentation that might have informed its decision-making?

---

313   See Article 76, para. 8, Article 3, para. 1, and Article 6, para. 3, of Annex II to the LOS Convention.

4.6.5.2 Reason-Giving in Global Administrative Law

The requirement to provide reasons for decisions has been described as a staple element of the exercise of administrative authority in modern states.[314] Legal authority and legal reasons are often perceived as interdependent. Thus also international courts and tribunals generally have an explicit obligation to provide reasons for their binding decisions.[315]

In international law, the duty to provide reasons for decisions does not, however, exclusively apply to courts and tribunals. The procedures and mechanisms pertaining to the Compliance Committee under the Kyoto Protocol require that decisions shall include reasons; the relevant branch of the Committee shall forthwith, through the secretariat, notify the party concerned in writing of its decision, including 'conclusions and reasons therefor'.[316] An obligation to provide reasons for decisions also applies to certain institutions dealing with international standard-setting, for instance with regard to the recommendations on banking regulations issued by the Basel Committee on Banking Supervision (BCBS). Banking regulations have been gradually improved through the Basel Accords (Number I, II and III) by the adoption of new mechanisms, including by providing reasons for decisions. The recommendations on banking laws and regulations drafted by the BCBS are not binding, but they have had a strong impact on state legislation since compliance

---

314 Perju, Vlad, 'Reason and Authority in the European Court of Justice', in *Virginia Journal of International Law*, Vol. 49, 2009, pp. 307–377, at p. 316.

315 For instance, Article 30 of Annex VI to the LOS Convention provides that any judgment of the ITLOS 'shall state the reasons on which it is based'. A similar rule is found in Article 56 of the Statue of the ICJ. Under Article 68 of the ICJ Statute it is also provided that in the exercise of its advisory functions, the Court shall be guided by the provisions of the Statute which apply in contentious cases to the extent to which it recognizes them to be applicable. Also, Article 45 of the ECHR determines that the ECtHR shall provide the reasons for its judgments. Under Article 49, the ECtHR shall also give reasons for advisory opinions. The ECJ also has a statutory duty to give reasons. Article 36 of the ECJ's Statute reads: 'Judgments shall state the reasons on which they are based. They shall contain the names of the Judges who took part in the deliberations'. Notably, the ECJ's obligation to provide reasons for its judgments is shared with EU's political institutions. Pervu takes note in this regard of (the current) Article 296 of the Treaty on the Functioning of the European Union: 'Regulations, directives and decisions adopted jointly by the European Parliament and the Council, and such acts adopted by the Council or the Commission, shall state the reasons on which they are based and shall refer to any proposals or opinions which were required to be obtained pursuant to this Treaty'. See Perju, 'Reason and Authority in the European Court of Justice', p. 313.

316 UN Doc. FCCC/CP/2001/13/Add.3 ('Decision 24/CP.7: Procedures and mechanisms relating to compliance under the Kyoto Protocol, Annex'), Section VIII, para. 7.

with them is often a requirement for being granted loans by international financial institutions.[317] As regards the requirement to provide reasons for global administrative decisions, however, it has been argued that international practice outside adjudicatory tribunals is relatively thin.[318]

4.6.5.3 The Commission's Reason-Giving

Regardless of the sparse practice at the international level outside courts and tribunals, the Commission should, in my view, be required to provide reasons for its recommendations. *First*, reason-giving promotes transparency and facilitates accountability. Providing reasons along with the recommendations would enable states to determine whether the Commission has acted according to the parameters embodied in the LOS Convention. Reason-giving would be an efficient tool in controlling and supervising the legal basis of the recommendations. Reason-giving, moreover, creates a record. In the wider context, providing reasons would make the Commission accountable by facilitating review by the legal subjects affected by its recommendations.

Second, requiring reasons to be stated should encourage members of the Commission to be attentive and precise while reviewing the matter at hand. Reason-giving might therefore have a preventive function in the sense that it would contribute towards that the Commission does a proper job.

Third, reasoned recommendations would be better suited to persuading states that the recommendations are correct. Legal scholars have argued that a court's authority 'ultimately rests on giving persuasive legal reasons in support of [its] holdings'.[319] This can be applied to non-binding recommendations— and perhaps even more so, precisely because they are non-binding.[320]

Finally, stating the reasons for the recommendations would enable the Commission to follow its own precedent by contributing to consistency in the application of Article 76.

Through its procedural rules, the Commission has addressed the LOS Convention's lack of regulations with regard to reason-giving. According to

---

317 See generally Barr, Michael S., and Geoffrey P. Miller, 'Global Administrative Law: The View From Basel', in *The European Journal of International Law*, Vol. 17, 2006, pp. 15–46.

318 Kingsbury, Krisch and Stewart, 'The Emergence of Global Administrative Law', p. 39.

319 Ferejohn, John, and Pasquale Pasquino, 'Constitutional Adjudication: Lessons from Europe', in *Texas Law Review*, Vol. 82, 2004, pp. 1671–1704, at p. 1680.

320 Ulfstein, Geir, and Andreas Føllesdal, 'Den europeiske menneskerettighetsdomstolen og Høyesterett—uavhengighet og demokratisk kontroll', in Engstad, Nils Asbjørn, Astrid Lærdal Frøseth og Bård Tønder (eds.), *Dommernes uavhengighet* (Fagbokforlaget, 2012), pp. 443–461, at p. 461.

Rule 12, paragraphs 4 and 5, of Annex III, the Commission in its recommendations shall include the 'rationale' on which they have been based:

4. If the submission contains sufficient data and other material upon which the outer limits of the continental shelf are based, the recommendations shall include the rationale on which such recommendations are based.

5. If the submission contains sufficient data and other material supporting outer limits of the continental shelf which would be different from those proposed in the submission, the recommendations shall contain the rationale on which the recommended outer limits are based.

At the international level, there is no consistent pattern of what a duty of reason-giving requires as to form and content.[321] However, the provisions of the Commission seem suited to ensure that it will give sufficient reasons for its recommendations. But how has the Commission practised its self-imposed duty to give reasons?

First of all, it should be noted that the Rules of Procedure use the phrase 'rationale' without further elaboration. The term can be variously interpreted. It might imply that the Commission must provide details on the content of discussions. An alternative interpretation is that the Commission is required to include only the most fundamental reasons for its recommendations. The 'rationale' might simply imply that it is sufficient for the Commission to state that the submission failed to meet certain requirements, followed by advice that the coastal state should provide further information in a new and revised submission.

We can illustrate the uncertainty with regard to the content of the duty to give reasons with the Commission's recommendations to Norway.[322] As also noted in Chapter 3, a key issue was whether the Jan Mayen Micro-Continent/Iceland Plateau was a submarine elevation, i.e. a natural component of the continental margin of Jan Mayen in the sense of Article 76, paragraph 6, of the LOS Convention. The Commission argued:

---

321   Perju, 'Reason and Authority in the European Court of Justice', p. 323.
322   The Commission's recommendations referred to here are set out in the executive summary of the recommendations to Norway. The full recommendations may contain more detailed statements of reasons.

Based on the morphological and geological evidence in the Submission, the additional material provided by Norway [...] and the literature, the Commission agrees that on balance the JMMC/IP composite high is a submarine elevation that is a natural component of the continental margin of Jan Mayen in the sense of article 76, paragraph 6. Hence, to delineate the outer limits of the continental shelf, a valid depth constraint could be applied to fixed points used to establish the outer edge of the continental margin that are derived from the JMMC/IP composite high; in particular, Jan Mayen South-East FOS 8.[323]

Here, although the Commission's argumentation seems to indicate uncertainty with regard to the nature of the seafloor highs in question, it still concluded in favour of Norway in approving the more generous depth criterion. The Commission, however, does not explain how morphological evidence can substitute the lack of geological evidence. When is morphology sufficient? And what literature is the Commission referring to? Neither does the Commission explain how it achieved the 'balance', or why such an approach had not been used in the other cases involving similar problems.[324]

A second example is the recommendations made to Australia. In Chapter 3, we focused, *inter alia*, on the Commission's rejection of Australia's method of linking the last segment of the outer limit to the 200 nautical mile limit. Even though Article 76, paragraph 7—if read in isolation—allows of an interpretation leading to the use of straight bridging lines to connect the outer limit and the 200 nautical mile limit so as to maximize the area of the continental shelf, the Commission did not approve of Australia's application of paragraph 7. In a general comment before examining each separate region, the Commission stated:

> Australia is of the view that it is possible to use lines not more than 60 M in length to join fixed points on the formula line beyond 200 M to any fixed point on the 200 M line. However the Commission is of the view that the determination of the last segment of the outer limits of the continental shelf shall be established either by the intersection of the formula line, in accordance with article 76, paragraphs 4 and 7, and the

---

323   Summary of recommendations to Norway, para. 77. Available at the website of the Commission: <www.un.org/Depts/los/clcs_new/commission_recommendations.htm> (accessed 1 January 2014).

324   Gao, Jianjun, 'The Seafloor High Issue in Article 76 of the LOS Convention: Some Views from the Perspective of Legal Interpretation', p. 132.

200 M limit from the baselines from which the breadth of the territorial sea is measured, or it shall be determined by the line of shortest distance between the last fixed formula point and 200 M limit.[325]

Here the Commission does not, however, explain why it cannot permit the coastal state to 'maximize' the extent of the continental shelf through the use of paragraph 7 when the outer limit is to be connected to the 200 nautical mile limit. Neither does the Commission provide adequate justification for its application of Article 76 when it deals with the specific regions of Australia's continental shelf claim—here exemplified by the Macquarie Ridge Region:

> In accordance with paragraph 26 above, the Commission does not agree with the method submitted by Australia on how the outer limits of the continental shelf beyond the 200 M line is to be connected with that 200 M line at points MAC-ECS-31 and MAC-ECS-431a, since this method creates area of continental shelf that falls outside of the continental margin as defined for the purposes of the Convention in accordance with article 76, paragraphs 4 and 7.[326]

The Commission's reasoning—'since this method creates area of continental shelf that falls outside of the continental margin'—is far from clear. How was the conflict of norms between paragraph 4 and paragraph 7 resolved? Why does the Commission apply the main rule that the continental shelf in a legal sense does not extend beyond the continental margin? How does the Commission justify that paragraph 7 can be applied anywhere else on the outer limit, and in such cases create area of continental shelf that falls outside of the continental margin? What exactly does the Commission mean by 'for the purposes of the Convention in accordance with article 76, paragraphs 4 and 7'? With stricter requirements for reason-giving, the coastal state could have been given answers to such questions.

4.6.5.4   Dissenting and Separate Opinions
A concrete issue with respect to the Commission's obligation to provide reasons is whether the Commission should be required to explain dissenting or separate opinions. Consider for instance two of the full recommendations

---

which so far have been posted on the Commission's website: the recommendations to Ireland in respect of the area abutting the Porcupine Abyssal Plain; and to Mexico in respect of the western polygon in the Gulf of Mexico.

While the recommendations to Mexico were adopted by consensus,[327] the recommendations to Ireland were split between a majority of 14 and minority of 2, with 2 abstentions,[328] but no explanation was provided for the dissenting or separate opinion. If, for example, members dissented because the Commission did not endorse Ireland's proposal to adjust the proposed outer limit by introducing a new fixed point generated from a specific slope point, this could easily have been clarified if the Commission had been bound by and observed regulations requiring it to explain dissenting or separate opinions.[329]

Such a rule could have strengthened the authority of a particular recommendation, because a separate or dissenting opinion involves more than publicly indicating a disagreement with the majority; the key here is to offer reasons for the disagreement. When the Commission does not allow its members to enter separate or dissenting opinions, however, the conflicting views of these members are neither brought into the open nor made available to the coastal state or others.

The Commission's practice of only revealing the voting count through the descriptive statements by the Chairman is also at variance with how dissensions and separate opinions are dealt with in certain other treaty regimes. For instance, under Rule 104 of the Rules of Procedure of the HRC it is provided that '[a]ny member of the Committee who has participated in a decision may request that his or her individual opinion be appended to the Committee's Views or decision'.[330]

Publication of individual opinions is also observed as a general rule by international courts and tribunals. The ECJ finds itself alone among supranational and international courts, and is one of only a handful of international courts to ban judges from writing concurring or dissenting opinions.[331] For instance, Article 30 of Annex VI to the LOS Convention provides that if a judgment of the ITLOS does not represent in whole or in part the unanimous opinion of the Tribunal, 'any member shall be entitled to deliver a separate opinion'.

---

327   Doc. CLCS/62, para. 26.

328   Doc. CLCS/54, para. 37.

329   See recommendations to Ireland, paras. 63–67. Available at the website of the Commission: <www.un.org/Depts/los/clcs_new/commission_submissions.htm> (accessed 1 January 2014).

330   Rules of Procedure of the HRC; adopted 11 January 2012. In UN Doc. CCPR/C/3/Rev.10.

331   Perju, 'Reason and Authority in the European Court of Justice', p. 309.

Provisions with a similar content are found in Article 57 of the Statue of the ICJ and Article 49, paragraph 2, of the ECHR. Thus, while dissenting and separate opinions are published in the decisions of the HRC and international courts, the interested outsider can only speculate as to what may have prompted the Commission to disagree.

4.6.5.5   Preliminary Conclusions

The LOS Convention has no provisions relating to the requirement of reason-giving for the Commission's recommendations. It would definitely be an added burden to the Commission to have to draw up comprehensive rationales. In the Rules of Procedure, however, the Commission has imposed on itself a duty to provide reasons for its recommendations, specifically so that the recommendations shall include the 'rationale' on which they have been based. Yet—as we have noted—the Commission's statements of reasons are often not sufficient to verify that the recommendations have been drafted in accordance with Article 76. It is also an obvious weakness that the recommendations do not include dissenting or separate views of those members disagreeing with the majority opinion of the Commission.

4.6.6   *Review*

4.6.6.1   Introduction

The LOS Convention and the Commission's Rules of Procedure do not contain rules allowing coastal states—or any others—to appeal against the Commission's recommendations. There is no 'second degree Commission' or different and independent body to control or verify whether the Commission has adopted its recommendations in accordance with Article 76. From the coastal state's perspective, the only option for testing the validity of the recommendations under the present system seems to be to establish the outer limits inconsistent with the outer limits proposed by the Commission—that is, at a more seaward position—and then leave it to any other state to pursue a case against it concerning the placement of the outer limit. But then it will become a matter for the court or other appropriate dispute settlement body how (or whether) to use the Commission's recommendations in interpreting Article 76.

   Also, the possibility to submit a new or revised submission in case of disagreement with the Commission, as provided by Article 8 of Annex II of the LOS Convention, is not a proper review mechanism. Firstly, it is the very same Commission that deals with a new or revised submission—contrary to the principle that review should be independent and impartial. Furthermore, Article 8 is not a suitable avenue if the coastal state considers the Commission's *legal* interpretation of Article 76 to be incorrect. As emphasized by Serdy, it seems pointless to make a new or revised submission in such cases, since a new submission then must necessarily rely on legal, and not scientific, reasoning.[332] Therefore we ask: should coastal states—and possibly other states—have the opportunity to take the Commission's recommendations to another body for independent review?

4.6.6.2   Comparisons and Considerations

The opportunity to have acts of administrative institutions reviewed is a fundamental constitutional guarantee in domestic legal settings. Numerous international legal instruments also specify requirements of review for domestic administrations and judicial bodies.[333] In the field of global administra-

---

332   Serdy, 'The Commission on the Limits of the Continental Shelf and its Disturbing Propensity to Legislate', p. 382.

333   For instance, the Aarhus Convention determines that each party shall, within the framework of its national legislation, ensure that any person who considers that his or her request for information under the Convention has been ignored, wrongfully refused, whether in part or in full, inadequately answered, or otherwise not dealt with in accordance with the provisions of the Convention, has access to a review procedure before a court of law or another independent and impartial body established by law (Article 9, para. 1, of the Convention). Also human rights instruments impose some basic procedural requirements on domestic administration. For instance, Article 13 of the ICCPR determines that an alien lawfully in the territory of a State Party may be expelled only after a decision in accordance with law. If there are not compelling reasons of national security, the person shall be allowed to be represented before and have his case reviewed by the competent authority or persons designated by the competent authority. Entitlement to review by national authorities was also highlighted in the WTO case *US—Import Prohibition of Certain Shrimp and Shrimp Products*. The measure at issue was the US import prohibition of shrimp and shrimp products from non-certified countries, i.e. countries that had not used a certain net-type in catching shrimp. India, Malaysia, Pakistan and Thailand then jointly brought a case against the USA. In reaching its conclusion that the US ban could not be justified, the AB not only reasoned that the measure was unjustifiably discriminatory because of its intended and actual coercive effect on the specific policy decisions made by foreign governments that were members of the WTO. The measure also constituted 'arbitrary' discrimination because of the rigidity and inflexibility in its application, and the lack of procedural fairness in the administration of trade regulations. The AB stated that with respect to neither type of certification under US law is there 'a transparent, predictable certification process that is followed by the competent United States government officials [...]. No procedure for review of, or appeal from, a denial of an application is provided' (*United States—Import Prohibition of Certain Shrimp and Shrimp Products*, para. 180).

tive decision-making, however, it has been argued that the right to review is reflected only to some extent.[334]

The right to review nevertheless exists in numerous international decision-making processes. Notably, the AB is a standing body of seven persons that hears appeals from reports issued by panels in disputes brought by members of the WTO. Appeals are conducted according to the procedures established under the Dispute Settlement Understanding and the Working Procedures for Appellate Review.[335] Each appeal is heard by three members of the AB, set up by the Dispute Settlement Body and representing the range of WTO membership. The AB may uphold, modify or reverse the legal findings. Reports of the AB are subsequently adopted (or not) by the Dispute Settlement Body.

The procedures relating to compliance under the Kyoto Protocol also contain regulations for a limited type of appeal. A State Party in respect of which a final decision has been taken may appeal to the Conferences of the Parties (COP) against a decision of the Enforcement Branch relating to Article 3 of the Kyoto Protocol if that state believes it has been denied due process.[336] The appeal shall be lodged with the secretariat within 45 days after the state has been informed of the decision, and the COP shall consider the appeal at its first session after the lodging of the appeal.[337] The COP may then override the decision of the Enforcement Branch, in which event the COP is to refer the matter of the appeal back to the Enforcement Branch.[338]

Perhaps a more sophisticated and pertinent example in the context of the Commission is the appeal procedure before the EPO. The Convention on the Grant of European Patents (EPC) has, in its Articles 106 to 111, rules that give a party who has been adversely affected the right to appeal a decision by, for instance, an Examining Division that refuses to grant a European patent application.[339] Decisions can be challenged before the Boards of Appeal. Also an Enlarged Board of Appeal is set, to deal exclusively with questions of law. These review bodies are to be fully independent from the EPO, and bound only by the EPC when examining an appeal. Part VI of the EPC thus has an appeal procedure reminiscent of a national administrative complaint

---

334   Kingsbury, Krisch and Stewart, 'The Emergence of Global Administrative Law', p. 39.

335   Doc. WT/AB/WP/6 ('Working procedures for appellate review').

336   UN Doc. FCCC/CP/2001/13/Add.3 ('Decision 24/CP.7: Procedures and mechanisms relating to compliance under the Kyoto Protocol, Annex'), Section XI, para. 1.

337   *Ibid.*

338   *Ibid.*

339   Convention on the Grant of European Patents, adopted in Munich on 5 October 1973; entered into force on 7 October 1977. Published in *UNTS*, Vol. 1065, p. 199.

mechanism: Article 106 specifies which decisions are subject to appeal; Article 107 specifies which persons are entitled to appeal and to be parties to appeal proceedings; Article 108 specifies the time limit and form of an appeal; Article 109 contains provisions on interlocutory revision; Article 110 specifies how the appeal shall be processed; Article 111 contains rules on the decisions of the appeal; Article 112 contains rules on the decisions or opinions of the Enlarged Board of Appeal; and Article 112a has rules concerning petitions for review by the Enlarged Board of Appeal.

Nonetheless, the issue of review is not uniformly resolved in international law. The vast majority of international dispute resolution bodies have no tradition of rules concerning appeal. Judgments of the ICJ are final and without appeal.[340] Article 33 of Annex VI to the LOS Convention specifies furthermore that the ITLOS' judgments are without appeal and shall be final.[341] Likewise, many ad hoc arbitrations adopt decisions that are final and without appeal or review. Thus, in the procedures before international judicial bodies there is most often only one first and last instance—with international criminal courts as notable examples of the opposite arrangement.[342] Not having the possibility of an independent review of the Commission's recommendations is therefore

---

340 Articles 60–61 of the Statute of the ICJ.

341 In the event of dispute as to the meaning or scope of a judgment, a party may make a request for its interpretation, but this must be distinguished from the concept of appellate or judicial review (Article 33 of Annex VI to the LOS Convention and Article 126, para. 1, of the Rules of the Tribunal). A separate issue is also the possibility of having a court decision revised (or annulled). Request for revision of an ITLOS judgment may be made in certain circumstances, for instance, if new decisive facts are produced. A final and binding decision will then be subject to a new evaluation (Article 127, para. 1, of the Rules of the Tribunal). The issue of revision is not an irrelevant issue with respect to the Commission's recommendations either. For example, if the physical conditions at the seabed changes, should the Commission adopt new recommendations?

342 The review mechanisms available in international criminal courts are notable examples. In *Tadic*, the Appeals Chamber of the International Criminal Tribunal for the former Yugoslavia stated that an international criminal court 'ought to be rooted in the rule of law and offer all guarantees embodied in the relevant international instruments' (*Prosecutor v. Duško Tadić, Decision on the Defence Motion for Interlocutory Appeal on Jurisdiction*, Case IT-94-1-AR72, 2 October 1995, para. 42). A judgment of the ICC can be appealed both by the convicted and the prosecutor in accordance with the rules in Part 8 of the Rome Statute. Article 81 determines that a decision may be appealed on the grounds of procedural error, error of fact, error of law or (by the convicted person or the Prosecutor on that person's behalf) on any other ground that affects the fairness or reliability of the proceedings or decision.

a legal arrangement that is neither fully in line with, nor fully contradicts, the rules applying to other international institutions.

Since the Commission's recommendations are not binding *strictu sensu*, it can be argued that a review opportunity is not needed. Klabbers holds that it is not obvious that judicial review should encompass non-binding decisions of international institutions.[343] The counter-argument, however, is that the recommendations of the Commission produce significant legal effects. Ignoring them entails certain legal disadvantages for the coastal state. And if they are used as the basis of national legislation, they contribute to the final and binding nature of the outer limits of the continental shelf. These effects speak strongly in favour of expanding review to encompass the Commission's recommendations as well.

However, it may seem excessive to permit an appeal mechanism in respect of the Commission's recommendations when not even the judgments of the ICJ or the ITLOS can be reviewed. And if we look at processes providing access to review, for instance the ICC, there are obvious differences as regards the Commission and its recommendations. The ICC sentences individuals to prison in cases regarding human rights and war crimes violations, whereas the Commission's recommendations are non-binding and concern a public law matter of inter-state character. Thus, although review mechanisms in the form of appellate bodies are available in international criminal courts, we should not automatically consider it a deficit if no such possibility exists with regard to the Commission's recommendations. It can indeed be argued that it is more serious for an innocent person to be sentenced to decades in prison, than for the Commission to misplace a slope point on a given part of the outer continental shelf.

On the other hand, the degree of intrusiveness should not obscure the fact that *every* legal decision—whether about war crimes or the placement of a resource limit at the seabed—should be correct. In my view, a review mechanism in the context of Article 76 would serve to protect this important interest. First, review would contribute to ensure that the Commission follows the legal procedures set out in the LOS Convention. Second, review would contribute to ensure that the Commission's recommendations are substantively correct and adopted 'in accordance with article 76'.[344] The question of whether a review mechanism is needed should also be considered in relation to the other

---

343 Klabbers, Jan, 'Straddling Law and Politics: Judicial Review in International Law', in MacDonald, Ronald St. John, and Douglas M. Johnston (eds), *Towards World Constitutionalism* (Martinus Nijhoff Publishers, 2005), pp. 809–835, at p. 820.

344 See Article 3, para. 1 (*litra* a), of Annex II to the LOS Convention.

challenges to legitimacy facing the Commission. As noted, the Commission is similar in composition to a scientific and advisory body, while its statutory functions and competences very much resemble those of purely legal institution. In my view, this very lack of legal expertise in the Commission indicates a *particular* need for a second opinion. It is a deficit that most other institutions which deal with treaty interpretation do not suffer from.

It is also worth recalling why many decisions by international legal institutions cannot be appealed, in whole or in part. It is primarily due to the fact that in international law—as opposed to national law—there is no obligatory, hierarchical system of institutions. For instance, when a state accepts the ICJ's jurisdiction, it also has to accept the finality of the Court's decisions. The reason, for instance, why the judgments of international courts cannot generally be appealed is the absence of what in domestic legal settings are seen as basic constitutional elements—appeal bodies—and not that review as such is an unwanted or presumed ineffective instrument. It is not known whether anyone, as a matter of principle, has stated that there is no need for appeal concerning legal decisions rendered by international institutions. On the contrary, scholars are increasingly asking whether the empowerment of international institutions is balanced by constitutional guarantees, including the right to review.[345]

4.6.6.3   Preliminary Conclusions

In my view, a review mechanism would definitely contribute to mitigate other legitimacy challenges facing the Commission, and should thus have been provided for. The submitting coastal state should have been granted the right to have the Commission's recommendations reviewed, involving a *de novo* consideration of facts and law. Such a review could then also cover the procedural requirements to the Commission's decision-making.

Alternatively, coastal states could have been granted the right to a type of reasonable review, that is, allow states to appeal the Commission's recommendations to an appellate body authorized to review the adequacy of, say, the Commission's reasoning. For instance, the ITLOS or the ICJ could be empowered to determine whether the Commission provided sufficient reasons in its recommendations to enable an effective examination of them, whereby making it possible to reveal any recommendations that might be 'arbitrary and capricious'.[346] Here we may note that the ITLOS' Seabed Dispute Chamber—

---

345   See generally Klabbers, Peters and Ulfstein, *The Constitutionalization of International Law.*
346   Tobler, Claudia, 'The Standard of Judicial Review of Administrative Agencies in the U.S. and EU: Accountability and Reasonable Agency Action', in *Boston International & Comparative Law Review*, Vol. 22, 1999, pp. 213–228, at p. 215.

established in accordance with Article 14 of Annex VI and Section 5 of Part XI of the LOS Convention—has limited jurisdiction with regard to decisions by the ISA, i.e. the Authority's 'discretionary powers'.[347]

Given the lack of formal legal expertise among the members of the Commission, it is the *legal* element which is in need of review under the Article 76 implementation process. An arrangement along the lines, for instance, of the aforementioned appeal-mechanism under the Kyoto Compliance System—with the Meeting of States Parties given the role as 'Chamber of Appeal'—is therefore not advised. Having a 'political' body as appellate authority would not enhance the legitimacy of the Commission or its recommendations in the context of Article 76 and the Commission.

4.6.7   *Conclusions*

The lack of detailed and sufficient procedural rules is one of the most conspicuous aspects of Article 76 and Annex II to LOS Convention. It has therefore been imperative for the Commission, of its own volition, to compile extensive regulations through its own Rules of Procedure. These provisions are characterized by a willingness to achieve a satisfactory process. However, as we have seen, the procedures of the Commission are not sufficient in all instances.

We have noted the unsatisfactory nature of the rules concerning admissibility of facts and evidence. Only the coastal state has the opportunity to contribute information regarding the properties of the seabed, and it is on the basis of this information that the Commission in turn shall base its recommendations. Further, it is unclear how, if at all, the Commission deals with information

---

347   Article 189 of the LOS Convention—titled 'Limitation on jurisdiction with regard to decisions of the Authority'—provides that the Seabed Disputes Chamber shall have no jurisdiction with regard to the exercise by the ISA of its discretionary powers in accordance with Part XI of the LOS Convention and that it in no case shall substitute its discretion for that of the Authority. Also, without prejudice to Article 191, in exercising its jurisdiction pursuant to Article 187, the Seabed Disputes Chamber shall not pronounce itself on the question of whether any rules, regulations and procedures of the Authority are in conformity with the LOS Convention, nor declare invalid any such rules, regulations and procedures. The jurisdiction of the Seabed Disputes Chamber in this regard shall accordingly be confined to deciding claims that the application of any rules, regulations and procedures of the ISA in individual cases would be in conflict with the contractual obligations of the parties to the dispute or their obligations under the LOS Convention, claims concerning excess of jurisdiction or misuse of power, and to claims for damages to be paid or other remedy to be given to the party concerned for the failure of the other party to comply with its contractual obligations or its obligations under the LOS Convention.

submitted by other states. This is a weakness that neither the LOS Convention nor the Commission's Rules of Procedure has resolved in a satisfactory manner.

The LOS Convention contains no provisions on coastal state participation in the procedures before the Commission, except that the coastal state shall have the opportunity to send representatives to participate in the 'relevant proceedings'—and, of course, that the coastal state shall file a submission. However, the Commission's Rules of Procedure include regulations for safeguarding coastal state participation. Hence, although the Commission's proceedings have certain shortcomings as regards the coastal state's right to be heard and participate—notably, the usually lengthy intervals between the submission phase and the advanced stage of the proceedings—we may conclude that the procedures attending to this matter are within the margins of permissible norms.

The LOS Convention has no provisions to ensure transparency and openness in the Article 76 process to the benefit of other states, NGOs or the general public. States and other actors may not attend sub-commission and Commission meetings, so they do not have unfiltered access to the Commission's decision-making or a complete picture of the debates and issues discussed. The way in which the Commission examines submissions—mostly written—is cited to justify that meetings are closed. However, the lack of official record-keeping is a weakness. The Chairman of the Commission produces and circulates an annual report to all States Parties, and it is reprinted on the Commission's website. However, this report does not include the specifics of the debate and discussion that informed the recommendations. Third states, non-members and the general public should be allowed to attend an open hearing at an advanced stage of the proceedings, perhaps between the adoption by the sub-commission of draft recommendations and the plenary Commission which adopts the final recommendations.

With regard to documentation, the Commission has improved transparency in its procedural rules by deciding that a summary of the coastal state's submission shall be made public. In addition, the full recommendations are to be made public when the coastal state has established the outer limits in its national legislation and then submitted charts and coordinates of these limits to the UNSG. This represents a major step forward in openness and transparency. In practice, however, some states have resisted the Commission's attempts to increase transparency through regulations which have no legal foundation in the LOS Convention.

The Commission's Rules of Procedure stipulate that the Commission shall state the rationale on which its recommendations have been based. However, we have seen that the Commission does not always provide sufficient reasons for its recommendations. This may be because there are no detailed regulations on the form and content of recommendations. Another weakness is that the Commission does not specify the reasons for dissenting and separate opinions. Finally, we have concluded that the absence of an independent review body is a procedural weakness, particularly given the absence of legal expertise in the Commission itself.

4.7   Assessment

The Commission is a unique legal institution insofar as its novel functions and competences for the purpose of setting the outer limits of the continental shelf distinguish it from other international bodies. However, in the performance of its functions, the Commission also bears resemblance to several other international institutions—for instance, in interpreting and applying Article 76, the Commission's tasks do not differ much from those of, say, any traditional dispute settlement body. But we have also observed that the Commission exercises a type of legal-administrative function which is neither primarily legislative nor adjudicative in character. The Commission in that sense resembles many other global administrative treaty bodies, although complete comparisons are difficult to identify.

Since the Commission has been delegated broad powers for the purpose of establishing the outer limits of the continental shelf under the LOS Convention, it has been the assumption that in exercising this power, the Commission should also be subject to certain normative standards in terms of its composition and procedures. Power should be controlled. In the analysis of legitimacy, the focus of attention thus shifted from legal aspects of the Commission's decision-making to the adequacy of its composition and procedures. Basically, there ought to be a proper relationship between these two 'sides'. The main concern—and the subject of the analysis—was therefore whether the Commission and its procedures were in fact in line with acceptable normative standards of institutional design and due process of law: whether the Commission's procedures and composition were legitimate in a normative sense. This is how the notion of 'legitimacy' in Chapter 4 is understood.

First, in terms of composition, it appears that the LOS Convention has not managed to balance the demand for a specialist expert regime against the demand for a legal decision-making system. The Commission should have had both scientific expertise and legal expertise. Legal expertise would have provided the Commission with greater legitimacy, for example by enabling it to give legally based reasons for its recommendations, to resolve conflicts of norms, or decide whether sufficient, legally relevant evidence for a factual circumstance had been produced by the coastal state.

The LOS Convention, however, emphasizes only scientific—not legal—expertise among the qualifications required for service on the Commission, even though its mandate and powers are also of a legal nature. So, while the Commission is presumably well-qualified to evaluate the factual information contained in submissions and the technical complexity of the rules in Article 76, it appears that the Commission is *not* sufficiently well equipped to interpret and deal with the legal challenges entailed in the implementation of that provision.

The Commission should therefore, I conclude, have been made up of both lawyers and relevant scientific experts. The current arrangement under Article 76 is a Commission consisting solely of scientists—and whose (possible) interaction with its legally well-qualified secretariat is not familiar to the outside world. This represents a deficiency which significantly undercuts the Commission's legitimacy in a normative sense. Legal bodies that deal with treaty interpretation generally consist of lawyers, wholly or in part.

Some concern about the Commission as regards the independence and impartiality of its members has also been expressed. It is unsatisfactory that the operating expenses of the individual Commission member—notably their salary—is reimbursed by the state that nominated the member. It would promote greater confidence—and conform with international standards—if the LOS Convention had a more neutral scheme whereby, for example, all Commission operating expenses were covered by the States Parties over a joint budget. Moreover, the size of the remuneration for the individual Commission member is determined by the state that nominated the person—also an unfortunate practice.

The LOS Convention rules on how Commission members are nominated and elected emerge as rather politicized. The nomination process is non-transparent. Governments approach individuals and encourage them to stand for election. It can therefore also be questioned whether Commission members are selected on the basis of qualifications and suitability, or whether political motives lie behind the choices. Procedures for nomination and election could be improved to increase the chances that the best candidates are elected. A nominating committee—as practised in several other treaty regimes—could be relevant here.

That Commission members may engage in extra-professional activity is also negative with respect to the independence and impartiality of the Commission. It would be an advantage for Commission members to serve on a full-time basis. We have seen that Commission members have held positions and received salaries from their nominating states, while the same state's continental shelf claims were being dealt with by the Commission. While serving on the Commission, members have also worked for oil companies, whose interest in a continental shelf's outer limits needs no further explanation. It is only natural that people who are experts in the field of, say, continental shelf geology may have held positions in the oil industry or worked with international law issues relating to the continental shelf in states' governmental administration or foreign services. But surely it is detrimental to the Commission's legitimacy that such activity continues while these persons are serving on the Commission. This is not only an issue of legitimacy, it impinges the Commission's efficiency. Average processing time for a continental shelf submission is several years. In the current situation, with the Commission being faced with a row of submissions, permanent membership positions could also help to speed up the Commission's work.

We have also seen that certain aspects of the Commission's procedures can be questioned in terms of legitimacy. First, as regards the adequacy of the rules on admissibility of facts and elucidation of evidence in the Article 76 implementation process. According to the LOS Convention, the Commission shall rely on information contained in the submission from the coastal state—that is, information produced by the party that stands to gain most from having the outer limits placed at the most seaward position as possible. The LOS Convention does not give other interested parties an opportunity to supplement the coastal state's production of evidence; and in practice, the Commission has rejected input from other states. Also problematic in this context is that the Commission has no legal mandate to initiate its own investigations in order to determine whether the description of the seabed given by the coastal state represents the true picture. There is the risk that the coastal state may be withholding or manipulating relevant information.

Through its Rules of Procedure, the Commission has taken important steps to improve conditions in terms of openness and transparency favouring the *coastal state* in the Article 76 implementation process. However, it can be argued that the interests of actors other than the coastal state itself are not satisfactorily protected for this purpose. The establishment of the outer limits of the continental shelf is a matter of interest to all States Parties, and may also be of interest to IOs, NGOs and non-parties, as well as the general public. Yet according to the LOS Convention, the Article 76 implementation process is completely closed—with regard to meetings and documents.

With regard to documents, however, the Commission has adopted important regulations concerning transparency, including making public a summary of the coastal state's submission and a summary of the recommendations.

When the outer limits have been established domestically, the Commission's procedural rules also provide that the recommendations in their entirety shall be made publicly available on the Commission's website. But as these regulations are not based on the provisions of the LOS Convention, it is difficult to see how the Rules of Procedure will improve transparency and openness if individual states demand secrecy.

Coastal states (and other states) will probably be concerned with the need of the Commission to respect the scope of obligations as ratified in Article 76 when making recommendations. According to the LOS Convention, however, the Commission has no explicit duty to provide reasons for its recommendations. Through the Rules of Procedure, the Commission has imposed on itself the duty to provide reasons: the Commission shall specify the 'rationale' for the recommendations. A few examples have shown, however, significant space to improve the clarity of interpretive reasoning in the Commission's recommendations. Furthermore, the recommendations do not contain, or annex, any dissenting or separate opinions. In those cases where the Commission's recommendations are not adopted unanimously or by consensus, the coastal state is therefore not informed about the reasons for the dissenting opinion(s), or why a Commission member abstained from voting. Surely, if the coastal state disagrees with the Commission's recommendations, it would be of particular interest for that state to know why one or more Commission members dissented.

One control mechanism which is also lacking in the Article 76 implementation process is the possibility to have the Commission's recommendations reviewed by an independent appeal authority, in whole or in part. If the Commission concludes that the outer limits should be placed somewhere else than the coastal state has provisionally delineated, that state must—given our conception of 'on the basis of'—abide by the Commission's view if it seeks to have legally final and binding outer limits established. Therefore, in case of disagreement by the coastal state with the Commission's recommendations, the coastal state—or other stakeholders—might wish to obtain a 'second opinion'. However, in accordance with Article 5 of Annex II, a new and revised submission is to be submitted to the same Commission. There is no genuine appeal mechanism involved.

Accordingly, the discussion of the legitimacy of the Commission and its decision-making has shown that the current regulations and practices concerning the Commission's composition and procedures—its legitimacy—are not ideal, nor are they ideally suited to safeguard the legitimate interests of all affected parties. An important general finding of this study is thus that the

Commission lacks several of the key legitimacy and accountability mechanisms that it should have had—mechanisms that are available to comparable legal institutions. Therefore, in many areas—from a normative legitimacy perspective—there is a remarkable mismatch between the Commission's functions and competences on the one side, and its composition and procedures on the other side.

CHAPTER 5

The Future of the Commission

5.1   Article 76 of the LOS Convention: An Opportunity Lost?

The legal historical review presented in Chapter 2 showed that when the UNGA decided to convene a new global conference on the law of the sea in 1973, one of the main purposes was to adopt 'a clear and precise definition of the outer limits of coastal state jurisdiction'.[1] It had been argued that there was 'nothing sacred in existing legal categories; they were created haphazardly to meet in some ways needs of coastal states that could no longer be adequately satisfied under existing international law, a law that [was] largely obsolescent and in part obsolete'.[2] The time had therefore come 'to consolidate the multiplicity of limits of coastal state jurisdiction in ocean space into an overall clearly defined outer limit of national jurisdiction'.[3]

It can be discussed to what extent the drafters actually achieved their mandate. For one thing, Article 76 of the LOS Convention does not provide for only *one* criterion on which to set the outer limit of the continental shelf. The outer limit is either 200 nautical miles from the baselines from which the breadth of the territorial sea is measured, *or* at 'the outer edge of the continental margin' where this margin extends beyond that distance. The first option is easy to apply: it involves simply measuring the distance from the baselines. The second would seem precise enough in view of the remaining specific and detailed formula of Article 76 concerning how exactly that outer edge shall be established. In fact, however, these provisions have intricate normative implications.

First, as a treaty provision, Article 76 is extraordinary in its complexity and legislative technique. Its provisions switch between precise rules which provide a specific solution to clearly defined situations on the one hand, and general and discretionary rules that allow of specific evaluations for the individual circumstances of the case, on the other. As we have seen, the implementation of Article 76 has so far shown that both the interpretation of its provisions and their application to a specific case at hand may give rise to controversy.

---

1   UN Doc. A/AC.138/SR.56 ('Report from the Sea-bed Committee'), pp. 27–28.
2   *Ibid.*, p. 45.
3   *Ibid.*

Second, there is the check on coastal state unilateralism in the application of Article 76 by the Commission. The making of recommendations places decision-making beyond the control of individual coastal states. The Commission exercises a type of law-bound discretion. But there exists a judicial discretion which allows the Commission to make recommendations within a range of possible interpretive options.

A simple distance criterion from the coast would make it just as easy to practise the rules of the outer limits of the continental shelf as the outer limits for the territorial sea, the contiguous zone and the exclusive economic zone. Moreover, there would be no need to have an international body to oversee the application of the rules. UNCLOS III nevertheless chose the more complex option for the continental shelf. From the perspective of international politics, this was a fundamental choice. Even larger subsea areas are currently being nationalized, basically to the coastal state's advantage—an option that clearly was preferred on the basis of a desire to exploit petroleum and other mineral deposits as far out to sea as possible. Coastal state jurisdiction prevailed at the expense of other interests. The price to pay, however, was a treaty provision that in no way is distinguished by its accuracy or is otherwise exemplary from a legal-technical perspective, but which will necessarily in many cases imply controversial application by an international body of experts. To quote Churchill and Lowe, in their renowned work on the law of the sea: 'Despite its detail, the formula in the 1982 Convention leaves room for considerable uncertainty'.[4]

And so it seems, on the basis of what has been discussed in this study. Even though the adoption of Article 76 was definitely a step in the right direction in relation to the 1958 Convention on the Continental Shelf, it remains to be seen whether, in the longer term, Article 76 will prove adequate in reconciling the diverging interests of the states in one of the most controversial issues of international law in our time—while a minority of those states, owing to their favourable geographical placement, continue to divide up the ocean floor.

5.2   Obstacles to Reform

As we have seen, the LOS Convention and the Rules of Procedure of the Commission are not fully suited to protect the legitimate interests of all parties as regards establishing the outer limits of the continental shelf. With many states having submitted claims to seabed areas beyond 200 nautical miles, the

---

4   Churchill and Lowe, *The Law of the Sea*, p. 149.

discussion over the Commission's procedures and composition will doubtless intensify in the years to come.[5] States might argue for changes in relation to the current regime, for example that procedural rules should be adopted by the Meeting of States Parties instead of the Commission, or that there should be created a permanent review mechanism for coastal states wishing a second opinion from a neutral appeals body, concerning the Commission's recommendations.

This study has discussed such reforms without regard to whether they can be realistically implemented. Regardless of their practical feasibility, however, any proposed changes would probably face fundamental challenges on several levels. First, making improvements to the Commission's Rules of Procedure might be problematic in relation to those states which have already initiated the process of implementing Article 76, and, most of all, those who have come to the stage of establishing the outer limits of the continental shelf in their national legislation. Should, for instance, new and more sophisticated procedural rules only apply to states that have yet to start implementation of Article 76 due to late ratification? Should an appeals mechanism apply to Myanmar, when there was none in place for Norway? And if it is decided that the composition of the Commission needs greater breadth with regard to academic qualifications in order to safeguard the coastal state's rights, should not *all* continental shelf submissions be reprocessed? Somewhat ironically, precisely because the Commission has already dealt with many continental shelf submissions, it must—for the sake of equal treatment—be cautious about making significant changes to its procedural rules in the future.

Another challenge in relation to any improvement to the Article 76 implementation process is that fundamental changes will require amendments to the LOS Convention, formal changes or even a completely new regime for the outer limits of the continental shelf. The latter option is hardly a feasible scenario. But also revisions or formal amendments to the Convention would be difficult to implement. First, such changes would not apply to the continental shelf submissions already processed. As a result, the above-mentioned issue of treating equally all shelf submissions again arises.

Second, although it is formally possible to revise or change the LOS Convention, it is a long and uncertain political process. For instance, is it so that the Meeting of the States Parties—through an 'authoritative interpretation' of how the deadline for making submissions is to be understood—can adopt *de facto* changes to a straightforward treaty provision? That is not among the Meeting's

---

5   As of 1 January 2014, the Commission has received 70 submissions, including two 're-submissions'. The Commission has adopted 18 recommendations as of 1 January 2014.

explicit functions under the LOS Convention.[6] An extension of the Meeting's functions could potentially be supported only by Article 319, paragraph 2 (*litra* e), of the LOS Convention, according to which the UN Secretary-General shall convene the 'necessary' meetings of the States Parties, or based on an effective interpretation of the LOS Convention because such changes would better serve to achieve the Convention's object and purpose as per Article 31, paragraph 1, of the Vienna Convention. The context nevertheless seems to favour reading 'necessary' as *necessary for the purpose of exercising the functions explicitly allotted to the Meeting of States Parties in the LOS Convention.* To the extent that 'improvements' in the Convention are to be adopted, the Convention's formal amendment procedures must therefore be employed.[7] Thus, attempts already undertaken by the Meeting to change the Convention's provisions by way of a 'simplified' procedure are actually questionable in terms of the Meeting's formal competences, even though these changes have 'strong support' among the States Parties and were considered necessary for the sake of the Commission's workload. In all probability, therefore, the Article 76 implementation process will, by and large, apply in the future, as it applies today.

In the wider context, these limitations to reform illustrate general challenges at the international level as to how treaty regimes can adjust to new demands and issues. Since the adoption of new rules is complicated and often proceeds more slowly in international law than at the national level, outdated or inadequate rules will often become a persistent drag on that treaty regime, precisely because revision mechanisms are complex and cumbersome. As regards the Commission, this problem has been highlighted by the emergence of modern international legal disciplines, notably global administrative law, focusing on the degree to which there is a proper balance between empowerment and control of international institutions.

5.3   Dislocation of Decision-Making

Globalization is confronting international law with ever new and more complex issues. Any chronological list of international treaties and other

---

6 The specific task of the Meeting of States Parties set out in the LOS Convention are only these: to elect the members of the ITLOS (Article 4, para. 4, of Annex VI), elect the members of the Commission (Article 2, para. 2, of Annex II) and to decide on the expenses of the ITLOS (Article 19, para. 1, of Annex VI).

7 Articles 312, 313 and 314 of the LOS Convention.

instruments will reveal their increasing number in the course of the past few decades. Closer and increasingly complex international relations require legal collaboration in more and more areas. The emerging pattern—fragmentation of international law—has been described in detail by the ILC.[8] International law is today divided into a number of highly specialized branches, like 'law of the sea', 'international environmental law', 'international refugee law', 'international criminal law', or 'European law', each with its own set of sub-categories and sub-regimes. In theory, there is nothing wrong with this: fragmentation is essentially a response to a need.

One aspect of this development is the proliferation of international bodies tasked with various functions under international treaties. The Commission is a notable example, yet only one among many. Legally speaking, these bodies must all be considered international institutions *sui generis*. They cannot be gathered under the same umbrella—even though all originate from the decision made by the states concerned not to establish an IO but a different sort of international institution. These international bodies vary widely in functions, competences, composition and procedures. However, given their creation and existence, they also reflect a general tendency, which is a relatively recent form of how international cooperation is being organized.

Tuori speaks of the process of 'de-nationalisation' in *The Law's Farewell to the Nation State*.[9] International law has always responded to transnational activity, but it has conventionally done so through substantive rules of law that were inseparable from states as subjects of international law—also expressed through the activity of IOs as subjects of international law. Today's international law, however, is opening the doors to different types of participation. States remain the principal actors, but the proliferation of sub-systems is a dominant trend, followed by functional differentiation and autonomous institutions with membership characterized by independence and expertise.[10] Koskenniemi describes an international law which is, on the one hand, uni-

---

8   See Koskenniemi, Martti, 'The Fate of Public International Law: Between Technique and Politics', in *The Modern Law Review*, Vol. 70, 2007, pp. 1–30.

9   Tuori, Kaarlo, 'The Law's Farewell to the Nation State?', in *Finnish Yearbook of International Law*, Vol. 19, 2008, pp. 295–328.

10   See Teubner, Gunther, and Andreas Fischer-Lescano, 'Regime-Collisions: The Vain Search for Legal Unity in the Fragmentation of Global Law', in *Michigan Journal of International Law*, Vol. 25, No. 4, 2004, pp. 999–1046. See also Churchill, Robin, and Geir Ulfstein, 'Autonomous Institutional Arrangements in Multilateral Environmental Agreements: A Little-noticed Phenomenon in International Law', in *American Journal of International Law*, Vol. 94, 2000, pp. 623–659.

versal in character and dominated by normative force.[11] On the other hand, he sees—and warns against—the accelerating slide from formalism to anti-formalism and marginalization of normative influence, as international law becomes increasingly infiltrated by technocratic regimes.[12]

In the Commission, we see one notable example—perhaps one of the clearest—of how and to what extent international law and decision-making currently are being influenced by such epistemic communities. Given the legal frame of reference contained in Article 76 of the LOS Convention, it was in my view both advantageous and necessary to include experts such as geologists, geophysicists and hydrographers in procedures to establishing the outer limits of the continental shelf. However, it seems less certain whether the drafters were sufficiently attentive to the specific functions and authority actually entrusted to the Commission as regards the implementation process of Article 76. In an overall perspective, the research conducted for this study thus also serves to illustrate—through the example of the Commission on the Limits of the Continental Shelf—what contemporary international law theory sees as a dislocation of decision-making in the law among nations.

---

11   Koskenniemi, 'The Fate of Public International Law'.
12   *Ibid.*

Bibliography

Books and Articles

Allott, Philip, 'Power Sharing in the Law of the Sea', in *American Journal of International Law*, Vol. 77, 1983, pp. 1–30.

Alston, Philip, and James Crawford (eds), *The Future of UN Human Rights Treaty Monitoring* (Cambridge University Press, 2009).

Alvarez, J.E., 'Constitutional Interpretation in International Organizations', in Coicaud, Jean-Marc, and Veijo Heiskanen (eds), *The Legitimacy of International Organizations* (UN University Press, 2001), pp. 104–154.

Amerasinghe, C.F., 'Interpretation of Texts in Open International Organizations', in *British Yearbook of International Law*, Vol. 45, 1994, pp. 175–209.

Anderson, David, 'Developments in Maritime Boundary Law and Practice', in Charney, J.I., David A. Colson, Lewis M. Alexander and Robert W. Smith (eds), *International Maritime Boundaries* (Martinus Nijhoff Publishers, 2005), pp. 3199–3222.

Anderson, David H., 'Delimitation of the Maritime Boundary in the Bay of Bengal (Bangladesh/Myanmar)', in *American Journal of International Law*, Vol. 106, 2012, pp. 817–824.

Ando, Nisuke, 'General Comments/Recommendations', in Wolfrum, Rüdiger (ed.), *The Max Planck Encyclopedia of Public International Law*. Online edition.

Ando, Nisuke, Edward McWhinney and *Rüdiger* Wolfrum (eds), *Liber Amicorum Judge Shigeru Oda* (Kluwer Law International, 2002).

Andrassy, Juraj, *International Law and the Resources of the Sea* (Columbia University Press, 1970).

Annand, Ram Prakash, *Legal Regime of the Sea-Bed and the Developing Countries* (A.W. Sijthoff International Publishing, 1976).

Armage, David (ed.), *The Free Sea* (Liberty Fund, 2004).

Aznar-Gómez, Mariano J., 'Organization of the Court', in Zimmermann, Andreas, Christian Tomuschat and Karin Oellers-Frahm (eds), *The Statute of the International Court of Justice: A Commentary* (Oxford University Press, 2006), pp. 205–218.

Barr, Michael S., and Geoffrey P. Miller, 'Global Administrative Law: The View From Basel', in *The European Journal of International Law*, Vol. 17, 2006, pp. 15–46.

Black, Julia, 'Constructing and contesting legitimacy and accountability in polycentric regulatory regimes', in *Regulation & Governance*, Vol. 2, 2008, pp. 137–164.

Blake, G.H. (ed.), *Boundaries and Energy: Problems and Prospects* (Kluwer Law International, 1998).

———, *Maritime Boundaries and Ocean Resources* (Croom Helm, 1987).

Bodansky, Daniel, Jutta Brunnée and Ellen Hey (eds), *The Oxford Handbook of International Environmental Law* (Oxford University Press, 2008).

Bodansky, Daniel, 'Legitimacy', in Bodansky, Daniel, Jutta Brunnée and Ellen Hey (eds), *The Oxford Handbook of International Environmental Law* (Oxford University Press, 2008), pp. 704–743.

————, 'The Legitimacy of International Governance: A Coming Challenge for International Environmental Law?', in *American Journal of International Law*, Vol. 93, 1999, pp. 596–624.

Bonzon, Yves, 'Institutionalizing Public Participation in WTO Decision Making: Some Conceptual Hurdles and Avenues', in *Journal of International Economic Law*, Vol. 11, 2008, pp. 751–777.

Bosch, Miguel Marín, *Votes in the UN General Assembly* (Martinus Nijhoff Publishers, 1998).

Bothe, Michael, 'Fact-Finding as a Means of Ensuring Respect for International Humanitarian Law', in Epping, Volker, and Wolff Heinstel von Heinegg (eds), *International Humanitarian Law Facing New Challenges* (Springer, 2007), pp. 249–267.

Boyle, Alan, 'Some Reflections on the Relationship of Treaties and Soft Law', in *International & Comparative Law Quarterly*, Vol. 48, 1999, pp. 901–913.

Brekke, Harald, and Philip Symonds, 'Submarine Ridges and Elevations of Article 76 in Light of Published Summaries of Recommendations of the Commission on the Limits of the Continental Shelf', in *Ocean Development & International Law*, Vol. 42, 2011, pp. 289–306.

Brown, E.D., *Sea-Bed Energy and Minerals: The International Legal Regime (Volume 1: The Continental Shelf)* (Martinus Nijhoff Publishers, 1992).

Brownlie, Ian, *Principles of Public International Law* (Oxford University Press, 2003).

Brunnée, Jutta, 'COPing with Consent: Lawmaking Under Multilateral Environmental Agreements', in *Leiden Journal of International Law*, Vol. 15, 2002, pp. 1–52.

Brunnée, Jutta, and Stephen J. Toope, *Legitimacy and Legality in International Law* (Cambridge University Press, 2010).

Buchanan, Allen, and Robert O. Keohane, 'The Legitimacy of Global Governance Institutions,' in *Ethics & International Affairs*, Vol. 20, 2006, pp. 405–437.

Burke, William (ed.), *Towards a Better Use of the Oceans: Contemporary Legal Problems in Ocean Development* (Almqvist & Wiksell, 1969).

Caron, David, 'The Legitimacy of the Collective Authority of the Security Council', in *American Journal of International Law*, Vol. 87, 1993, pp. 552–588.

Cass, Deborah, *The Constitutionalization of the World Trade Organization: Legitimacy, Democracy, and Community in the International Trading System* (Oxford University Press, 2005).

Cassese, Antonio, *International Law* (Oxford University Press, 2005).

Cavnar, Anna, 'Accountability and the Commission on the Limits of the Continental Shelf: Deciding Who Owns the Ocean Floor', in *Cornell International Law Journal*, Vol. 42, 2009, pp. 387–440.

Chapman, Wilbert McLeod, 'Concerning Fishery Jurisdiction and the Regime of the Deep-sea Bed', in Burke, William (ed.), *Towards a Better Use of the Oceans: Contemporary Legal Problems in Ocean Development* (Almqvist & Wiksell, 1969), pp. 154ff.

Charney, J.I., and L.M. Alexander (eds), *International Maritime Boundaries* (Martinus Nijhoff Publishers, 1993).

Charney, J.I., and Robert W. Smith (eds), *International Maritime Boundaries* (Martinus Nijhoff Publishers, 2002).

Charney, J.I., David A. Colson, Lewis M. Alexander and Robert W. Smith (eds), *International Maritime Boundaries* (Martinus Nijhoff Publishers, 2005).

Churchill, Robin, and Alan Vaughan Lowe, *The Law of the Sea* (Manchester University Press, 1999).

Churchill, Robin, and Geir Ulfstein, 'Autonomous Institutional Arrangements in Multilateral Environmental Agreements: A Little-noticed Phenomenon in International Law', in *American Journal of International Law*, Vol. 94, 2000, pp. 623–659.

———, *Marine Management in Disputed Areas: The case of the Barents Sea* (Routledge, 1992).

———, 'The Disputed Maritime Zones around Svalbard', in Nordquist, Myron H., Tomas H. Heidar and John Norton Moore (eds), *Changes in the Arctic Environment and the Law of the Sea* (Martinus Nijhoff Publishers, 2010), pp. 551–593.

Clark, D.H., *Natural Justice: Substance and Shadow* (Stevens, 1975).

Clingan, T.A. (ed.), *The Law of the Sea: What Lies Ahead?* (University of Hawaii, 1988).

———, 'Dispute Settlement Among Non-Parties to the LOS Convention with Respect to the Outer Limits of the Continental Shelf', in Clingan, T.A., (ed.), *The Law of the Sea: What Lies Ahead?* (University of Hawaii, 1988), pp. 497–499.

Coicaud, Jean-Marc, and Veijo Heiskanen (eds), *The Legitimacy of International Organizations* (UN University Press, 2001).

Colson, David A., 'Delimitation of the Outer Continental Shelf Between States with Opposite or Adjacent Coasts', in Nordquist, Myron H., John Norton Moore & Tomas H. Heidar (eds), *Legal and Scientific Aspects of Continentals Shelf Limits* (Martinus Nijhoff Publishers, 2004), pp. 287–297.

Colson, David, 'The Delimitation of the Outer Continental Shelf Between Neighboring States', in *American Journal of International Law*, Vol. 97, 2003, pp. 91–107.

Conti, Joseph A., 'Producing Legitimacy at the World Trade Organization: Role of Expertise and Legal Capacity', in *Socio-Economic Review*, Vol. 8, 2009, pp. 131–155.

Cook, P.J., and C.M. Carleton (eds), *Continental Shelf Limits: The Scientific and Legal Interface* (Oxford University Press, 2000).

Cot, Jean-Pierre, 'The Law of the Sea and the Margin of Appreciation', in Nidiaye, Tafsir Malik, and Rüdiger Wolfrum (eds), *Law of the Sea, Environmental Law and Settlement of Disputes* (Martinus Nijhoff Publishers, 2007), pp. 389–404.

Crawford, James, *Brownlie's Principles of Public International Law* (Oxford University Press, 2012).

———, 'The UN Human Rights Treaty System: A System in Crisis?', in Alston, Philip, and James Crawford (eds), *The Future of UN Human Rights Treaty Monitoring* (Cambridge University Press, 2009), pp. 1–15.

Dallmeyer, Dorinda, and Louis De Vorsey (eds), *Rights to Oceanic Resources: Deciding and Drawing Maritime Boundaries* (Martinus Nijhoff Publishers, 1989).

Eckert, R.D., *The Enclosure of Ocean Resources* (Hoover Institution Press, 1979).

Ehring, Lothar, 'Public Access to Dispute Settlement Hearings in the World Trade Organization', in *Journal of International Economic Law*, Vol. 11, 2008, pp. 1021–1034.

Elferink, Alex G. Oude, and Constance Johnson, 'Outer Limits of the Continental Shelf and "Disputed Areas": State Practice Concerning Article 76(10)', in *The International Journal of Marine and Coastal Law*, Vol. 21, 2006, pp. 461–487.

Elferink, Alex G. Oude, 'Article 76 of the LOSC on the Definition of the Continental Shelf: Questions Concerning its Interpretation from a Legal Perspective', in *The International Journal of Marine and Coastal Law*, Vol. 21, 2006, pp. 269–285.

———, 'Openness' and Article 76 of the Law of the Sea Convention: The Process Does Not Need to Be Adjusted', in *Ocean Development & International Law*, Vol. 40, 2009, pp. 36–50.

———, 'The Establishment of Outer Limits of the Continental Shelf Beyond 200 Nautical Miles by the Coastal State: The Possibilities of Other States to Have an Impact on the Process', in *The International Journal of Marine and Coastal Law*, Vol. 4, 2009, pp. 535–556.

Engstad, Nils Asbjørn, Astrid Lærdal Frøseth and Bård Tønder (eds), *Dommernes uavhengighet* (Fagbokforlaget, 2012).

Epping, Volker, and Wolff Heinstel von Heinegg (eds), *International Humanitarian Law Facing New Challenges* (Springer, 2007).

Esty, Daniel C., 'The World Trade Organization's Legitimacy Crisis', in *World Trade Review*, Vol. 1, 2002, pp. 7–22.

Evensen, Jens, *Working Methods and Procedures in the Third United Nations Conference on the Law of the Sea* (Martinus Nijhoff Publishers, 1986).

Ferejohn, John, and Pasquale Pasquino, 'Constitutional Adjudication: Lessons from Europe', in *Texas Law Review*, Vol. 82, 2004, pp. 1671–1704.

Franck, Thomas, 'The Power of Legitimacy and the Legitimacy of Power: International Law in an Age of Power Disequilibrium', in *American Journal of International Law*, Vol. 100, 2006, pp. 88–106.

———, *The Power of Legitimacy Among Nations* (Oxford University Press, 1990).

Gao, Jianjun, 'The Seafloor High Issue in Article 76 of the LOS Convention: Some Views from the Perspective of Legal Interpretation', in *Ocean Development & International Law*, Vol. 43, 2012, pp. 119–145.

Gardiner, Piers R.R., 'The Limits of the Area Beyond National Jurisdiction—Some Problems with Particular Reference to the Role of the Commission on the Limits of the Continental Shelf', in Blake, G.H. (ed.), *Maritime Boundaries and Ocean Resources* (Croom Helm, 1987), pp. 63–76.

Gardiner, Richard, *Treaty Interpretation* (Oxford University Press, 2008).

Goldsmith, Jack L., and Eric A. Posner, *The Limits of International Law* (Oxford University Press, 2005).

Gudlaugsson, S.T., 'Natural Prolongation and the Concept of the Continental Margin for the Purposes of Article 76,' in Nordquist, Myron H., John Norton Moore and Thomas H. Heidar (eds), *Legal and Scientific Aspects of Continental Shelf Limits* (Martinus Nijhoff Publishers, 2004), pp. 61–90.

Gutteridge, J.A.C., 'The 1958 Geneva Convention on the Continental Shelf', in *British Yearbook of International Law*, Vol. 35, 1959, pp. 102–123.

Hall, Christopher Keith, 'The Duty of States Parties to the Convention against Torture to Provide Procedures Permitting Victims to Recover Reparations for Torture Committed Abroad', in *The European Journal of International Law*, Vol. 18, 2007, pp. 921–937.

Hedberg, Hollis D., 'Ocean Floor Boundaries', in *Science*, Vol. 204, 1979, pp. 135–144.

Henkin, Louis, *Law for the Sea's Mineral Resources* (Institute for the Study of Science in Human Affairs: Columbia University, 1968).

Henriksen, Tore, and Geir Ulfstein, 'Maritime Delimitation in the Arctic: The Barents Sea Treaty', in *Ocean Development & International Law*, Vol. 42, 2011, pp. 1–21.

Herz, John, 'Legitimacy—Can We Retrieve It?', in *Comparative Politics*, Vol. 10, 1978, pp. 317–343.

Hey, Ellen, 'International Institutions', in Bodansky, Daniel, Jutta Brunnée and Ellen Hey (eds), *The Oxford Handbook of International Environmental Law* (Oxford University Press, 2008), pp. 749–769.

Higgins, Alexander, and Constantine John Colombos, *The International Law of the Sea* (Longmans, 1943).

Highet, Keith, 'Evidence, the Chamber and the ELSI Case', in Lillich, Richard (ed.), *Fact-Finding by International Tribunals* (Transnational Publishers, 1992), pp. 33–79.

———, 'Whatever became of natural prolongation', in Dallmeyer, Dorinda, and Louis De Vorsey (eds), *Rights to Oceanic Resources: Deciding and Drawing Maritime Boundaries* (Martinus Nijhoff Publishers, 1989), pp. 87–100.

Hollis, Duncan B. (ed.), *Oxford Guide to Treaties* (Oxford University Press, 2012).

Hornby, A.S, *Oxford Advanced Learner's Dictionary of Current English* (Oxford University Press, 1989).

Howse, Robert, 'Adjudicative Legitimacy and Treaty Interpretation in International Law: The Early Years of WTO Jurisprudence', in Weiler, Joseph H.H. (ed.), *The EU, the WTO, and the NAFTA* (Oxford University Press, 2000), pp. 35–70.

————, 'The Legitimacy of the World Trade Organization', in Coicaud, Jean-Marc, and Veijo Heiskanen (eds), *The Legitimacy of International Organizations* (UN University Press, 2001), pp. 355–407.

Howse, Robert, and Kalypso Nicolaïdis, 'Legitimacy and Global Governance: Why Constitutionalizing the WTO Is a Step Too Far', in Porter, Roger B., Pierre Sauve, Arvind Subramanian and Americo Beviglia Zampetti (eds), *Efficiency, Equity, and Legitimacy: The Multilateral Trading System at the Millennium* (Brookings Institution Press, 2001), pp. 227–252.

Hurd, Ian, 'Myths of Membership: The Politics of Legitimation in UN Security Council Reform', in *Global Governance*, Vol. 14, 2008, pp. 199–217.

Jares, Vladimir, 'The Work of the Commission on the Limits of the Continental Shelf', in Vidas, Davor (ed.), *Law, Technology and Science for Oceans in Globalisation—IUU Fishing, Oil Pollution, Bioprospecting, Outer Continental Shelf* (Martinus Nijhoff Publishers, 2010), pp. 449–475.

Jensen, Øystein, 'Towards Setting the Outer Limits of the Continental Shelf in the Arctic: On the Norwegian Submission and Recommendations by the Commission', in Vidas, Davor (ed.), *Law, Technology and Science for Oceans in Globalisation—IUU Fishing, Oil Pollution, Bioprospecting, Outer Continental Shelf* (Martinus Nijhoff Publishers, 2010), pp. 521–538.

————, 'Treaty Between Norway and the Russian Federation concerning Maritime Delimitation and Cooperation in the Barents Sea and the Arctic Ocean', in *The International Journal of Marine and Coastal Law*, Vol. 26, 2011, pp. 151–168.

Jiuyong, Shi, 'Maritime Delimitation in the Jurisprudence of the International Court of Justice', in *Chinese Journal of International Law*, Vol. 9, 2010, pp. 271–291.

Jodoin, Sébastien, 'Enhancing the Procedural Legitimacy of the U.N. Security Council: A Normative and Empirical Assessment', in *Sri Lanka Journal of International Law*, Vol. 17, 2005, pp. 1–54.

Johnson, D.H.N., 'The Legal Status of the Sea-Bed and Subsoil', in *Zeitschrift für ausländisches öffentliches Recht und Völkerrecht*, Vol. 16, 1957, pp. 474–487.

Jonas, Davis S., and Thomas N. Saunders, 'The Object and Purpose of a Treaty: Three Interpretive Options', in *Vanderbilt Journal of Transnational Law*, Vol. 43, 2010, pp. 565–609.

Joshua, Julian, 'The Right to be Heard in EEC Competition Procedures', in *Fordham International Law Journal*, Vol. 15, 1991, pp. 16–91.

Karagiannis, Symeon, 'Observations sur la Commission des Limites du Plateau Continental', in *Espaces et Ressources Maritimes*, Vol. 8, 1994, pp. 163–194.

Katin, Ernest, *The Legal Status of the Continental Shelf as Determined by the Conventions Adopted at the 1958 United Nations Conference on the Law of the Sea: An Analytical Study of an Instance of International Law Making* (University of Minnesota Press, 1969).

Keller, Helen, and Geir Ulfstein (eds), *UN Human Rights Treaty Bodies—Law and Legitimacy* (Cambridge University Press, 2012).

———, 'Introduction', in Keller, Helen, and Geir Ulfstein (eds), *UN Human Rights Treaty Bodies—Law and Legitimacy* (Cambridge University Press, 2012), pp. 1–15.

Keller, Helen, and Leena Grover, 'General Comments of the Human Rights Committee and their legitimacy', in Keller, Helen, and Geir Ulfstein (eds), *UN Human Rights Treaty Bodies—Law and Legitimacy* (Oxford University Press, 2012), pp. 116–198.

Kemp, Roger L. (ed.), *Documents of American Democracy: A Collection of Essential Works* (McFarland, 2010).

Kingsbury, Benedict, Nico Krisch and Richard B. Stewart, 'The Emergence of Global Administrative Law', in *Law and Contemporary Problems*, Vol. 68, 2005, pp. 15–61.

Klabbers, Jan, 'Straddling Law and Politics: Judicial Review in International Law', in MacDonald, Ronald St. John, and Douglas M. Johnston (eds), *Towards World Constitutionalism* (Martinus Nijhoff Publishers, 2005), pp. 809–835.

Klabbers, Jan, Anne Peters and Geir Ulfstein, *The Constitutionalization of International Law* (Oxford University Press, 2009).

Klemm, Ulf-Dieter, 'Continental Shelf, Outer Limits', in Bernhardt, Rudolf (ed.), *Encyclopedia of Public International Law*, Vol. I, 1992, pp. 804–806.

Koskenniemi, Martti, 'The Fate of Public International Law: Between Technique and Politics', in *The Modern Law Review*, Vol. 70, 2007, pp. 1–30.

Krisch, Nico, and Benedict Kingsbury, 'Introduction: Global Governance and Global Administrative Law in the International Legal Order', in *The European Journal of International Law*, Vol. 17, 2006, pp. 1–13.

Krisch, Nico, 'The Pluralism of Global Administrative Law', in *The European Journal of International Law*, Vol. 17, 2006, pp. 247–248.

Kumm, Mattias, 'The Legitimacy of International Law: A Constitutionalist Framework of Analysis', in *The European Journal of international Law*, Vol. 15, 2004, pp. 907–931.

Kunoy, Bjørn, 'The Admissibility of a Plea to an International Adjudicative Forum to Delimit the Outer Continental Shelf Prior to the Adoption of Final Recommendations by the Commission on the Limits of the Continental Shelf', in *The International Journal of Marine and Coastal Law*, Vol. 25, 2010, pp. 237–270.

Kunoy, Bjørn, Martin V. Heinesen and Finn Mørk, 'Appraisal of Applicable Depth Constraint for the Purpose of Establishing the Outer Limits of the Continental Shelf', in *Ocean Development & International Law*, Vol. 41, 2010, pp. 357–379.

Lauterpacht, Hersch, 'Sovereignty over Submarine Areas', in *British Yearbook of International Law*, Vol. 17, 1950, pp. 376–433.

Lillich, Richard (ed.), *Fact-Finding by International Tribunals* (Transnational Publishers, 1992).

Livermore, Michael, 'Authority and Legitimacy in Global Governance: Deliberation, Institutional Differentiation, and the Codex Alimentarius', in *New York University Law Review*, Vol. 81, 2006, pp. 766–801.

Macnab, Ron, 'The Case for Transparency in the Delimitation of the Outer Continental Shelf in Accordance with UNCLOS Article 76', in *Ocean Development & International Law*, Vol. 35, 2004, pp. 1–17.

Macnab, Ron, and L. Parsons, 'Continental Shelf Submissions: The Record to Date', in *The International Journal of Marine and Coastal Law*, Vol. 21, 2006, pp. 309–322.

Mahmoudi, Said, *The Law of Deep Seabed Mining* (Almqvist & Wiksell International, 1987).

Mahoney, Paul, 'The International Judiciary—Independence and Accountability', in *The Law and Practice of International Courts and Tribunals*, Vol. 7, 2008, pp. 313–349.

Malone, David M., 'Eyes on the Prize: The Quest for Non-permanent Seats on the UN Security Council', in *Global Governance*, Vol. 6, 2000, pp. 3–23.

McDorman, Ted, 'The Role of the Commission on the Limits of the Continental Shelf: A Technical Body in a Political World', in *The International Journal of Marine and Coastal Law*, Vol. 17, 2002, pp. 301–324.

———, 'The Continental Shelf Regime in the Law of the Sea Convention: A Reflection on the First Thirty Years', in *The International Journal of Marine and Coastal Law*, Vol. 27, 2012, pp. 743–751.

McDougal, M.S., and W.T. Burke, *The Public Order of the Oceans* (Yale University Press, 1962).

McNair, Arnold D., *International Law Opinions* (Cambridge University Press, 1956).

———, *The Law of Treaties* (Oxford University Press, 1961).

Mechlem, Kerstin, 'Treaty Bodies and the Interpretation of Human Rights', in *Vanderbilt Journal of Transnational Law*, Vol. 42, 2009, pp. 905–947.

Nandan, Satya, and Shabtai Rosenne (eds), *United Nations Convention on the Law of the Sea, 1982, A Commentary*, Vol. II (Martinus Nijhoff Publishers, 1993).

Nelson, L.D.M., 'The Continental Shelf: Interplay of Law and Science', in Ando, Nisuke, Edward McWhinney and *Rüdiger* Wolfrum (eds), *Liber Amicorum Judge Shigeru Oda* (Kluwer Law International, 2002), pp. 1235–1253.

———, 'Claims to the Continental Shelf beyond the 200-Mile Limit', in Götz, Volkmar, Peter Selmer and *Rüdiger* Wolfrum (eds), *Liber Amicorum Günther Jaenicke—Zum 85 Geburtstag* (Springer Verlag, 1998), pp. 573–588.

Nidiaye, Tafsir Malik, and Rüdiger Wolfrum (eds), *Law of the Sea, Environmental Law and Settlement of Disputes* (Martinus Nijhoff Publishers, 2007).

Nordquist, Myron H., and John Norton Moore (eds), *Current Maritime Issues and the International Maritime Organization* (Martinus Nijhoff Publishers, 1999).

Nordquist, Myron H., John Norton Moore and Tomas H. Heidar (eds), *Legal and Scientific Aspects of Continental Shelf Limits* (Martinus Nijhoff Publishers, 2004).

Nordquist, Myron H., Tomas H. Heidar and John Norton Moore (eds), *Changes in the Arctic Environment and the Law of the Sea* (Martinus Nijhoff Publishers, 2010).

O'Connell, Daniel P., *The International Law of the Sea* (Clarendon Press, 1982).

Oda, Shigeru, *The International Law of the Ocean Development: Basic Documents* (Sijthoff, 1972).

Orth, John V., *Due Process of Law: A Brief History* (University Press of Kansas, 2003).

Oxman, B.H., 'The Third United Nations Conference on the Law of the Sea: The Eighth Session (1979)', in *American Journal of International Law*, Vol. 74, 1980, pp. 1–47.

Oxman, Bernhard, 'The Territorial Temptation: A Siren Song at Sea', in *American Journal of International Law*, Vol. 100, 2006, pp. 830–851.

Pardo, Arvid, 'Whose Is the Bed of the Sea', in *American Society of International Law*, Vol. 62, 1968, pp. 216–229.

Perju, Vlad, 'Reason and Authority in the European Court of Justice', in *Virginia Journal of International Law*, Vol. 49, 2009, pp. 307–377.

Peters, Anne, 'Dual Democracy', in Klabbers, Jan, Anne Peters and Geir Ulfstein, *The Constitutionalization of International Law* (Oxford University Press, 2009), pp. 261–341.

Picciotto, Sol, 'The WTO's Appellate Body: Legal Formalism as a Legitimation of Global Governance', in *Governance*, Vol. 18, 2005, pp. 477–503.

Platzöder, Renate, (ed.), *Third United Nations Conference on the Law of the Sea: Documents*, Vol. I (Oceana Publications, 1982).

———, *Third United Nations Conference on the Law of the Sea: Documents*, Vol. II (Oceana Publications, 1982).

———, *Third United Nations Conference on the Law of the Sea: Documents*, Vol. IV (Oceana Publications, 1982).

———, *Third United Nations Conference on the Law of the Sea: Documents*, Vol. V (Oceana Publications, 1982).

———, *Third United Nations Conference on the Law of the Sea: Documents*, Vol. IX (Oceana Publications, 1982).

———, *Third United Nations Conference on the Law of the Sea: Documents*, Vol. XI (Oceana Publications, 1982).

———, *Third United Nations Conference on the Law of the Sea: Documents*, Vol. XV (Oceana Publications, 1982).

Porter, Roger B., Pierre Sauve, Arvind Subramanian and Americo Beviglia Zampetti (eds), *Efficiency, Equity, and Legitimacy: The Multilateral Trading System at the Millennium* (Brookings Institution Press, 2001).

Prescott, V., 'Natural Rights to Hydrocarbon Resources of the Continental Margin Beyond 200 Nautical Miles', in Blake, G.H. (ed.), *Boundaries and Energy: Problems and Prospects* (Kluwer Law International, 1998), pp. 51–81.

Razzaque, Jona, 'Changing Role of Friends of the Court in the International Courts and Tribunals', in *Non-State Actors and International Law*, Vol. 1, 2001, pp. 169–200.

Reidy, D.A., and W.J. Riker (eds), *Coercion and the State* (Springer, 2008).

Reus-Smith, Christian, 'International Crises of Legitimacy', in *International Politics*, Vol. 44, 2007, pp. 157–174.

Rose, Gregory, and Saundra Crane, 'The Evolution of International Whaling Law', in Sands, Philippe (ed.), *Greening International Law* (The New Press, 1994), pp. 159–179.

Ruud, Morten, and Geir Ulfstein, *Innføring i folkerett* (Universitetsforlaget, 2011).

Salzman, James, 'Decentralized Administrative Law in the Organization for Economic Cooperation and Development', in *Law and Contemporary Problems*, Vol. 68, 2005, pp. 189–224.

Sands, Philippe (ed.), *Greening International Law* (The New Press, 1994).

Sands, Philippe, Campbell McLachlan and Ruth Mackenzie, 'The Burgh House Principles on the Independence of the Judiciary', in *The Law and Practice of International Courts and Tribunals*, Vol. 4, 2005, pp. 247–260.

Sato, Tetsuo, 'The Legitimacy of Security Council Activities under Chapter VII of the UN Charter at the End of the Cold War', in Coicaud, Jean-Marc, and Veijo Heiskanen (eds), *The Legitimacy of International Organizations* (UN University Press, 2001), pp. 309–354.

Serdy, Andrew, 'Some Views Are More Equal Than Others: Submission to the Commission on the Limits of the Continental Shelf and the Strange Loss of Confidence in Article IV of the Antarctic Treaty', in *Australian Yearbook of International Law*, Vol. 28, 2009, pp. 181–195.

———, 'The Commission on the Limits of the Continental Shelf and its Disturbing Propensity to Legislate', in *The International Journal of Marine and Coastal Law*, Vol. 26, 2011, pp. 355–383.

Shany, Yuval, 'Toward a General Margin of Appreciation Doctrine in International Law?', in *The European Journal of International Law*, Vol. 16, 2005, pp. 907–940.

Sinclair, Ian, *The Vienna Convention on the Law of Treaties* (Manchester University Press, 1984).

Sloan, Blaine, 'The Binding Force of a 'Recommendation' of the General Assembly of the United Nations', in *British Yearbook of International Law*, Vol. 25, 1948, pp. 1–33.

Smith, Herbert Arthur, *The Law and Custom of the Sea* (Stevens and Sons Limited, 1959).

Smith, Robert W., and G. Taft, 'Legal Aspects of the Continental Shelf', in Cook, P.J., and C.M. Carleton (eds), *Continental Shelf Limits: The Scientific and Legal Interface* (Oxford University Press, 2000), pp. 17–24.

Smith, Robert W., Noel Newton St. Claver Francis and Richard Haworth, 'The Continental Shelf Commission', in Nordquist, Myron H., and John Norton Moore (eds), *Ocean Policy: New Institutions, Challenges and Opportunities* (Martinus Nijhoff, 1999), pp. 135–169.

Stewart, Terence, and David Johanson, 'The SPS Agreement of the World Trade Organization and International Organizations: The Roles of the Codex Alimentarus
Commission, the International Plant Protection Convention, and the International Office of Epizootics', in *Syracuse Journal of International Law and Commerce*,
Vol. 26, 1998, pp. 27–53.

Stokke, Olav Schram, Jon Hovi and Geir Ulfstein (eds), *Implementing the Climate
Regime: International Compliance* (Earthscan/James and James, 2005).

Suarez, Suzette, *The Outer Limits of the Continental Shelf—Legal Aspects of their Establishment* (Springer, 2008).

Szasz, Paul C. (ed.), *Administrative and Expert Monitoring of International Treaties*
(Transnational Publishers, 1999).

Teubner, Gunther, and Andreas Fischer-Lescano, 'Regime-Collisions: The Vain Search
for Legal Unity in the Fragmentation of Global Law', in *Michigan Journal of International Law*, Vol. 25, 2004, pp. 999–1046.

Tobler, Claudia, 'The Standard of Judicial Review of Administrative Agencies in the
U.S. and EU: Accountability and Reasonable Agency Action', in *Boston International
& Comparative Law Review*, Vol. 22, 1999, pp. 213–228.

Traavik, Kim, *Et nytt territorium åpnes—en studie av forhandlingene om kontinentalsok-
kelkonvensjonen av 1958* (Fridtjof Nansen Institute, 1973).

Trechsel, Stefan, *Human Rights in Criminal Proceedings* (Oxford University Press, 2005).

Treves, Tullio, 'Remarks on Submissions to the Commission on the Limits of the Continental Shelf in Response to Judge Marotta's Report', in *The International Journal of
Marine and Coastal Law*, Vol. 21, 2006, pp. 363–367.

———, 'The Development of the Law of the Sea since the Adoption of the UN Convention on the Law of the Sea: Achievements and Challenges for the Future', in
Vidas, Davor (ed.), *Law, Technology and Science for Oceans in Globalisation—IUU
Fishing, Oil Pollution, Bioprospecting, Outer Continental Shelf* (Martinus Nijhoff Publishers, 2010), pp. 41–58.

———, 'The Law of the Sea "System" of Institutions', in *Yearbook of UN Law*, Vol. 2,
1998, pp. 325–340.

Tuori, Kaarlo, 'The Law's Farewell to the Nation State?', in *Finnish Yearbook of International Law*, Vol. 19, 2008, pp. 295–328.

Ulfstein, Geir, and Andreas Føllesdal, 'Den europeiske menneskerettighetsdomstolen
og Høyesterett—uavhengighet og demokratisk kontroll', in Engstad, Nils Asbjørn,
Astrid Lærdal Frøseth and Bård Tønder (eds), *Dommernes uavhengighet* (Fagbokforlaget, 2012), pp. 443–461.

Ulfstein, Geir, and Jacob Werksman, 'The Kyoto Compliance System: Towards Hard
Enforcement', in Stokke, Olav Schram, Jon Hovi and Geir Ulfstein (eds), *Implementing the Climate Regime: International Compliance* (Earthscan/James and James,
2005), pp. 39–62.

Ulfstein, Geir, 'Den rettslige betydningen av avgjørelser fra menneskerettslige konvensjonsorganer', in *Lov og Rett*, Vol. 51, 2012, pp. 552–570.

———, 'Individual Complaints', in Keller, Helen, and Geir Ulfstein (eds), *UN Human Rights Treaty Bodies—Law and Legitimacy*, pp. 73–115.

———, 'Institutions and Competences', in Klabbers, Jan, Anne Peters and Geir Ulfstein, *The Constitutionalization of International Law* (Oxford University Press, 2009), pp. 45–80.

———, *The Svalbard Treaty: From Terra Nullius to Norwegian Sovereignty* (Scandinavian University Press, 1995).

———, 'Treaty Bodies and Regimes', in Hollis, Duncan B., *The Oxford Guide to Treaties* (Oxford University Press, 2012), pp. 428–447.

Van Alebeek, Rosanne, and André Nollkaemper, 'The Legal Status of Decisions by Human Rights Treaty Bodies in National Law', in Keller, Helen, and Geir Ulfstein (eds), *UN Human Rights Treaty Bodies—Law and Legitimacy* (Oxford University Press, 2012), pp. 356–413.

Vice, Daniel, 'Implementation of Biodiversity Treaties: Monitoring, Fact-Finding, and Dispute Resoution', in Szasz, Paul C. (ed.), *Administrative and Expert Monitoring of International Treaties* (Transnational Publishers, 1999), pp. 135–163.

Vidas, Davor (ed.), *Law, Technology and Science for Oceans in Globalisation—IUU Fishing, Oil Pollution, Bioprospecting, Outer Continental Shelf* (Martinus Nijhoff Publishers, 2010).

Viljoen, Frans, 'Fact-Finding by UN Human Rights Complaints Bodies—Analysis and Suggested Reforms', in *Max Planck Yearbook of United Nations Law*, Vol. 8, 2004, pp. 49–100.

Villiger, M.E., *Commentary on the 1969 Vienna Convention on the Law of Treaties* (Martinus Nijhoff Publishers, 2009).

Voeten, Erik, 'The Political Origins of the UN Security Council's Ability to Legitimize the Use of Force', in *International Organization*, Vol. 59, 2005, pp. 527–557.

Wade, William, *Administrative Law* (Oxford University Press, 1982).

Weil, Prosper, 'The Court cannot Conclude Definitively…Non Liquet Revisited', in *Columbia Journal of Transnational Law*, Vol. 36, 1998, pp. 109–119.

Weiler, Joseph H.H., 'The Geology of International Law—Governance, Democracy and Legitimacy', in *Zeitschrift für ausländisches öffentliches Recht und Völkerrecht*, Vol. 64, 2004, pp. 547–562.

———, (ed.), *The EU, the WTO, and the NAFTA* (Oxford University Press, 2000).

Whitemann, Marjorie M., *Digest of International Law* (Department of State Publication, 1965), pp. 756–757.

Wolfrum, Rüdiger, 'IMO Interface with the Law of the Sea Convention', in Nordquist, Myron H., and John Norton Moore (eds), *Current Maritime Issues and the International Maritime Organization* (Martinus Nijhoff Publishers, 1999), pp. 223–236.

————, 'Legitimacy of International Law and the Exercise of Administrative Functions: The Example of the International Seabed Authority, the International Maritime Organization (IMO) and International Fisheries Organizations', in *German Law Journal* (*Special Issue: The Exercise of Public Authority by International Institutions*), Vol. 9, 2008, pp. 2039–2080.

————, Peter-Tobias Stoll and Karen Kaiser (eds), *WTO—Institutions and Dispute Settlement* (Martinus Nijhoff Publishers, 2006).

Zimmermann, Andreas, Christian Tomuschat and Karin Oellers-Frahm (eds), *The Statute of the International Court of Justice: A Commentary* (Oxford University Press, 2006).

Zinchenko, Alexei A., 'Emerging Issues in the Work of the Commission on the Limits of the Continental Shelf', in Nordquist, Myron H., John Norton Moore & Tomas H. Heidar (eds), *Legal and Scientific Aspects of Continentals Shelf Limits* (Martinus Nijhoff Publishers, 2004), pp. 215–250.

Zürn, Michael, 'Global Governance and Legitimacy Problems', in *Government and Opposition*, Vol. 39, 2004, pp. 260–287.

UNCLOS I Official Records

United Nations Conference on the Law of the Sea, Official Records (*Plenary Meetings*), Vol. II. UN Doc. A/CONF.13/38.

United Nations Conference on the Law of the Sea, Official Records (*Fourth Committee*), Vol. VI. UN Doc. A/CONF.13/42.

UNCLOS III Official Records

Third United Nations Conference on the Law of the Sea, Official Records, Vol. III (New York: United Nations, 1977).

Third United Nations Conference on the Law of the Sea, Official Records, Vol. V (New York: United Nations, 1976).

Third United Nations Conference on the Law of the Sea, Official Records, Vol. VI (New York: United Nations, 1977).

Third United Nations Conference on the Law of the Sea, Official Records, Vol. VII (New York: United Nations, 1976).

Third United Nations Conference on the Law of the Sea, Official Records, Vol. VIII (New York: United Nations, 1977).

Third United Nations Conference on the Law of the Sea, Official Records, Vol. IX (New York: United Nations, 1980).

Third United Nations Conference on the Law of the Sea, Official Records, Vol. XI (New York: United Nations, 1980).
Third United Nations Conference on the Law of the Sea, Official Records, Vol. XIII (New York: United Nations, 1980).
Third United Nations Conference on the Law of the Sea, Official Records, Vol. XV (New York: United Nations, 1982).
Third United Nations Conference on the Law of the Sea, Official Records, Vol. XVI (New York: United Nations, 1983).
Third United Nations Conference on the Law of the Sea, Official Records, Vol. XVII (New York: United Nations, 1983).

UNCLOS III Documents

Compromise suggestions by the Chairman of negotiating group 6. UN Doc. A/CONF.62/L.37.
Draft convention on the law of the sea. UN Doc. A/CONF.62/L.78.
Final Act of the Third United Nations Conference on the Law of the Sea. UN Doc. A/CONF.62/121.
Informal composite negotiating text, revision 1. UN Doc. A/CONF.62/WP.10/Rev.1.
Informal composite negotiating text, revision 2, correction 2. UN Doc. A/CONF.62/WP.10/Rev.2 and Corr.2.
Informal composite negotiating text, revision 2. UN Doc. A/CONF.62/WP.10/Rev.2.
Informal composite negotiating text, revision 3. UN Doc. A/CONF.62/WP.10/Rev.3*.
Informal suggestion (anonymous). UN Doc. NG6/20.
Preliminary study illustrating various formulae for the definition of the continental shelf. UN Doc. A/CONF.62/C.2/L.98 and Add.1–3.
Report by Mr. Andres Aguilar M., Chairman of the Second Committee, on the work of the Committee. UN Doc. A/CONF.62/L.17.
Report of the Chairman of the Drafting Committee on behalf of the President and the Chairmen of the First, Second and Third Committees. UN Doc. A/CONF.62/L.160.
Report of the Chairman of the Drafting Committee. UN Doc. A/CONF.62/L.152/Add.23.
Report of the Chairman of the Drafting Committee. UN Doc. A/CONF.62/L.67/Add.14.
Report of the Chairman of the Drafting Committee. UN Doc. A/CONF.62/L.67/Add.14 (1981, mimeo.).
Report of the Chairman of the Drafting Committee. UN Doc. A/CONF.62/L.67/Add.4.
Report of the Chairman of the Drafting Committee. UN Doc. A/CONF.62/L.67/Add.4/Corr. (1981, mimeo).
Report of the Chairman of the Drafting Committee. UN Doc. A/CONF.62/L.67/Add.4/Corr.1–5.

Report of the Chairman of the Second Committee. UN Doc. A/CONF.62/L.51.

Report of the President of the Drafting Committee on behalf of the President of the Conference and the Chairmen of the First, Second and Third Committees. UN Doc. A/ CONF.62/L.72.

Report to the Plenary by the Chairman of the Second Committee, Annex A. UN Doc. A/ CONF.62/RCNG/1.

Revised single negotiating text (part II). UN Doc. A/CONF.62/WP.8/Rev.1/Part II.

Statement by the delegation of Bahrain dated 4 April 1980. UN Doc. A/CONF.62/WS/7.

Statement by the delegation of Canada dated 2 April 1980. UN Doc. A/CONF.62/WS/4.

United Kingdom of Great Britain and Northern Ireland: amendments. UN Doc. A/ CONF.62/L.126.

United States of America: draft articles for a chapter on the economic zone and the continental shelf. UN Doc. A/CONF.62/C.2/L.47.

Other UN Documents

Agreement on Cooperation and Relationship between the United Nations and the International Tribunal for the Law of the Sea. UN Doc. A/RES/52/251.

Conditions of service and compensation for officials other than Secretariat officials: members of the International Court of Justice and judges and ad litem judges of the International Tribunal for the Former Yugoslavia and the International Criminal Tribunal for Rwanda. UN Doc. A/RES/61/262.

Declaration of Principles Governing the Sea-Bed and the Ocean Floor, and the Subsoil Thereof, Beyond the Limits of National Jurisdiction. UNGA Res. 2749 (XXV).

Declaration on Fact-finding by the United Nations in the Field of the Maintenance of International Peace and Security. UN Doc. A/RES/46/59.

Examination of the Question of the Reservation Exclusively for Peaceful Purposes of the Sea-Bed and the Ocean Floor, and the Subsoil Thereof, Underlying the High Seas Beyond the Limits of Present National Jurisdiction, and the Use of Their Resources in the Interests of Mankind. UNGA Res. 2467 (XXIII).

Examination of the question of the reservation exclusively for peaceful purposes of the sea-bed and the ocean floor, and the subsoil thereof, underlying the high seas beyond the limits of present national jurisdiction, and the use of their resources in the interests of mankind. UN Doc. A/RES/22/2340.

Examination of the question of the reservation exclusively for peaceful purposes of the sea-bed and the ocean floor, and the subsoil thereof, underlying the high seas beyond the limits of present national jurisdiction, and the use of their resources in the interests of mankind. UN Doc. A/6695.

Examination of the question of the reservation exclusively for peaceful purposes of the sea-bed and the ocean floor, and the subsoil thereof, underlying the high seas beyond the limits of present national jurisdiction, and the use of their resources in the interests of mankind. UN Doc. A/RES/2467 (XXIII, A).

Final report of the Ad Hoc Committee on a Comprehensive and Integral International Convention on the Protection and Promotion of the Rights and Dignity of Persons with Disabilities. UN Doc. A/61/611.

Fragmentation of International Law: Difficulties Arising from the Diversification and Expansion of International Law: Report of the Study Group of the International Law Commission. UN Doc. A/CN.4/L.682.

International Conference of Plenipotentiaries to Examine the Law of the Sea. UNGA Res. 1105 (XI).

Law of the Sea. UN Doc. A/RES/49/28.

Meeting of the Parties to the Convention on Access to Information, Public Participation in Decision-making and Access to Justice in Environmental Matters: Report of the First Meeting of the Parties. UN Doc. ECE/MP.PP/2/Add.8.

Oceans and the Law of the Sea. UN Doc. A/RES/55/7.

Oceans and the Law of the Sea: Report of the Secretary-General. UN Doc. A/57/57/Add.1.

Optional Protocol to the Convention on the Rights of the Child on a Communications Procedure. UN Doc. A/RES/66/138.

Organization of the Secretariat of the United Nations. UN Doc. ST/SGB/1997/8.

Presidential Decree No. 781 [of Peru] Concerning Submerged Continental or Insular Shelf, 1 August 1947. Reprinted in *Laws and Regulations on the Régime of the High Seas* (Division for the Codification and Development of International Law: United Nations publication, Sales No. 1951.V.2). Also in UN Doc. ST/LEG/SER.B/1.

Presidential Declaration [of Chile] Concerning the Continental Shelf, 23 June 1947. Reprinted in *Laws and Regulations on the Régime of the High Seas* (Division for the Codification and Development of International Law: United Nations publication, Sales No. 1951.V.2). Also in UN Doc. ST/LEG/SER.B/1.

Question of the Reservation Exclusively for Peaceful Purposes of the Sea-Bed and the Ocean Floor, and the Subsoil Thereof, Underlying the High Seas Beyond the Limits of Present National Jurisdiction, and the Use of Their Resources in the Interests of Mankind. UNGA Res. 2574 (XXIV).

Report of the Human Rights Council. UN Doc. A/63/435.

Report from the Sea-bed Committee. UN Doc. A/AC.138/SR.56.

Report of Sub-Committee I, Annex III, Texts Illustrating Areas of Agreement and Disagreement on Items 1 and 2 of the Sub-Committee's Programme of Work. UN Doc. A/AC.138/94/Add. 1.

Report of the Conference of the Parties on its Seventh Session, held at Marrakesh from 29 October to 10 November 2001. UN Doc. FCCC/CP/2001/13/Add.3.

Report of the Human Rights Committee. UN Doc. A/48/40.

Report of the Seabed Committee to the General Assembly. UN Doc. A/9021.

Report of the World Conference on Human Rights. UN Doc. A/CONF.157/24.

Reservation Exclusively for Peaceful Purposes of the Sea-Bed and the Ocean Floor, and the Subsoil Thereof, Underlying the High Seas Beyond the Limits of Present National Jurisdiction and Use of Their Resources in the Interests of Mankind, and Convening of a Conference on the Law of the Sea. UNGA Res. 2750 C (XXV).

Reservation exclusively for peaceful purposes of the sea-bed and the ocean floor, and the subsoil thereof, underlying the high seas beyond the limits of present national jurisdiction and use of their resources in the interests of mankind, and convening of the 3rd United Nations Conference on the Law of the Sea-Bed and the Ocean Floor beyond the Limits of National Jurisdiction. UNGA Res. 3067 (XXVIII).

Reservation exclusively for peaceful purposes of the sea-bed and the ocean floor, and the subsoil thereof, underlying the high seas beyond the limits of present national jurisdiction and use of their resources in the interests of mankind, and convening of a conference on the law of the sea. UN Doc. A/RES/2750 (XXV, C).

Resolution of the Fifth Assembly of the League of Nations of 22 September 1924. Reprinted in *American Journal of International Law,* Vol. 20, 1926, pp. 2–3.

Second Report on the Regime of the High Seas by Mr. J.P.A. François, Special Rapporteur. UN Doc. A/CN.4/42.

Statement by Ambassador Pardo (Malta). UN Doc. A/C.1/PV.1515.

Yearbooks of the International Law Commission

Yearbook of the International Law Commission, Vol. I (New York: United Nations, 1949).

Yearbook of the International Law Commission, Vol. II (New York: United Nations, 1950).

Yearbook of the International Law Commission, Vol. I (New York: United Nations, 1953).

Yearbook of the International Law Commission, Vol. II (New York: United Nations, 1953).

Yearbook of the International Law Commission, Vol. II (New York: United Nations, 1956).

Yearbook of the International Law Commission, Vol. II (New York: United Nations, 1972).

Documents of the Commission

Modus Operandi of the Commission (CLCS/L.3, 12 September 1997).

Internal procedure of the subcommission of the Commission on the Limits of the Continental Shelf (CLCS/L.12, 25 May 2001).

Statement by the Chairman of the Commission on the Limits of the Continental Shelf on the Progress of Work in the Commission—First session (CLCS/1, 30 June 1997).

Statement by the Chairman of the Commission on the Limits of the Continental Shelf on the Progress of Work in the Commission—Second session (CLCS/2, 17 September 1997).

Rules of Procedure of the Commission on the Limits of the Continental Shelf (CLCS/3, 12 September 1997).

Rules of Procedure of the Commission on the Limits of the Continental Shelf (CLCS/3/ Corr.1, 27 April 1998).

Rules of Procedure of the Commission on the Limits of the Continental Shelf (CLCS/3/ Rev.1, 14 May 1998).

Rules of Procedure of the Commission on the Limits of the Continental Shelf (CLCS/3/ Rev.2, 4 September 1998).

Rules of Procedure of the Commission on the Limits of the Continental Shelf (CLCS/3/ Rev.2/Corr.1, 28 March 2000).

Rules of Procedure of the Commission on the Limits of the Continental Shelf (CLCS/3/ Rev.3, 6 February 2001).

Rules of Procedure of the Commission on the Limits of the Continental Shelf (CLCS/3/ Rev.3/Corr.1, 22 May 2001).

Letter dated 11 March 1998 from the Legal Counsel, Under-Secretary-General of the United Nations for Legal Affairs addressed to the Chairman of the Commission on the Limits of the Continental Shelf (CLCS/5, 11 March 1998).

Statement by the Chairman of the Commission on the Limits of the Continental Shelf on the Progress of Work in the Commission—Third session (CLCS/7, 15 May 1998).

Statement by the Chairman of the Commission on the Limits of the Continental Shelf on the Progress of Work in the Commission—Fourth session (CLCS/9, 11 September 1998).

Scientific and Technical Guidelines of the Commission on the Limits of the Continental Shelf (CLCS/11, 13 May 1999).

Scientific and Technical Guidelines of the Commission on the Limits of the Continental Shelf—Annexes II–IV to the Guidelines adopted by the Commission on 3 September 1999 at its sixth session (CLCS/11/Add.1, 3 September 1999).

Scientific and Technical Guidelines of the Commission on the Limits of the Continental Shelf Annexes II–IV to the Guidelines adopted by the Commission on 3 September 1999 at its sixth session (CLCS/11/Add.1/Corr.1, 19 November 1999).

Scientific and Technical Guidelines of the Commission on the Limits of the Continental Shelf (CLCS/11/Corr.1, 24 February 2000).

Scientific and Technical Guidelines of the Commission on the Limits of the Continental Shelf (CLCS/11/Corr.2, 17 May 2000).

Statement by the Chairman of the Commission on the Limits of the Continental Shelf on the Progress of Work in the Commission—Fifth session (CLCS/12, 18 May 1999).

Establishment of a Trust Fund to Assist in Financing the Participation of Members of the Commission on the Limits of the Continental Shelf From Developing Countries (CLCS/16, 19 August 1999).

Statement by the Chairman of the Commission on the Limits of the Continental Shelf on the Progress of Work in the Commission—Sixth session (CLCS/18, 3 September 1999).

Statement by the Chairman of the Commission on the Limits of the Continental Shelf on the progress of work in the Commission—Seventh session (CLCS/21, 5 May 2000).

Statement by the Chairman of the Commission on the Limits of the Continental Shelf on the progress of work in the Commission—Eighth session (CLCS/25, 1 September 2000).

Statement by the Chairman of the Commission on the Limits of the Continental Shelf on the progress of work in the Commission—Ninth session (CLCS/29, 25 May 2001).

Statement by the Chairman of the Commission on the Limits of the Continental Shelf on the progress of work in the Commission—Tenth session (CLCS/32, 12 April 2002).

Statement by the Chairman of the Commission on the Limits of the Continental Shelf on the progress of work in the Commission—Eleventh session (CLCS/334, 1 July 2002).

Statement by the Chairman of the Commission on the Limits of the Continental Shelf on the progress of work in the Commission—Twelfth session (CLCS/36, 2 May 2003).

Statement by the Chairman of the Commission on the Limits of the Continental Shelf on the progress of work in the Commission—Thirteenth session (CLCS/39, 30 April 2004).

Rules of Procedure of the Commission on the Limits of the Continental Shelf (CLCS/40, 2 July 2004).

Rules of Procedure of the Commission on the Limits of the Continental Shelf (CLCS/40/Rev.1, 17 April 2008).

Statement by the Chairman of the Commission on the Limits of the Continental Shelf on the progress of work in the Commission—Fourteenth session (CLCS/42, 14 September 2004).

Statement by the Chairman of the Commission on the Limits of the Continental Shelf on the progress of work in the Commission—Fifteenth session (CLCS/44, 3 May 2005).

Letter dated 25 August 2005 from the Legal Counsel, Under-Secretary-General of the United Nations for Legal Affairs, addressed to the Chairman of the Commission on the Limits of the Continental Shelf: Legal opinion on whether it is permissible, under the United Nations Convention on the Law of the Sea and the rules of procedure of the Commission, for a coastal State, which has made a submission to the Commission in accordance with article 76 of the Convention, to provide to the Commission in the course of the examination by it of the submission, additional material and information relating to the limits of its continental shelf or substantial part thereof, which constitute a significant departure from the original limits and formulae lines that were given due publicity by the Secretary- General of the United Nations in accordance with rule 50 of the rules of procedure of the Commission (CLCS/46, 7 September 2005).

Internal code of conduct for members of the Commission on the Limits of the Continental Shelf (CLCS/47, 8 September 2005).

Statement by the Chairman of the Commission on the Limits of the Continental Shelf on the progress of work in the Commission—Sixteenth session (CLCS/48, 7 October 2005).

Statement by the Chairman of the Commission on the Limits of the Continental Shelf on the progress of work in the Commission—Corrigendum (CLCS/48/Corr.1, 3 November 2005).

Statement by the Chairman of the Commission on the Limits of the Continental Shelf on the progress of work in the Commission—Seventeenth session (CLCS/50, 10 May 2006).

Statement by the Chairman of the Commission on the Limits of the Continental Shelf on the progress of work in the Commission—Eighteenth session (CLCS/52, 6 October 2006).

Statement by the Chairman of the Commission on the Limits of the Continental Shelf on the progress of work in the Commission—Nineteenth session (CLCS/54, 27 April 2007).

Statement by the Chairman of the Commission on the Limits of the Continental Shelf on the progress of work in the Commission—Twentieth session (CLCS/56, 4 October 2007).

Statement by the Chairman of the Commission on the Limits of the Continental Shelf on the progress of work in the Commission—Twenty-first session (CLCS/58, 25 April 2008).

Statement by the Chairman of the Commission on the Limits of the Continental Shelf on the progress of work in the Commission—Twenty-second session (CLCS/60, 26 September 2008).

Statement by the Chairman of the Commission on the Limits of the Continental Shelf on the progress of work in the Commission—Twenty-third session (CLCS/62, 20 April 2009).

Statement by the Chairman of the Commission on the Limits of the Continental Shelf on the progress of work in the Commission—Twenty-fourth session (CLCS/64, 1 October 2009).

Statement by the Chairperson of the Commission on the Limits of the Continental Shelf on the progress of work in the Commission—Twenty-fifth session (CLCS/66, 30 April 2010).

Statement by the Chairperson of the Commission on the Limits of the Continental Shelf on the progress of work in the Commission—Twenty-sixth session (CLCS/68, 17 September 2010).

Statement by the Chairperson of the Commission on the Limits of the Continental Shelf on the progress of work in the Commission—Twenty-seventh session (CLCS/70, 11 May 2011).

Statement by the Chairperson of the Commission on the Limits of the Continental Shelf on the progress of work in the Commission—Twenty-seventh session—Corrigendum (CLCS/70/Corr.1, 25 May 2011).

Progress of work in the Commission on the Limits of the continental Shelf—Statement by the Chairperson—Twenty-eighth session (CLCS/72, 16 September 2011).

Progress of work in the Commission on the Limits of the continental Shelf—Statement by the Chairperson—Twenty-ninth session (CLCS/74, 30 April 2012).

Progress of work in the Commission on the Limits of the continental Shelf—Statement by the Chairperson—Thirtieth session (CLCS/76, 5 September 2012).

Documents of the Meeting of States Parties to the LOS Convention

Draft Rules of Procedure of the Commission on the Limits of the Continental Shelf (SPLOS/CLCS/WP.1, 1996).

Draft decision on the day of commencement of the ten-year period for making submissions to the Commission on the Limits of the Continental Shelf set out in article 4 of Annex II to the United Nations Convention on the Law of the Sea (SPLOS/L.22, 2001).

Report of the fifth Meeting of States Parties (24 July–2 August 1996) (SPLOS/14, 1996).

Election of the Members of the Commission on the Limits of the Continental Shelf (SPLOS/15, 1997).

List of Candidates Nominated by States Parties for Election to the Commission on the Limits of the Continental Shelf English (SPLOS/16, 1997).

Curricula Vitae of Candidates Nominated by States Parties for Election to the Commission on the Limits of the Continental Shelf (SPLOS/17, 1997).

Curricula Vitae of Candidates Nominated by States Parties for Election to the Commission on the Limits of the Continental Shelf (SPLOS/17/Add.1, 1997).

Report of the sixth Meeting of States Parties (10–14 March 1997) (SPLOS/20, 1997).

Report of the seventh Meeting of States Parties (19–33 May 1997) (SPLOS/24, 1997).

Letter dated 15 May 1998 from the Chairman of the Commission on the Limits of the Continental Shelf addressed to the President of the Eighth Meeting of States Parties (SPLOS/28, 1998).

Decision regarding the establishment of a voluntary trust fund for the purpose of the Commission on the Limits of the Continental Shelf (SPLOS/58, 2000).

Report of the tenth Meeting of States Parties (22–26 May 2000) (SPLOS/60, 2000).

Decision regarding the date of commencement of the ten-year period for making submissions to the Commission on the Limits of the Continental Shelf set out in article 4 of Annex II to the United Nations Convention on the Law of the Sea (SPLOS/72, 2001).

Report of the eleventh Meeting of States Parties (14–18 May 2001) (SPLOS/73, 2001).

Election of the members of the Commission on the Limits of the Continental Shelf—Note by the Secretary-General (SPLOS/79, 2002).

List of candidates nominated by States Parties for election to the Commission on the Limits of the Continental Shelf—Note by the Secretary-General (SPLOS/80, 2002).

Curricula vitae of candidates nominated by States Parties for election to the Commission on the Limits of the Continental Shelf—Note by the Secretary-General (SPLOS/81, 2002).

Report of the twelfth Meeting of States Parties (16–26 April 2002) (SPLOS/91, 2002).

Rules of Procedure for Meetings of States Parties (SPLOS/2/Rev.4, 2005).

Election of the members of the Commission on the Limits of the Continental Shelf—Note by the Secretary-General (SPLOS/149, 2007).

List of candidates nominated by States Parties for election to the Commission on the Limits of the Continental Shelf (SPLOS/150, 2007).

Curricula vitae of candidates nominated by States Parties for election to the Commission on the Limits of the Continental Shelf—Note by the Secretary-General (SPLOS/151, 2007).

Report of the seventeenth Meeting of States Parties (14 to 23 June 2007) (SPLOS/164, 2007).

Decision regarding the workload of the Commission on the Limits of the Continental Shelf and the ability of States, particularly developing States, to fulfil the requirements of article 4 of Annex II to the Convention, as well as the decision contained in SPLOS/72, paragraph (a) (SPLOS/183, 2008).

Arrangement for the allocation of seats on the International Tribunal for the Law of the Sea and the Commission on the Limits of the Continental Shelf (SPLOS/201, 2009).

Report of the nineteenth Meeting of States Parties (22–26 June 2009) (SPLOS/203, 2009).

Election of the members of the Commission on the Limits of the Continental Shelf (SPLOS/238, 2012).

List of candidates nominated by States Parties for election to the Commission on the Limits of the Continental Shelf—Note by the Secretary-General (SPLOS/239, 2012).

List of candidates nominated by States Parties for election to the Commission on the Limits of the Continental Shelf—Note by the Secretary-General: Addendum (SPLOS/239/Add.1, 2012).

Curricula vitae of candidates nominated by States Parties for election to the Commission on the Limits of the Continental Shelf (SPLOS/240, 2012).

Report of the twenty-second Meeting of States Parties (4–11 June 2012) (SPLOS/251, 2012).

Election of one member of the Commission on the Limits of the Continental Shelf—Note by the Secretary-General (SPLOS/252, 2012).

Reports and Papers

Consumers International's Decision-Making in the Global Market. Paper written by Steve Suppan. Published by the Institute for Agriculture and Trade Policy, 2004.

Continental Shelf: The Last Maritime Zone. Report edited by Tina Schoolmeester and Elaine Baker. Published by UNEP/GRID-Arendal, 2009.

Judicial Independence: Law and Practice of Appointments to the European Court of Human Rights. Report prepared by Jutta Limbach, Pedro Cruz Villalón, Roger Errera, Anthony Lester, Tamara Morshchakova, Stephen Sedley and Andrzej Zoll. Published by INTERIGHTS, 2003.

Legitimacy in International Law and International Relations. Paper written by Daniel Bodansky for the 2011 Annual Meeting of the American Political Science Association.

Nomination of candidates and election of judges to the European Court of Human Rights. Report of the Committee on Legal Affairs and Human Rights of the Assembly of the Council of Europe. Doc. 11767, 1 December 2008.

Proactive Transparency: The future of the right to information? A review of Standards, Challenges, and Opportunities. Report by Helen Darbishire. Published in Governance Working Paper Series of the World Bank Institute (Washington, D.C., 2010).

Report of the Berlin Conference (2004): Committee on International Human Rights Law and Practice of the International Law Association.

Report of the Berlin Conference (2004): Committee on Legal issues of the Outer Continental Shelf of the International Law Association.

Report of the New Delhi Conference (2002): Committee on Legal issues of the Outer Continental Shelf of the International Law Association.

Report of the Sub-Committee on Territorial Waters. Reprinted in *American Journal of International Law*, Vol. 20, 1926, p. 126.

The Burgh House Principles On The Independence Of The International Judiciary. Drafted by The Study Group of the International Law Association on the Practice and Procedure of International Courts and Tribunals, in association with the Project on International Courts and Tribunals.

Transparency and Public Participation in WTO Dispute Settlement. Report written by Christiane Ahlborn and James Headen Pfitzer. Published by the Centre for International Environmental Law, 2009.

EC Regulations

Council Regulation (EEC) No 2136/89 of 21 June 1989 laying down common marketing standards for preserved sardines. *Official Journal L 212, 22/07/1989*, pp. 79–81.

Commission Decision 93/619/EC of 19 November 1993 relating to the institution of a
Scientific, Technical and Economic Committee for Fisheries. *Official Journal L 297,
02/12/1993*, pp. 25–26.

Commission Decision 2005/629/EC of 26 August 2005 establishing a Scientific, Technical and Economic Committee for Fisheries. *Official Journal L 225, 31/08/2005*,
pp. 18–22.

Commission Decision 2010/74/EU of 4 February 2010 amending Decision 2005/629/
EC establishing a Scientific, Technical and Economic Committee for Fisheries.
Official Journal L 37, 10/02/2010, pp. 52–54.

Commission Decision 2012/C 72/06 of 9 March 2012 on appointment of three new
members of the Scientific, Technical and Economic Committee for Fisheries.
Official Journal, L 72, 10/03/12, p. 26.

Table of Cases

Permanent Court of International Justice

International Tribunal for the Law of the Sea

Arbitration

Tardieu-Jasper Dispute (Belgium v. France). Decision of 1 March 1937. Reprinted in *UNRIAA*, Vol. 3, p. 1701.

Case Concerning the Delimitation Maritime Areas between Canada and the French Republic (St. Pierre and Miquelon). Arbitral Award of 10 June 1992. Reprinted in *ILM*, Vol. 31, 1992, p. 1149.

WTO Dispute Settlement

European Communities—Measures Concerning Meat and Meat Products (Hormones), Appellate Body Report, WT/DS26/AB/R, WT/DS48/AB/R, 16 January 1998, in *DSR* (1998), Vol. I, p. 135.

United States—Import Prohibition of Certain Shrimp and Shrimp Products, Panel Report, WT/DS58/R and Corr.1, 6 April 1998, in DSR (1998), Vol. VII, p. 2821.

United States—Import Prohibition of Certain Shrimp and Shrimp Products, Appellate Body Report, WT/DS58/AB/R, 12 October 1998, in *DSR* (1998), Vol. VII, p. 2755.

Australia—Measures Affecting Importation of Salmon, Appellate Body Report, WT/DS18/AB/R, 20 October 1998, in *DSR* (1998), Vol. VIII, p. 3327.

Japan—Measures Affecting Agricultural Products, Panel Report, WT/DS76/R, 27 October 1998, in *DSR* (1999), Vol. I, p. 315.

Japan—Measures Affecting Agricultural Products, Appellate Body Report, WT/DS76/AB/R, 22 February 1999, in *DSR*, Vol. I, p. 277.

Canada—Measures Affecting the Export of Civilian Aircraft, Appellate Body Report, WT/DS70/AB/R, 2 August 1999, in *DSR* (1999), Vol. III, p. 1377.

European Communities—Trade Description of Sardines, Appellate Body Report, WT/DS231/AB/R, 26 September 2002, in *DSR* (2002), Vol. VIII, p. 3359.

Japan—Measures Affecting the Importation of Apples, Appellate Body Report, WT/DS245/AB/R, 26 November 2003, in *DSR* (2003), Vol. IX, p. 4391.

Japan—Measures Affecting the Importation of Apples, Panel Report, WT/DS245/R, 15 July 2003, in *DSR* (2003), Vol. IX, p. 4481.

United States—Continued Suspension of Obligations in the EC—Hormones Dispute, Appellate Body Report, WT/DS320/AB/R, 16 October 2008, in *DSR* (2008), Vol. X, p. 3507.

Canada—Continued Suspension of Obligations in the EC—Hormones Dispute, Appellate Body Report, WT/DS321/AB/R, 16 October 2008, in *DSR* (2008), Vol. XIV, p. 5373.

United States—Continued Suspension of Obligations in the EC—Hormones Dispute, Panel Report, WT/DS320/R, 31 March 2008, in *DSR* (2008), Vol. XI, p. 3891.

Index